Other river titles from Fretwater Press

Every Rapid Speaks Plainly
the River Journals of Buzz Holmstrom
Brad Dimock, editor

Sunk Without a Sound
the Tragic Colorado River Honeymoon of Glen and Bessie Hyde
Brad Dimock

The Very Hard Way
Bert Loper and the Colorado River
Brad Dimock

The Brave Ones
the River Journals of Ellsworth and Emery Kolb
William Suran, editor

Glen Canyon Betrayed
a Sensuous Elegy
Katie Lee

Riverman
the Story of Bus Hatch
Roy Webb

Desert Riverman
the Free-Spirited Adventures of Murl Emery
Robert S. Wood

The Books of the Colorado River & the Grand Canyon
a Selective Bibliography, 1953
Francis P. Farquhar

The Books of the Grand Canyon, the Colorado River,
the Green River & the Colorado Plateau
a Selective Bibliography, 1953 — 2003
Mike S. Ford

THE DOING OF THE THING

the brief, brilliant, whitewater career of

BUZZ HOLMSTROM

THE

DOING

the

brief

brilliant

OF THE

whitewater

career

THING

of

BUZZ

HOLMSTROM

Vince Welch
Cort Conley
Brad Dimock

FRETWATER
· PRESS ·
FLAGSTAFF · ARIZONA
1998

FRETWATER PRESS
1000 Grand Canyon Avenue
Flagstaff, Arizona 86001
www.fretwater.com

17 • 9 8 7

ISBN (cloth) 1-892327-37-6
Limited edition of 500

(trade paper) 978-1-892327-07-9

Library of Congress Catalog
Card Number: 98-86745

This book was created on
Macintosh computers.
Text is set entirely in the Adobe
Minion family of fonts.

To the Holmstroms

... the Bad Rapid—

Lava Cliff—

that I had been looking for,

nearly a thousand miles.

I thought—

once past there—

my reward will begin—

but now

everything ahead

seems kind of empty

and I find I have already had my reward—

in **the doing of the thing**—

the stars

the cliffs

and canyons—

the roar of the rapids—

the moon—

the uncertainty

worry—

the relief when through each one—

the campfires at nite,

the real respect of the rivermen I met

and others...

NOVEMBER 21, 1937

Contents

Preface

BUZZ HOLMSTROM is all but forgotten in his home town of Coquille, Oregon. A handful of older folks remember him, or recollect hearing the name. Some know his sister Anna, or knew his brother Carl, who died there in 1997. Yet for a brief moment in the late 1930s, Buzz Holmstrom was known across America as the brave young man who rowed the Green and Colorado Rivers alone in a hand-made wooden boat. At his death, less than ten years later, his name had faded into obscurity.

It is only along the whitewater stretches of the Green and Colorado Rivers of the Southwest that Holmstrom's name is recognized today, among the fraternity of men and women who guide tourists through the whitewater canyons. Any boatman can tell you that Holmstrom was the first to row the eleven hundred miles of river alone; the first to run every rapid of the two rivers. In the Belknap's *Grand Canyon River Guide*, 1969, there is a small photograph of Holmstrom with a caption saying as much, but nothing more. In 1986 David Lavender published his excellent account of river running history, *River Runners of the Grand Canyon*. His chapter on Holmstrom helped to fill the gaps in the pioneer boatman's story, but, like any overview, asked more questions than it answered.

What brought Holmstrom into the mainstream of Grand Canyon lore was a typewritten transcript of his 1937 journal. Photocopies circulated among boatmen, and passages were read aloud by the campfire at night. Holmstrom's humor, humility, and love of the river called for more than a snapshot.

"THERE IS ONLY ONE WORSE THING that a river-rat can do than turn turtle, and that is to turn historian," wrote Lewis R. Freeman, author, historian and boatman in 1923. Three authors, all professional boatmen, combined efforts to bring Holmstrom's tale to light. Vince Welch, in his home state of Oregon, wrote of Holmstrom's family background and upbringing, his voyages on the Rogue River, and his untimely death. Brad Dimock, in Arizona, covered Holmstrom's adventures on the Colorado Plateau. Cort Conley, of Idaho, wrote of the Salmon River trip, the Clegg–Holmstrom cross-country river trip, and Holmstrom's years in the navy.

The story that evolved is far more than a string of whitewater tales. It tells of a deep and complex young man, caught between the old and new, between duty and desire, between pride and humility. Buzz Holmstrom's life, river voyages, and death, tell of a lone man's struggle in a difficult and changing world.

*O*N SUNDAY MORNING, MAY 19, 1946, Rolf Holmstrom was walking home from his friend's house when Floyd Smith, his brother-in-law, drove up in his Model-A. "Where have you been?" Smith asked sharply as he flung the car door open. Caught off guard, Rolf was startled by Floyd's abrupt manner. "Get in!" said Floyd. "You're needed at your mother's house immediately." As they drove, it became obvious to Rolf that Floyd was upset about something. "What's going on?" he asked. For a moment Floyd looked away. Then he broke the news. "Buzz is dead. He died on the Grande Ronde River yesterday."

Rolf was stunned. His brother? Dead? Did the family know? Yes, everyone was over at the house. They rode in silence the rest of the way home.

Earlier that morning, Pastor Munger had knocked on the back porch door of the Smith house. They were getting ready for Sunday services when seven-year-old June answered the door.

"Is your daddy here?" Munger asked. Her father had come up behind her. A moment later Anna, Buzz's younger sister, arrived at the back porch door as well. When Pastor Munger told the Smiths what had happened, Anna cried out, "How can that be?" "I don't know," Munger answered.

Immediately the children, June and Shirley, were sent off to Sunday school. At the church June announced importantly to anyone who would listen, "My Uncle Buzz was murdered." Meanwhile Anna and Pastor Munger went directly to Frances's house which was a few steps across the creek. Carl, Buzz's older brother, greeted them at the door.

Frances, in the kitchen when they arrived, sensed something was wrong. Munger handed her the telegram: "ELGIN, OREGON, MAY 18, 1946. MRS. FRANCES HOLMSTROM: HALDANE DIED LAST NIGHT ON THE RIVER. IRA C. RUBOTTOM, COMM. OF EXPEDITION."

Frances felt weak, nauseous. Disbelief washed over her. Her son had been home just three weeks ago, happy and excited. She had recently received a letter from him; he had signed it with his usual "Everything O.K. Buzz."

The Holmstroms did not attend church that Sunday. They gathered in the small sitting room of Frances's house and tried to make sense of the telegram. What could have happened? Buzz could not have drowned. He was always cautious on the river. Maybe he had an accident.

Neighbors prepared food, but the Holmstroms did not eat. Numb with grief, Frances lay down on the davenport to nap, then went into her bedroom, never resting for long in either place. Anna walked back and forth between houses, keeping an eye on the children while also trying to comfort her mother. Rolf circled the nearby field again and again, stopping in front of the *Julius F.*, Buzz's overturned boat. Carl just stood and stared out the window. With no idea of how Buzz died, they were left to imagine the circumstances on the Grande Ronde. Perhaps, they hoped, it was all a mistake.

HALDANE "BUZZ" HOLMSTROM's *life ended on a remote river in northeast Oregon. It was a life inseparable from rivers, born out of the necessities the geography of his home state placed upon his working parents, Charles and Frances. Introduced to the world of water and boats at a young age by his Scandinavian father, Buzz would return as an adult again and again to the western rivers he loved. His story begins with his father, at the turn of the century, in a small logging town on the southern coast of Oregon...*

opposite: Logging camp at Schofield Creek

Braided Currents

1903–1909

I N GARDINER in the summer of 1903, the evening air smelled of the sea and lumber and steam engines. The same type of engines that powered the locomotives and "steam donkeys" in the woods propelled the sternwheeler *Eva* toward the wharf of this coastal logging town at the mouth of the Umpqua River. Rowboats, skiffs, and the new gasoline-powered launches crowded the docks. Nearby, a schooner sat idle, awaiting its cargo of lumber from the Gardiner Mill. So many of the coastal ships had captains of Scandinavian origin that the locals referred jokingly to the fleet as the "Scandinavian navy."

A procession of horse-drawn wagons passed along Gardiner's waterfront main street. Several townspeople, including Charles Holmstrom, paused to watch the

Eva dock. Twenty-one years before, after a lengthy stage ride down the Willamette Valley from Portland, Holmstrom himself had taken the sternwheeler to Gardiner. Now he waited for the upriver news and the promise new faces sometimes offered. Captain Cornwall, skipper of the *Eva,* signaled the deckhands to prepare for landing.

That June evening, the *Eva* carried its usual freight: lumber, cord wood, bales of hay, and crates of fish crowded the fore and aft lower decks; sacks of mail and ten gallon containers of milk destined for the local creameries obstructed the gangways. Along the railing of the upper deck, passengers stood searching the wharf for acquaintances and relatives. When they finally disembarked and made their way to the Gardiner Hotel, the travelers aroused the usual curiosity and comment. The Johnson family, especially the two young women, Frances and Emma, did not go unnoticed. A year would pass before Charles Holmstrom encountered Frances Johnson again.

CHARLES MAGNUS HOLMSTROM was born in the province of Värmland, Sweden, on May 27, 1863. West of Stockholm, the Värmland region is laced with more than three thousand lakes and watercourses. Vanern, the largest lake in Sweden, is at the heart of the province. For centuries the Scandinavians named themselves after the natural features of their landscape, rather than the work they did or the town or village they came from. In Swedish, Holmstrom means "home stream."

Holmstrom spent his boyhood playing in the creeks, streams, and lakes around his village. By age ten, his father had taught him the rudiments of boat handling, and later, of boat building. In the Värmland region a boat was a necessity—as much for transportation and work as for pleasure. Custom and economics spawned generations of backyard boat builders.

In 1876 the Holmstrom family immigrated to the United States. Like many Scandinavian immigrants, they chose the Great Lakes region—Michigan, Wisconsin, Minnesota—for one obvious reason: it reminded them of home. Those arriving in the United States from Europe tended to migrate "horizontally," settling within the general latitudinal bounds of their former countries. Here they easily recognized the "rules of nature," and found a familiar climate, geography, and growing season. These Scandinavian families, many of which were headed by dairy farmers, woodsmen, fishermen, and shipwrights, were usually able to secure the kind of work they were most familiar with while they learned the less visible cultural rules of their new country. After experiencing hunger and deprivation in their native lands, they hoped to find new opportunities in cities like Minneapolis.

Once in Minneapolis, the Holmstrom family took whatever work was available. Like many boys his age, Charles Holmstrom, then twelve, went to work in an iron foundry. He pounded sheets of molten metal with oversized wooden mallets in preparation for castings. The hours were long, the pay poor, the working conditions dangerous. Charles Holmstrom's formal education ended early.

At sixteen he left home and hired on with the Northern Pacific Railroad, working the Dakota and Montana lines. Hard, physical labor at minimal pay convinced him to look for something better. Over the next few years he learned how to operate and maintain steam locomotives. He was a quick learner, with a natural aptitude for engines and machinery. Decades later, Charles Holmstrom's youngest son Rolf remembers his father reading over and over about the mechanics and operation of steam engines in the hefty *Handbook of the Locomotive*. Although he had operated locomotives and steam donkeys in the woods for years, Charles Holmstrom wanted to know more. Rolf said his father "was mostly self-taught; he had a mechanical mind, he understood how machines worked, and he could really apply what he knew to different and novel situations. He liked working with his hands and he was a very good boat builder." Charles Holmstrom's skills and knowledge were in demand in the woods.

He traveled farther west. In 1880 he landed at Greys Harbor on the coast of Washington Territory. The first "steam donkey" was being unloaded at the same time. This stationary, steam-powered engine was used to pull logs out of the forest to a landing, or staging area; it quickly replaced the "hay-burners" of the woods, the bull teams and horses. Great Lakes lumbermen, many of them Scandinavian, flooded into the area. The rush for timber claims had begun.

After Greys Harbor, Charles Holmstrom traveled south to Portland, Oregon. In 1882, he arrived in North Bend, a town on the edge of Coos Bay on the Oregon coast. He had heard encouraging reports while in Portland and, at nineteen, he was eager to confirm them. The year he arrived in North Bend, Holmstrom found work operating a locomotive on the construction of the first rock jetty at the entrance to Coos Bay. The jetty, inside the harbor at Fossil Point, was intended to impede the buildup of sandbars in the vital shipping channel at Coos Bay. (Jarvis Landing, across from Empire, was the southern end of the coastal area's main transportation corridor—the beach highway.) After seven years, the depth of the channel had not changed appreciably and the city fathers, discouraged, halted the project. Holmstrom was unemployed. Ships continued to run aground at the bay's entrance, and by 1892 a more ambitious North Jetty Project was begun. After a brief stint in one of the numerous Scandinavian-run boatyards, Holmstrom was rehired as a locomotive engineer.

Seventeen years after his arrival in America Charles M. Holmstrom finally became a United States citizen. He was thirty years old. In front of Judge J.C. Fullerton, witnesses George Lighthall and Mary Holmstrom swore that Charles Holmstrom had lived in the U.S. for the last five years and was a man of good moral character. Mary Holmstrom was most likely Charles Holmstrom's first wife, although information on the subject is sparse. The couple had a baby girl (Holmstrom may or may not have been the father) and not long after, filed for divorce. Holmstrom continued to support mother and child.

In 1897, the North Jetty was completed and the depth of the channel now reached twenty feet. Believing this to be a permanent solution to a perennial problem, city fathers dropped their plans for construction of a south jetty. Holmstrom was out of work again. Taking the beach stagecoach from Jarvis Landing, the thirty-four-year-old Holmstrom rode twenty miles north up the coast to Gardiner. He was going to work for the Gardiner Mill Company.

Gardiner, "The White City of the Umpqua," had been a company town for at least twenty-five years when Holmstrom arrived. The proximity of the Umpqua River and the Gardiner Mill Company's network of logging camps, coupled with brisk sailing ship trade, had made the town one of the busiest ports on the Oregon coast. After the fire of 1881 destroyed many of the town's homes and businesses, the owners of the Gardiner Mill Company offered to supply the townspeople with unlimited quantities of free white paint, but no contrasting colors for trim. Every waterfront home and building was painted white, a stark but not unpleasant contrast with the surrounding forested hillside. The reward for this conformity was a unique-looking town and rejuvenated civic pride. Travelers passing through the area always remembered Gardiner.

Charles Holmstrom made his living in the logging camps, operating and repairing the steam donkeys and the Shay steam locomotives. The steam donkey had revolutionized logging while the Shay locomotive, with its three-cylinder engine and gear drive on the side, was well suited for hauling logs out of the steep-hilled forests of the Pacific Northwest. Holmstrom knew both pieces of machinery well. Because the logging sites were still in the vicinity of the mill, he lived in the camps during the logging season; in the off-season he boarded at his friend Charles Walker's farm, across the Umpqua River from Gardiner. In between logging stints, he also operated a locomotive hauling rock for construction of the Fort Stevens jetty at the mouth of the Columbia River. It was not long before Holmstrom purchased a few acres on Eel Lake near the Ten Mile Lakes area, five miles south of Gardiner, where he built a cabin and a small boat for himself.

In late summer of 1899, Holmstrom joined the Masonic Lodge in Gardiner. Old Aurora Lodge #59 served as a business and social network for its members who supported one another and the general community. He passed through the Masonic degrees quickly: August 19, "Entered Apprentice;" September 16, a "Fellow of the Craft;" October 14, he graduated to "Master Mason." After twenty years in the area,

Holmstrom was an accepted member of the community. He called Gardiner home.

Charles Holmstrom was a compact, solid-looking man. At five feet, seven inches, he stood as if rooted to the ground. His weathered hands, accustomed to physical labor, were large for a man his size. His face had an expansive forehead, thick brows, clear eyes, a firm jaw. The thick, drooping mustache suited him. As many men did at the time, he wore a hat when having his photograph taken. Holmstrom neither smiled nor scowled at the photographer, but appeared quietly amused. His expression, although it did not reveal much, invited trust and confidence.

IN THE SUMMER OF 1904, Holmstrom met a young, dark-haired woman at the local creamery in Ten Mile, Oregon, south of Gardiner. As was the custom for rural female school teachers, twenty-four-year-old Frances Johnson was boarding with the Landrith family on their farm. Holmstrom, nearly forty, had finished work on the jetty at Fort Stevens near Astoria and had come to Ten Mile to make repairs on his cabin before he started back to work in the woods on Schofield Creek.

More than by any other geographical feature, the town of Ten Mile was defined by the narrow reaches of Ten Mile Lake and North Ten Mile Lake. The town itself, at the head of Ten Mile Lake, consisted of a store, a hotel, the one-room schoolhouse and a baseball diamond. Schroeder's Creamery was at the hub of the small lakeside community. Along the Oregon coast creameries like Schroeder's provided a reliable market for the products of the local dairy farmers. Each morning and evening, they rowed down the arms of Ten Mile Lake to deliver their raw milk to Schroeder. After processing, butter and cheese was hauled by wagon south along the beach highway to North Bend, where coastal schooners waited to carry the product to San Francisco.

The post office, usually based at the postmaster's residence, changed location so often at Ten Mile the local people gave up and went to Schroeder's to collect their mail. There they left messages, met visitors, and exchanged gossip. Schroeder was even known to hold a dance occasionally.

At the Creamery, Holmstrom and Frances Johnson struck up a conversation,

7

discovering they had mutual friends. Although they had never met before, each seemed familiar to the other. Frances told Charles she had come from Oregon City a year earlier, riding the train, stagecoach, and finally the sternwheeler to Gardiner. Holmstrom suddenly recognized her as the young woman he had seen at the dock that summer evening. He invited Frances Johnson out for a row on Ten Mile Lake. She accepted.

FRANCES JOHNSON was born in Thomas, Michigan on May 2, 1881, to Anna and Sylvester Johnson. From an early age, Fanny (as she was called by her family) revealed a talent for drawing and rhyming. Mrs. Johnson encouraged her oldest daughter's artistic abilities and upon completing her elementary education, the shy country girl was sent to the Cleveland School of Art in Cleveland, Ohio. She thrived in her new surroundings. Considered "a budding genius, but a beautiful soul," she was well-liked by students and faculty. Her drawing and painting talents were recognized and encouraged by her instructors. She also wrote poetry for the school newspaper. Frances wanted to become an illustrator. By the standards of the time, she was an educated young lady.

After two years, she was summoned home. Her instructors urged her to stay in school. Without a trace of resentment, Frances would only say that her mother needed her. In an article written before her departure, the tenor of the times was revealed with a telling line, "But better for the world to lose her talent than that she should have failed in her devotion to her mother." Soon after Frances came home, the family left for Oregon, arriving in 1897.

Upon their arrival, the Johnsons purchased a home at Eleventh and Madison Streets in Oregon City, fifteen miles up the Willamette River from Portland. At the time, Frances was sixteen, her sister Emma thirteen, her brother Seth nine. Perched on the banks above Willamette Falls, Oregon City had been the terminus of the Oregon Trail for the early pioneers. Mrs. Johnson wrote to a friend back

Frances Johnson with her pupils

in Michigan, "From my window I can see the silvery Willamette winding through the valley and boats tracing its course. It rains nearly all the time at this season, but when it does stop everything is lovely."

The Johnsons' reasons for migrating were as hopeful, numerous, and complex as those of any emigrants before them. They also had family-related motives. Anna's brother, Joseph Hall, lived in North Bend, Oregon, and was struggling with the recent death of his wife. Left with eight children (six were girls,) Hall had written often to the Johnsons, encouraging them to come west. He assured Sylvester Johnson that a land boom was in the making.

Frances immediately took a job teaching in Oregon City; her youth and calm manner were appreciated more than her arts background. The drab single-room schoolhouse, crowded with children, was difficult to heat; during the interminable rains, the roof leaked. The usual shortage of teaching supplies and materials came as no surprise. What frustrated Frances most, however, were her students. Many of the children, with an astonishing range of abilities, were tired and listless and often came to school sick. Attendance was haphazard. Education, while valued, came second to the more immediate needs of their families, whose survival depended on the labor of their children.

A year after arriving, Sylvester Johnson departed for the gold fields of Alaska. His family remained behind. Johnson had been a successful farmer, landlord, and businessman in Michigan. The *Oregon City Courier* reported, "Mr. Johnson expects to engage in business somewhere in Oregon in the future, but has not yet selected a location." Another newspaper account described him as a restless individual with a "pioneering instinct." Johnson had been caught in the economic depression that had swept over the country in the 1890s, and the lure of the Alaskan gold fields proved irresistible. Two years later, in 1900, Johnson returned from Alaska empty-handed; the failed venture was never mentioned again. Another three years passed before Johnson followed his brother-in-law's advice, uprooting the family and moving to North Bend.

That first year in North Bend, Frances again took a job teaching. Her sister Emma helped her mother with the running of the household as well as looking after Uncle Joe's children. Seth found work in a sash and door factory on Coos Bay. Sylvester Johnson—Michigan farmer, Oregon businessman, Alaskan gold seeker — found what he was looking for in North Bend. Anna Johnson regained her cherished extended family. Within a year, Frances accepted another teaching position fifteen

Loggers in camp. Charles Holmstrom, right of door

miles north of Marshfield (later, Coos Bay) in the tiny coastal community of Ten Mile.

Not long after their meeting at Schroeder's Creamery, Frances and Charles went Sunday boating on Ten Mile Lake. The smooth surface of the lake reflected the pale blue of the summer sky and the discreet shades of green of the surrounding forest. Bird song slipped from the stands of fir and pine along the shore. Charles rowed the wooden boat toward the center of the lake, the rhythmic stroke of the oars portioning the silence they both enjoyed. Occasionally, a breath of wind brushed the glassy surface. Charles pointed out farms and cabins as well as familiar landmarks. They ate and made small talk. Frances read her book while the boat drifted, the panoramic views unfolding lazily past her. Hours passed unnoticed. It was the first of many outings that summer.

Over the coming weeks, Charles and Frances explored numerous arms of Ten Mile Lake—Shutters, Colemans, Devores, and Templeton Slough—all named after the earliest settlers in the area. At Charles's insistence, Frances even tried her hands at the oars.

These sallies on the lake served Frances well, reminding her of girlhood excursions on Nolan Lake near her hometown of Thomas, Michigan. On the water, unhurried, she had time to think and to sort her feelings. She liked Charles Holmstrom's quiet reserve, which some mistook for a chilly distance. His Swedish heritage came through, a certain reticence mixed with a dry humor. Frances sensed that the ruggedness of a life spent in the woods had not taken away Charles's innate gentleness and although he was not a churchgoer, he seemed a believer nevertheless. Neither was he threatened by her education nor her ease with words or books. He also seemed friendly toward children.

Their courtship continued after Charles moved over the ridge to Schofield Creek that fall. He had taken a job with the Gardiner Mill Company, operating a Shay locomotive: six days of work, dawn to dusk. On Sunday mornings, however, Holmstrom hiked up the switchback trail to the ridge and down the other side to meet Frances at the Landriths' farm. Their usual routine was to visit a short while and then excuse themselves. They hiked up to the top of the ridge above Schofield Creek and had lunch, with views of the forest and Pacific Ocean.

The following summer (1905) Frances moved over the hill from Ten Mile to Schofield Creek to teach school. When Charles Holmstrom mentioned to Charles Walker that the new school teacher was looking for room and board, Walker took the hint. Three of the Walker children attended the one-room schoolhouse where Frances Johnson taught the first year.

Poor seating, a lack of sanitary facilities, the usual shortage of books and materials—Frances worked with what came her way. Being the only school teacher

in the area, she slipped easily into the life of the community. She liked the simplicity and the nearness to nature at Schofield Creek. Through good times and bad,
people stuck together; despite difficult conditions, they carried themselves with a
rough-hewn dignity.

But one afternoon, as she went hiking, she noticed enough bare spots on the
steep hillsides and the surrounding valleys to give her pause. When she reached one
of the higher ridges, a green sea of trees stretched as far as her eye could see. Surely
there was more than enough here to guarantee steady work and a secure future. Still,
the bald spots troubled her. She later wrote a poem about the single spar-pole tree
left standing to hoist logs by block and and tackle from the surrounding forest.

The High Lead Tree

My brothers' trunks upon the hillside lie,
And I, who live, envy the ones who die,
For I am slave. Steel woven cables bind
My living body, torn, dismembered, blind,
To the betrayal of my forest kind.
For such as I there is no day, no dark.
No circling seasons wind within my bark
Their secret record, like a silken thread.
My live heart pulses in a body dead.
Not log I am, not bough, no longer tree
I am a thing that men have made of me.

They shout below: the heavy fetters thrum.
The singing cable winds about the drum.
The donkeys shriek, the timber-fallers cry
Warning: the forests take the ax and die,
While I stand high in nakedness, and swing,
Above the carnage and the clamoring,
My brothers' flesh down to the marketing.

IN APRIL OF 1906, after an earthquake devastated San Francisco, the demand for
Oregon lumber soared, and the mills along the south coast were busier than ever. In
October, the four-masted, 280-foot sailing bark *Peter Iredale,* en route to pick up a
cargo of wheat in Portland, ran aground near Astoria north of Gardiner. (The iron
skeleton of the ship remains embedded in the sand to this day.) In between these
crises, Frances Johnson and Charles Holmstrom were married.

On Saturday afternoon, September 15, 1906, the two met in the Walker's front room for the ceremony. School, held in the dry seasons in logging camps, had ended. The early fall weather was pleasant and unseasonably warm. Frances's relatives and friends came from North Bend for the celebration. Charles Holmstrom's long-time acquaintances from North Bend, Gardiner, and Ten Mile attended as well.

In her new journal, Frances described their life together on Schofield Creek that first year:

> Our first home was a little three-room cabin up in the canyon, just at the edge of the camp, with steep hills all around, and the creek and the railroad tracks running in front. It was a very humble house, but we made it cozy with books, pictures, home manufactured furniture, and bright draperies.... Charlie went to work repairing the locomotive and the donkey engines. Though the winter was so pleasant for us, yet it was really a dark and stormy one. The canyon was deep, and for nearly three months the sun could not come into it, though we could see a few weak rays on the hilltop across the canyon. Then in February there came a day when it flickered just a minute on the kitchen wall, and was gone—such a welcome sight that I wanted to kiss the place where it had shone. The next day it stayed a little longer....
>
> Then there were the storms. Ever since I first discovered Schofield I had longed to see a real freshet, such as the Keiths described to me, and my wish was much more than granted, for that winter there were three. Each time the rain fell steadily, and the shallow creek rose, for several days, till it filled its banks, covered meadows and railroad, and made the whole valley a broad river, with the mountains for its banks and the cabins standing out like Noah's Arks from the flood. The storms that brought the freshets also softened the earth on the steep hills, and caused several landslides, one of which I shall never forget....
>
> It had rained for days, the house was surrounded by water, and Charlie had made the little foot-bridge fast to the house with a rope, so that our only connection with the outer world might not be lost. About two o'clock that night we were wakened by an awful sound—the rushing of water, cracking and splintering and crashing of trees, and all awful sounds mingled, coming from somewhere up the canyon. We ran to the windows, but it was pitch dark, and the crash and the roar came nearer every minute. We did all we could—we ran, without stopping to dress either, our minds filled with pictures of the Johnstown flood [Pennsylvania, 1889], of the whole mountain side sliding in, of all the horrors we ever heard of. But we hadn't run far, when with a last, loudest and nearest crash, it ended, and all was still. We went back, lit a lamp and dressed and by that time we could see lanterns and hear the voices of the boys out investigating. A large slide had come down and destroyed Abbott's house, about fifty yards above us. It was the most terrible sound I ever heard, and the darkness made it more dreadful.

A year later Frances wrote again in the family journal, "A great change has taken place in this little cabin, for here, almost a month ago, on the 25th of June, our little boy was born." Frances's mother had arrived from North Bend on the beach stage a day before the birth. The morning was hot and dry and they were canning strawberries when Frances began labor. Mrs. Walker was called and sent one of the children into the woods to fetch the father-to-be. Later that day, Frances gave birth to a ten-

Holmstrom cabin, Ten Mile

and-a-half-pound baby boy whom they named Carl Francis. Soon after, the children from the camp and nearby farms crowded into the small cabin to admire their teacher's baby.

Two months later, in August 1907, the new family moved back to the cabin at Ten Mile. The thought of another dreary winter, or a middle-of-the-night freshet, did not appeal to the Holmstroms. Frances wrote that Charles was fed up "with things in general and the boss in particular," not for the first or last time.

In jest, they called their place on Eel Lake "the ranch." It had a cabin and two outbuildings, but nothing more. Their nearest neighbor, Mr. Schroeder, was almost a mile away at the creamery. Charles cut a trail through the pines and brush to get there. The edge of the forest ran along the back of their property, and was the haunt of stray cattle, deer, even an occasional bear. Sandy hills covered with huckleberry bushes ringed the front of the cabin. The ocean, three miles away, was an easy walk.

That fall Charles cleared a portion of the land and planted apple trees. He spent hours digging irrigation ditches and fencing ten acres of the sand hills to pasture their cow. With firewood to cut, a roof to mend, and tools to sharpen, Charles kept busy. He also found time to play the mouth organ, entertaining Carl for hours in the evening. After they returned from a Thanksgiving in North Bend, Charles began building another rowboat. The following summer Frances's parents visited and kept house while she, Charles, and Carl made a trip to Schofield Creek. Frances wrote:

> We had a beautiful trip over to Schofield. We started about sunrise one morning, thru' the narrow trail to the boat landing, then went off up the cool, still lake. After a five mile pull we reached the head, left our boat at the Wilkins landing and began our walk. After passing Wilkins's house, the road entered the woods, and followed a cool, damp canyon draped in ferns and moss and ceiled over with leaves. Soon the trail turned up the mountain and became rocky, zigzagging, and in places almost impassable steep.

We climbed for a mile or so, then reaching the ridge, began to go down, down, down. Then through another long dewy canyon where the sun never reached, and out into lovely Schofield, the lost Garden of Eden, it seems to me. Charlie carried Carl in a sort of sack on his back, Indian fashion, and he rode very comfortably.

In November of 1908, the Holmstroms moved back to Schofield Creek. They had been planning to go back the following spring, but money pulled them back earlier. Mr. Henderson, in charge of the lower logging camp at Schofield, desperately needed Holmstrom's services. Charles and Frances knew what awaited them over the long, often gloomy months. Furthermore, Frances was pregnant again, due the following May. In spite of their circumstances, they rented out their place at Ten Mile and Holmstrom immediately went to work at the new logging site.

When Frances arrived at the lower camp, she was dismayed. She wrote:

I think it was as horrid a place as anyone ever lived in. It did not contain over an acre of cleared ground, and what there was, was just mud, deep and soft and stinking mud. There was no sunshine, and every few days the tide would rise to a depth of a few feet over the whole place. Three times it came into the house, covered the floor to a depth of eight or ten inches, and drove us out for a few hours.

By March, camp life had improved. Two months before Frances's delivery date, the family moved to one of the upper camps, where the cabins were above the tidal fluctuations of Schofield Slough. These small cedar shake cabins, resting on a foundation of logs, were more mobile than they looked. As soon as enough track had been laid, the cabins were lifted aboard the flat beds of the train and hauled along the track to the new site. So close were the railroad tracks to the cabin's front yard that Charles nailed a chicken wire fence around the yard to keep Carl out of harm's way.

The days lengthened and the weather warmed. Frances's mother visited for a week. After the ordeal at the lower camp, the three-room cabin was comfortable and relatively dry. Frances discovered her new neighbors were old friends: Mollie Wilson lived on one side of the Holmstroms' cabin, the Swaggerts just above, and the newly-wed Whismans directly across the tracks. Mollie Wilson assured Frances she would assist at her birth. Charles, ever busy, was happy. Whenever Carl heard the sound of the "lokey" coming down the tracks, he scampered outside to the chicken wire fence and waited. When at last the locomotive appeared, he waved; his father tooted the whistle and waved back.

opposite: Buzz, Charles and Anna on the farm

A Place of Their Own

1909–1934

T HE LOCAL DOCTOR did not reach the upper camp at Schofield Creek in time. On May 10, 1909, Frances Holmstrom gave birth to another son. Once again Frances's mother and Mollie Wilson served as midwives. Nine-and-a-half pounds, with soft dark hair, the infant had, in his mother's words, "a very cunning little face, with a saintly fashion of folding one dimpled little hand over the other." They named the boy Haldane: Hal(l), which was Frances's mother's maiden name and Dane, to acknowledge Charles's Scandinavian ancestry. Later that summer, Frances wrote of the newborn, "He is a great, fat, happy little fellow, who spends his time sleeping, kicking, thinking and eating. He has a happy look all the time and he laughs quite uproariously sometimes." She was twenty-eight; Charles was forty-five.

When the logging camp closed down for the holidays that winter, the Holmstroms went to North Bend to visit Frances's family. After only a week,

Charles returned to their cabin on Eel Lake. He was building a new boat and wanted to finish it as soon as possible. He relished the idea of cruising the Umpqua delta with his family during the Sunday morning boat fairs, which reminded him of the Sunday church races he had participated in as a boy in Sweden.

Despite the thousand-dollar cost, every farmer, logger, and fisherman along the coast wanted a gasoline-powered launch. Local boatwrights could not keep up with the demand. Holmstrom, of course, could not imagine paying someone else to build a boat. By mid-January 1910, the twenty-foot launch was finished, and Charles picked up Frances and the two boys at the wharf in Gardiner. They motored across the Umpqua River and south up Schofield Slough in the *Chiquita*—the first of many boat rides for Haldane, now eight months. Two-year-old Carl was already a veteran.

The following summer Charles took Frances, the two boys, and the Walker family camping for four days. They motored down the Umpqua estuary below Gardiner and found a place in the dunes sheltered from the ocean winds, with a wide flat beach in front and the forest behind. When the high tides ebbed, the strand turned into a wide, sandy playground strewn with kelp and shells, and spotted with warm, shallow pools. The children played all day and slept well at night. Except for Haldane. Frances wrote, "Poor little 'Buzz' enjoyed it least of all, as he could not walk on the uneven ground, the beds were hard and he was afraid of the water."

This is the first mention of Haldane's nickname, which originated with three-year-old Carl's attempts to pronounce "brother." The word sounded like "Buzz," and the name stuck, more out of rhyme than reason. For the rest of his life, everyone called him "Buzz." Only his mother used the name "Haldane."

On the Fourth of July, Frances's sister Emma and her new husband Roy Lawhorne visited for a few days. Healthy children, close friends, warm weather, the fading memory of the rigors of winter—Frances called it a "delightful summer." She hung a hammock in the yard and moved the dining room table outside under the trees where they ate every night. Demand for Charles's services slackened, allowing him to spend more time with the family. He built toys, made minor repairs on the cabin, and played with his two sons. On impulse, he often loaded Carl and Buzz aboard the *Chiquita* and crossed the Umpqua to Gardiner for a treat or to examine the sailing ships and coastal steamers moored along the waterfront.

In the logging camp Carl and Buzz chased the cats mercilessly, squabbled over their hand-made toys, and played in the nearby creeks and ponds with the other camp children. Frances wrote of the fifteen-month-old, "We used to fear he was going to lack spunk, but he is developing a very peppery temper—will fling himself down wailing, and fly about like a little skating-bug, but it is all over in a minute."

Another year and the Holmstroms moved again. Charles had been in charge of the upper camp at Schofield Creek that winter, repairing and maintaining the machinery and serving as watchman. When the logging operation started up, he ran the locomotive and Scottsburg steam donkey. A new boss was put in charge, and soon after, Holmstrom quit. Neither Charles nor Frances seemed concerned. Holmstrom had always been able to find work. For the first time, however, Frances abandoned the habit of recording only facts and events in her journal. She mentions "breaking loose from the camp life entirely, of getting a place of their own, perhaps a farm." Suddenly the Holmstrom's discontents, as well as their wishes and dreams, floated to the surface. They were ready for a change, but once again steady wages drew them back to the Gardiner Mill Company. This time they relocated directly across the Umpqua River at a logging camp on the Smith River, named after mountain man and fur trader Jedediah Smith, who narrowly escaped an Indian massacre here in 1828.

Rough and raw, the camp at Smith River had not yet taken shape. The cabins were dropped, without the usual forethought, on their log foundations in the first available spot. More important, fresh water, so necessary for cooking and cleaning, had to be hauled some distance. Frances rolled up her sleeves and went to work. Shortly after the Holmstroms settled into camp, the Shay locomotive arrived and needed Charles's immediate attention. A few days later, two steam donkeys were delivered and the logging began. But Charles, like Frances, was already looking beyond the forests of the Umpqua. Under the Gardiner Company's employ for the last fifteen years, Holmstrom sometimes struggled with the hand that fed him. Eight decades later his youngest son Rolf remembers, "If my father was dissatisfied with the boss or working conditions, he took immediate action—he walked off the job. He might have missed some opportunities doing that. He was impetuous that way."

Over the course of the year, Frances grew weary of the cramped quarters and the constant concern for Carl and Buzz. The boys needed open space to play safely. Regular schooling was also on her mind. The short winter days, the waiting for goods and supplies to arrive, the seasonal mud that made housekeeping difficult—annoyed her.

In July of 1913, Charles and Frances reached a joint decision to "quit the Company and move to Harbor, in Curry County." The previous February, Charles Holmstrom had traveled by wagon south down the coast. Unable to find transportation out of Gold Beach, he walked the final forty-three miles to Harbor. After a day in the village, he decided there were opportunities for a man with his skills.

That year *The Curry County Reporter* in Gold Beach crowed:

> To Curry County, with an area of 1,000,000 acres, belongs the unique distinction of not having a single incorporated town, no railroad mileage, no telegraph lines, but one barber, and no policeman. This county, located at the extreme southwest corner of Oregon, has the raw wealth of many a well-populated section, a land area nearly equal to that of the state of Delaware, and estimated population of less than 2,500. Fronting on the Pacific Ocean, and being almost surrounded to the rear by the Coast Range, Curry County is naturally rough and isolated. This very mixture of mountain, valley and coast, however, is the assurance of the future.

When the Holmstroms left Smith River in early September, Buzz was four and Carl, six. The family crossed the Umpqua River and met the beach stagecoach at Winchester Bay for the ride down to North Bend. As the horses trotted along the hard-packed sand, the driver kept an eye on the incoming tide. Carl and Buzz were thrilled by what they viewed as a race with the surf. Another wagon, loaded with trunks, bedding, Frances's sewing machine, and Charles's tool chest, followed behind, the driver squinting while he inhaled spray and sand. They forded Ten Mile Creek without incident and reached Jarvis Landing, where they caught a launch to Empire.

The Holmstroms stayed in North Bend for two weeks, visiting Frances's family. Seth, Frances's younger brother, had quit his job at one of the local mills and gone into the transportation business with two friends, purchasing a small number of automobiles. When Uncle Seth drove the family to the Marshfield depot to catch the train to Coquille, Carl and Buzz sat in shocked amazement: their first automobile ride.

The Holmstroms rode the spur line of the Southern Pacific to Coquille. From there, they traveled west down the Coquille River to Bandon aboard the *Dispatch*, one of three sternwheelers on the river. Frances called their journey a "dreamland ride." The Coquille Valley impressed both the Holmstroms.

At Bandon, Holmstrom hired a man to take them by auto to Gold Beach, sixty miles down the coast. After fifteen miles, they stopped in the small town of Langlois for the night. Worn out by the long day, neither Carl and Buzz had trouble falling asleep, nor did Charles. But Frances lay awake most of the night, annoyed by the music from a nearby dance hall.

The next morning they were off early–the narrow dirt track was the only north-south route in Curry County at the time. Up and over Introductory Mountain they went. Frances wrote:

> The road was barely wide enough for a team or auto, steep with a drop of hundreds of feet below us, and turns so sharp we had to stop to make some of them. I glued my eyes to the uphill side and held my grit with both hands. We kept meeting teams and having to back up to find a place where we could pass. Once, when we took the outside to let someone pass, I knew there was trouble, but didn't dare look down. Charlie told me afterward that the hind wheel slid outside the log that banked the road, and we had been hung for a few minutes right over the precipice.

After a meal in Wedderburn, they ferried across the Rogue River to Gold Beach, the seat of Curry County, and their auto ride ended.

Their belongings arrived from Bandon aboard a gasoline schooner. Now Holmstrom hired a wagon to carry family and belongings the last thirty-five miles to Harbor. The next afternoon they finally reached Harbor, across the Chetco River from Brookings, Oregon. The hundred-mile journey had taken nearly three days.

CHARLES HOLMSTROM was looking for a fresh start. He found work at the Brookings Lumber Company, at the time the most modern mill on the Oregon coast. Brookings promised much: steady wages, safer working conditions, decent accommodations for the men and their families. One observer stated, "The large locomotives, steam shovels, scrapers, etc. that are at work, together with the number of logging cars and dining cars standing on sidetracks reminded the casual observer more of a railroad division than a logging camp." Experienced engineers like Holmstrom were in demand.

The southern Oregon coast's temperate climate, along with its forests and beaches, offered Carl and Buzz plenty of room to wander. They played in the

Nina Benham and Frances Holmstrom

nearby sand dunes and waded in the tide pools, ponds, and streams. In nearby Chetco River, they sailed hand-made boats and commandeered oversized pieces of driftwood for rafts.

Charles resumed his boat-building. On Sundays, he took the boys out on the Chetco in yet another new rowboat. Mrs. Nina Benham, a French woman, "on whom household cares sit lightly, and who loves children," often escorted the two Holmstrom boys to the beach, where she cooked their supper of fried potatoes and boiled eggs. Then Benham would throw herself into their games, playing with them until they were worn out and it was time for bed.

Frances immersed herself in the local Sunday School activities. Like her mother and sister, she was an able organizer. Church picnics, bake sales, poetry readings, and school plays all had Frances's mark. When she was not running the household, Frances continued to paint and write poetry. One of her paintings portrayed a woman, her back to the artist, at the kitchen sink with the window open. The woman appears to have paused in the middle of her summer task to look out across the expanse of ocean.

At the end of their first year in Harbor, Frances wrote:

> Last September, when we came here, our little tract of land was covered with hazel and fern so thick we couldn't go through it. Now we have a comfortable house, a good big woodshed and workshop, a little barn filled with hay for the yellow Jersey and a fine, up-to-date hen house, where about forty fowls, mostly Brown Leghorns, dwell and lay eggs. All the fern and hazel is cut and burned and we had one acre planted to garden this summer. It did reasonably well, supplying us with all we needed ourselves, a supply put away for winter, and a little to sell. We have made friends, and feel at home in our new place.

That September Carl began school in the white one-room schoolhouse nearby. His teacher, Mr. Kendricks, ran a tight ship. Buzz, only five, was eager to go to school but had to wait another year. To the north nineteen-year-old Glen Wooldridge was running the Rogue River for the first time. (Twenty years later, he helped Buzz Holmstrom during his second run down the same river.) In Bandon, a fire gutted the entire business district of the town of eighteen hundred. In eastern Europe, Austria declared war on Serbia and World War I began.

> Jan. 30, 1915. It is a rainy night. The surf is roaring, and the wind and rain come in bursts, with calm spells between. It is very warm, and feels like spring. I found a bunch of spring flowers in bloom today, and have a few early seeds planted. Up at our old Gardiner home they report weather that froze over the Umpqua River so that boats could not go up for several days.

LIKE THE WEATHER Frances wrote about, an unsettled period was beginning for the Holmstroms. Prices for basic necessities had begun to rise because of World War I. Charles had been injured on his job at the Mt. Emily gold mine on the Chetco River. While operating a diesel engine, a piece of the heavy machinery broke off and fell on his foot, breaking bones. Money was scarce and Frances, thinking of going back to work, began preparations for the teacher's examination. In one of her few political opinions stated in her journal, Frances wondered aloud how the commodity dealers were allowed to make so much money by selling products overseas to foreigners, while Americans went hungry.

Christmas 1915 was difficult for the Johnsons, the Lawhornes, and the Holmstroms. Frances wrote, "Our gifts were ordinary, but we did our best. Charlie made a pair of candlesticks for Mother and a pair for Emma. I sent Roy and Emma a book of poems to read beside their fireplace on winter evenings and Mother a couple of watercolors of the beach." Charles built a toy water-wheel which, when placed in the creek, operated a miniature saw and steam donkey for the boys. On Christmas Day the weather cooperated, and Charles, Frances, and the boys picnicked with friends on the beach.

On the afternoon of February 23, 1916, long-suffering Anna Johnson died. She was sixty-eight. Frances arrived late and kept a vigil at her mother's bedside throughout the night. Later, she remembered her Mother as "an ailing woman. Always suffering, but making light of it—sitting on a stool to wash dishes, iron, etc., because she was not able to stand up." She was buried in the Pioneer Cemetery in Marshfield. The same year Mrs. Johnson died, the Southern Pacific linked Coos Bay to the Willamette Valley.

In September 1917, the Holmstroms left Harbor. Four years was the longest the family had remained in one place. Until his accident, Charles had worked regularly. Frances had become a guiding light within the congregation and the community at large. Carl was entering fourth grade, and Buzz, third grade. The Holmstroms had made friends, established themselves, seemed to have a stake in the town's future. Frances, however, mentioned "being discouraged, for Harbor seemed to be a sinking ship.... The news of good times on Coos was very tempting." They rented out their place for a year and sold all their furniture, crops, and stock. Abruptness characterized their departure.

They spontaneously decided to visit San Francisco. Frances wrote, "As we had never visited Frisco since we were married, and had always planned a trip, we suddenly determined to take our wedding trip right then, accompanied by the two children." Carl and Buzz had reached the age where they could appreciate an adventure to a new place. The trip took twenty-four hours. First-class fare, one way, fourteen dollars; second-class fare, nine dollars. The Holmstroms took the latter.

Three hundred yards offshore from Brookings lay the steamer *Quinault*. For two days she had been taking on a cargo of lumber from the Brookings Mill and now the signal to bring the paying passengers aboard was given. The Holmstroms found themselves seated in a nine by twelve-foot carriage, attached to a cable that ran from a point on the cliffs out to the waiting ship. "Before we knew it, we swung out over the water, lightly, swiftly and smoothly to the ship, landing before we realized that we had started." Buzz and Carl were thrilled. The *Quinault* was so heavily loaded that she rode smoothly on the voyage down the coast to San Francisco. Nevertheless, all the Holmstroms were seasick.

Early the next morning, the *Quinault* steamed into San Francisco Bay. A spectacular fall day, typical of that time of year, inspired Frances to write, "We entered a fairyland." Carl and Buzz stood on deck, entranced by the skyline.

As Charles, Frances, and the boys disembarked, they were met by a colorful noisy scene. Since the streetcar drivers were on strike, the streets were thick with traffic. Cars and trucks honked their horns as they jockeyed for position; the pedestrians, ignoring the traffic, moved with undisguised purpose. Carl and Buzz clung to their father, excited, yet fearful.

They stayed at the Hotel St. Cecile on Van Ness Avenue, overlooking the recently built Civic Center and spent their days sightseeing. Frances wrote:

> My general impression of San Francisco is of its greatness, its crowds, its kindness and the riches that seem to overflow so that even the poorest may reap a little of its benefit, in the wonderful Golden Gate park, museums, lectures, concerts, greenhouses and zoo.
>
> There seems such a spirit of friendliness everywhere and handsomely dressed men and women would go out of their way to show kindness to us poor greenhorns. The boys were most of the time astonished simply beyond words, but during our first streetcar ride up Market, Haldane had everybody's attention, standing up and pointing and hollering, 'Oh Mamma, look... See those women in the windows!' meaning the wax figures (mannequins). He has told me since then that when we had secured our lodging, and went into the elevator to be taken up to it, he thought the elevator was our room.

After their impromptu family holiday, the Holmstroms took the steamer *Breakwater* back to Coos Bay. (Frances noted offhandedly in her journal that the

Quinault, on its return voyage to Brookings, had hit a rock and gone down.) Coming up the coast, the *Breakwater* bucked ocean swells and the prevailing winds for the entire voyage. Frances and the boys remained in their cabin; Charles walked the decks, immune to the pitch and roll of the coastal steamer.

By the time they passed over the bar at Coos Bay, the Holmstroms were eager to be home. For ten days they stayed with cousin Eva Hall in North Bend. They began house-hunting and found a place to rent in Bunker Hill, a neighborhood to the south of Marshfield. With its dismal view and its back to the ocean, Bunker Hill was not the Holmstrom's first choice. The shipyards along Coos Bay were bustling, however, and Charles put to use his skills as a boat builder. Carl and Buzz enrolled in the local grammar school.

Frances enjoyed being near her family and relatives, especially her sister Emma. Uncle Joe's six girls looked toward the two sisters for advice and direction. Yet, Frances wrote in her journal:

> We felt like cats in strange garrets all the time we were there, for none of us liked town life, and all longed to escape it.... The rest of the memories of that year are of German measles, Carl's sore eyes, Charlie's lame leg, grocery bills, paychecks that never could be persuaded to do more than balance expenses, and a longing for a place of our own.

AFTER A YEAR the Holmstroms found their long-sought place near McKinley, fourteen miles east of Coquille and the Coquille Valley, in the Coast Range. Isolated by the Blue Ridge and the Hungry Mountains, McKinley occupied a small valley along the edge of Fairview Valley. The Coos Bay Wagon Road (the Willamette Valley-to-coast route) was still in use in August, 1918, when the Holmstroms moved to their farm. The twenty-five mile section of wagon road through Sumner, Fairview, McKinley, and Dora was a single lane constructed from local timber. Logs were set end to end and then four-by-twelve planks laid horizontally across the logs and nailed in place. Lumber was so inexpensive at the time that the planks were replaced routinely. Carl Holmstrom recalled that he and Buzz sometimes walked out to the wooden road and waited to see the lone horse-drawn wagon or Model-T passing through McKinley. "Kept us out of trouble. Not that there was much trouble to be found in McKinley in those days."

McKinley was off the beaten track. The one-room schoolhouse, which Carl and Buzz would attend, stood at the center of town. A grange hall, where the local farmers met, served as the post office. Nothing more. The road intersected a few small homesteads. Most people lived in the outlying areas, working their farms, coming into "town" only when necessary; subsistence farming required long hours and ceaseless effort.

Land around McKinley was a bargain. With the sale of their place at Harbor and their savings, Charles and Frances paid most of the fifteen hundred dollar sale price for the twenty-seven-acre farm. The remainder was scraped together with help from Frances's family. Neither of the Holmstroms were inclined to borrow money, certainly not from outside the family, but they could not pass up this chance. They had found their haven.

When the Holmstroms moved to the farm at McKinley that summer, Buzz was just past his ninth birthday. He had grown into a broad-faced boy with color in his cheeks; a perpetual grin that he struggled to contain; and like his father, a compact, square-shouldered body that already suggested strength and efficiency. In his bib overalls, with his shirt sleeves rolled up, and straddling the plow horse, Buzz looked the quintessential country boy.

Used to living in logging camps and on small plots of land, Carl and Buzz could not believe their good fortune when they first saw the farm. Nor could they believe that their family owned such an immense tract. The acreage, a good portion of it bottom land, occupied one of the many small valleys surrounded by the thickly forested McCarthy hills, near McKinley. The boys quickly took to the fields and woods, learning the lay of the land as they explored. In short order they located the game trails, the thickest berry patches, the fishing holes, and with the help of one of the neighbor boys, the secret shortcut over the hill to school, cutting travel time in half. Most important, Middle Creek looped through the property, giving an island-like appearance to the farm during the spring runoff.

The Holmstrom house squatted beneath an enormous black walnut tree whose branches stretched over the roof. At first sight of the house, Frances was discouraged. The rooms were small and plain — a kitchen, a bedroom, a sitting room, a storage area, and the attic. Rough vertical cedar planks, board and batten, covered the exterior. Wads of newspaper provided meager insulation; an east wind could still finger its way in on cold days. But Frances had always managed to turn the logging camp cabins into suitable homes and it would be no different here.

What furniture there was—a table, chairs, two trunks, a chest of drawers, simple platform beds—Charles built. In winter the round black stove in the sitting room fended off the worst of the cold, as did the wood-burning cook stove in the kitchen. Buzz and Carl slept in the attic where the heat collected. "You kept bundled up and got used to the chill that set in when the fires burned low in the morning," Carl remembered. "It wasn't so bad. Besides, we didn't know any better. Come summer, we slept outside."

The Holmstroms had few material possessions and little ready cash. Food came from the garden planted between the house and Middle Creek. Occasionally, Charles hunted game in the surrounding forest. They drew well-water for drinking,

cooking, and washing. When it went dry in summer, Carl and Buzz took turns hauling creek water to the house. Candles and kerosene lanterns furnished light until
they left the farm in 1934, the same year the Rural Electrification Administration
began to string its lines out to McKinley. Even then, the Holmstroms could not
have afforded the connection costs.

Clothes were handmade, passed down and around the neighboring farm families as the children outgrew them. With a piece of cardboard, shoes were made to
last until the hole outgrew the shoe. Everything was used, then reused, until it
simply wore out. The boys' toys were simple and few, often the found objects
around the farm, or something Charles made out of available materials. Frances
read to Carl and Buzz from the Bible and the monthly *National Geographic*. She
encouraged both boys to write poetry, although she often shook her head at their
youthful efforts.

MIDDLE CREEK rises on the slopes of Coos Mountain, two thousand feet above the
valley floor. After a relatively straightforward descent, the creek enters Fairview
Valley and meanders toward McKinley. There it redoubles on itself, carving two
distinct bights within a short distance before emptying into the larger North
Fork of the Coquille a few miles downstream. The Holmstroms, each time they
came and went, had to cross Middle Creek to reach their house, the barn, and the
outbuildings. In summer and fall crossing the creek was a minor inconvenience:
walk down a shallow dip in the bank, along a worn trail, step over the creek, and
climb up the other side. Come winter and early spring, however, the trail disappeared as the creek overflowed its banks and spread toward the fields. Even the
footbridge the Holmstroms used was temporarily submerged under the swirling
brown water. Then the farm became an island and the Holmstroms stayed put.

If the Holmstroms were going to make a living off the farm, they would need
easier access to their property. A year after arriving, Charles Holmstrom and a
hired man began work on a bridge across Middle Creek. They searched the forested hillsides above the farm, found four tall cedars to serve as foundation posts,
felled them, and dragged them by horse to the creek. With the creek a trickle, they
set the posts in its bed. No small task. They felled four more cedars, larger still,
and used them as stringers across the creek. Once more timber was sawed into
planks, Charles was able to finish the job himself. A significant addition to the
farm, the new bridge allowed them to drive their Model-T, nicknamed "Cooty,"
onto the farm in any season, to graze the cows in the pasture on the other side
of the creek, and to place their dairy products within easy reach of the creamery
truck.

Running the farm required a coordinated effort on the part of everyone.
Buzz and Carl were always doing chores—before and after school, weekends,

Young Buzz reaping

summers — collecting eggs from the hen house and honey from the beehives; hanging meat in the smokehouse; collecting, chopping, and stacking wood in the woodshed. The garden had to be spaded, planted, weeded, and watered, as did the seasonal cash crops. The livestock required care and feeding, pens and stalls needed cleaning. Equipment had to be maintained, outbuildings repaired, fences mended. In order to take on the other projects that sprung up, Charles taught the boys the most vital chores. Lately, Charles was out of breath and needed afternoon naps on a cot beneath the walnut tree, if he was to continue working.

Soon after arriving on the farm, the Holmstrom's purchased a DeLavall Separator and Milker. The separator, first marketed in 1917, soon proved to be indispensable to anyone dependent on a monthly cream check. The Holmstroms, needing a steady income, named their first and favorite milk cow Goldie. Twice a day, morning and evening, Charles, Frances, Carl or Buzz sat in the barn, cranking the handle as fast as possible until the bell signaled the cream had separated from the milk. Carl thought it a mundane chore; Buzz thought it was like winning a prize.

In addition to the monthly cream check, the Holmstroms made money "truck farming." They grew corn, potatoes, and strawberries, harvested them and sold them to the local markets in Coquille. Their strawberries soon gained a local reputation for excellence. But picking strawberries, as Wallace Ohrt recalled in *The Rogue I Remember,* "is absorbing for awhile, then tedious and finally backbreaking."

While Charles and the boys tended to the farming, Frances kept up with the other demands—housekeeping, meals, canning, and curing meat; mending and washing clothes; tending the garden. If all went well, it was a break-even proposition.

THAT FIRST YEAR Buzz and his new friend, Ross Brown, were in fourth grade; Carl was in fifth grade. The Browns, long-time residents of McKinley, lived within shouting distance of the Holmstrom farm. Each day the boys walked to school together. Class began with the pledge of allegiance and a song that everyone had to learn by heart. Resources in District #27 were limited and the standard curriculum prevailed—

arithmetic, geography, reading, penmanship, social studies. Pupils' attendance varied, depending on the farm work. Mrs. Harry grouped students by grade, rotating them to the front of the room for their lessons. Carl believed even then his brother had an uncanny memory:

Buzz, Anna, and Goldie

> I think he had one of those photographic memories. He'd read a book and weeks later tell you all about it. Buzz absorbed everything so easily that he finished his assignments quickly and often had time on his hands. Too much time. He would get into mischief with the other boys in class.

Lois Sheperd Shinkle recalls the time she and a number of other school children were standing in front of the post office in McKinley when a runaway team of horses, dragging a log, came racing by. Buzz ran out into the road and somehow managed to steer the horses in between two myrtlewood trees. Once the team stopped, however, one of the horses stepped on a bottle and cut its foot. When Buzz saw that the horse was hurt, he put his arms around the horse's neck and cried and cried.

A year after arriving on the farm, Frances wrote:

> We are all happy and contented, though we all work hard and so far haven't made much more than a living. The house is a horrid shack of a thing, and I used to think it would never seem like home, but it does. The barn, smokehouse and woodshed are also shacks, but they are old and picturesque, and I like them. The land is fertile, and it is a joy to look across the field of clover and the bloomy rippling grain and the cool, tender old orchard and feel that it is all ours — ours to labor with, to reap, and finally be rewarded for. But when our five milk cows come pacing into the picture our pride is at its height, for we, who never dreamed of such a thing a few years ago, are actually milking cows, separating, sending cream, and above all, receiving a monthly cream check. We feel sure we can make a living as farmers if — we always include in all our plans for future success — if we keep our health.

Over the next decade, Frances's words proved prophetic. Both Charles and she suffered minor health problems, complicated by the demands of the farm. Further,

27

Carl in the Bennett "boat"

at the age of thirty-seven, Frances was pregnant with her third child, due the following summer. Nearly ten years had passed since Carl, then Buzz, were born in the logging camp up Schofield Creek. She worried about the pregnancy but said little to Charles.

She fretted more about her husband's precarious health. The thought of what might happen if Charles were too sick to run the farm made her anxious. That first winter on the farm the pandemic Spanish influenza swept across the United States and finally reached Oregon. One quarter of the American population contracted the virus, and nearly seven hundred thousand died. The Holmstroms, like many others along the isolated Oregon coast, weathered it with only minor illness.

On April 22, 1919, Frances gave birth to a baby girl, whom they named Anna Hall, after Frances's mother. The doctor had a difficult time reaching the farm in McKinley, arriving only at the last moment. Martha Bennett and Edna Brown, Ross's mother, proved competent midwives. They labor-sat with Frances through-out the birth and kept her new household running the first weeks after Anna's arrival.

In October 1919 Frances's father died in North Bend. He was buried next to his wife in the Pioneer Cemetery at Marshfield, but his passing went unrecorded in Frances's journal.

Like most farmers in the valley, Charles Holmstrom could not afford regular hired help. The survival of the farm depended on Carl and Buzz's labor. Years later, when asked what he remembered most about his brother Buzz, Carl replied with-out hesitation, "His work on the farm. Buzz was a boy doing a man's work back then!" So was Carl. Rural, working people along the southern Oregon coast had always said the Great Depression had been going on years before it officially started and continued for years after it had officially ended.

In July of 1920, Frances wrote:

> The boys are big fellows now. Carl will soon be thirteen and Haldane, though only eleven, is bigger than Carl. He takes the bigger interest in the farm work, too, and can harness and drive the team, plow, and milks his two cows night and morning, while he watches the filling cream cans with as jealous an eye as either Charlie or I. Carl is glad to do his share, but he does it in duty only, and hoes corn and feeds pigs while his spirit is falling timber or climbing up to grease the blocks in the high lead tree on top of the hill.

When they were not going to school or doing their chores, Buzz and Carl headed for Middle Creek. For a couple of months each summer it was a sparkling, tree-lined stretch of water. All the farm kids—the Browns, the Hansens, the Masts, and the Holmstroms—gravitated to the creek on hot days.

Both Buzz and Carl had grown up within sight or sound of moving water. As young children, they traveled by rowboat, launch, sternwheeler and coastal steamer. They knew the motion of water as well or better than the ground beneath their feet—the heave of an ocean swell, the smoothness of a lake, the tug of a stream, or the pull of a river. They could tell the difference between a trickle, a freshet, a riffle, and a rapid. Most important, Carl and Buzz had witnessed their father's alert yet comfortable way around water. Whether rowing his skiff across Ten Mile Lake or piloting the launch on the Umpqua delta, Charles Holmstrom had always been careful. The boys' instinctive attraction to a rollicking stream was tempered by a degree of caution. Not enough, however, to quell their enthusiasm.

By early summer the water subsided and warmed enough for swimming. The gravel bars were exposed and in the deeper sections of the creek swimming holes appeared. Frances wrote in her journal, "The boy's chief relaxation this summer is in the water. They can swim and dive and do all sorts of water tricks, and Carl especially can roll a log splendidly."

Hours passed with the adults away and the boys left to their own devices. Buzz and Ross skipped stones and floated crude homemade boats. They caught crawdads in coffee cans and later boiled them and ate the tails. Each boy had his favorite spot, a place where the wind could not reach, or the branches of a willow were strong enough to bear his weight as he dangled over the water. Blackberry bushes crowded along the banks, offering easy pickings. The willow trees provided shade. They chewed the roots of licorice fern, a kind of natural candy, that grew on maple trees. It stuck between their teeth for days afterwards.

One morning Ira Bennett, whose wife had helped deliver Anna, showed up with a boat he had built and proudly presented his creation to Buzz and Carl. Made from barn wood and nailed haphazardly, the rectangular box somehow managed to float, despite a constant two inches of rising and falling water inside; Bennett never claimed to be a boat builder, just a good neighbor. The boys gracefully accepted.

The winter of 1920 brought heavy rains and Middle Creek, now a muddy brown, turned into a fast-moving torrent that regularly overran its narrow banks and flooded the surrounding fields. Over the years, Charles took care to warn both of his sons about fast water. Frances, from her kitchen window, often teased the boys: Watch out, a freshet might be coming down river any minute now and sweep you away! But for the most part, Buzz and Carl were left to figure it out for themselves.

Although wary of the high water at first, Buzz and Carl eventually decided the excitement outweighed the danger. They patched Ira Bennett's boat (it had taken a beating over the previous summer) and, along with Ross Brown, dragged it upstream as far as they could, slid it down the bank of the creek and jumped in. Away they went, mostly out of control, careening down the waterway until they somehow managed to pull into a rare eddy. More often, one of them ended up in the creek.

Buzz and Carl discovered another means for getting down Middle Creek. They began riding the stray logs that washed down the creek and into the adjacent fields whenever the loggers breached a splash dam upstream. Each fall Jay Freeman, (who lived with his wife Audrey across from the Holmstrom farm) and the other gyppo loggers would begin cutting timber high up one of the drainages. They cold decked the logs or held them behind a splash dam, waiting for the winter freshets. Too much rain and the logs would float out of the river channel and onto the farmers' fields, much to the latter's displeasure. Too little rain, and the logs wedged in the river. The loggers waited for the right moment and when it came, off they went down the river. Freeman recalls following log runs down Middle Creek in a rowboat, right past the Holmstrom place. As he put it, "The river was the key to the whole thing. The river was the road and without it there was no logging and no work." In the mid 1930s, farmers in the region obtained an injunction to halt the practice.

Walking upstream, the Holmstrom boys searched for a log wide enough to be stable and short enough to slip down the channel. Some they tried to ride standing, most they straddled and held on for dear life; success was measured in tens of seconds. Sooner or later, everyone ended up in the river. Afterward, all the boys stood on the banks shivering—except Buzz. He fell off as often as Carl or Ross, but the cold did not seem to bother him. Carl Holmstrom wondered aloud why they all did not drown. Years later Katie Brown, Ross's older sister, wrote to Buzz, "I was sorry you didn't have your collaborator mention the wild desire you boys used to have to drive logs during high water. That used to be the height of your individual and collective ambitions as I can remember."

To discourage the log-riding, Charles built a pram for Buzz and Carl. Ten feet long, lightweight, flat-bottomed with a broad transom and a squared-off bow, the boat was best suited for slow-moving water, but performed adequately on a narrow creek with fast water. It was stable and easily repaired, something the boys appreciated. Ross Brown, however, remembers the boat as prone to tipping, always taking on water because there were usually two or three boys crowded in it at one time. Buzz and Carl fashioned paddles and off they went. In late spring and summer they would paddle upstream as far as possible, often a mile or more. Once they reached unbearably slow water, they would turn the pram around and drift lazily back downstream. As they moved down the creek, they would maneuver the craft away from the rocks, snags, and overhanging branches. Over and over again, the boys floated the river until they were called to do a chore or were simply too worn out to paddle.

During the winter and early spring, when the water ran high and fast, they dragged the flat-bottomed pram along the banks to their launching point, slid the boat in and hopped aboard, paddles in hand. Immediately they were swept downstream, the banks shoulder-high now, at a speed they had only imagined. Obstacles were few, but there was no ignoring the bridge their father had built. Every so often, one of the boys forgot to duck and into the creek they went, delighted with themselves. Soaked to the bone after these winter runs, Buzz and Carl huddled around the wood stove in the kitchen, shivering with glee.

IN FEBRUARY OF 1922, Frances was pregnant again. She was forty-one; Charles was almost sixty. Despite the long hours, they made only a slim living on the farm. Anna needed looking after and Charles was constantly short of breath. Frances was not feeling well either. They went to see a doctor at the Keizer Hospital in North Bend. His diagnosis was sobering; Charles had a heart problem and needed rest, a need of which the Holmstroms were well aware. Frances's chest pains were the result of overwork and constant worry.

Carl, never keen on farming, finished eighth grade and went to work in the woods. He hired on as a whistle punk (usually a young boy whose job was to signal the steam donkey operator when it was time to pull the log to the landing)over on Cunningham Creek; starting pay was three dollars a day, plus room and board in the logging camp. Only four men to a cabin, decent bunks, and plenty of good food. Carl was glad to have the job, even if it was at the bottom of the chain. Just fourteen, his dream was to become a high-lead climber (a logger who would rig blocks and lines high above the ground on a spar tree), then sail the seas.

In October of 1922, Buzz entered his final year at the McKinley grade school. He would graduate from eighth grade the following June and was excited about going to high school, especially about the opportunity to play football on an organized team. Frances, too, had set her mind on Buzz going to high school, perhaps college after that. Like her mother, Frances pinned many of her hopes and aspirations on her second son. Buzz was bright, liked school, and had always done well with little effort. Frances, however, was unsure how she and Charles would manage the farm, with Carl gone so often.

On October 28, Frances gave birth to a boy named Rolf. Later she recorded his birth in the family journal.

> So now we have two small children and two big ones. Rolf, having followed the usual route of babies, is now out of babyhood, beginning to think and reason and having a very strong personality of his own. Tow-headed and round-faced, like all the rest, and usually healthy and normal. He has a merry and loving nature, and has never been bashful a moment, or seen anyone he considered a stranger. He and Buzz seem quite alike.

With an ailing husband, two young children to look after, and chores that could not wait, Frances needed Buzz at home more than ever. High school was postponed.

AFTER A YEAR-AND-A-HALF on the farm, fifteen-year-old Buzz Holmstrom entered Coquille High School in September 1924. Two other McKinley boys, Ross Brown and Ken Hansen, started high school with Holmstrom that fall and all were eager to venture beyond the boundaries of their rural community. Holmstrom and Hansen were especially interested in joining Coach "Brick" Leslie's football team.

At first, Carl and Buzz planned to find an inexpensive house in town to rent. Carl would continue to work in the woods and Buzz would go to school. They would help on the farm when needed. No inexpensive place could be found, however, and the plan fell through. Buzz ended up boarding with Ken Hansen at the McCloud Apartments. Over the years, many of the farm youth from the outlying areas around Coquille had roomed there. Conditions were Spartan, but the rent was negligible and a degree of independence was gained. Buzz took a part-time job baby-sitting in the Walker household to cover a portion of his living expenses. Ed Walker and his wife Rio liked Buzz immediately. Before long, Ed offered him a job at his recently opened Standard Oil service station.

By the summer of 1925, Charles Holmstrom's health was deteriorating and Buzz moved back to the farm. With Mr. Brown and other neighbors, he kept the farm running.

In early June, Carl joined the Merchant Marine. Since boyhood he had harbored the dream of going to sea. With Buzz back at home, Carl decided the time was right—one of the few occasions when he allowed his yearning for adventure to override his strong sense of duty toward his family. Carl shipped out of Portland for six months aboard the M.S. *Seekonk*, a ship built for service in World War I. It was bound for the east coast with a load of white fir lumber and then to Europe.

While Carl was at sea, Buzz began his sophomore year at Coquille High. That September, he boarded at the McCloud Apartments again. After school and on the weekends he started working regularly at Walker's station. Business was thriving and Ed Walker was delighted to have Buzz back.

Walker—a slender, wiry man with a quick smile and boundless energy—spoke fluent French, was a renowned storyteller, and had been a welterweight boxing champion at the University of California at Berkeley. A member of the Masonic Lodge, he was known to give dazzling, impromptu speeches. Around Coquille, Walker was also known for his unsolicited generosity. On more than one occasion the Holmstroms themselves were the recipients of his kindness. Like his three brothers—Archie, Dewey, and Paul—Ed enjoyed gambling of any kind. His willingness to place a wager on matters of chance or ability—weather, football games, the time it took to change a tire—was common knowledge around town.

In the center of the Coquille business district, Walker's location proved ideal. All the local and long distance traffic passed by the station daily. One entire wing of the station was reserved for tire repair. The three grease pits used for lubrication and oil changes were always busy. Four gas pumps meant prompt service, though most folks were not in a hurry, preferring to chat with the amiable young men the Walkers always seemed to hire. The Walkers ran an efficient business, but treated their employees more like an extended family. Young Buzz Holmstrom fit right in.

Buzz assumed the usual duties—pumping gas, changing oil and batteries, and repairing tires. He learned fast. Ross Kistner, who played football with him, recalls that Buzz eventually preferred working in the "pits" lubing and changing oil rather than pumping gas. Kistner believed that working at the station more or less forced Holmstrom out of his shell. "It was impossible to walk or drive through Coquille without passing by the Walker's," he said. "After awhile everyone knew Buzz."

Ken Hansen and Buzz alternated at the guard position on Coach Leslie's football team their second year. With only twenty players on the squad, and a number of untimely injuries and illnesses, the two sophomores played enough to earn the first stripe on their letterman's sweater. The team struggled that

"The McKinley Boys," Ross Brown, Buzz Holmstrom, Harry Mast, Ken Hansen

year, winning only two out of seven games. Only Bandon had a worse record, losing all seven of its games. The losses failed to quash Holmstrom's enthusiasm. He also discovered that he was the academic equal of the best of the town kids and was invited to join the recently formed Honor Society.

The friendships Holmstrom made his first two years in Coquille lasted throughout his life. Thurman Hickam, who later lived across the street from Holmstrom, had moved into Coquille from the small farming community of Arago to go to school. Phyllis McCurdy, who met him in the Honor Society, became a life-long friend and confidant. She recalls:

> Buzz was never shy around me. He played pranks and jokes and the such. He did seem to become very shy around girls, in the romantic sense I guess. He grew up on a farm that was quite isolated in those days. Sometimes he walked into town, or thumbed his way in if he could. Some of the old farm people didn't get to town often, except when they had to. So sometimes their social skills were limited. In those days the boys didn't have the social skills they do today. But I wouldn't say Buzz was particularly shy. He especially liked the older people.

Holmstrom eventually became friends with Earl Hamilton, who courted and married Phyllis after high school. Jim Watson, a year behind Buzz in school, saw him nearly every day at Walker's. Buzz also met Clarence Bean.

In 1926 Clarence Bean was a senior at Coquille High. Because of his delayed start, Buzz, the same age as Clarence (seventeen), was a sophomore. A yearbook photograph of Bean reveals a thin young man, standing with his weight on one leg,

Clarence Bean

the other leg bent slightly in front. His hands reach together tentatively across his stomach, fingertips to fingertips, as though he were holding a piece of string. His short brown hair is parted on one side, and a trace of melancholy is conveyed in the pose. Class vice-president his sophomore year and then class president the last two years, he participated in the school plays and the executive council and had recently been chosen editor for the school newspaper, the *Hi-Times*.

In a small rural town where football, farming, and logging were the mainstays, Clarence Bean was a bit out of step. He was not much of an athlete, and though he liked the outdoors, he was neither a fisherman nor a woodsman. His popularity rested on a ready wit, a superior intelligence, and a willingness to try anything new or different. Jim Watson remembers his friend as soft-spoken, well read, something of the town literate. During his high school years, Bean often stayed with Jim Watson's family, growing especially close to Watson's mother. Coquille rumors claimed there were drinking problems in Bean's home.

Bean recognized a kindred spirit in the quiet, unassuming Holmstrom. Although from different backgrounds, the two teenagers were curious, intelligent, and hungry for wider experience. Both had adventurous spirits and were well-liked, with numerous friends and acquaintances. Yet each displayed a certain reticence.

Neither had a steady girlfriend in high school nor did either marry in later life. Both were close to their mothers and later helped support them. Ross Kistner, a life-long friend of Bean's, saw both his friends as mavericks and loners.

> It wasn't like Clarence was one or the other, a friendly guy or a loner. They were just different aspects of his personality. Buzz was pretty smart, but Clarence was brilliant. He got top grades and learned everything easily, perhaps too easily. He sometimes didn't seem to have much ambition. It was funny. Clarence was one that always wanted to try different things, though he wasn't particularly adept at outdoor pursuits. Once he figured it out, he'd get bored and look around for something else to do.

In later years a story circulated that Clarence, along with his friend Pete Gould, initiated Buzz into the "Knitting, Tatting and Tattooing Club." Members were supposedly taught "how to drink, swear like a man, and other things man-like." The president was the one who could get the drunkest, the vice-president was runner-up, and the sober one became the janitor. Kistner never heard of this club. He laughs, "If there was any club, I would have been in it. Buzz never drank that much. One time Clarence and I got him drunk just because he didn't drink at all, kind of an innocent. He couldn't go to work the next morning. But I wouldn't call him a drinker."

In late 1926, Frances wrote:

> Haldane is a junior in Coquille High. He has made his own way, working spare time in the Walker Brother's Service Station and making good there and in his studies and on the football team. But he is home now this semester, getting acquainted with the family he has hardly known for two and a half years. Anna is seven. She is in the second grade and fond of school and her teacher, Miss Shone. She is full of pep and life, singing and dancing and racketing all the day…. Rolf has turned four and has always been his Papa's boy, and it is very hard for him now that his best comrade comes no more to play with him…. Carl came home from sea and has been here ever

since. He is now the man of the family, since our Daddy, who was the life and mainstay of us all, has gone away to live in a better country than this. I cannot write about it.

After months of illness, Charles was taken to the Keizer Hospital in North Bend. His chest pains had become intolerable and he had serious difficulty breathing. While Frances watched over Charles at the hospital, Rolf and Anna were sent to their Uncle Seth's for an extended stay. Carl continued working for a local logging outfit and returned to the farm each night to keep an eye on things while Buzz remained in school. Charles improved, only to relapse and finally fall into a coma. On November 7, 1926, he died from "heart trouble and complications." He was sixty-three.

Frances's worst fear, mentioned years earlier, had come true. She was now a widow with two small children, a farm to run, and no regular means of support, except Carl's seasonal logging and Buzz's part time work at Walker's. Adding to the family difficulties, eight-year-old Anna fell off a swing and broke her leg. Then four-year-old Rolf contracted impetigo, a contagious childhood skin disease. Frances, too, was ill, a result of overwork and continual anxiety. Rolf remembers his mother was devastated by Charles's death.

> That's when religion really started to play a bigger part in her life. She asked for divine help. She placed her trust in God's will and the belief that Charles had gone to a better place. I think it helped her get through that difficult time....
>
> I think she kind of grew into Christianity rather than grew up with it.

Funeral services were held in North Bend. In a special to the *Coos Bay Times*, the reporter wrote:

> Mr. Holmstrom was a good man. My acquaintance with him was limited. He was a man whom it did me good to meet for he struck me as a man with whom a child or a blind man could do business and get the best part of the deal for he seemed like a man who had no desire to over-reach or get the best of anyone in any shape, manner or form. I always felt like more of a man after meeting Mr. Holmstrom.

His son would later have the same effect on people.

IN MID-DECEMBER Buzz finished the first semester of his junior year, then returned to the farm. Ed Walker assured Buzz a job was waiting for him whenever he needed it. That winter Buzz put in long hours doing chores. In the evening he studied Latin, English, and a Bible course, determined to complete enough courses so that he could rejoin his class in the fall and graduate from high school.

Frances's sister, Emma, arrived at the farm to look after Frances and the children. Anna and Rolf returned to the one room schoolhouse in McKinley. After a few days, Emma realized how ill Frances was and called a doctor, who told Frances she must rest, preferably in a drier climate, if her health was to improve.

Emma suggested that Frances move to Santa Barbara, California where she and Roy now lived. The rents were cheap, the winters warm, and she and Roy could help with the children. Initially, Frances balked at her sister's offer. She and Charles had always made their own way since they first met at the Creamery in Ten Mile. But Emma's proposal made sense. Frances knew that if her health worsened, Emma and Roy would take the children and raise them as their own. She agreed.

One relative recalls that Aunt Emma, "carried herself like an aristocrat. She didn't just walk; she strode out into the world." She loved to socialize, mix with different kinds of people, and proved a good conversationalist on a variety of subjects. An excellent seamstress, she was much in demand by the rich and famous of Southern California.

Uncle Roy had been a commercial artist for the Seaside Oil Company; he also taught photography at Santa Barbara State College. In time he became a professor at the Brooks Institute, where he was one of the last teachers hired without a college diploma. He painted landscapes; he was a world-class archer; he tinkered with inventions.

While Anna and Rolf attended the Mesa grade school, Frances enrolled in the Santa Barbara Art School. She resumed painting and writing poetry. The incongruity of returning to school after all these years was not lost on Frances. She wrote, "I did very well, holding my own, after all the years on the farm, with the young moderns." With sunshine and with the support of Roy and Emma, Frances's health improved.

Back in Coquille, the football team did not fare well during Buzz's senior year. "Every game, except the one with Riverton, was lost after a stiff battle, but it almost goes without saying that if every class could have offered men such as those from the midst of the 'mighty seniors' the championship would easily have been won for C.H.S." read the 1928 Senior Class Book.

Buzz was elected vice-president of his senior class. He remained in the Honor

Society and participated in the senior play. On May 17, 1928, Holmstrom graduated from Coquille High School with his twenty-two classmates. He had turned nineteen a week earlier. Mr. Higbee, the principal, handed out the diplomas; Ed Walker stood in for Frances, who was still in Santa Barbara. She sent her son a congratulatory note, reminding him that he was the first Holmstrom to complete high school.

The evening program included the "Class Will" read by Holmstrom. In it the seniors bequeathed their rights to the juniors, a tireless convention in this age-old rite of passage. Jokes were scattered throughout the Senior Class Book. One read, "Do you mean to say that Haldane is the strongest senior in school? Strong? Why that guy is so powerful he takes two pianos, puts them together, and plays them like an accordion." Two weeks later, the "strongest senior" was working his way down to Santa Barbara aboard the coastal steamer, *Breakwater,* to bring Frances and the children home.

By now the gravel road from Myrtle Point to Bandon on the coast was complete; thirty years of river boating on the Coquille ended. State Highway 42 brought progress to the Coquille Valley. Cost and travel time shrank, convenience and personal freedom grew. Instead of watching the fields and homesteads from the deck of a paddlewheeler, people sped along the river in their Model-Ts. The paddlewheelers—*Dora, Telegraph, Dispatch, Charm, Echo, and Liberty*—became obsolete. A powerful notion—that mobility equaled freedom—was being reinvented by the automobile.

After the *Breakwater* docked in San Pedro, Buzz made his way to Uncle Roy and Aunt Emma's home in Santa Barbara. Holmstrom had always admired and respected Uncle Roy and was in no hurry to return home. He lingered with Frances and the children in the balmy weather. When it was time to go, Emma and Roy presented Frances with a car they had purchased weeks before. Frances wrote, "We loaded ourselves, typewriter, bedding, grub, many resurrection lily bulbs and other things into the rickety Ford and drove back to Coquille—a glorious trip!"

Recalling that trip up the coast, Anna Holmstrom Smith chuckles at her mother's description.

> Yes, Buzz came down and got us. And it was a nice ride back for a while, until we got to Crescent City, California, and the roads got so bad we had to stop overnight a few times. We started to get short on money and nearly ran out of gas. And then we hit some wet weather which made the roads even more difficult to navigate. I think we barely made it back home. I remember we walked up a hill to have a picnic and there were some Indian graves with stuff around them. Buzz told Rolf and I not to touch the graves, I remember.

The next few years proved to be difficult ones for the Holmstroms. The lease agreement on the farm ran for another year, so upon arriving in Coquille, they rented a house in town. Carl had signed on for another stint with the Merchant

Marine and continued to send a portion of his paycheck home, but he would not return until August. Buzz went back to Walker's, although not as enthusiastically as before. The larger question facing all of them was what to do with the farm.

Town living, Frances discovered, had its advantages. She renewed old friendships and soon met a group of women who belonged to the Coquille Tabernacle Church, a Pentecostal denomination. Before long she was asked to join their congregation. Now that she could attend church services regularly, she also became involved in the church's informal social work. Rolf, in seventh grade, attended Lincoln Junior High; Anna was a sophomore at Coquille High.

In August 1928 Carl returned to Coquille with stories of his adventures in the Merchant Marine. He encouraged Buzz to give it a try. Throughout his high school years, football had taken much of Buzz's energy. Now he was looking for something else. With Carl back to look after the family, he signed on for a tour after Christmas.

When Buzz told Ed Walker that he had joined the Merchant Marine, Walker urged him on. "Silver Dollar Eddie," as some called him, appreciated Holmstrom's yearning for adventure. Walker, a fervent gambler, made regular forays to Reno and Las Vegas. Often he returned a winner, his suitcase full of silver dollars. He came up with an original idea—cementing a portion of his winnings into the pavement surrounding the gas station. Walker knew that people would stop and try to pick the silver dollars up. Of course they would appear foolish, but have a good laugh.

Later, they would tell their friends about the peculiar gas station in the heart of Coquille with the silver dollars in the pavement. Cheap advertising.

In February of 1929, Holmstrom traveled to Seattle, Washington, and earned his "Certificate of Efficiency to Man Lifeboat" from the U.S. Department of Commerce, Steamboat Inspection Service. Upon returning to Portland, he signed on with the Dollar Steamship Company as an ordinary seaman, earning twenty dollars a month plus room and board. He also took flying lessons from Tex Rankin, a well-known pilot in the area. Although he quickly grew proficient enough for solo flight, he did not try for a pilot's license. Two weeks later, Holmstrom was in Seattle aboard the *President Jefferson*, bound for the Orient.

When the Holmstrom family moved back to the farm in the fall of 1929, the stock market crash was only weeks away. That winter President Hoover asked Congress to help create jobs by increasing funds for public works. A portion of the money was directed towards the completion of Boulder Dam on the Colorado River.

By this time Buzz had returned from overseas and had gone immediately to work at Walker's. He had not been able to save much money. A family friend in Salem, Oregon, urged him to continue his education, offering him part time work as well as room and board. After Charles's death, the Gardiner Masonic Lodge reminded Buzz that he was eligible for one of the scholarships they gave deserving students. But the opportunity passed, or he let it pass; the needs of Frances and those of his younger brother and sister took precedence. Carl continued to be the main provider and a father-figure to the younger children. Anna believed that Buzz sometimes felt guilty for not doing more, but Rolf thought that his two older brothers had come to an agreement about who would do what. Family came first.

Over the next five years, the Holmstrom farm gradually ceased to be a working farm. Rolf recalls those days:

> We didn't have a pot to pee in or a window to throw it out of. I don't think Carl was cut out for farming. It must have been pretty frustrating for him. Besides it was hard times. Poor equipment, not enough money to buy anything modern. We had a horse or two, an old plow and disc. And the soil, it needed a lot of work, even though it was bottom land. After a couple of years the work probably got under his skin. For Carl, it was more of a burden than a choice.... And after my father died, that farm work nearly killed my mother... the endless chores and raising two small children.... I remember people in the area though who were worse off, squatters and such who lived in these rude shacks. No land, no money, no tools. They survived by making moonshine and poaching. They cut firewood in the forest, fished the streams, worked the local harvests.... They were hard up against it.

Frances carried on. Her arrhythmia, which had frightened her so much a few years before, returned. She went to the doctor and was told that if she did not slow down, she would die sooner rather than later. When these spells became intolerable, Frances curled up beneath the giant walnut tree just as Charles had done when he needed to rest. She lay there quietly, stilling herself, until the spell had passed. Then she would go back to the job at hand.

During one of these attacks, she experienced a spiritual reawakening. Years later, Frances wrote to Catherine Marshall, the novelist, about her experience on the farm after Charles's death. Marshall fashioned a character after Frances Holmstrom in her novel *Christy* [1967], a story about the hill people who lived in the Smoky Mountains at the turn of the century. Aunt Polly Teague, the fictional character, is a ninety-two-year-old woman who lives in the mountain hamlet of Cove.

In 1969 Anna wrote to Catherine Marshall, inquiring if the character of Aunt Polly was indeed based on her mother. Marshall wrote back,

> Dear Mrs. Smith, You guessed correctly and I am intrigued that you spotted in Aunt Polly Teague, the material from your mother's letter. It was taken directly, with her letter actually by my side as I wrote.... Aunt Polly Teague, along with Fairlight Spencer, turned out to be two of my favorite characters in Christy. Thus you can record this in your scrapbook, along with this letter

and be on very sure ground in telling your friends that a great deal of the
inner life and thinking of Aunt Polly is really your mother....

Religious practice and writing poetry, inherently acts of faith, sustained Frances
through those difficult years.

DURING THE GREAT DEPRESSION YEARS, Ed Walker kept everyone working at the
station by spreading the hours around and cutting the wages. Family men were
usually given the extra shift. For Holmstrom and the other young men of Coquille,
the station remained the hub of their social life. Hal Howell, George McClellan,
Clarence Bean, Thurman Hickam, Ross Kistner, Jim Watson, and Ken Hansen—all
were in their early twenties. They had graduated from high school and taken what
work they could find, often in the lumber mills, out in the woods, or working for
the county. Some had married.

After jumping from one job to another, Clarence Bean landed a desirable position with Standard Oil Company. He sold and delivered fuel and oil to the gyppo
loggers out in the woods around Coquille. He had joined the volunteer fire department and appeared to be settling down. When prohibition ended, he opened the
first "bottle club" in Coquille. He rented a space, put in some tables, chairs, and
a back bar and opened for business. The locals brought their liquor bottles in,
labeled with their name, and paid for the privilege of having someone pour their
own drinks for them.

At Walker's they caught up on local news, made fishing plans, constantly played
pranks on one another.

One warm day, two ladies passing through Coquille stopped for gas. The
women had been down at the coast near Bandon. Holmstrom was on duty at the
time and one of the ladies asked him, "Do you have a rest room?" Holmstrom,
looking at the inside of the car, thought she said, "Do you have a whisk broom?"
He replied, "Oh, you won't need one of those. Just pull around back and I'll blow
it out for you." Needless to say, the woman was upset and demanded to speak with
the owner. Ed Walker, with as straight a face as he could manage, did not believe his
favorite attendant would have said such a thing. He reassured the two women that
there must have been a misunderstanding. Holmstrom apologized profusely, more
embarrassed than they. For years afterwards the story made the rounds in Coquille.

Occasionally Buzz made money fishing wood out of the Coquille River and
selling it as firewood to the townspeople; country folk would never have considered paying for it. At the time, the Johnson Mill kept its logs corralled in the river
inside floating "booms." Each log had to be a standard length to accommodate
the saws in the mill; if it was too long, the ends were sawed off and chucked into
the river. When the mills were particularly busy, Buzz and his friends searched the
larger eddies along the Coquille River for these "lily pads," as the locals called them.

Sometimes they drove the eighteen miles to the river mouth at Bandon, where, piled up on the beach, the pads that had escaped the eddies came to rest.

Throughout the early 1930s Holmstrom continued to fish the local rivers along the southern Oregon coast—the Elk, Sixes, Rogue, and Pistol—with George McClellan and Earl Hamilton. Occasionally the young men from Coquille engaged in what was known as "outlaw fishing," fishing out of season or without a license. One evening Buzz, George, and Earl were camped along the banks of the Sixes River near Cape Blanco, Oregon, when three drunken gill-netters saw their fire and invited themselves over to warm up. The gill-netters, who also happened to operate the local still, asked if the young men would like a drink. Sure! As the night progressed, one of the gill-netters asked if they had ever petted a wild deer. George looked at Buzz, who looked at Earl, who looked back at George. "No, not lately," said Earl. "Well, come have a look," the other gill-netter replied. Down the beach they found a half-dozen deer laid out, apparently asleep. The moonshiners had dumped the mash from their still on the ground and the deer had made a meal of it. Now they were at least as drunk as the fishermen.

Another time, the three friends were trolling the Sixes River from the banks when Buzz hooked a tremendous salmon. The fish began to drag him along the shore. Hysterical with laughter, Hamilton and McClellan soon realized the fish was pulling their friend toward the ocean. Knowing Holmstrom well enough to know that he was not going to let go, they ran after him. Earl Hamilton finally caught hold of his friend around the waist. The fish dragged the pair a few more yards before the line snapped.

Phyllis Hamilton recalled their times together: "Both Earl and Buzz worked at the local sawmill off and on during that time. They'd get off the night shift around 1:00 A.M. and come over to my parent's house. I'd have all the camping gear ready and off we'd go. Buzz and Earl wanted to be fishing first thing in the morning... I think Buzz wanted something more to do with his life at that time. He was restless and used to making his own way. He wasn't one to sit around. I think Buzz always wanted something more than the gas station."

IN THE SPRING OF 1934, Buzz, Carl, and Frances sat down around the kitchen table and reached a decision about the farm. This time they decided to sell it to the Rhule family. Later, Frances wrote of the Rhules, "they love the place and keep it up much better than we ever did." With the move to town, Frances relinquished her dream of a farming life. No matter how hard they had worked, the Holmstroms were always "hard up against it." Many families in McKinley endured similar fates. Carl was never keen on the farming and Buzz, though he liked it at one time, had lost interest.

They bought a blue, two-story house in Coquille on a hill above an acre of bottom land. It needed paint and repairs. Given time and a group effort, Frances decided they could make it comfortable. She paid fifteen hundred dollars for it.

For the first time in years, all the Holmstroms lived under the same roof. Anna and Rolf were enrolled in school; Carl came and went from his logging jobs, spending weekends at home. Buzz moved back in with the family. Since he was helping Frances with his weekly check, it no longer made sense for him to pay room and board at McClouds. Together, they could stretch their dollars.

Frances Holmstrom drawing

Rogue River Tale

1934–1935

URING THE SUMMER OF 1934, Buzz began to build a boat in the dirt-floored basement of the house. The previous owners had partially excavated it, leaving mounds of dirt outside the narrow doorway. But they had neglected to put in any windows. The upstairs wiring ran along the overhead floor joists, providing electricity for a single light and an outlet. Buzz built a crude workbench along one wall and a tool rack above it; two sawhorses stood on the uneven floor. The back of the house faced south, catching the sunlight and breezes that slipped through the gaps in the siding. It was not much of a workshop, but pleasant enough to spend summer evenings in.

The tool chest, the one their father had left to Buzz and Carl, rested beneath the workbench. Inside was an assortment of woodworking tools—two mallets and a brace and bit; planes, handsaws, and chisels of various widths; a complete set of clamps, three or four adzes, and a draw knife for shaping the curves and lines of a boat. The chest, lined with red cedar, seasoned the basement with its familiar fragrance.

Holmstrom started with little more than an idea: he needed a boat to go down the Rogue River. Small, sturdy, and stable, it would be a craft he could easily maneuver and haul in and out of the water by himself. Unwittingly, he pictured himself on the local lakes, coastal bays, and the Coquille River, the river he knew best and fished often. Yet, everyone along the southern coast of Oregon knew the reputation of the Rogue as a white water river.

LIKE MOST PEOPLE in the area, Holmstrom had heard of Zane Grey, the famous novelist who, in the late 1920s, regularly fished the Rogue during the fall salmon runs. Grey had written two popular books about the Rogue during this period: *Tales of Fresh-Water Fishing* (1928), a nonfiction account of his fishing trips, and *Rogue River Feud* (1929), a novel. Both are full of exciting descriptions not only of fishing, but of the hazards and beauty of running the whitewater river. Holmstrom, an avid reader, had read them both.

He had heard of river men like Bob Pruitt and Claude Bardon, Cal Allen and Glen Wooldridge. In September of 1915, Allen had said to Wooldridge, "Let's make a boat and go down the Rogue River." That fall, in a crude handmade boat, Wooldridge and Allen made the first known whitewater run of the Rogue. It took them five days to cover the hundred-mile stretch to Gold Beach on the Oregon coast. Two years later, in 1917, Wooldridge took his first dudes on a guided river trip down the Rogue. By the 1920s celebrities such as Babe Ruth, Jack London, Irvin Cobb, and even Winston Churchill had made pilgrimages to the Rogue. In the early 1930s, Wooldridge was guiding notables such as Ginger Rogers, Clark Gable, and President Herbert Hoover on commercial fishing trips. Some of the rapids were unrunnable and Wooldridge, in the late 1930s and early 1940s, began to dynamite many of them. Not everyone appreciated his efforts. Miners and trappers along the river were certain that opening up the river would invite more outsiders.

As a boy, an adolescent, and a young man, Holmstrom had crossed the mouth of the Rogue River by ferry any number of times. He had also fished the lower reaches near Gold Beach. And he certainly remembered his boyhood adventures on Middle Creek at the farm. In one respect, however, it was a startling decision for the twenty-five-year-old gas station attendant to make. He was building a flat water boat—low sides, no decking, shallow draft—better for fishing and floating than whitewater. A river like the Rogue was obviously different and Holmstrom knew its reputation: excellent fishing, dangerous whitewater. He had heard the stories of impassable rapids, all-day portages, unseen rocks that would suddenly tear a hole in one's boat. The boat he built was not suited for whitewater, certainly not the Rogue.

But decades later, Rolf claims that Buzz knew during construction that he was going down the Rogue. Holmstrom built the kind of boat he knew best, just as other river runners had before him when they ventured into unknown waters. It did not matter if the boat was ill-suited to the task; he wanted to run the Rogue River. He was not the first to run that reach of river, but he was certainly one of a handful to attempt it alone, arriving on the scene before Wooldridge's dynamiting reordered the rapids.

ALTHOUGH HE HAD NO FORMAL TRAINING, Buzz had watched and helped each time his father built another boat. The feel of a plane running over a block of wood, the sound of hammering and sawing, the inevitable splinter in his hand—in these ways he absorbed spoken and unspoken lessons from his father. What he learned about boat building had been so gradual as to go unnoticed, as much to do with attitude as with the actual use of tools, although the two were inseparable. Simple lessons—take your time, learn from your mistakes, take care of your tools, finish what you start, enjoy what you are doing—learned more by example and imitation than by instruction.

George McClellan, whose father supervised one of the local mills, kept a good supply of red cedar underneath his house for boat-building. McClellan, however, never got around to building a boat. Buzz was welcome to as much of it as he needed. More than once, he took up his friend's offer.

He also stopped by Art Ellingsen's boatyard up the Coquille Valley near Arago for advice. For years, Ellingsen, of Norwegian heritage, had built or supervised the building of wooden boats of all sizes—rowboats and launches; tugs and stern-wheelers for Coos Bay and the Coquille River; coastal schooners for the cargo trade. His father, uncle, and brothers had all been shipwrights on Coos Bay. Now his son, Denton, who was Buzz's age (twenty-five), was learning the craft. Ellingsen offered Holmstrom the offsets or forms that would dictate the basic lines and the distinct V-hull of his first rowboat.

Back in the basement, Holmstrom began laying down a strongback, or wooden beam, that supported the offsets Ellingsen had given him. One by one, he mounted these temporary "ribs" to the strongback. Then he went to work setting a perma-nent bow stem and stern. At this stage, the basic shape of the boat emerged; a clean skeleton, twelve feet from bow to stern, twelve inches from gunwale to chine, with a broad transom and flared sides.

With its temporary "bones" in place, the boat was ready for its "clinker-built" or lapstrake siding. Holmstrom employed this traditional method of overlapping each plank, or "strake," with the one above. It was a time-consuming process. After cutting the planks to length, he fitted them on the form, took them off, planed them, refitted them, took them off again, worked the wood until he got the fit and the shape perfect. Only then could he attach the planks to one another permanently, fashion a keel, and finally turn the boat upright.

Replacing the offsets with permanent ribs was equally time-consuming. Holmstrom removed each one and replaced it with a four-piece rib laid across the keel and up both sides. Each piece was cut, shaped, notched, and sanded to fit the interior lapstrake of the hull. Once he was satisfied with the fit, he attached each rib. He proceeded slowly, as much by instinct as by trial and error.

Years later, Jack Bailey, a former resident of Coquille, described Holmstrom's abilities:

> He was an extraordinary carpenter. He would study, then move in with a saw and hammer to get results. He would fit and joint as much as twenty-five times to make it right. It had to be right. Anybody that is that careful fitting things doesn't get into trouble.

Often on those warm summer evenings, Holmstrom liked to work alone, but his pals dropped in regularly. Rolf, eleven at the time, remembers a steady flow of visitors to the basement. Clarence Bean and Jim Watson stopped by to check Buzz's progress, then lured him down to Bill's Place, the local bar, for a beer and a game of snooker. Thurman Hickam, who lived across the street, always offered a hand or loaned a tool. Some came to help, others just to watch. Like his father, Holmstrom was too polite to chase them away. For a boy Rolf's age, it meant the chance to mix with the older fellows. Buzz often sent Rolf down to Coquille Hardware for nails, wood screws, or sandpaper. After a couple of years, Eva and Stanton Stevens, the owners, could tell when Buzz was building a boat. Eventually, they extended him credit on his purchases. Thirty years after Holmstrom's father built his boats, backyard boat-building provided the young men with the same pleasures.

One August afternoon, Holmstrom surveyed the nearly completed boat. There was still work to do: oarlocks to mount, chines to set, gunwales to finish, seats midship and stern. And equipment to assemble: oars, stern line, extra rope, a repair kit and camping gear. He decided he could finish the rest of the work outdoors. Buzz called upstairs to Rolf to help him carry the boat outside. Together they managed to lug the two-hundred-pound craft through the narrow doorway into the sunlight.

NAMED BY FRENCH TRAPPERS in the 1830s for the apparently hostile Indians in the area, the Rogue is within easy reach of Coquille. It begins its two-hundred-and-fifteen-mile run on the western slope of Crater Lake in the Cascade Mountains of southern Oregon. The stretch of river that Holmstrom would run begins in the relatively flat water that passes through the middle of the town of Grants Pass. Thirty or so miles downstream from Grants Pass, in the heart of the Siskiyou Mountains, the river drops into a deep, often narrow canyon. Eventually dissecting the gentler Coast Range, the Rogue emerges at the ocean, eighty miles down the coast from Coquille.

On November 11, 1934, Holmstrom set out in a rainstorm for Grants Pass. As far he was concerned there was no time to waste. Ignoring the pleas of his mother, Buzz told her, "You're just jealous that you can't go!" Years later, Frances wrote in the family journal:

> It was on that night [Armistice Day] eight or so years ago that Haldane left town with the old open Dodge roadster and his first attempt at a boat on the trailer, in a howling tempest, the streets running like rivers, for his first river trip, the one down the Rogue.

With winter coming on, it was a difficult time to begin a river trip. Once Holmstrom got his teeth into something, there was no letting go. Out to Bandon and down the coast he went in the open Dodge, at the mercy of the weather. At Wedderburn he crossed over the recently completed Gold Beach Bridge. He drove south to Crescent City, California, where he turned inland along the Smith River, and finally back over the Coast Range into Grants Pass.

Clarence Bean said of his friend, "The wetter, the colder, the more uncomfortable it was, the happier he was. Sometimes Buzz would make things tough. He seemed to thrive on it." Rolf recalls a time when he, a friend, and Buzz went for a three-day hike up the North Fork of the Coquille.

> It was miserable, raining the whole time. We ran out of food, except for some cocoa and I think we got lost. I was really hungry by the time we got out. But it didn't bother Buzz very much. Buzz would say, "We'll get out, or know the reason why." Another thing, he didn't seem to require as much sleep as other people.

At dawn on an ashen Tuesday morning (November 12), Holmstrom put his boat in the muddy water beneath the Fifth Street Bridge in Grants Pass. He left the old Dodge at a lot in town—a local fellow assured him that no one would bother a topless Dodge, much less steal one. The rain stopped temporarily but a mist lingered over the river. With no previous whitewater experience, no map of the river, and no fanfare, he pushed off from shore in the open boat and drifted downstream.

In the bottom of the boat were Holmstrom's bedding, canned food, cooking gear, clothes, and fishing tackle. Although he had always preferred fishing to hunting, he also brought along an expensive rifle he had borrowed. Jim Watson had dug up a set of oars for him to use. Holmstrom, however, had not been able to find a tent.

Most of the gear he carried in the boat was second-hand, mended, and made to last. What he did not own, he had borrowed from friends. It was a habit that arose from a chronic lack of money and continued throughout his brief river-running career. In a town the size of Coquille, Holmstrom's fledgling adventures had an unexpectedly salubrious effect. "Everybody wanted to pitch in once Buzz got started on the rivers," says Hal Howell. "We were all interested in Buzz's adventures."

That morning, the stretch of river below Grants Pass gave no indication of things to come. Two hundred yards wide and clay-colored, the river flows steadily, uneventfully, with barely a riffle, much less a rapid. The current was sluggish and so Holmstrom, trying to make time, pulled on the oars while he surveyed the scene. Side streams seeped in from both sides of the river and their gurgle mixed comfortably with the morning song of the few remaining sparrows.

Overhead the Oregon sky slumped a familiar gray, dampening the appearance of the surrounding countryside. Along shore, the berry thickets and tangles of vegetation lay limp and shriveled; the ferns—deer, sword, bracken, and maiden hair—curled, brown along their edges. The willows and birches still clutched the last of their colorful leaves—yellows, reds, and oranges defying the overcast. The lively shades of green that overwhelmed the senses in springtime were subdued to a monotonous uniformity. Winter's front edge had arrived.

Intermittently Holmstrom spied the derelict gill-netter camps, their drying racks folded at acute angles and the shacks collapsing. Deserted ramshackle cabins peered from the riverbank. Behind them, barn roofs and outbuildings appeared and quickly disappeared as Holmstrom floated by. Stray cattle marked the distant fields. In 1927 the entire area had been flooded by the Rogue. Downstream the Hellgate Bridge had been washed away.

Mid-river a cobblestone island, littered with driftwood and patches of sand, split the river into two narrow channels. Slow water quickened into riffles, making a sound disproportionate to its size. Overhanging branches on the right shore spread a dense shadow over the curve of swift water; the small boat responded to the current's faint acceleration. Hesitantly, Holmstrom guided his boat down the right-hand channel, waiting for a thump, or worse. No sooner had the water shallowed over the gravel bars, then the river flattened and resumed its course. He relaxed, his hands light on the oars, thinking about the river, trying to get a feel for the boat.

Holmstrom may have picked up some rowing tips from Julius F. Stone's 1932 account of his Grand Canyon trip, *Canyon Country, The Romance of a Drop of Water and a Grain of Sand* and from Ellsworth Kolb's book, *Through the Grand Canyon from Wyoming to Mexico*. There are some descriptions of rowing in Zane Grey's books as well. Still, except for his childhood exploits on Middle Creek, most of his rowing had been on flat water. Rapids, fast water, and river currents demanded different skills. Now he sat with his back to the bow, facing the downstream, pulling slowly upstream on the oars. He could see where he was going. This position let him slow his downstream momentum, position himself in the current, and avoid rocks and gravel bars. When the larger, more hazardous rapids appeared, he could pick a route and maneuver the boat into position above the rapid. But in the swifter water, he would need swifter decisions. He could not row upstream indefinitely.

Holmstrom at Sunset Bay (near Coos Bay) with his first Rogue boat

Holmstrom found the answer by experimenting with a technique that is now called a "ferry angle." By maintaining the boat at an upstream angle across the current, with the bow pointed approximately sixty degrees towards shore rather than directly downstream, he gained a degree of control and maneuverability over his craft while he was carried downstream by the current. With additional time to anticipate the numerous obstacles and various conditions of the river—entry point, current velocity, direction, water depth, rocks, boils and eddies—he could better position himself for a successful run and avoid being forced to make costly, last-second decisions. Anticipation was everything.

He maneuvered the craft in and out of eddies, ran the riffles, studied the water, took note of his boat's response. Soon he was experimenting in the more modest, forgiving rapids that had begun to appear. Wheeling the bow around, he pulled downstream. On a wide river, one with enough current and relatively free of obstacles, the traditional position was better for making time.

Upriver, the distant black ridge of the Siskiyou Range cut the eastern horizon. To the west, in front of Holmstrom, lay the same mountains, their tops buried in cloud cover and their flanks tinged a dark, shadowy blue. Another storm was blowing in from the Pacific.

Six miles downstream, the Applegate River entered from the left. As Holmstrom drifted by, he noted a crude boat ramp across the river from the mouth of the Applegate; it was a reassuring landmark. A large gravel beach lay just below the mouth and immediately below it, the river braided. Another cobble-stone island appeared, accompanied by the peculiar sound of gravel bars that warned he was entering shallow water. Along the rocky shore burned-out snags stood guard, an abandoned osprey's nest set solidly atop one of them. He chose a channel and maneuvered into position.

Downstream he went and, without warning, the boat knocked, scraped bottom, and ground to a halt in the middle of the river. He felt helpless and a little foolish. With the river flowing past him, he stepped out and began to rock and push the boat. Just as it floated free, he hopped in.

Stands of conifers appeared on shore and the river slanted downward as the canyon walls rose and redefined the skyline. The spicy odor of pine drifted to the river as Holmstrom rowed, snacking between strokes. He passed beneath the recently constructed Robertson Bridge and before he saw it heard the sound of a large creek coming in from the right: Jump-off Joe Creek. After another hour, Holmstrom entered Hellgate Canyon. He pulled upstream, slowing the boat enough to take in the dramatic scenery.

Abruptly, the canyon tapered to a twenty-foot channel between two jagged black outcrops of rock. To the earliest miners and packers in the area these outcroppings might well have appeared to be the gates of hell. The river surged though the constricted passage. As Holmstrom edged his boat down toward the gap, the river boiled up without warning, first beside the boat, then behind it. It seized the boat and carried it toward the gnarled walls of the canyon, only to let it go at the last moment. Now the craft was washed back toward the other side of the river and spun around. All Holmstrom could do was to try to avoid a wreck. Then pausing capriciously, as though it were gathering its energy for one final implosion, the river dropped away, and the boat seemed to be pulled down toward the bottom of the river. Foam, bubbles, swells, boils, and eddies on the surface—no rapids yet. Rapids, at least, stayed put and repeated themselves. Holmstrom detected no discernible pattern or rhythm to the water's movement as he careened downstream.

For the first time that day, Holmstrom was anxious, uneasy—overcast sky, the gloomy, dark rock rising above him, surging water, the unfamiliar canyon. He felt helpless, or worse, useless. Had he known that Hellgate Canyon ran for less than a mile, he might have relaxed, but he did not. He braced himself. When the canyon suddenly opened up a short while later, he was as surprised as he was relieved.

Below Hellgate Canyon the river broadened considerably. Forest crowded the river's edge where rocky outcrops alternated with small sandy beaches and extensive grassy benches. The canyon walls soared vertically, the gray sky narrowed, and for the first time the river deepened. Instead of gravel bars, Holmstrom watched for submerged rocks, which would cause as much damage as any rapid. As more serious rapids began to appear—Ennis, Upper Gallis, Rocky, Chair, Alameda, Argo—Holmstrom tested his boat and his raw technique. Late that afternoon, under a still-threatening sky, he pulled ashore above Grave Creek and made camp.

On shore a chill cut the autumn air. Holmstrom lit a fire and began fixing his supper of pork and beans and coffee. The day had gone well. The boat was intact, handled well enough, and hardly shipped water. He estimated that he had made at least thirty miles and, except for Hellgate Canyon, had not encountered any major problems. With a full stomach, his apprehension slipped away. He crawled into his borrowed sleeping bag and curled close to the fire, his back to the cold.

The next morning Holmstrom woke up wet and exhausted. During the night, the storm had pushed in from the coast. The brief drizzle turned into a continuous downpour whose sound he might have enjoyed if he had been inside a tent. The wet limbs of trees and bushes slumped toward the ground. The fire was out, the firewood soaked. Unable to cook breakfast or dry his clothes, he changed, ate another can of pork and beans, and drank last night's coffee. He bailed out the boat, surprised by the amount of water that had accumulated in it.

Pushing off from shore, he floated beneath the Grave Creek Bridge, and then reached Grave Creek Riffle; riffle was a misnomer. Running the left-hand channel between a rocky island and the shore the boat plunged down the chute and took on gallons of water. To avoid some of the submerged rocks, Holmstrom had to ship his oars at one point. Two-hundred feet downstream, Grave Creek Falls beckoned. Holmstrom bailed as quickly as he could.

In 1925 the jagged rocks at Grave Creek Falls tore a hole in one of Zane Grey's skiffs and it sank before anyone could react. Holmstrom suddenly realized how swiftly the current was carrying him and how quickly he would have to commit. Downstream, like a train thundering through a snowstorm, came a muffled roar. Heart racing, he stood up to gain a better view. A large boulder blocked the middle of the river. He dismissed the rocky, nearly invisible right run and focused his attention on the left. As his boat slipped downstream, the rain fell harder, pocking the surface of the water. Now the patter of the rain was subdued by the growing growl of the rapid. Holmstrom spotted the narrow tongue that signaled a deeper channel between the rocks. With a few light strokes, he pulled the boat toward the left shore just above the tongue and spun the stern downstream. Dipping first one oar and then the other, he held his position. Pushing down on the handles, he lifted his oar blades above the water. The boat dropped over the glassy lip, between protruding rocks and others visible just beneath the surface. Then the river swallowed him.

Holmstrom came out of the rapid right side up, his boat full of water and difficult to steer. He began bailing, keeping an eye as he drifted downstream. Looking back upstream, he realized that Grave Creek Falls had been a straightforward run, if one were familiar with the river. Though his instincts had served him well, he knew he had been caught off guard and that worse rapids lay ahead. He would scout every one if necessary.

Passing to the left of Sanderson's Island, Holmstrom continued. On either side of the river stood the concrete piers of an old trail-bridge destroyed by the 1927 flood. After less than a mile of calm water, his new resolution was put to the test. A familiar sound traveled up the narrow canyon, growing louder and louder. From his boat, he could see the surface of the river and its apparent horizontal edge. Surely below that line the river resumed its course. Closing the distance, he could see spray spouting from the middle of the rapid. Holmstrom had heard of Rainie Falls in Grey's book. He pulled to the left shore, tied his boat, and went to have a look.

Rainie Falls was named for J.N. Rainey, who had lived in a cabin at the foot of the rapids. When Rainey first arrived, he purchased a placer mining claim and started to work. By 1915, he was gaffing salmon at the falls and packing the fish out to Glendale, Oregon, which provided him with a steady income. In the late 1920s, he was found dead in his cabin; his murder, like many others along the Rogue, was never solved.

By 1915, when Glen Wooldridge began running the Rogue, a tradition of *not* running Rainie Falls had taken hold among the local river men—they always lined or portaged. No boulders, no tricky currents to remember, more waterfall than rapid, the river simply plunged fourteen feet off a ledge into a keeper hole. At the bottom, a standing wave curled and broke upstream. Some locals swore it was illegal to even *attempt* the run.

For a long time Holmstrom stood on the rocky outcropping, slick with rain and river spray, and viewed the tumult. The sound enveloped him. With no intention of running the rapid, he searched the lip of the falls, mesmerized by their power and beauty. Even if he chose the right path, so much was left to timing and chance.

On this side of the river, there was no way he could carry or even drag his boat over the rocky ledges. On the opposite shore, Holmstrom noticed the vague outlines of a trail winding through the boulders. He had heard of an alternative run as well: a man-made channel called the Fish Ladder. He got back in his boat, rowed upstream, and pulled across the river to the right shore. After exploring it, Holmstrom decided to line his boat down the narrow chute. Unloading his gear, he carried it down to a small eddy, making five round trips.

In higher water or with a larger boat, lining the Fish Ladder would have been a difficult chore for one man. In 1925, after his party spent hours lining their five heavy boats down it, Zane Grey wrote

> We sat and lay around George Takahashi's camp fire, a starved, exhausted, silent group, wet to the skin and suffering from bruises, rope burns and aches.... The next morning disclosed a bunch of cripples, several lost articles of baggage, two leaky boats and various other things that might have been expected.

But Holmstrom's rowboat was relatively light and maneuverable and he was able to manage the rocky, terraced ladder, with its slower pool-and-drop water.

A steady succession of rapids followed—China Gulch, Whiskey Creek, and Big Slide. Above Tyee Rapid, Holmstrom again pulled ashore to scout. At first glance, the rapid appeared to be a spidery maze of boulders and rocky ledges. The entry was littered with rocks just above and below the surface, offering no recognizable path. The current swept towards the right, piled up on boulders, and rebounded ferociously back into the current. Fingers of rock reached out into the surging river, forming small eddies. To be swept into one of these rocky pockets in a wooden boat would be disastrous.

The river pounded a massive boulder midstream, creating its own waves and recirculating holes. Holmstrom studied the two options. A channel ran between the boulder and the right shore, but he would have to deal with the velocity of the water, and the need for considerable maneuvering as well as the immediate consequences of a mistake. The margin for error would be small. The other option, hugging the left bank, meant reacting quickly and repeatedly to a partially hidden maze of rocks and ledges. Shallow, a bit slower, and less powerful, the run had its own particular hazard: too many obstacles to commit to memory. Seat-of-the pants rowing. Holmstrom took the right run and just managed to avoid a wreck.

Holmstrom faced a series of similar decisions throughout the rest of the afternoon. Wildcat Rapid, sister of Tyee, was immediately around the bend. Then came Russian, Montgomery, and Howard Creek Chutes, one right after another. Slim Pickins, Washboard, Plowshare, and Windy Creek Rapids—each had its idiosyncrasies—followed with unrelenting regularity. The novice boatman relied on his natural abilities and homework to get him through.

By late afternoon Holmstrom was tired. It was late and his thoughts drifted to finding a suitable campsite. It was then that he wrecked in Black Bar Falls, and was soon separated from his boat. (He later mentions the wreck as having taken place at "Lookout Point," possibly a landmark or a bit of droll humor.)

As he later described it to a reporter from *The Coquille Sentinel*:

> Sometimes the mountains crowded in until the river was walled by sheer precipice on either side. Then the water galloped madly down a narrow course, and my boat buffeted about like a leaf. I was so busy dodging rocks that I did not have time to be cold, although my clothes were soaked. Suddenly the boat struck a partially submerged boulder....

Evening was coming. Boatless, perched on the rock in the middle of the river, Holmstrom stripped down to his long underwear and his life jacket, made a bundle of the clothes he had been wearing, and threw the bundle across the channel. It missed and was swept downriver. Now there was nothing left to do but swim ashore. Once on the rocky bank, he started walking, though he had no idea what he was going to do. For all he knew, the overturned boat was long gone and he was in the middle of nowhere. He kept walking. After an hour, he spotted the boat in an eddy on the opposite shore and swam over to it.

Surprisingly, it had sustained only minor damage. An oarlock was sheared, but it hardly mattered since the oars were gone. If he were to continue, the boat needed repairs. Tired and cold, Holmstrom pulled the boat up on the sand and tried to climb the steep, rocky bank to gain his bearings. It was hard going in the dark, and he stumbled over the bank's sharp-edged boulders. Once on top of the lava rock bench, things got worse. The boulder-strewn field, the forest, and the skyline were submerged in thickening darkness. As he hesitated, he noticed a single electric light in the distance and fumbled along a rocky trail towards it. He heard dogs barking.

A year earlier, with the help of local miners, Hal and Bea Witherwox had begun construction of Black Bar Lodge. It was the first such accommodation along this isolated stretch of the river. Most of their clients were packers who brought supplies in to miners and trappers.

Bea Witherwox heard the dogs. She stuck her head out the window and asked "Who's there?" not expecting an answer. From the nearby trees, Holmstrom replied, identifying himself. Bea told him to come in, but he would not budge. Hal Witherwox finally went out and found the young man shivering in his long underwear and life jacket. After a brief introduction, Witherwox gave him a blanket and led him up to the lodge, where Bea was waiting at the door. After a hot bath, warm clothes, and a meal, Holmstrom sat in front of the fire and gave the Witherwoxes a detailed account of what had happened. The wreck had not surprised him as much as how swiftly his situation had deteriorated. In a flash, his boat was gone and he was stranded. The Witherwoxes listened sympathetically to the likable river runner.

They wanted to know if he would finish the trip. Holmstrom nodded. It had never occurred to him to not finish something he started. Hal offered advice on the rapids downstream, cautioning him about Blossom Bar. Had Buzz ever met Glen Wooldridge or Bob Pruitt, local boatmen? He had not. Claude Bardon had a place downriver and Witherwox suggested talking with him. Of course, that depended on whether or not his herd of goats liked you; if the goats acted in a way that Bardon considered favorable, then he would come down from his homestead and visit. If the goats acted strangely, forget it.

The next morning after a breakfast of Bea's sourdough pancakes, Hal outfitted Holmstrom with the equipment necessary to get down the river: an oarlock, new oars, bedroll, shoes, extra clothing, and fishing tackle. Bea put together some bread, canned food, and jerked venison. They carried the gear down to the river, went to work on the boat, and before noon, it was river-worthy. Witherwox encouraged Buzz to stay with them another night, but he was ready to go—his mother would start worrying if he did not show up on time, and he did not want to let Ed Walker down. He thanked the couple repeatedly for their kindness, promising to repay them as soon as he got back to Coquille. They urged him to visit again.

Now Holmstrom headed into the most isolated stretch of the canyon; more serious water awaited him. After talking with Hal, he was fully aware of the challenge he had undertaken. Somewhere between Black Bar Lodge and Blossom Bar, twelve miles downstream, he overturned two more times. Each time he got into trouble he was able to right the boat and carry on.

Mule Creek Canyon, eleven miles downstream from Black Bar, was an intimidating and dramatic piece of whitewater. It had always been a trouble spot for early boaters; Glen Wooldridge recalled how frightened he and Cal Allen were the first time they encountered it in 1915. In 1925 Zane Grey nearly lost another one of his boats here. Grey considered the Narrows section of Mule Creek Canyon to be the most dangerous place on the entire Rogue. Then as now, the canyon offered no practical way to portage.

Holmstrom floated under the swinging footbridge just above Mule Creek Canyon, and saw two large boulders marking the entrance to the gorge-within-a-gorge. Once past these megaliths, he was committed. The skyward-reaching canyon walls narrowed abruptly as the constricted river gathered velocity and turned nasty. No slow water, no beaches, no reliable eddies. As the river rushed toward the first of three blind turns, Holmstrom was unable to see more than a hundred yards downstream. The narrowing canyon twisted and bent the current—he rowed by instinct alone. At certain spots, the walls were so close that he could have touched them with his oars. The river boiled and surged and tugged, threatening to capsize the boat. Without warning, it shoved the craft toward the wall, trying to pin it against its side, then suddenly releasing it.

Zane Grey had described The Narrows as:

> Two low points of rock, one slanting down from the opposite side, and the other, a ledge of cliff on my side, reached out diagonally toward each other across the stream. All the tremendous volume of the Rogue River had to pass between them at sharp speed.

Facing this chute of water, Holmstrom kept his boat centered in the river, gave a last push, and shipped his oars to avoid shattering them. Two hundred yards downstream at Coffeepot, the river narrowed even further. With its unpredictable water, Coffeepot has trapped boats for as long as twenty minutes, circulating them helplessly around this cauldron, bumping and slamming them into the jagged cliffs. Some boats broached on the vertical walls, filled with water, and overturned. Once again he had to take his chances.

Blossom Bar Rapid, two miles downstream from Coffeepot, was named for its shoreline azaleas. Before Wooldridge blasted a channel through it in the late 1930s, it was considered unrunnable; half-day portages were common. Given the steep series of rocky ravines and the weight of the boat, a portage was nearly impossible for one man. Holmstrom lined his boat around Blossom Bar that afternoon, then rowed until dusk and made camp above Foster Bar. Another thirty-mile day.

Early on the morning of November 15, Holmstrom broke camp and began rowing, intent on making miles. Near Clay Hill Rapid, the scenery altered dramatically and he sensed that the worst of the rapids were behind him. The steep canyon walls gave way to rounded, smoother stone formations along shore. In the distance, the tattered ridge lines softened and gradually became insubstantial. A series of mounds and hills, obscured by the morning fog, rolled on one after another. As the overcast sky widened, so did the river, slaty and silver; the air salty, refreshing.

Holmstrom had entered the lower reaches of the Rogue, thirty-five miles from the ocean. Although he could have taken out at any number of places along the river, he was determined to row all the way to the sea, which he considered a proper conclusion to his journey. The river meandered through the broad river valley and the current weakened. He pulled with a rhythm, his strokes as steady as the wing beats of a heron. With any luck, he might reach Gold Beach by evening.

On he rowed, through the afternoon, past the village of Agness, where the Illinois River made its meager contribution to the Rogue. The current slowed to a crawl and an upstream breeze further slowed his progress. Holmstrom let the boat drift while he ate lunch. Afterward, he set himself to the task again, hoping to cover twenty miles. He found his rhythm, half-enjoying the endless repetition that flat water rowing requires. He sang aloud to relieve the monotony and maintain the rhythm of his strokes.

Once past Elephant Rock Island, the sound and smell of the sea grew stronger. Coastal clouds hung low over the water; a steady drizzle tapped against the wooden boat. Holmstrom heard the distant thunder of breakers, punctuated by the lonely toll of a buoy and the raucous cries of gulls. Flocks of gulls rose above his boat, hovered, and then plunged towards the water, pulling back at the last instant. Ahead he saw the outline of the Gold Beach bridge.

Gill-netters and purse-seiners materialized out of the mist. When they noticed the lone boatman, the fishermen raised a hand or nodded their head, but kept to their work. Holmstrom maintained his rhythm and finally reached the bridge. Despite the hour, he kept on rowing. As darkness gathered, he rowed across the river mouth, where he drifted, rising and falling with the swell, accompanied by the sound of the buoy. When he felt the tide pulling his boat out to sea, he reluctantly made for shore.

The next morning he thumbed a ride down to Crescent City, California, and then across the Coast Range to Grants Pass to pick up his car. Though he had taken a thrashing, he had already decided to return to the Rogue the following spring. In typical fashion, he later understated his difficulties to a local reporter at the *Coquille Sentinel,* who wrote, "Although he said there was nothing very exciting about his four day trip down the Rogue from Grants Pass to Gold Beach, Haldane

Holmstrom does not care to try it again—in the winter time at least."

"Nothing very exciting… but did not care to try it again." Secretly, Holmstrom thought otherwise. It was as challenging as anything he had ever done, though he would never say so directly, certainly not in a newspaper. The line between private and public expression was sharply drawn in the Holmstrom family.

Holmstrom's maiden voyage down the Rogue had taught him a number of lessons. He now knew there was a difference between the perception of a rapid one held while standing on shore and the perception of the same rapid one saw from a boat on the river. Bridging that gap required mental acuity, physical prowess, a proper regard for the river, and even then, some luck.

He also thought it risky to discuss his river plans before attempting them. Saying he was going to do something, then not doing it, might sound like empty boasting. Nevertheless, his accomplishments would draw unsought encouragement, even admiration. And this, in turn, elicited his own self-deprecating humor, innate modesty, and perhaps a quiet pride—all attributes of his father as well.

Holmstrom had also shaken Coquille out of his system temporarily. He had met people such as the hospitable Witherwoxes, made friends with the suspicious miners and self-reliant fishermen, and been accepted into their fraternity. He felt he somehow fit in with them. As for the mishaps, he was not entirely satisfied with his skills or his boat, but knew he would do better next time.

IN THE RAINY FIRST MONTHS OF 1935, Holmstrom began construction of another boat, one very different from his first. This time he was building a boat that would suit the whitewater of the Rogue. He did his figuring in a pocket-sized notebook, scratching out rough drawings and making material lists. He checked in regularly with Art Ellingsen at the Arago boatyard. Down at Coquille Hardware, Eva and Stanton Stevens kidded Buzz about constructing a second boat to get down the river. All Buzz knew was that he would have to work quickly to make a spring run on the Rogue.

Although it was not hard to find quality lumber around Coquille, Buzz decided to use plywood on the hull and decking of his new boat. Rolf recalls that his brother was in a hurry to complete this second boat and took some short cuts in the construction. "It was a step back, not his best work. Afterwards, he got better and better with each boat."

After the first Rogue trip, Holmstrom had told the reporter from the *Coquille Sentinel* that he needed a boat "six feet longer, with a prow at each end for the best navigation of the turbulent stream," which meant that the new boat would be eighteen feet long. It would also have a higher bow which would serve two purposes: it would decrease the amount of water taken in over the bow and increase the freeboard (the distance between waterline and gunwale). More freeboard meant less water over the flared sides. He knew firsthand the difficulty of trying to maneuver a boat with water sloshing back and forth inside.

He decided to deck the bow and stern, forming a cockpit for the boatman. This simple alteration reduced bailing and provided much-needed storage room below decks. More importantly, if the boat overturned, he would not lose his gear again.

As the design of the boat progressed, Holmstrom decided that a wider beam (the distance across the boat at its widest point, gunwale to gunwale) would increase stability. He also chose to retain the stern design of his first boat, recalling that river veterans like Galloway, Stone, and Kolb had all used boats with a blunt stern. Throughout the remaining weeks, he worked steadily in the damp basement. By early April 1935, the boat neared completion. In jest, he named it the *Silver Streak*, after the new streamlined trains.

Throughout the construction of the *Silver Streak*, Buzz had considered taking someone with him on the trip. Strong practical arguments favored another pair of hands—the increased weight of the *Silver Streak* made portaging or lining by one man extremely difficult; even with two people, it would be a chore to move the boat through the boulders at Blossom Bar. A wreck or a turnover was certainly possible. All in all, a partner would be helpful. He would not mind the company either.

Who was available? Earl Hamilton was a married man now. Hal Howell had expressed an interest in going, as had Thurman Hickam. But taking time-off from work could be a problem. Clarence Bean, though not much of a boater or boat builder, had been considerable help over the past months.

Although Bean was not an outdoorsman, he was always game. According to Bean's life-long friend, Ross Kistner, "Clarence would have never gone off on his own or initiated a journey without someone like Holmstrom. Clarence admired Buzz's sense of adventure, his physical courage, and his can-do attitude." When Buzz asked Clarence if he wanted to go down the Rogue, he agreed at once.

Holmstrom wanted to put the new boat on the trailer and take it down to Walker's to paint its name on the bow and stern. One mild April morning, Jim Watson and Clarence Bean arrived to help carry the *Silver Streak* out of the basement. They lifted the boat and carried it toward the doorway. Halfway through, they realized they were stuck. They backed up, tried turning the boat at different angles and still they could not get it out the door. Finally, the three of them found an angle that worked, and shoved the boat through. "You need to do something about that doorway," said Bean.

Down at Walker's, Buzz found the free paint he was looking for. For unknown reasons, he painted a 13 in large letters on the right side of the bow, with *Grants Pass to Gold Beach* in smaller letters next to it. Bean and Watson pitched in. On the left side of the bow, one of them painted "SILVER STREAK OF COQUILLE" and below it, "*Gas 22 cents.*" "SINK OR SWIM" was lettered across the transom. The three friends then went for a beer at Bill's Place. By the time they returned, the paint was dry. As they circled the boat, Clarence noticed something: "STREAK" had been misspelled and now read "STEAK." No one owned up to the mistake. An amused Holmstrom left it.

The Silver Steak

On Saturday, May 4, 1935, Buzz and Clarence set off down the Rogue River. Together, they made the same drive down the coast to Crescent City and over the mountains to Grants Pass that Holmstrom had made the previous winter. The weather was fair and forecasts for the following week predicted temperatures above normal, with light winds along the coast.

The two young men began their trip where the Applegate River flows into the Rogue, six miles downstream from Grants Pass. Off they went, Holmstrom rowing, while Bean sat uncomfortably on the bow deck, camera in hand. They floated along at a good clip. The higher water meant fewer rocks and less maneuvering which allowed Holmstrom to adjust to his new boat. Although heavier than the rowboat, the *Silver Steak* was a vast improvement over the nameless first boat. It handled well, was more stable, and certainly more comfortable to row. Bean, who was riding the stern deck, may not have agreed. By afternoon, they had floated fifteen miles or more and were about to enter Hellgate Canyon. They decided to stop for lunch, then hike up above the river; Bean wanted to take some distance shots of the narrow, rocky canyon.

Back on the river, Bean took photos from the stern. By nightfall, they had covered nearly twenty-five miles. With Rainie Falls just downstream and the task of portaging and lining ahead, Holmstrom decided to camp.

At Rainie Falls the next morning, he told Bean about the local tradition of never running this rapid. After looking the rapid over, Bean agreed that the tradition was one they should abide by, and they worked the boat down the Fish Ladder.

At Tyee Bar, Buzz met Glen Wooldridge for the first time. He was guiding a group of fishermen and had stopped for lunch. Holmstrom and Wooldridge talked boats: building them, rowing them, wrecking them. Holmstrom told Wooldridge how he had wrecked and temporarily lost his boat at Lookout Point last fall. Wooldridge smiled. After twenty years on the river, he knew every rock, riffle, and rapid. Lookout Point was just around the bend. As a gesture of respect, Holmstrom offered to let Wooldridge row the *Silver Steak*. He accepted and rowed through Tyee without incident. He thought the boat handled well.

They drifted downstream, ran Slim Pickens, Plowshare, and Big Windy easily enough. Holmstrom pointed out the black rock where he had wrecked the previous November. Bean took a picture. A mile and a half downstream, Holmstrom photographed Bean sitting gloomily in the stern of the *Silver Steak* in an eddy. Holmstrom wrote "Here I found my boat and had to swim from the other side across to reach the boat." By the time they pulled ashore at Black Bar Lodge to visit with the Witherwoxes, the afternoon drizzle had turned to rain.

The Witherwoxes were pleased and surprised to see Holmstrom so soon again. After introductions, Bea insisted that the two river runners come up to the lodge for something to eat. Hal peppered Buzz with questions about the new boat. How did it handle? Had they had any trouble so far? He also offered the two river runners an empty cabin just below Little Windy Creek if they wanted it. Neither Holmstrom nor Bean relished a night in the rain and accepted his offer.

The next morning Holmstrom and Bean rowed across the river, and in spite of the dreary weather, they spent most of one day hiking up to the rim of the gorge. Their effort yielded a panoramic view of the surrounding watersheds. Looking north toward Bear Camp, they saw the endless forests of the Klamath Range; spotted Saddle Mountain, near Mule Creek, and glimpsed Horseshoe Bend on the river below it. They attempted to reach an unnamed peak along the rim, but turned back. On their way down, they spotted the roof of the Witherwoxes lodge. After another gloomy day lounging around the cabin, both men were ready to head downriver.

The next morning the weather broke fair; they floated downstream, the river looking less menacing in the morning sunshine. They approached Horseshoe Bend, where the river made a sharp right hand turn. The current piled into a rock wall on the left, creating another set of waves that caromed into the main channel. Bean grew quieter than ever as Holmstrom steered the *Silver Steak* through unharmed. For the next few miles, the canyon narrowed and the river surged. With Bean holding on as best he could and catching most of the waves, Holmstrom guided the boat through.

Holmstrom and Bean stopped at Winkle Bar, Zane Grey's place, to visit. As they walked up the trail they found two cabins, but no one in residence. They wandered the grounds, enjoying the chance to snoop around the famous writer's retreat. The boathouse, with its hip roof and open sides, sheltered three of Grey's drift boats. Holmstrom inspected them carefully, commenting to Bean on the workmanship. Built in Grants Pass, Buzz guessed.

By late morning, they were back on the river, heading for Mule Creek Canyon. This time Holmstrom had some idea of what was coming; Bean had none. No time for pictures or lengthy explanations—once past the two large rocks, the current forced the boat down the left wall closer than Buzz wanted. He pulled away and the broad-beamed boat, buffeted by the pent-up energy of the waves, was shot immediately down the narrow corridor. A patch of calm water appeared and the boat slowed. Then the river turned a corner and picked up speed; once again the boat was propelled forward. The walls flashed by. After Coffeepot, the *Silver Steak* emerged—Bean soaked and bailing as fast as he could, Holmstrom doing his best to keep the boat away from the walls.

A half-mile downstream at Stair Creek Falls, they met two men on horseback and Buzz rowed across the river to chat with them. They talked boats, weather, miners, and their mutual acquaintance, Wooldridge. Holmstrom mentioned that Wooldridge had rowed his boat through Tyee Rapid two days earlier. One of the men told Holmstrom that Blossom Bar was just around the corner. Though it was still early in the day, he decided to camp above Blossom Bar before attempting the arduous portage.

When Holmstrom and Bean arrived at Blossom Bar the next morning, the usual portage on the left side of the river was underwater. They had no choice but to take the boat over the jumbled outcropping of boulders on the right side of the river. Lifting and shoving, pushing and pulling, they finally wedged the wooden boat up the face of one large boulder. They stopped to rest and then tried again. After eight hours, they had moved the boat no more than one hundred feet. Enough. Holmstrom decided to run the rest of Blossom Bar alone, while Bean took pictures.

Before ferrying out to midstream, he eased the boat down a series of eddies on the right shore and quickly found himself in trouble. Surrounded by waves, pourovers, and boulders, Holmstrom was momentarily lost and out of control. He flailed with his oars—the left one crabbed beneath the boat, the right one beat the air. The boat spun toward the left bank, nearly smashed against the cliff, and appeared to be headed for more trouble when he finally managed to get both oars in the water. After dodging more rocks and pourovers, he slipped through the lower half of the rapid and picked up Bean. Later Holmstrom wrote two captions in his photo album: "No one who had ever gone over it in a boat lived to tell about it," and "We felt relieved when we got this place behind us." They camped a few miles downstream at Solitude Bar.

With the most difficult rapids behind them, the two men set off early the next morning intent on making miles. Through Tacoma and Clay Hill Rapids, past Foster Bar and Illahe, they slipped by the Illinois River before noon. With high water, mild weather, and Buzz doing most of the rowing, they made good time in the lower reaches of the Rogue. On the evening of May 9, under partly cloudy skies, they landed at Gold Beach.

There would be no stirring accounts of this trip in the local newspapers. Things had gone well, except for the two days of rain. Most importantly, the boat had proven river-worthy and Holmstrom had avoided any serious wrecks or turnovers. He enjoyed visiting with the Witherwoxes and the opportunity to scrutinize Zane Grey's boats. Finally, he had met Glen Wooldridge. And Bean, despite his moodiness, had been good company.

As they drove along the coast toward Coquille the next day, Holmstrom was not enthused about going back to work. He wondered aloud which river they should run next.

River of No Return

1936

W ITH HIS SLENDER yet significant triumph on the Rogue River behind him, and the successful construction of two river boats, Holmstrom was now a local river runner of note. Nonetheless, he was back seven days a week in the workaday world of Walker's, not a place of lush possibilities. That did not impede his whittling daydreams into sharp reality, however. The Snake and the Columbia Rivers were burnished borders on two of Oregon's four sides, and each represented a larger challenge than the Rogue, but Holmstrom chose a less voluminous yet more remote compromise for his next venture.

In October 1935, the National Geographic Society, jointly with the U.S. Geological Survey, sponsored a three-week expedition on the Salmon River in Idaho, from Salmon City to Lewiston on the Snake River. Ostensibly, the trip was to furnish answers about the extent and nature of an immense granitic mass known as the Idaho Batholith, which underlies several thousand square miles of central Idaho. The director of the Idaho Bureau of Mines and Geology, and two other geologists, accompanied the single-boat trip, as did an Idaho Congressman and the U.S. Forest Service regional forester.

The *Geographic* story, "Down Idaho's River of No Return," was reported in forty-plus pages of the July 1936 issue of the Society's monthly magazine. As soon as Holmstrom read it, the old itch demanded scratching. He would row the same stretch in a smaller boat with oars instead of the thirty-two-foot sweep boat used by the National Geographic Expedition. The ever-available Clarence Bean could accompany him. They would build the boat before the season slipped away—the two men had eight weeks to prepare.

The Salmon, entirely contained within Idaho, is undammed, and for most of its four hundred miles courses through wilderness. In 1805, Captain William Clark had explored the upper reaches of the river and, discouraged by his observations as well as by reports from local Nez Perce Indians, decided against attempting a passage with canoes. By the early 1900s, it was touted as the River of No Return because its convoluted terrain forestalled any attempt to pull a boat back upriver once it journeyed through the canyon. It was no place for amateurs who might have to hike out.

Holmstrom located a suitable white cedar log in the Coast Range mountains above the South Fork of the Coquille, near Powers, about thirty miles south of Coquille. Bean helped him split it up and haul it to the mill at home, where at an affordable price it was sawed into boards.

Holmstrom, with an assist now and then from Bean and Rolf, fashioned a fourteen-foot decked boat with a five-foot beam. The sides were lapstraked three boards high, the bow pointed, the stern broad and blunt. He inserted watertight bulkheads at each end, attached a six-inch cowling around half of the cockpit, and enameled the boat lobster-red. Finished it weighed 270 pounds.

Although he had planned a vacation at September-end, sometimes nature shuffles plans. Fall 1936 was exceptionally dry. On Saturday night, September 26, sparks from a slash burn near a logging camp in southwestern Oregon ignited a fire that flared through thickets of highly flammable Scotch broom, an aggressive, introduced shrub. Quickly crowning in the trees, and pushed by a brisk wind, the blaze soon engulfed Bandon, a small seaport and logging town (population 1,800) at the mouth of the Coquille River, eighteen miles west of Coquille. Only a single building in the five downtown blocks survived; over four hundred houses burned and twenty-one people perished. The fire, torching mostly Port Orford cedar, at one point flamed along a hundred-mile front. Although initially threatened, Coquille was ultimately spared by a capricious wind. As with most large forest fires, however, only a weather change brought it under control. By October 8, mop-up efforts had begun.

Coquille families opened their homes to Bandon's homeless. Although the Bandon mill had survived, much hardship ensued. The Holmstroms took in a man and his two children for several months. At Walker's station, once preliminary aid had been dispensed, a much-relieved Buzz asked Walker for two weeks of vacation. Before leaving town, he spent five dollars on a five-thousand-dollar life insurance policy, and then, boat in tow, he drove north to Eugene, then east to Springfield, Oregon, where he planned to meet Bean. The car, rescued from the town dump and rebuilt, was a 1929 two-door Chevrolet with a wooden frame and a steel roof. En route he ran out of gas and slept in his car.

The next morning in the Eugene paper he learned that hammers were swinging on a hundred new homes in Bandon. Bean, originally involved in fire-fighting, was now too busy there to go with him. So Holmstrom drove east alone on the McKenzie Highway, towing his trailer and stopping often to let his engine cool on the climb up the lava slopes of McKenzie Pass. He lugged extra water in a carbide can.

Holmstrom spent the next night alongside the John Day River near Dayville, Oregon. Before turning in, he pulled a small spiral notebook from his shirt pocket and noted the day's events. It represented the beginning of a habit.

Holmstrom kept diaries or journals—the terms are interchangeable for our purposes—on all his river trips. Small and spiral-bound, invariably with entries in pencil, they sometimes consisted of nothing more than abbreviated phrases; other times in the long twilight or the predaylight hours, awaiting sleep or enough light to row, he would write at length. His motives for keeping the diaries are an open question. Obviously, he had Major John Wesley Powell of the first Colorado River expedition as influence and example. Moreover, hoarding the sights, sounds, and impressions of a canyon to which he might never return would allow Holmstrom

Crossing the Sawtooths

to carry his favorite world back to a more ordinary one—"keeping now for then." And the fact that he only kept journals on river trips is persuasive evidence that he thought of the river world as the worthier one.

But there was probably more to it than that. Arguably, no one ever kept a diary just for himself, but his intended reader is unknown. His cozy habit armored him against shyness, loneliness, and mortality.

Leaving the John Day River next day, and despite additional car problems...

> still carrying the carbide can full of water—the natives think the middle of the desert out here is a funny place for a boat.... Having an awful time... get ignition fixed—looks like it might quit out here 40 miles from town—trailer is coming apart—think it will hold together to get to town...."

Holmstrom reached Ontario, Oregon, near the western border of Idaho, by evening. He continued east into Idaho, past Mountain Home, and north to the outskirts of Hailey, Idaho. It was four in the morning by the time he stopped and crawled into his sleeping bag.

Hailey, rebounding from the Great Depression, was riding a resurgent lead and silver mining boom. Holmstrom stayed in town long enough to enjoy a late breakfast before "having at," in his words, Galena Pass (8,750 feet), an hour north of Sun Valley, where the first chair lifts were being installed just two months before the ski lodge opened. Holmstrom's sedan required three gallons of gas and three gallons of water to hump its way over the summit. From the top, he could see the Salmon River threading its way down out of the Sawtooth Range before it flowed north 170 miles to Salmon City, a mining town dating to 1867.

He followed the twisting gravel road fringed with chrome yellow cottonwoods, its meanders dictated by the river. Calling it "the worst road I ever saw"—and Holmstrom was not given to gratuitous complaints—he persevered until he reached Salmon City, well after dark.

The next day, October 13, on the northern outskirts of the town, he prepared to launch below the bridge where all the scows began their trips. It was late fall in this country—after the first of November, ice floes could start running in the river at any time. Water was skimpy: just 800 cubic feet per second (CFS). A dry year indeed, but Holmstrom counted on picking up additional water at the confluence with the Middle Fork of the Salmon sixty miles downstream. He heard that "Cap" Harry Guleke had left with a party a day earlier.

SWEEP BOATS had been plying the River of No Return for forty years. Sweeps are a steering device: two poles, up to thirty feet in length, each fitted with a ten-foot blade that rests in the water, pinned at a pivot point, one at the bow, one at the stern. Holding the handles of the leveraged poles, the guide stands in the center of the boat on a raised platform, using the momentum gained from the fastest

Launching in Salmon City

current to maneuver with the sweep blades around obstacles in slower currents. The sweep handles operate above the heads of the passengers seated in the boat. In larger scows, the captain took the front sweep, reading the water and shouting his directions to the rear pilot.

The scows, which could be built in three days at a mill alongside the Salmon, were roughly eight feet in width and thirty-two to forty feet in length, raked at a forty-five degree angle at the bow and stern. The double hull was formed from longitudinal green lumber, one-by-twelve planks, with interior planks running athwart the barge; raised floorboards kept supplies dry when the craft shipped water. The gunwales were generally three feet high, double-walled to facilitate grocery storage. The seams were caulked with pitch or tar. Most scows carried a stove and an ice box. Sufficient canvas was on board to tent over the boat in foul or frigid weather.

The sweep boat was an efficient craft, able to carry tons of freight to the mines along the Salmon while drawing only fourteen inches of water. Its chief shortcoming became apparent when docking: it was necessary to bump along the bank until someone could get a bowline around a tree or boulder.

The craft was not an Idaho invention. Flatboats, or broadhorns as they were called elsewhere, were in use on the Ohio and Mississippi Rivers a hundred years before they appeared on the Salmon.

Harry Guleke was the boatman who brought the sweep boat and the River of No Return to national prominence. Although other boatmen had been freighting cargo downriver to Shoup for several years before Guleke arrived, the muscular and friendly boatman soon established himself as the most charismatic, knowledgeable, and successful pilot on the river. He made over two hundred trips in his career, many to Lewiston and one all the way to Portland. At first he carried heavy mining equipment, but after 1912 he began taking hunting and tourist parties into a canyon that became renowned for its scenery and big game. Documentary movies and magazine articles about the trip received widespread circulation.

When old-timers strolled by, looked over Holmstrom's boat, and suggested he rig it with sweeps, he listened respectfully to the codgers, then quietly expressed renewed confidence in his oars. He had never run a sweep boat and this was not the trip on which to learn.

He launched at three in the afternoon—the only leak proved to be an unplugged knothole—ran ten miles, and camped on a gravel bar studded with grizzled cottonwoods whose limbs hosted flocks of chattering magpies. Since a few problems had become apparent—the center-load was so great that he lacked freeboard for his oars in the shallows and consequently shattered an oar-block—he shifted supplies to the stern compartment.

In the morning, once he was back on the river, he was pleased by the results: "[it] handles 100% better.... I like it better all the time." By midafternoon he was at Shoup, a collection of abandoned mining buildings, some dating to the 1880s, on the north shore. He beached his boat and walked downstream to scout Pine Creek Rapid, a noisy and rocky predicament for the larger sweep-scows. He "looked it over good," left his camera on shore as a precaution, ran the rapid, then walked back to Shoup and mailed some postcards at the rustic post office. While returning to his boat, he stumbled over a castoff cowboy boot and, always the opportunist, cut it apart into leather sleeves to sheathe the oar shafts where they rubbed in the oarlocks.

Nine miles below Pine Creek, Holmstrom drifted the inside of a riverbank curve and surprised Lieutenant Tindall and his wife, who were fishing on the bank. The officer supervised the Civilian Conservation Corps camp, Camp Panther Creek F-176, where young men were housed while constructing the road down the river. (World War II ended the project.) Lt. Tindall invited Holmstrom to dinner, and he spent the evening in cordial conversation with the young workers.

After an early breakfast of sourdough pancakes, Tindall gave all the men time to see Holmstrom off. Acknowledging their good-byes, he waved once and disappeared around the bend. Three cars followed him as far as the new road allowed. By noon he was past the mouth of the Middle Fork and boating on twice the water. In rapids, a stiff wind blew water off the waves, making it difficult to see. "Made me so mad I could bite myself," he wrote.

Six miles farther down at the Avery ranch at Proctor Falls, he spotted a river bungalow and a dredge he remembered from the *National Geographic* article. He pulled in to call on the miners. They were busy, but not too busy to offer him lunch, which he accepted.

From 1863–1883, rich gold placer mines had been located in the mountain basins four thousand feet above the Salmon River Canyon, and miners flocked to camps such as Florence, Leesburg, and Warren's. Later, significant hard-rock quartz-gold lodes were discovered, and still a generation later, less productive sandbars along the river itself were placer mined, particularly during the Great Depression. Holmstrom was to encounter a fair number of these miners, better known as "snipers," just as he had on the Rogue River.

Back on the Salmon, it was scarcely a mile before he saw another cabin that he recalled from among the forty-some photographs in the magazine story: on the south bank, it was the home of John "Jack" Cunningham, an experienced sweep boat pilot and assistant on last year's Geographic Society trip. Holmstrom, never one to miss an opportunity for advice, pulled for shore. Cunningham was home. The two boatmen struck up a friendship, and when they parted after an hour, the younger boatman not only had a headful of advice, but handfuls of peaches and canned grape juice as well.

Another mile down the river, another stop. This time to visit with Jack and Mary Killam, who were placer mining for gold on the riverbank. Killam, a former attorney from San Diego, had a Ph.D. in English from the University of Michigan; his wife was from an upper-class Georgia family. When a doctor in California diagnosed an aneurysm and told Jack that he had six months to live, the Killams sold everything, built a camper on a Model-A Ford frame, and took their five children traveling around the West. In 1934 they came down the Salmon on a scow and settled in a cabin they built at "Killam Point."

On learning from Killam that Bert Loper, a Utah boatman already fairly well-known, had been down the Salmon only a month earlier in a similar boat on higher water, and that Killam had Loper's address in the family's cabin, Holmstrom gave the couple a lift in his boat down to their place to get it. (Loper, sixty-seven at the time, was accompanied by a friend, Charles Snell. They began at Challis, Idaho, well above Holmstrom's launch, but only went as far as Riggins.)

From the doorway of Killam's cabin, they noticed a man on the far shore, walking upriver. Hailing him, they discovered he was Monroe Hancock; after Guleke, Hancock was the most experienced sweep boatman on the river and captain of the Geographic Society trip. They rowed over for a visit.

Once again, the older boatman took to the younger. Hancock told Holmstrom he thought his boat the best of its type he had ever seen—although he could not resist suggesting that sweeps might be an improvement. Since wooden rowboats were not rare on the Salmon—even a party with three rubber rafts had run the river eight years earlier—Hancock's estimate was a high compliment indeed. Hancock also remarked that someday he would like to run the Colorado River with a sweep boat. As boatmen will, they talked about the river, and Hancock said Holmstrom "should make it OK." For his part, Holmstrom noted that Hancock "impressed me very favorably—quiet, slow spoken, lean, intelligent...." Holmstrom, after saying his good-byes, ran another mile to camp—it was almost dark, time to seek his "kapok kouch" as he called it.

His log entry that night reflected an amalgam of declining worries, growing confidence. In part, he wrote:

> Since leaving Salmon, I have not met one person who ever heard of Coquille or has been anywhere near it…. I will sleep with one eye half open tonight as Jack Killam says a couple of days ago he saw the biggest grizzly bear he ever saw in his life—I hope he doesn't like sal-man meat…. I write this lying by the fire with the hatchet for a pillow waiting…. It occurred to me that I am what you might call bait for the Salmon—whether or not the Salmon gobbles up the bait remains to be seen.

October 15. After a breakfast of eggs, bacon, hotcakes, and coffee, he cast off again. Snow dusted the ridge tops above Horse Creek. Four miles downriver, at the mouth of Cottonwood Creek, he caught up with Captain Harry Guleke, the local grandee, encamped with four hunters. "Cap" as he was affectionately known, was at the shank end of his career that reached back to 1896. Holmstrom noted, "Pretty old—can't bend over good—not as big as I thought but Hancock says he is the best riverman on the river." Holmstrom had written Guleke for advice and the old boatman remembered him from his letters. Hancock had also cautioned Holmstrom that Guleke was very jealous of his own preeminence on the river, and that he had been aground three or four times already on this trip. Still, the elder boatmen (in his early seventies) acknowledged the quality of the Oregon boat, "and said I probably would get thru though I might swamp first…. I had the privilege of towing the scow out of an eddy…." (Guleke made his last trip in 1939, died in 1944.)

By noon, loaded with gifts of venison and bear meat, Holmstrom got underway. He ran Rainier, Lantz Bar, and Devil's Teeth Rapids without problems. "The deck has been wet all forenoon." He noted the wreckage of a scow below Devil's Teeth.

Until it was repeatedly dynamited, Salmon Falls, a spectacular batholithic exposure of granite, was a serious obstacle for sweep boats. Known earlier as the Black Canyon Falls, it floods out in high water; at low flows there are three slots, depending on the size of the craft. It was four in the afternoon and cold when Holmstrom, alerted by its sound, reached the rapid. He stopped to scout—this was only the second rapid to merit a look. "It was a bad one… the wickedest looking place I ever saw…." In his own words:

> The total fall is probably not more than 10 feet but it comes in less than 100 feet—when I first looked at it I would have sworn it impossible to run, but by going close against the rock on the left side and over the top of a rock on a pour—which looks like a knob on top & from the top of which the water runs 3 ways—if the boat didn't end over & I could get between the two rocks—15 or 12 feet below I could make it—I really didn't think it possible

but it was either that or walk out & give up—took off my shirt—fastened life jacket—unloaded boat at head on right side—emptied pockets—and had at her—there is an approach of 50 feet of very swift water with bad boils—very narrow—not enough room to handle oars properly—on account of rocks on sides—went through there crossways almost trying to line up with the pair over which I must go exactly in the center—with the last stroke of the left oar before it struck the rock on left I straightened the boat up & over she went exactly in center—stood on end and, impossible as it seemed to me, the stern shot out of the water & the boat leveled out taking on hardly any water at all & I went between the rocks—dead center—& pulled ashore below

As soon as the boat leveled out & I saw it was OK, I started yelling—hollering at the top of my lungs and whistling & singing as I absolutely couldn't help it & as I would not admit it as soon as the excitement is over I write it down now using a flat granite boulder for a table & looking at the boat safely parked below the fall with the duffel all ready to load in—Peculiar formation here—apparently the granite on both sides slopes toward the gorge at an angle of 45°—it is slick with practically no vegetation & very smooth—there are two very tall peaks sharp & almost bare towering almost straight above on the right side of the falls (north) & a gully has been formed here running down from their direction & down it has tumbled these huge granite blocks from 20 to 50 feet in diameter forming a dam & the falls—will load the boat now & head on down—G's party gave me some deer & bear meat—I am now enjoying the finest feeling of satisfaction & relief & some thing I can't express I ever had—this is what makes the trip worth while....

Two more miles running on adrenaline, then Holmstrom pulled in on the right at Sabe Creek to camp for the night. He wrote in his journal:

Am now lying with the life jacket for a pillow writing by light of fire—am camped by a good sized stream on right 1 to 2 miles below Salmon F—down here the mountains are still somewhat the same granite forms as at the falls but are more broken down—not so steep & more vegetation—don't know what creek this is & am totally lost—have not passed a man or horse since the one above Devils [T]eeth—the forestry map is worse than nothing as there is nothing on it for me to identify things by—good thing there is only one way out or I would probably try my old trick of finding a shortcut & get into trouble.

Have had a very fine repast consisting of a "thing" with butter & jam on it—the thing is made as follows: dump in some biscuit flour—add some water from the nearest ck—dump in a small can of condensed milk add two eggs—stir well & add a liberal mixture of sand if you happen to be camped on a sand bar—try & cook in a frying pan over open fire—It is really very good but I am not going to make another till I am camped on solid ground as the sand makes it necessary to be careful not to close your teeth clear together when eating it.

> I think the boat is the finest one ever built—it behaves better than I hoped—if some wild animal doesn't steal my bear meat during the nite I think I will have some for breakfast—It ought to put me in the mood for [running?] lots of bad rapids—so far I have not stopped to look over one single one but Pine Ck & S.F.—This is surely a beautiful country....

On the morning of October 16, after a bear-meat breakfast, he launched early. The canyon slopes steepened; ponderosa pines quilled the upper heights, while closer to the river Oregon grape, syringa, ninebark, and mountain mahogany flourished in granitic soil between the yellow pines. He drank it in. "This sure is beautiful country." He stopped for a scrub and a soak at Barth Hot Springs, where water too hot for comfort spilled in rivulets into the river. On a flat on the bench above and out of sight of the river, Guleke maintained a small cabin. Holmstrom examined the inscriptions carved in the riverside rocks by earlier parties, but had neither the time nor hubris to add his own.

For ten miles he had easy, tranquil going. He stopped at a vacant cabin (Monroe Hancock's) and left a quarter for the melon he cut from the garden. Just after noon, he started down the tongue of Bailey Rapid — a long, steep string of breakers — got soaked, and took on water in his front hold. Unruffled, he pressed on, only to be taken by surprise in Big Mallard Rapid at the foot of a blind curve. He missed the pour-over rock at the bottom of the rapid but got sucked back in behind it, spun around, lost an oar in the river, then finally was spit out of the hole. He chased his cedar oar and recovered it undamaged. (Guleke often had his problems here, as did the Hatch-Swain trip in 1936.) After bailing the water out of his cockpit, he proceeded on, more attentive than before — "worst stretch I have seen so far — continuously soaked and bailing" — onward through Elkhorn and Growler Rapids.

That night Holmstrom camped on the flat below Painter Mine on the right side of the river and across from Five Mile Bar at Five Mile Creek. He found John Painter's grave, only two months old, up on the slope behind his camp. He dried out his sleeping bag by the fire, then fell asleep staring at the stars.

At dawn, October 17, he watched as a buckskin-clad figure," young—30—medium size good looking fellow," accompanied by a brown spotted dog, rowed his odd boat across to Holmstrom's camp and invited him back across the river to breakfast. Holmstrom had just met Sylvan Ambrose Hart, the Salmon River's "Last of the Mountain Men."

Hart, born in 1906 in a sod dugout in Oklahoma Indian Territory, had gone to college in Kansas and Oklahoma, finishing with a B.A. in English Literature at the University of Oklahoma. In 1932, the core of the Great Depression, he had found his way to Five Mile Bar, where he could live on fifty dollars a year. He reflected, "I always had a garden. It was easy to get fruit, and I made moccasins and clothing out of animal skins. There were copper plates lying around at Painter's mine that I made into utensils." Hart was also a gunsmith and a crack shot. (He died in 1980, still at Five Mile Bar.)

Hart, Holmstrom recorded, "cooked a lot of venison—made gravy—baked sourdough biscuits in an iron Dutch oven in fireplace—butter—tomato preserves —and chocolate—not bad...." The small stucco cabin reminded him of Robinson Crusoe. After breakfast they hiked four miles up a side stream to look at some Nez Perce pictographs.

It was late afternoon when the men parted. Holmstrom accepted a bar of homemade soap: "...guess I looked like I need it." He took up his oars and pushed downriver, through Ludwig Rapid, then Jackson Bar Rapid, and past Mackay Bar— an expansive flat on the left at the mouth of the South Fork, once used to raise hay and cattle, but in 1936-1938 the site of a dubious placer mining operation. Thinking he might reach the town of Riggins (forty-five miles) the next day, he did not stop. In camp that night, the sound of fall Chinook thrashing in their redds lulled him to sleep.

Holmstrom was up before daylight. He built a large warming fire from drift-wood, then wrote in his diary:

> 7:15 boat loaded & ready to leave — earliest yet — either watch fast or gets light late as I had breakfast before daylite — nice place to camp here — no houses within miles tho there is a trail here — big sand bar — lots of driftwood and a large quiet eddy — Salmon jumping in it last nite & a lot of trout this A.M. — If I had time sure I could catch some — campfire just about burned out now & sun just hitting tops of hi mts. — I can see where my housekeeping is going to get to be a little more complicated soon as my sweatshirt & overalls are getting so dirty I can't get the dishes very clean by wiping them that way any more — of course a good wet day like day before yesterday would give me a fresh start — Breakfast 4 slices bacon 4 eggs 2 cups coffee & 3 slices bread — will have to last all day tho — few of Jack C's peaches left but in bad shape — good thing I didn't get wrecked in the upper end of trip & have to live off country with gun as the shells I got won't fit the gun — Each morning I have to fill some more seams in the boat with tar where the plastic wood moved out. I am going to try to find the Riggins hot springs so I can wash again —
> 8:30 Burned hole in life jacket this A.M. — built big fire up & went to find water & spark got in jacket — yesterday a sock & this A.M. jacket —

Days were getting shorter. Since launching, he had dropped over two thousand feet in elevation, but the cold was numbing; he remarked on the ice on his decks. He was still over two hundred miles from Lewiston. "Can't stop to figure date," he wrote.

The canyon opened up; rapids were less frequent and less technical. Dried Meat, Chittam, Vinegar Creek, Carey Falls—he did not know or care what the rapids were named—he had "miles to go before he slept." By noon he was boating alongside the CCC construction crews at work on the southern extension of the road intended to connect with Salmon City. An audience followed him along the road above the river, taking photographs. In midafternoon, he reached Riggins. He was a god-awful sight: unwashed, unshaved, old tar on his fingers, char holes in his grimy shirt.

He was in town less than an hour—long enough to visit the post office and the Mercantile. The item that did snag his eye and camera was one of Russell "Doc" Frazier's boats abandoned alongside a small house.

Holmstrom swung back out into the river, a river whose flow, augmented by the South Fork and the Little Salmon, had grown to 3,000 CFS, low for most years, but more than three times that at his launch site. The river wheeled due north. The mountains lay well back from the river now; timber was sparse, sage and cheat-grass and bunchgrass predominant. He got a wake-up call at Fiddle Creek Rapid, where he went sideways into a hole and nearly capsized. It put him on notice that the water here was stronger, more insistent. "This is a real river now." Ten miles below Riggins, he put in for the night at Cow Creek (present-day Lucile). Just a few miles west of the ridge behind his campsite, the Snake River flowed northerly. Not enough driftwood for a fire, so earlier than usual he wormed into his sleeping bag. Over fifty miles in a day, some of it through deadwater; not bad. He wrote in his diary:

> 7:00 camped at Cow Creek 11 miles below Riggins—Below R[iggins] the river is of a different nature—much swifter—larger waves by far—when the boat enters a rapid it is almost impossible to do anything with it—she almost stands on end—Pursuing my usual pattern of carelessness I broke an oar & nearly wrecked in Fiddle Ck—if the boat had not been wide as it is she would have went over—slid over a big rock sideways into a hole below —she tipped up on her side—hesitated—oar went under & broke off & she righted herself—a number of bad ones between here & R[iggins]—I still think I can make it tho by being more careful—no damage done yet except to my pride on account of the miserable handling I did this P.M.

At dawn on his seventh day, he shrugged into his wet clothes and pressed on. At noon he boated past the point where Highway 95 left the river in the direction of Lewiston. Holmstrom would get to Lewiston the hard way, the colorful way, the river-road-way.

Once again, bare, rugged mountains loomed ahead; the canyon shouldered in. The geology increased in complexity and color. Few subjects fascinated Holmstrom more: "…beautiful scenery—something like Grand Canyon on a small scale… wish

I knew more geology…." He had not seen Grand Canyon yet; this gorge was known locally as Green Canyon because of its serpentine-hued tinge. Walls steep-to-sheer made it impassable to placer miners. After stashing some rock samples, he wrote:

> 2:30 River here turns toward N.W.—Rock—Reddish brown & hard as iron— has a grain sloping up toward west—so there will naturally be some bad drops—at one now—lot of rocks at top but straight shot only back curling waves—Had a very attentive audience down here—horses and cows all stand on the hillsides like statues as I go by—3 of them—soaked on 1st—2nd not so bad & 3 better—very nasty sheer walls—
> lonely

Pine Bar Rapid looked scratchy: it is a ledgy rapid with closely scattered boulders washed down from Hells Gate Creek and most difficult at low water. To get through, he unloaded his ungainly canvas tent, debating about leaving it. Then, confused about where he was (thinking this was Snow Hole Rapid) he jotted in his diary, "…Am I happy—this is one of those places where you either do or don't—no compromise—" He ran it easily enough and camped three miles below Rice Creek, a forty-mile day. Holmstrom was so tired that he decided against fixing dinner; he would eat in the morning. Mapless now, he fell asleep thinking he still might make Lewiston the next day.

At 5:30 A.M., Tuesday, October 20, day eight, with the stars still out, his boat packed, Holmstrom stood by his campfire, watching his coffee come to boil:

> coffee actually fit to drink this A.M.—In fact drank three cups—toast & 3 burned eggs & burned bacon—fine fire—got to get an early start & try to get to Lewiston today—getting a little homesick now—hope everything is OK.… I like this camping out… wish I could find another hot spring so I could wash—glad I haven't a mirror… been looking up at the stars every night since leaving home—even the night it rained—I'll bet I hold the world's championship for quick washing & stowing away of dishes—nothing to it—— new system.

He was off, deeper into a green canyon still seized by shadows. But for all his haste, the going slowed. At White House Bar, a spacious, sandy bench on the right, he stopped to visit with a miner on shore. Bill Herwig lived in a fissure in the basaltic cliff with a canvas entry-wall. He made coffee and they talked river-talk. "Wild Bill" Herwig had apparently once boated into Cataract Canyon on the Colorado River in Utah and wrecked. Then he had tried a scow down the Middle Fork of the Salmon. (Unfortunately, Holmstrom did not record the year or the outcome of that venture, but if Herwig made it, it would have been either the first or second trip through there.)

Afloat again, Holmstrom added several penciled pages to his diary as he drifted:

Bill Herwig's home

Here everywhere is the crystal shaped rock—in all positions cropping out all over the mts—some funny shapes but mostly as sort of Rimrock—some places it will radiate like spokes on a wheel in all directions from a center—some places perpendicular & some horizontal.

I suppose the water in the river is cleaner than it looks—the miners all use it without boiling & when you are in Rome—but every time I think of the two dead horses 1 dead cow & 1 dead dog below Salmon I kind of wonder.

Beginning 1 mile below camp got into green rock—all green now—apparently under the crystal brown formation—fast going—no bad ones.

All thru here can be seen that mark of civilization that the old Indian never saw—old tires—hi up on the banks sometimes where the eddys have put them at hi water—kind of spoils the primeval aspect—should row forwards thru the quieter places but prefer to back down—slower but can see downstream & enjoy the beauty....

In midafternoon he arrived at Snow Hole Rapid. Here the canyon became more precipitous, the river knotted with impressive, rough-hewn boulders that spawned equally impressive holes. He scouted from the right shore, unloaded his gear, and made a flawless run. "Ran thru OK—fastest water I ever saw—once start, fairly fly...." Just below the rapid, he encountered another miner who was living on a twenty-seven-foot scow, and they visited.

In late afternoon, Holmstrom turned his bow and back downstream and rowed against the predictable upstream wind. Then another stop—this time to palaver with Jack Shelby, who had spent two years coming down the river in a crude, sixteen-foot canvas-over-frame boat from Salmon City, placer mining as he went. Wrote Holmstrom: "...hauls everything he owns in it—quite diff from me—when he takes chances on a rapid he loses everything if he tips over while I lose nothing but boat & a few trinkets—has no life preserver—had inner tube on Snake but it got a leak so he threw it away...." Shelby had also run the Snake River from Weiser through Hells Canyon to Lewiston, Idaho (over two hundred miles). More boatman talk. Said Holmstrom of his new friend;

> big, tall, rangy—about 50 or more but very healthy & strong looking—hated to see me leave & I hated to [leave] as we were running the Salmon rapid by rapid.... News travels slowly here. He asked if I were Dr. Frazer [who] has been gone home from Riggins over 6 weeks....

By now, Holmstrom knew he shared a special fraternal bond: what might be called the Benevolent and Protective Order of River Runners.

Something more than icy weather compelled Holmstrom to keep moving: he was down to four slices of bread, three eggs, a half can of milk, a little coffee. Miners wintering in the canyon, however large-hearted, could scarcely afford to grubstake him.

Before daylight on Wednesday morning, he wrote by the amplifying light of his campfire:

> Had breakfast—stowed everything away & waiting for it to get light enough to move—will have to make L soon—Built such big fire this A.M. couldn't get close enough to cook very well—cold last nite—sheeting of clear ice all over boat this A.M.—Hate to get out of sleep bag but forced now—put pants & sweatshirt under bag & they are fairly warm in A.M.—fellow with scow above China Bar said 50 miles from junction of S & S to L[ewiston]—must be at least 15 from here to junct—hope he was wrong—if wind blows wrong way again won't make it.

At first light, he pushed off once again. He made good time, noted the remarkable hexagonal formations of columnar basalt, and immediately detected the start of Blue Canyon, revealed by yet another transition in geology. (The Slide—a famed rapid today, would not form here for two more decades.)

Still early in the morning, he reached the confluence with the Snake River. There he overtook two Finnish brothers, Ed and Eno Luoto, for whom he had a message from another miner upriver. The Finns dropped everything to make coffee and a meal for their visitor aboard their large scow, which was so fastidiously clean that they removed their shoes before going aboard. The Luotos, who went by "Og" and "Oke," were raised in Minnesota, and came west to Astoria, Oregon, to work as ocean fishermen. Before coming to the Salmon, they had worked as trappers along the Rogue River; later they trapped the high country of the Salmon Mountains as well. In support, one of the Luotos rowed a seventeen-foot, squared-stern rowboat behind the scow. Holmstrom took to them on the spot. "...they know everyone on the river & everyone knows & likes them...."

In the course of their exchange, the brothers confided that the following year they intended to bring a scow down the Snake River, loaded with a car engine to run a pump that would facilitate their hydraulic mining operations. Holmstrom was impressed, although he wrote, "...nice fellows—will probably kill themselves in the end but said they don't care if they have a good time doing it...." Men after his own heart. They would cross trails again less than three years hence.

The Snake River was nearly quadruple the Salmon's flow; Holmstrom estimated its width at four hundred feet, but remained unsure how far he was from Lewiston. Other encounters with miners riding out the Great Depression—one in his seventies with "the worst boat I ever saw," and the other "working like a mad-man"—slowed him like a head wind. "Spent too much time with them... the gold bug bites pretty deep—I may have the river bug a little but I hope the gold one never bites me—it is almost pathetic to see how lonesome some of them are...." He weighed running by moonlight, but since the light was inferior, he stopped, ate one of his eggs, and curled up on a pocket of sand below a cliff. His journal entry reveals his frustration with the torpid "Snake Lake":

> bad whirls & boils—current eddys back & forth & can't make any headway at all—to top it all off—very strong wind blowing upstream—whitecaps in some of stillwater made me awfully mad—tonite I am in a fine fix—thot maybe I could see by moon to run on in to L[ewiston]or Asotin 6 mi above but light no good & came to rapid—couldn't see so ran ashore on right bank.

The next morning, October 22, broke cloudy, with sleety rain carried on the wind. Before he cast off, Holmstrom ate the last of his food, picked the stick-tight burrs out of his clothing, and treated himself to a pair of dry socks. The landscape impressed him less than that of the Salmon: grass-clad rolling hills with an occa-

The Luoto brothers and their giant rowboat. Scow in back-ground

sional forlorn hackberry tree clinging to the eroding shore; not a sign anyone lived in the area save for a burro, the skeleton of a horse, a mile of barbed wire fence, and a placer claim marker.

The Snake River packs a burly current, however, and despite the frustrating goad of a constant upstream wind, he rowed ashore at Lewiston at nine in the evening—after fifteen hours on the river. He hauled his boat out of the water, left his things with an old fellow, J. J. Hastings, at Brady's dock, and went into town. There he got himself a razor, a tube of shaving cream, a bar of soap, and clean underwear. Then he went to a bathhouse and looked in a mirror. "Didn't realize how I look till then." He used the entire twenty-five-cent tube of shaving cream.

Holmstrom walked around Lewiston, a ranching and logging town at the confluence of the Clearwater with the Snake, finding it "...a strange town—everything is grain elevators—buyers, sellers or else wool—stores have window displays of lariats spurs chaps bridles etc...." He made plans to leave the next day for Salmon on the afternoon bus, hoping to catch Hancock in town at work on his winter scow.

That night Holmstrom wrote his most poignant journal entry:

> I am sorry the trip is over—scared most of the time but now I find I would like to do it over right now—know I lost some weight but no doubt will have it all back by the time I get home—felt so good all time—felt like whistling or singing—no doubt natives think I am a very musical man— my biggest regret is that someone wasn't along to enjoy the trip with me —Clarence or Carl for instance—Seems like hoarding for one person to have so much all to himself.

Old prospector and his boat

Never very lonely as so many interesting people along river—slept looking up at the stars every nite since leaving home—2 weeks—wish I were home now as next few days isn't going to be very much fun—hope the car performs OK.

The next day, he rode the bus up Lewiston Grade—a two-thousand-foot climb through sixty-four curves—onto the Palouse plateau. "...all wheat [soft white] far as can see,... rich looking country—like top of world—all work here seems to be done by horses—yellow fields dotted with horses & cows & pigs...." The bus traveled by way of Moscow, Idaho, to Spokane, Washington. The following day he rode to Missoula and Hamilton, Montana, then south to Salmon, where he arrived shortly after noon.

Holmstrom recovered his car, then chased the recently embarked Monroe Hancock downriver as far as the mouth of the Middle Fork. He narrowly missed overtaking him. It was getting dark, so on his way back up the river he stopped at the CCC camp, accepted a dinner invitation, and under friendly duress, regaled the men with an account of his trip.

After breakfast at the camp, he started for home. A flat tire and an empty gas tank kept him at the Shenon Hotel in Salmon for the night. (For someone who worked in a gas station, Holmstrom was oddly forgetful of his gas gauge.) He learned that the woman who owned the hotel was the mother of Philip Shenon, co-author of the *National Geographic* article that had inspired Holmstrom's journey.

He drove as far as Coeur d'Alene, Idaho, the next day, before a wheel came off of his empty trailer and required a stop to find a replacement. He grouched about the price: $4.50. By noon the next day, he was on his way again and drove into Lewiston that night.

In the morning, October 27, he loaded his boat and took it up on the Lewiston bench to the Lewiston State Normal School, a two-year teacher's college, where the National Geographic Society, along with the USGS, had donated its scow. He positioned his trusty boat alongside and photographed them together. Then he got back in his car and started home, just a gas jockey about a week late for his routine job at Walker's.

The Doing of the Thing

1937

N O ONE KNOWS just when or why Buzz Holmstrom decided to run the Colorado. To judge from appearances he was drifting from one whim to the next. Yet well before his Salmon trip, he had his sights on the Colorado. In the summer of 1936 he had written to Emery Kolb, a well-known river runner, about the possibility of joining a Grand Canyon trip. Kolb had steered him to Frank Dodge, who was to lead a scientific survey through Grand Canyon later that year. Dodge had not been encouraging. He had already picked all his boatmen and later wrote that the trip had been postponed a year. Later, on the Salmon River, Holmstrom had the foresight to secure Colorado River boatman Bert Loper's address from Jack Killam.

Upon returning from the Salmon, Holmstrom was a local celebrity for a few weeks, but was soon back at his job at Walker's. As he pumped gas and changed tires, he mulled over his next trip. Holmstrom wrote to Loper for pointers on running Grand Canyon, asking how it compared with the Salmon. He wrote Kolb again, describing his Salmon boat, how well it had handled, and asked if Kolb thought it good enough for the Colorado. If not, how big a boat should he build?

> Where can I secure plans for a boat like the ones you used? Can I get the dope on how to recognize the different rapids, their fall, and how they have been negotiated by the different parties? How long oars did you use? Are two spares enough? What type of oarlocks have been found to be the most successful on the Colorado?—P.S. what is the best type of life preserver for using on that trip?

Kolb sent Holmstrom plans for a Galloway-style boat—the type that Kolb and most Grand Canyon river runners had used since Nathaniel Galloway, a Utah trapper, began building them in the 1890s.

Holmstrom wrote to Colonel Claude Birdseye in Washington, D.C. for more pointers. Birdseye had been in charge of the 1923 USGS trip through Grand Canyon; Emery Kolb had been lead boatman, Frank Dodge a young surveyor about to earn his oars. Birdseye supplied USGS survey maps of the river, an invaluable gift, and referred Holmstrom back to Bert Loper, who he claimed was a riverman without equal.

In 1937, communication with Frank Dodge resumed, still with little promise. The trip, a joint geologic exploration for Carnegie Institution of Washington and California Institute of Technology, was scheduled to launch October 10, but there still was no room for another boatman. At one point Dodge mentioned the remote possibility of Holmstrom tagging along at his own expense, although he had doubts about a kid who wrote letters in pencil on lined school paper and signed his name "Buzz." "If you are interested, give me your age, weight, amount of schooling and better send a late photograph of yourself.... P.S. Please sign your correct name."

When Holmstrom asked his opinion of going alone or with a friend, Dodge wrote:

> In re to a lone trip in a 15 ft. boat through the canyons, I would advise against it, especially from Lees Ferry down through Marble and Grand Canyons for, there are places miles and miles long, that if one should loose their boat, he would be lost. No way of climbing out. A man would starve to death. From Wyoming to Lees Ferry it wouldn't be so bad, for a man can climb out most anywhere and reach a cow or sheep camp or a small settlement if one used his head but please don't try the lower canyons alone. It's almost sure to be fatal....

With little encouragement, Holmstrom methodically pursued his plan. By day he was the affable grease monkey down at Walker's. After hours he was busy with friends, playing handball, fishing, horsing around. At night he read anything he could find about the Colorado, about river running, about Grand Canyon. Rolf recalls his brother bringing home every river-related title he could find from the library, reading into the wee hours. Ian Campbell, who met him later in Grand Canyon, observed, "Buzz has apparently read—& remembered—every book written about the Colorado. Also sea stories—quoted from Joshua Slocum."

Slocum, a retired sea captain, was a hero to many young folk of the day. *Sailing Alone Around the World*, published in 1900, was his matter-of-fact tale of one man's quest, from building his own sloop, to being the first to sail solo around the world, with little in the way of finances, encouragement, or sophisticated equipment. Slocum described his encounters with gales, reefs, pirates, savages, and bouts of loneliness; all of which he mastered by his wit, skill, perseverance, and good luck. "To young men contemplating a voyage," Slocum wrote, "I would say go." Holmstrom took that to heart.

Holmstrom decided to build a bigger boat. As with his other boats, he would build it himself with whatever he could find, beg, or borrow. He lived where outstanding timber grew: white cedar, the locals called it; more accurately, Port Orford cedar. Although rare today, it still grows in a narrow stretch of southern Oregon, in the steep, rain-soaked forests of the Coast Range. In Holmstrom's day, Port Orford cedar was already well known for its unique strength, straight clear grain, and unusual resistance to decay. It was used for separators inside batteries, venetian blinds, arrow shafts, and boats.

In 1915, some thirty miles up the South Fork of the Coquille River, entrepreneur Albert Powers had built a railroad into a stand of Port Orford cedar and there named a town for himself. As he had for previous boats, Holmstrom went to Powers in pursuit of wood. There was no mistaking the areas he searched—at the service station he had used a tire-treading tool to melt his name into the tread of his bald trailer tires. Every dirt road he drove down read: BUZZ HOLMSTROM BUZZ HOLMSTROM BUZZ HOLMSTROM.

He found the perfect log, a windfall, not too far from the road, and hewed it into a manageable chunk. Later, with the help of friends, he trailered the block of wood into town and had Smith Wood Products mill it to order. After hauling the planks home and stacking them, he allowed the fresh lumber to dry for the next few months. The sweet, pungent odor of the curing cedar overpowered the dirt-floored basement.

Once the wood was dry, Holmstrom carted it back to Smith's for planing. He then had a large stack of clear, smooth lumber. But Rolf remembers that on the edges of the boards he could still see his brother's hand-hewing of the original log.

Into his daily routine Holmstrom now squeezed, between evening handball and late-night reading, several hours of crafting his boat. No one recalls a set of plans. Buzz designed his boats in his mind, complete with complicated bends and compound-mitered cuts, then built them. For this boat, he enlarged and modified his Salmon design for bigger water. Although he had plans for the classic Galloway-style Colorado River boats he did not adhere to them. He stayed with what he knew. He incorporated ideas from previous boats, adopting and adapting much of what he saw in the southern Oregon rapid-water drift boats, and using features of the Galloway boat when appropriate. In later years, river historian Otis "Dock" Marston claimed that Holmstrom's unique hybrid boat was the best white-water craft yet to see the Colorado.

His lumber ready, he began. On the coast Holmstrom found an old driftwood stump with the perfect bend and hewed out the stem piece. Friends offered handles, hinges, canvas, and tacks. Holmstrom scrounged paint, tools, oars, and leather.

Night after night, piece by piece, the boat took shape. Friends occasionally came by to see what he was up to, but for the most part Buzz worked late and he worked alone. Once again Rolf, now fourteen, would help, holding boards, clinching nails (bending them around backwards to grip the wood), running errands. Buzz explained to Rolf what he was doing on the immediate project without revealing the big picture. That is, he explained the cut he was making without letting on why he was building the boat.

Holmstrom looked at the boat, examined his lumber, thought for a bit, then cut the next piece. And the next. Slowly summer passed. He had started with a large splintery plank laid on the dirt floor. From this rose a series of thin boards that acted as forms, defining the graceful curves of the hull. Bent around these, large cedar planks formed the sides of the boat. Holmstrom cut them to approximate shape with a draw knife, fine-tuning the curves with a hand plane. Once the

Where the boats were built; basement workshop open to the world

planks matched each other in perfect bends, he planed an matching bevel onto the lower board. He then clinch-nailed the lapped boards together. When the hull was complete, he turned the boat right-side-up and removed the forms. He then cut permanent ribs to fit inside and screwed them into place.

The Terry twins, Duane and Wayne, stopped in on occasion. Recalls Duane: "One of my fondest memories was watching Buzz there in the basement building that boat. Nobody else in Coquille was doing much in those days. He was my boyhood hero."

For whitewater, the interior of the boat needed decking. Holmstrom nailed thin panels of wood tightly, side by side, to the cross thwarts, separating his rowing cockpit from watertight compartments at each end. He then nailed arched decks across these bulkheads and covered them with a layer of canvas to shed water. Small hatches gave access to the ample bow and stern compartments, and Holmstrom sealed lids securely over them with thumb screws. He gave it a coat of gray-green paint, a mix of left-over colors. Finally, the Holmstrom brothers went to pull the finished boat from the basement of the old house. This was the biggest boat he had yet built, and the earlier ones had been a tight fit—this time they had to remove the door and widen the doorway. The boat, complete, had cost around thirty-five dollars.

Buzz began tinkering with the old Dodge Brothers Touring Car, one of the family's endless string of jalopies. He and Carl had recently bought it for ten dollars, and taught Rolf to drive in it. It was a comical and archaic machine—the roof, damaged beyond repair, had been removed. Bailing wire held the doors shut; painted warnings adorned what remained of the body. Satisfied that the Dodge's demise was not imminent, Holmstrom began enlarging his trailer to accommodate the new boat. Rolf remembers it was only then that he asked his brother where he might be headed. "Oh, down the Colorado River," said Buzz.

At some point, Holmstrom invited Clarence Bean to go along, and Earl Hamilton as well. At first each talked of going, but as time passed, other matters intervened. Hamilton went back to school. He was studying dentistry, and his education did not allow time for adventures. Bean was in a bind. Two friends from Coos Bay were planning a sailing trip to the south seas and had invited him to go. Getting the sailboat ready would take time and they were headed south to San Diego to begin work. Bean had to choose one trip or the other and, as he later described it, he simply departed with the first expedition. The sailors left first.

Holmstrom was disappointed, but not about to give up. A year earlier, when Bean had been called away to the Bandon fire, Holmstrom had run the Salmon alone. Now it was happening again. Of course, Holmstrom had no commitment to go alone. He had made no deals, signed no contracts, shared no plans. It was simply something he wanted to do, something he was too hard-headed *not* to do, even though his friends backed out.

Bean, who had been in Santa Barbara visiting the Lawhornes, sent a card:

> Your Aunt said you are going down the river alone. Haven't you any sense at
> all, you dumb Swede? She and I think you had better come with us on the
> boat. Personally I don't know where or when we're going since I'm just a
> deck hand—Beans

America was crawling out of the Great Depression but its repercussions lingered. Few, especially in the logging communities of southern Oregon, had a cent
to spare. Families like the Holmstroms grew as much of their food as possible.
Those who had jobs were lucky and worked hard to keep them. Compounding
matters, Buzz and Carl were still supporting Frances, Rolf, and Anna. It was not
a time to go adventuring—that remained the privilege of the wealthy. Yet here
was Holmstrom, with his ten dollar car, the trailer and boat he built for nearly
nothing, a small camera and fifteen dollars' worth of film, a hundred dollars in
his pocket and seventeen in the bank. His net worth could not have topped two
hundred dollars. And although there was little likelihood he would be back on
time, Holmstrom arranged for a month of vacation from Walker's. Late the night
of September 29, 1937, he fired up the roofless Dodge and, with scarcely a word to
anyone, headed east into the Coast Range, boat in tow.

It took Holmstrom five days to travel the eleven hundred miles from Coquille,
Oregon, to Green River, Wyoming. The Dodge required nearly as much care and
maintenence as the horse it was designed to replace. He made it through the mountains the first night—it was stormy on the divide, but the car chugged on. On the
30th he wound east, up along the Snake River; the following day he arrived in Salt
Lake City. The clean, orderly city with its wide streets impressed Holmstrom. He
wrote to his mother, "I talked to quite a few people and as luck would have it didn't
say anything bad about the church before they let me know they belonged to it."

He visited every boatman he could find—Russell "Doc" Frazier, a general
practitioner and river runner; and Ralph Woolley of the USGS, who had been on
the 1922 survey of the upper Green River. Next he called on the head boatman
from the same expedition, Bert Loper.

If anyone qualified as the old man of the river, it was Loper. Orphaned young,
Loper had worked his way west doing odd jobs and mining. By the late 1890s, he
had discovered boating and begun rowing down the San Juan, Green and Colorado
Rivers, prospecting the gravel bars. In the early 1920s, the USGS hired Loper as head
boatman for surveys of the San Juan and Green Rivers. Twice he had started out to
run Grand Canyon, but each time his plans went awry.

In 1936, when Holmstrom had written, Loper considered joining him for the
Grand Canyon trip. Although not a young man, Loper had just run the Salmon
without problems. But again, it was not to be. Whatever the reason, Holmstrom
wrote that Loper "is 69 years old now and thought he'd better not."

When Holmstrom found him in Salt Lake, Loper was caretaking the old Masonic Temple, penniless. Holmstrom was surprised to find "a big strong man appearing to be about 50." Loper filled Holmstrom with tales of the river, its history, and its people. He spoke of dangerous rapids and techniques for coping with them. It may have been that Holmstrom and Loper found in each other reflections of themselves. Essentially loners, each had fallen in love with the river. Without adequate finances, each had begun building boats and running rivers. And without intending to, each had ended up doing most of his boating alone.

Holmstrom left Salt Lake with Loper's blessing and by late the next night was on the last leg of his road trip, heading into Wyoming. Growing drowsy, he pulled off the road to spend the night in the desert. When a hitchhiker riding along began shivering, Holmstrom gave him his sleeping bag and curled up contentedly in a small blanket by the car.

HOLMSTROM was not one to do things half-way. He could have quit the Rogue when he wrecked at Black Bar, and no one would have thought the worse of him. On his Salmon run he could easily have chosen a shorter trip—Salmon to Riggins, or Riggins to Lewiston. But he ran the entire river. Now there were several choices as he headed for the Green and Colorado. Between Green River, Wyoming, and Boulder Dam in Nevada, three highways crossed the river. If he wanted to get back to the gas station in a month, he could have chosen any of a number of shorter options and still had an excellent and challenging trip. But no. Holmstrom had decided to follow the entire route of Major John Wesley Powell.

In 1869, Powell, a one-armed Civil War veteran, was the first to explore and record the canyons of the Green and Colorado. Launching with nine sturdy men Powell spent one hundred days working his heavy, keeled boats downriver. There was no art to their river running; they just did the best they could. On June 9, two weeks out, they smashed a boat. One man quit. On August 28, near the end of Grand Canyon, half-starved and faced with ever-worsening rapids, three more men left the trip. Just thirty hours later, Powell emerged from Grand Canyon. His feat, lavishly (if not accurately) recorded in his *Exploration of the Colorado River of the West*, inspired those who followed his route: Flavell and Montez in 1896, Galloway and Stone in 1909, and the Kolb brothers in 1911. Holmstrom's would be the fifth trip to travel the entire route, and the first to attempt it alone.

Green River, Wyoming, was founded by the Union Pacific Railway as their regional headquarters. The three thousand residents ranched, mined soda ash, or worked for the railroad. Two hundred miles upriver in the pine forests of the Wind River Mountains, crews of railroad tie cutters worked year-round cutting, hewing, stacking, and hauling the ties down to the valley floor. Men then herded them down the Green River to the rail yards. Days before Holmstrom arrived, a major drive of 375,000 ties had ended.

Sitting beside the river Holmstrom began his journal:

> Green R—Oct 4
> Rained out last nite—got up at 3:30 to keep bed from getting wet—light-
> ning off to south west in mts—long jagged streaks blue lightning about 15
> seconds before hear thunder. People here don't know anything about the
> river—there is quite a rivalry between 3 families down by the river as to
> whose place I am going to leave the car at—the boat looks very good but
> leaks some—I hope a day or two of soaking will cure that—the seat is a little
> too hi and the oars should be 8 feet instead of 7½—according to the people
> here the big obstacle in my way is the tie boom a mile below here—I don't
> know but I shall have to give up the trip if it is as bad as they say....

Holmstrom needed to buy a few last things, but it was Sunday. He had to wait.
The river was low, lower than it had been for some time, a mixed blessing. The rapids would be less powerful, making it easier to control the boat and reducing the
chances of disaster. Starting so far up the river, however, there was barely enough
water to float the boat. The flow, in a river whose extremes ranged from 200 to
15,000 CFS, was just over 500—that of a respectable creek.

By midday October 5, Holmstrom finished packing. A few locals saw him off,
none with any encouragement. By now, Holmstrom did not expect any. With a
wave of his hand, he cast off.

Finally. Time to stop planning and preparing and get on with it. With the days
short and getting shorter, he would be rowing most of the daylight hours. The boat,
untested, would have to work, and the paltry flow of the river would have to suffice.
Within an hour he passed the last traces of town and entered the Great American
Desert. Between here and Boulder Dam lay more than a thousand miles of river
and rapids, dropping more than five thousand vertical feet.

A few hours downriver was the old Logan Ranch, where in 1911 the Kolb brothers had stopped to reforge their oarlocks. The Logans were gone and the ranch was
now run by Mrs. Arvice Kincaid; her husband was in jail for horse rustling. After
a brief visit, Holmstrom was off again, promising to send her a picture he took of
her ranch. He made camp three miles downriver in a grove of willows and cottonwoods.

> My greatest worry is the early October blizzard, which everyone says is due
> here now—am now engaged in thawing out my shoes so I can get them on—
> water froze solid in kettle overnite....

Before it was inundated by Flaming Gorge Reservoir in the 1960s, the seventy
miles of river below Green River, Wyoming, meandered slowly through badlands
of green and gray shale. Spires and buttes occasionally broke the rolling skyline;
cottonwoods and willows along the shore softened the desolation. Although mostly

uninhabited and uninhabitable, the land supported a few ranches and small settlements along the side streams. Holmstrom spent his second day dodging, hitting or dragging over sand and gravel bars. But the weather held and the days were warm enough for wet shoes to be tolerable. To the south, the great Uinta Mountains loomed, snow covered, across the river's path. Once Holmstrom reached them, the canyons and the rapids would begin.

Barren as this country was, the river had once teemed with beaver. In the 1820s General William Ashley engaged a group of men in St. Louis to explore and trap this untested but promising new area. They headed overland to the Green River, then known as the Seedskadee. From there they split up, agreeing to regroup at the river after working the region. Ashley himself took the most roundabout route to the rendezvous. With a group of fellow trappers, he headed downriver in bull boats—round contraptions made of saplings and branches bent into a hemisphere with buffalo hide stretched over them. Although nearly impossible to maneuver, the crafts carried them downriver. They portaged around the rapids, leaving the name *Ashley* scrawled on a cliff by one cascade, later named Ashley Falls. They continued on through the calm water of Browns Hole and into the fierce cataracts of Lodore. Somehow they survived—the first people known to pass through the upper gorges—and floated out into the Uinta Basin. From there they went overland, north through the Salt Lake Valley, and back to the rendezvous.

Luck had been as good for the trappers as bad for the beaver. When Ashley and his men regrouped at the junction of the Green and Henrys Fork, the famed mountain man rendezvous was born. For fifteen years thereafter, mountain men such as Jim Bridger, William Sublette, Hugh Glass, Joe Meek, Kit Carson, and Jim Beckwourth met annually to exchange pelts, stories, bottles, bullets, lies and fisticuffs. By 1840, as the beaver population diminished, the trappers moved on. By the time Holmstrom passed through, only a few ranchers remained.

> brush all along banks, all colors of rainbow—mostly red & yellow & mts in
> west blue in distance—one range rising higher behind the first & the hi ones
> white with snow—no wonder the first travelers on this river thought they
> had found an easy way....

On the evening of his second day Holmstrom stopped at the ranch of Walter and Eva Holmes, who had established themselves beside the river in 1910, and had entertained the Kolb brothers when they rowed though. The Holmeses' hospitality was impossible to refuse, especially with approaching weather, and Holmstrom spent a warm night in their bunkhouse. Anxious about the rapids that lay ahead, Holmstrom left early the next morning. Just below the mouth of Henrys Fork, the Green made a few bends in a vain attempt to avoid entering the Uinta Mountains. The monotony of the gray-green badlands could not have ended more abruptly. The rock strata, which until now had lain relatively flat, stood abruptly on end, exposing the vivid layers below. To the east a steep, forested mountain slope flanked the first bend of the river. To the west rose an abrupt cliff some two thousand feet high, a brilliant rust. In 1869, Major Powell had named it Flaming Gorge.

If this were not startling enough, the river then turned sharply east, cutting a deep narrow canyon straight into the mountain side. After only a mile, the river made a hairpin turn and exited just a few hundred yards from where it entered—Horseshoe Canyon. Showing little method in its madness, the river did another about-face and again dissected the mountain, meandering east through Kingfisher Canyon, named for the hundreds of birds that inhabited the high, jagged, cream-colored cliffs.

With the canyons came faster water and riffles. Early travelers found them thrilling, but they had more water than Holmstrom.

> good gravel rapids till horseshoe—1 mile of the most miserable rowing I ever put in—wide shallow and rocky, and the sun squarely in my eyes—couldn't see downstream at all—zigzagged back and forth....

Within three miles, the beige rocks of Kingfisher Canyon pitched skyward, exposing the ancient, dense, maroon rocks of Uinta Mountain quartzite. The channel narrowed; the current quickened. This was Red Canyon, home to the first rapid of any consequence, Ashley Falls. A rock fall here choked the river with boulders, and at high water the currents were tricky. Low water played in Holmstrom's favor and he easily missed the hazards.

A short distance below, a group of cowboys were crossing the river and stopped to talk. When Holmstrom told them he was going downriver through the Canyon of Lodore to Jensen, they were dubious. Said one, "I don't think you can make it. There ain't nobody ever made it, only Than Galloway."

Nathaniel "Than" Galloway is considered the father of modern rowing technique. A solitary trapper from Vernal, Utah, Galloway began building small boats in the 1890s, and working down stretches of the Green in pursuit of beaver pelts. Galloway discovered several things about whitewater navigation that had eluded Powell. He made his boats light and maneuverable, rather than heavy. He gave them flat bottoms for ease of pivoting, not keels for speed. And he slowed his boat in tricky waters by pulling upstream, running stern-first, looking where he was going, pivoting his craft as needed, and ferrying away from rocks and waves.

In 1896, Galloway and another trapper, William Richmond, launched near Flaming Gorge and ran all the way through Grand Canyon. In 1909, Galloway mounted a second expedition, this time with three boats, all built to specifications in Chicago. Julius F. Stone, a wealthy Ohio businessman, financed the trip and rowed the second boat. Seymour Dubendorff, a young friend of Galloway's, rowed the third. Said to be the first trip just for the sport of it, their expedition was a great success, and Stone had found a new joy in life.

Stone was eager to share his enthusiasm and gave the Kolb brothers plans for a Galloway boat and instructions on how to row it. Ellsworth Kolb's book, in turn, gave Galloway's design and techniques more exposure, and the USGS trips of 1922–1923 adopted the style. Holmstrom, too, rowed in classic Galloway form, although it is unclear where he learned it—from his reading, through trial-and-error, from Glen Wooldridge and others on the Rogue—most likely a combination. Holmstrom now followed in Galloway's wake.

> Oct 7, 6:00 P.M. Flaming Gorge, Horseshoe and Kingfisher Canyons are indescribably beautiful even at this late season—they are just full of birds and their songs echoed by the cliffs—here in Red Canyon the walls are high but not so unfriendly looking as some, as they are full of crevices with pine trees in them—but the rude awakening is not far off now....

Toward the end of Red Canyon, Red Creek enters from the north. The creek deposits a tremendous delta of debris, choking the river against the southern cliff. For years this rapid caused boatmen grief, not due to big waves, but to the number of unavoidable rocks.

> At 2:30 I came to Red Creek Rapid—it is a dirty son of a gun to put it mild—steep long & rocky—at its head is a steep drop with water shooting into right cliff—a channel there but no room to use right oar for the cliff—anyhow some lining had to be done below, as the river splits into 3 parts—I might have tried to run it if close to home & everything favorable, but here there is too much to lose by a smashing.
>
> Portaging the boat over a beaver dam, down a little side channel, then run down a way with oars, then slid over the rocks into another shallow channel & run down to the foot light—did not take over twenty minutes but then the trouble began—it was over ¼ mile from the duffel at the head to the boat at the foot. I made it all in 3 loads but I am sure a donkey's ears would have burned with shame watching me—I got away from that place, although it was dark by the time I got the stuff in the boat—as there is just a long windy rock bar to camp on there.
>
> I hated to break down and portage as I have not done so before, but what I am trying to do is see how far I can get, rather than how many I can run—If there are many more long portages, about half my stuff is going overboard....

After another mile, the current slowed as Holmstrom entered the broad, mountain-ringed valley of Browns Park, where Wyoming, Colorado, and Utah meet. A hard place to get to from any direction, Browns Park had long been a refuge for outlaws. Butch Cassidy and the Wild Bunch headquartered there. When lawmen managed to find it, the outlaws swiftly headed across the nearest border. Even reputable ranchers lived by their own laws in Browns Park. As large cattle companies began to encroach on this remote site, a range war erupted between local ranchers and the cattle barons—arguments and rustling were punctuated by assault and murder. By 1937, few ranchers remained in the area.

> Browns Park—Prettiest place I ever saw—Park is right—I have come many miles through it and have not seen a living soul—several ranches in the upper end, but deserted—beaver slides every fifty feet—duck & geese are thick—there are hi mountains all around the valley sort of protecting it, it seems—and I feel kind of guilty going through here myself—took quite a few pictures but know they can't do the place justice—the mts surrounding the valley rise higher and higher and bluer the farther away—There are birds of every description here—I think I will pay dearly for this peaceful cruise through here though when I hit the next canyon—Lodore.
>
> There is a little sliver of a moon tonite but the air is so clear it causes things to throw a good shadow—it was 110° in the sun today—I am well sunburned....

At the south end of Browns Park, the river again cuts directly into the Uintas through a dramatic and forbidding declivity: the Gate of Lodore. Two miles below, the river begins a series of steep rocky falls, dropping more than two hundred feet in six miles. Disaster Falls, Triplet Falls, and Hells Half Mile are among the severe drops. Lodore had long been known as a boat crusher. The year before Holmstrom's trip, two boats had wrecked and been abandoned. At the first rapid he saw one—the *Illinois Girl*, a scow deserted by Tony Backus from Salt Lake City.

Unlike Holmstrom, Backus had *planned* a solo trip. The Canyon of Lodore dissuaded him. He hiked out to a ranch where he spent two weeks collecting his wits, then left the river forever. Holmstrom examined the boat and pressed on.

Disaster Falls is a series of three rapids. The first, Upper Disaster, Holmstrom scouted, then ran fully loaded. In the middle reach he portaged his cargo, then rowed through. Lower Disaster rushes beneath the undercut right cliff. Holmstrom lined his boat along the left shore, reloaded, and continued. Triplet Falls was much the same—after running the boat through the first two sections, he lined part of the third, and camped at the foot.

After starting a campfire, he walked back to the top to fetch his duffel. When he got back to camp, his fire had escaped to a nearby driftwood pile. So fierce was the blaze that he had to build a smaller fire to cook dinner while he fought the bigger one. Nearby were mementos of another boat wreck—the oars and hull of the *Lota Ve*, undone in Disaster by the Hatch-Swain party a year earlier.

> This portaging duffel is real work—sure makes me tired but it will do me good I know—the water doesn't seem cold at all—I feel that I have done pretty well on the river so far, but tomorrow will tell the story—for the Green at least, for 1 mile below where I am now is Hells Half Mile—a certain half mile portage of everything except maybe the boat—over a steep hillside too, I think—the most difficult going in Green River—Today was my poorest day—

only about 42 miles but I will be awfully lucky to make 12 tomorrow—moon
is now lighting up top of canyon walls—pretty—going to bed now—late for
me to be up—7:20....

Holmstrom got a workout in Hells Half Mile—a seemingly endless chaos of
rocks, islands and drops. Bad as it looked, after emptying his boat, he attempted
the rapid. He hung on a rock at the bottom of the first drop, spinning away from
his intended route. Recovering, he rowed back into position for the middle. An
oarlock pulled out. While he was putting it back, he washed sideways onto another
rock. Flushing off, he got his oar back in the water and pulled to shore at the bottom.

boat started leaking & I am worried sick for fear I have smashed a plank—
when upon examination I find the paint has got knocked off a screw hole
without a screw in it....

After Hells Half Mile the river slackens for six miles then bends sharply east and
crosses the Mitten Park Fault. The Canyon of Lodore ends, and the Green meanders placidly through Echo Park, its creamy sandstone walls darkly varnished by
primeval stains and streaks. The river soon doubles back around Steamboat Rock,
retraces its route across the fault, and re-enters the dark Uinta Mountain quartzite
it left in Lodore. Whirlpool Canyon's several rapids are small, but Holmstrom
scouted a channel before running them.

Oct 13 eve—Camped just above Jones Hole Creek I think—long bar on left of
river—dead cow and horse on lower end of bar, but as I say it is a long one
and they shouldn't mind....

Below Whirlpool Canyon, he stopped briefly at the Ruple Ranch in Island Park
and spoke with the Ruples about the river and boaters they had known. After lunch
he examined their boat—a Galloway-type built in 1914 for the Utah Power and
Light survey. By four that afternoon, back on the water, he entered Split Mountain
Canyon, where again the river rips into the side of a mountain and saws through.
More rapids, shallow and rocky, and slow going. As evening fell, storm clouds gathered. He camped and, for the first time that trip, put up his tent.
   The next day, as he picked his way down through several more rapids, a second
storm struck.

12:00 Oct 15—Right in middle of storm—thunder, lightning—huddled under
rock with water streaming down all round—can't keep me dry above hips
though—wouldn't have missed this for anything—creeks falling over the cliffs
all around—right across river is almost a landslide—big creek bringing down
rocks by the ton—river turning dark red—almost black—maybe this will give
me a little more water to go on anyhow—only two more miles of this canyon.

> So far this trip I have looked all the rapids over carefully & lucky I have,
> as the channels through most of them are mighty complicated—All the can-
> yons so far have dealt very kindly with me & the weatherman did too until
> last nite & today....

Two more miles of easy going put him below Split Mountain Canyon and
into the 120-mile smooth water stretch of the Uinta Basin: a scrubby, featureless
expanse of open range. The next morning, on his twelfth day, he reached the
highway bridge at Jensen, Utah. He rented a room at Aunt Atta Chatwin's hotel,
then went to the post office for mail. Since little commerce took place in Jensen,
Holmstrom hitchhiked into Vernal, thirteen miles west, to pick up supplies and
look up the "Colorado River Club."

This informal group consisted of a local carpenter named Bus Hatch and two
of his brothers; Frank and Garn Swain, double cousins of the Hatches; and Royce
"Cap" Mowrey, married to Bus's sister Thelma. The "club" had its origins in 1931
when sheriff Frank Swain jailed Parley Galloway for child support; the prisoner
was the son of the early boatman Nathaniel Galloway. Parley had made several
trips with his father, and in 1927 had been hired as lead boatman for Clyde Eddy's
trip, joining a dozen college boys, a dog and a bear cub, on a floodwater journey
through Cataract, Marble, and Grand Canyons.

Galloway, luckless and impoverished, had little to do but sit in his cell and
tell Swain and Bus Hatch of his boating adventures. Swain and Hatch, fascinated,
eventually agreed to release Galloway. In recompense, he would show them how to
build a proper boat and teach them the art of running rapids. Galloway had not
been out of his cell a day before he vanished.

Undaunted, the cousins designed and built a few boats of their own. In August
of 1931 they launched in Kingfisher Canyon and ran down through Red, Lodore,
Whirlpool, and Split Mountain Canyons. By most standards, the trip was disastrous: flips, lost supplies, near-drownings. Hatch and Swain thought it was so
much fun they decided to run the entire river, one canyon at a time. Hatch said
it wasn't really a trip if you didn't flip. The important thing was to make sure you
brought along enough to drink, and he didn't mean water. The names of their
boats reflected their attitude: *What Next, Don't Know, Who Cares.* (Another of
Hatch's boats, *Lota Ve*, was the one Holmstrom saw wrecked at Triplet Falls.)

Frank Swain, who had been working at the Bingham copper mines south of Salt
Lake City, brought along a couple of new folks—Russell "Doc" Frazier, a medical
doctor from Bingham, and his friend Bill Fahrni. These men had a rare commodity
in the Great Depression: money. They immediately fell in love with river running,
became part of the club, and financed many of its outings.

Because none of them ever got a chance to boat with Parley Galloway before he
skipped town, the club members had to invent their own rowing style, and it bore

no resemblance to Galloway's. Their technique was closer to Powell's: they entered the rapid with their backs downstream, pulling hard and hoping for the best. They swam a lot. Their devil-may-care approach was unique among river runners in the 1930s. Years later, Bus Hatch's oldest son Don, a life-long professional river runner and authority on river history, observed with a chuckle, "Those guys probably set river running back twenty years."

Holmstrom had met Frazier in Salt Lake, and now hoped to meet the rest of the group. Bewhiskered and ragged, he had a tough time getting a ride, but finally made it into Vernal in the back of a truck. Unfortunately, Bus Hatch and Frank Swain were off deer hunting, but Cap Mowrey, Garn Swain, and Bay Hatch were in town. Although they could not answer all of his questions, they gave him plentiful advice, spun a few heroic tales, and sent him off encouraged.

The next day Holmstrom was rowing, the water low, the current indiscernible, and the wind wailing upstream. He made but four miles.

> Camped on island—trees—awfully windy—can't row—cloudy—bad—going to rain some more maybe—no real dry wood—tent up—be glad to get back in canyons—seem more friendly somehow....
>
> Oct 18—3:30 got stuck on sandbar—took off shoes & pulled it through— lot of the way river is 400 to 500 feet wide—then wind came up—in straight stretches waves 1½ feet hi—simply awful to try to do anything—can scarcely buck it—& when sideways go along sideways with one oar backing water and rowing with all my might on other....

From Jensen, the next strong current was over a hundred shallow, flat, meandering miles away, and Holmstrom knew it. All he could do was row. The next day, the Duchesne River added a bit more water. Around another bend, the White River gushed in from the east, swollen to a thick, chalky soup by the recent storms. Although he now had to boil water in order to make the fine silt settle out, the increased current was welcome.

> this A.M. I actually saw two red skies at once—in the east the sun made a big red sky & in the west the moon (which really shines bright here—I read the writing in this book by it last night) was shining up on a cloud & while it was not really red it was sort of pink—I will be sorry to see the moon go— it is like a friend now—waiting all lit up bright when the sun goes down & staying till the sun comes up again....

On October 20 Holmstrom stopped at Sand Wash to talk to the ferryman. At this remote outpost there was scant business until the ranchers brought their sheep down on the way to their winter range. Then, at five cents a head, twenty thousand sheep compensated for the slow business during the rest of the year. When Holmstrom asked why the floors of the out-buildings were two feet below ground level, the ferryman explained that two years earlier, a massive flash flood half-buried his ranch with mud.

Another twenty-three miles on the river carried Holmstrom well inside Desolation Canyon for the night, just three miles short of the next rapid. With faster current the next day, he soon arrived at the Seamount brothers' ranch at Rock Creek. Pulling in, he smacked a rock with the hull—the first one he had hit with much force—but the damage was slight. Rock Creek Ranch was a verdant oasis with russet sandstone buildings and tall cottonwood and mulberry trees irrigated from the clear, rushing stream. No one was home, however, and Holmstrom moved on.

A few miles farther he pulled in at the McPherson Ranch. Another enchanting site, but again, no one was home.

> Oct 22—moon so bright last nite it actually hurt eyes to look at it—absolutely clear this A.M.—no frost either—Probably raining at Coquille now & everyone snuffling around with colds etc.—while here am I in better shape than I have ever been, I am sure—except that due to the long spells of rowing I have put in the last few days, it is much more comfortable to stand up than to sit down—am going to try to get some kind of cushion at Green R.
>
> Right across river is big butte looking like a castle with battlements & towers—the boat just handles swell & rides the waves very good.
>
> For supper last nite—1 can pork & beans—1 can Vienna sausage—1 can condensed milk—4 slices bread—butter & jam—& some grape nuts—got up at 4:30 this A.M. as was hungry—and had very large plate cracked wheat mush—1 can milk—3 hotcakes same size as frying pan with butter & jam—3 cups coffee—& then as was still hungry 1 cupful of grape-nuts & 1 boiled egg—guess I will shove off now—as is 7:15 & sun is hitting tops of cliffs on west—that time is approximate though as watch stops sometimes & I set it by guess....

Holmstrom ran all the rapids in Desolation Canyon without difficulty. Below the McPherson Ranch the walls of the canyon rise and fall away to the east and west, the starker walls of Gray Canyon rising to replace them. A few rapids on his map concerned him, but he rowed them easily enough. Yet he always weighed the rapids ahead, having promised himself not to take unnecessary chances. Range Creek, Coal Creek, Rattlesnake. By nightfall the cliffs of Gray Canyon fell back and he was out in flatter land again. He pulled into Green River, Utah in the twilight.

> all way down from Jensen—through Des & Gray Can—couldn't find anyone at their homes—so I got in here at dark last night—saw a house up on the bank with the lights on—so tied up the boat at their pump & went up to make sure it was OK—Knocked & knocked but no one answered the door—Began to wonder if I was jinxed, or if when they saw my whiskers & general attire they wouldn't answer.

> Next house I hit though was Howland's—Eddy speaks of him—has been through Cataract with very poor boats too—very nice old man—am going to talk more to him—also to Tasker who runs this hotel—he was through with the geological survey in 1921 & has pictures.
>
> Green R town seems to be a mile from the river & is the most miserable dilapidated one horse town I ever saw—I guess I can get everything I need here though....

Green River, Utah, was little more than a whistle stop for the Rio Grande Western Railroad. Sporadic attempts to establish a steamboat line to Moab, Utah, had failed years before and Green River's sole claim to fame was being the watermelon capital of Utah.

Holmstrom searched out the local rivermen. Cap Yokey, a steamboat pilot, had been up and down the Green several times. Holmstrom, concerned that one of his spare oars was cracked and the other too bent to row with, asked about getting new ones. Yokey told Holmstrom not to worry, he would be sure to find some in the driftwood piles along the river. In fact, he would sell Holmstrom one he had found for twenty-five cents. Holmstrom declined, and ordered a new pair to be delivered to Lees Ferry. He ordered tennis shoes also, as his were "going very haywire." He bought a length of rope to rig life lines around the boat and jettisoned surplus gear, replaced his heavy pulleys with lighter ones, and restocked his food: salt, eggs, jam, flour, grease, pork, and beans. He also took time to write to his mother, assuring her that he was okay. Friends back home and folks he met along the way received progress reports.

Two local men, Harry Tasker and Harry Howland, had been through Cataract Canyon and had stories and pictures. Holmstrom made mental notes and prepared to head down river. The Green was flowing 2,000 cfs, four times what he began on in Wyoming. The local gager told him another 3,000 was coming down the upper Colorado, making for at least 5,000 cfs in Cataract Canyon—pleasantly more than he had expected. On October 25, he rowed south.

Holmstrom had to row 120 miles of flat water through the Utah canyon lands to reach the Colorado River. Although he had obtained excellent survey maps for most of river, with miles marked and elevation drops carefully noted, he had not been able to get charts for this stretch. Holmstrom did bring along Ellsworth Kolb's *Through the Grand Canyon from Wyoming to Mexico*. He used Kolb's vivid descriptions to navigate, studying the book each night before going to sleep.

> didn't work very hard today & am not as tired as should be—tomorrow I am going to use the old oars—tired of wearing out arms & twisting skin off palms of hands trying to use the warped one—Dodge's outfit should be out 15 days now—sure would like to have good luck so I could catch them....

Frank Dodge's trip—the one Holmstrom had tried for two years to join—was on his mind. He wanted to catch them, not so much to prove anything, as to meet a few more boatmen. A goal; something to shoot for, at least.

The bleak gray desert surrounding Green River gave way to salmon sandstone cliffs, first on the east side, then the west, then both. Holmstrom passed Ruby Ranch across from the mouth of the tiny San Rafael River. After another bend, he entered Labyrinth Canyon. The rusty Navajo Sandstone walls rose higher and grew more intricately carved by the mile. Holmstrom recognized the names of other river runners carved on the cliffs: the Kolbs, Cap Yokey's initials, Tom Wimmer—Holmstrom remembered Wimmer from Lewis Freeman's book about running the Colorado in the 1920s.

> quite a time finding good campsite tonite as everywhere there is a good bar with wood, about 100 feet of mud separate it from river—worked boat up to one though & it is much better than last nite—feel badly tonite as I can't find Kolb's book—could swear I put it in this A.M.—Perhaps can find it in A.M.—Swell night—warm & clear—not much wind today—cooking prunes this evening—This A.M. tied warped oar to hatch so it is sprung opposite way—will leave till hit Cataract & see if that helps any—sure glad to eat the last of that very old Jensen cheese—makes my mouth burn like I was a fire-eater.
>
> Oct 27—Feel fine this A.M.—found Kolb's book in sleeping bag—there is a stone arch opposite camp here & when I got up this A.M. the moon—only ¼ now but still bright—lighted it up beautifully—Last night a splashing around groaning jabbering & scraping & hammering sound for a long time across the river—sounds like some crazy people—finally concluded it was beavers at work—although maybe something else too as I didn't think beavers made any vocal noise & pretty soon I got up to see if one of them was chewing a hole in the boat as it sounded close....

The wind that had plagued Holmstrom in the Uinta Basin eased and he made good time through Labyrinth. Seventy miles downriver the cliffs broke away, exposing surreal vistas of spires, peaks and mesas in ghostly pastel hues of gray, rust and lavender. Then another set of cliffs ascended: Stillwater Canyon.

> Oct 28 7:20 vacation over today but can't very well get to work on time—oh well—have almost forgotten the gas business—those cataracts ahead seem quite important now—washed this morning—that high layer of sheer sandstone seems sort of like a prison wall—in some places it is way back—but it is always there just the same....

Four hours later Holmstrom reached the junction of the Green and Colorado Rivers. He was tempted to explore, but Cataract Canyon was right around the bend. Cataract, with its legendary rapids; Cataract, the graveyard of the Colorado. Although a mere forty miles long, its rapids had drowned more boaters than the 280 miles of Grand Canyon. An isolated tempest of whitewater amid three hundred miles of smooth current, it had lured dozens of unwary prospectors and trappers to their doom.

For a few minutes Holmstrom tinkered with his boat, rigging his lifeline, scooping the mud out of the cockpit, sealing his gear, and filling a bag with chocolate and prunes, "just in case of trouble." He jettisoned what food he could spare, leaving it in someone's recently occupied camp—their fire still smoldered. He was as ready as he could get. At 2:15 P.M. he headed downstream.

> Eve—camped just below #5 rapid—that is my count & will keep my own—sure came on the junction suddenly—walls went up quickly & there was I—scared & glad all at once—the proper thing is to go back a mile on right & climb up a creek bed & come out directly over junction but I was too anxious to see how the rapids were—the walls are supposed to be 1300 feet hi at junction but if they are then I am 10 feet tall.
>
> #1 I ran on left—#2 on right & some water slopped over left side onto seat—#3 down middle—no rocks at all—#4 is a long crooked riffle with a little island at head—#5 is the biggest—went down center through first reverse waves & pulled over to right—thought it was going to be bad but didn't even get rear deck wet—there are some swells just at the top above the reverse waves that must be 4 or 5 feet deep—the river here is much larger than the Salmon & all muddy now—travels fast & sure has power—have not come to any really steep drops yet—by tomorrow nite I should know how I am going to make out—am sure going to be careful of the boat as it is the best way out of here....

The next morning he came to Mile Long Rapid, a tight series of rock-infested cataracts. Scouting each section carefully, he ran them without incident. Next came three particularly steep rapids, known today as the Big Drops. The first drop was easy. The second was trickier, requiring several evasive maneuvers. The third rapid gave him pause.

> wide & steep & very rocky—looked a long time and thought I saw a possible channel by dodging around & going through an up shooting reverse wave—was about to walk back to boat when the water died down for a second & I saw a sharp rock stick out of this innocent wave—decided to portage much as hate to—too swift to line I thought—unloaded boat & at 1:00 started it down over the rock bar, got it in the water just at dark—awful job—will carry down things in A.M.—Hands very sore from handles on boat—big job carrying logs & poles to slide on—Possible chance of running on left—clear though narrow chute through, only right at head, row of submerged rocks which I thought boat sure to hang up on—not enough to gain and too much to lose—For all I know there may be another just like it around next bend—if there is I will portage it too....

Good judgment. At such low water, the right side of Big Drop Three would be

*Portaging
the boat
around
Big Drop
Three*

disastrous for a wooden boat. Instead he portaged his craft—over four hundred pounds empty—through the steep jagged boulders along the right shore. What else was there to do?

At each rapid, Holmstrom stopped, scouted, and figured a way through. Most went according to plan. He tapped a few rocks, but none very hard. As the trip went on, Holmstrom poured his thoughts into his small journal. Scribbled in pencil and tucked in his shirt pocket in rapids, the besmudged log revealed ever more of Holmstrom's insights, thoughts, and humor.

> Built my fire in front of a big sandstone rock & slabs 1 foot or more long keep popping off. There is a little riffle just ¼ mile above camp & it makes the darnedest noises—thumps for a while like a drum—then rattles like someone drawing their last breath & then sounds like someone drawing a rosined string through a hole in a tin can—of course the narrow steep walls here magnify the sound.
>
> The maps I had out only went to here & I would not let myself look at the next one last nite till I had fixed my bed & cooked & ate supper—when I did look I was agreeably surprised at the short distance out—only right around Dark C. looks bad.
>
> If there aren't some tennis shoes for me at Lees F, I will have to walk out to Salt Lake & get some as both my soles & heels are right on the ground.
>
> For the last few days I have been, & still am, in about as uninhabited & inaccessible place as there is anywhere—I believe one could get out of this canyon in quite a few places, but when you did you would be exactly nowhere—about 40 miles to the nearest town on north, or much farther to anything if you happened to miss it, and that is as the crow flies & no water

& country cut up with canyons etc.—and on the south nothing—& can't go
up or down river along bank....

Notorious Dark Canyon Rapid demanded Holmstrom's full attention. He knew
where the Kolbs had run in 1911, and where they had wrecked in 1921. He also knew
where Clyde Eddy had snuck down a side channel on the flood water of 1927—but
that was dry now. Holmstrom had read every book published about the Colorado,
and had consulted every riverman he could find. The details of each rapid and each
run were filed away in his mind. Few river runners before or since have done their
homework as well. And being a gifted athlete, Holmstrom was able, at each new
challenge, to translate his knowledge to action. Yet even while scouting a major
rapid, Holmstrom remained intrigued by his surroundings, ever curious.

> saw some kind of spider—about 4 inches across if legs straightened out—
> white back—not cross—two little feelers in front ½" long & 2 short legs
> behind—black and brown fuzzy all over—move very slow—touch its face
> with stick & it would turn slowly & rub its face with front feelers....

Although he was knocked around and took on a gallon of water, Holmstrom
came through Dark Canyon fine. He pulled in at the bottom of the rapid to look
at the inscriptions on the cliff. In 1927 Eddy's trip had signed in, as had the Pathé–
Bray movie trip later that year. Each trip had taken a dog along—Rags and Pansy
respectively, signed in as well. In 1933 the Hatch gang installed a copper plaque in
honor of themselves. Downriver Holmstrom stopped again. Another signature on
the sandstone caught his eye: HYDE 11/1/28.

Holmstrom had heard of this trip in Green River, Utah. Glen and Bessie Hyde, a
young couple from Idaho, had launched their honeymoon trip from there, headed
for Needles, California. They had planned to make not only the fastest trip yet
down the river, but to claim Bessie as the first woman ever to run the Colorado.
What captured the attention of the Green River locals was the craft Glen Hyde
built: a twenty-foot sweep scow. Up in Idaho, Hyde had run the Salmon River
with the great Cap Guleke and learned the art of sweeps. Hyde knew what he was
doing, but the Green River locals called the scow a floating coffin. Hyde ignored
them. Like Powell and others before him, Hyde was going with the boat he knew,
confident he could make it work.

The Hydes made it to Lees Ferry, and then Phantom Ranch in the heart of
Grand Canyon. Their trip had been fast and thrilling. What concerned many
people though, was that they brought no life jackets—both claimed to be strong
swimmers. At the South Rim of Grand Canyon, Emery Kolb *offered* them life
jackets, strongly *recommended* life jackets, and finally tried to get them to at least
take *inner tubes* from the gas station. No luck. They returned to the river, resupplied at Hermit Rapid, and were never seen again. Their boat was found marooned

midstream near the end of Grand Canyon with only two major rapids yet to run.

It was now November 1, the same day the Hydes had signed in nine years before. Wondering if he would share the same fate, Holmstrom signed his name with white lead and continued on.

After Dark Canyon, the river wound around jagged Mille Crag Bend, and straightened through Narrow Canyon where the Dirty Devil River entered. Here was one of the precious few breaks in canyon country, a place where the river could be reached from either shore and crossed.

Years earlier Cass Hite, a prospector, came looking for a legendary Navajo gold mine. He became friends with Hoskininni, a Navajo Chief who showed him something more valuable than gold: a river crossing. Hite established a ferry and named the spot Dandy Crossing. Later renamed Hite, it became a welcome stop for early river runners who, having survived Cataract Canyon, were ready to relax.

Hite had killed a man in a scuffle and served time; for years afterward he lived alone a few miles downstream from the crossing. Bert Loper, another semi-recluse, had his own hermitage at the mouth of nearby Red Canyon. A curmudgeon's paradise. Glen Canyon began here before inundation by Glen Canyon Dam in the 1960s. It was an attractive place for prospectors who placer mined the gravel bars. Few got rich, though many tried, and Hite was their access point between the placid river and the small town of Hanksville, fifty miles away.

By the time Holmstrom arrived, Hite and Loper were long gone. The first people he met were a road crew. A few men were surveying, while blowhards from Washington, D.C., and Salt Lake City, and Sheriff Skews of Moab, Utah, swatted flies, fished, and talked about putting a highway across the canyon. Holmstrom spent the night with them and, by the campfire, told of his journey.

The next day Holmstrom met the Gearharts, a German family who farmed the area. They had done a tremendous amount of work clearing and irrigating the land. Albert, the youngest son, took a liking to Holmstrom and gave him a tour, scrambling up onto the plateau to a small petrified forest. Later, Gearhart took him to a small Indian ruin under a ledge. Glen Canyon was rich with ruins of the Anasazi, a culture that inhabited the canyons of the Southwest from around A.D. 700 through the 1300s. Locals referred to them as Moqui, a term present tribes consider offensive. Looting the ruins was a common pastime. Holmstrom picked up a few pottery shards for his mother, but found ruins to be rather dreary. He preferred rocks.

The Gearharts relayed a radio report of Frank Dodge's trip. The group had made it to Phantom Ranch, midway through Grand Canyon, on November 1. There was still a good chance Holmstrom could catch them.

A short way below Hite, Arth Chaffin and his wife had established a sizable ranch and operated a ferry. The Chaffins' home was the hub of the small community; few boatmen escaped their hospitality. Nor did Holmstrom. He left after a substantial dinner, but not before the Chaffins had loaded his boat with eggs, squash, melons, tomatoes, and fruit preserves.

Holmstrom had been on the river only a short time when Billy Hay waved him in. Hay, who had bought Bert Loper's old claim on California Bar, had become something of an expert on ruins. He took Holmstrom to several sites, showed him a petroglyph panel at Smith Fork, and put him up for the night. Full of river stories, Hay told Holmstrom that Galloway believed if a person could get through Cataract Canyon, he need not fear Grand Canyon.

Having spent so much time socializing, Holmstrom leaned on the oars, passing places he had heard of rather than stopping to explore: the San Juan River, the Escalante River, and Hole-in-the-Rock. Holmstrom did not even stop at Aztec Creek, where a half-day hike would have taken him to Rainbow Bridge.

> Nov 4—looked at my squash in the coals this A.M.—poked around & seemed to be one coal a little bigger than the others—broke it in two—red hot clear through—all that remained of my squash.
>
> Have no light now—bought some flashlight batteries from Monky Ward & they went dead without scarcely any using at all—wish the fellow who sold them to me was here & I would push him into the creek.
>
> Nov 5—sky lighting up in east—Breakfast over & everything packed away— in about 5 minutes will be light enough to see river & I will be off—got up too early—watch stops at nite & I get up by the little dipper & didn't figure quite right this time—this echoing cliff would be a fine place for an orator to practice his speech—he could speak it at the cliff & hear it spoken back at him—Provided of course he was not a politician.
>
> Must be about 56 miles to store at bridge—will almost get there today if current holds good—have to wait for a little more light as I lost one of my sock supporters in sand & can't find it yet—stars are pretty dim now & I am off—spent quite a while drying out sleeping bag as very heavy dew & everything soaked.
>
> 7:05—By the time the sun touched the tops of the highest buttes I had made five miles....

Holmstrom reached Lees Ferry by midafternoon. Settled in the 1870s as a crossing for Mormon traffic to the Little Colorado Valley, the ferry had been run for several years by John D. Lee. A staunch Mormon, Lee was later apprehended, tried, and executed as a scapegoat for his part in the Mountain Meadows Massacre—the bloody slaughter, by Mormons, of a wagon train of Missouri gentiles.

Due to the completion nine years earlier of Navajo Bridge, four miles downstream, the ferry was now abandoned. Lees Ferry boasted only the USGS river gaging station, but the men who operated it, Frank Dodge and Owen Clark, were ahead on the river. Holmstrom, hoping to save time, rowed down to the bridge to get his mail and supplies. When he got to the bridge he found it nearly five hundred feet above him, with sheer cliffs rim to river on both sides.

> the only way to get up to the top is up an almost sheer cliff. I managed to climb up myself but didn't relish the job and am sure going to have my work cut out getting the stuff down. Will probably leave for Bright Angel Monday if I don't break my neck getting down to the boat first....

When he reached the Marble Canyon Lodge at the west end of the bridge, Holmstrom was again disappointed. He had hoped to find his new oars and tennis shoes, but they were in Flagstaff, 130 miles south by road. He did receive a few letters. Uncle Roy sent back some of his developed photographs. And Holmstrom's mother had written. He replied, boasting that he had not wet his feet since it rained in Split Mountain Canyon, and finishing, "It sure is nice to have someone like you to write cheerful letters instead of giving reasons why I should quit and worrying all the time. I know now that carelessness is the one thing that can stop me...."

The bus ride to Flagstaff was long and uncomfortable. At 7,000 feet above sea level, Flagstaff was cold and rainy when he arrived. One of his new oars had warped to worthlessness. He slept on the floor of the bus terminal amid a group of Civilian Conservation Corps workers, but got little rest. His clothes were dirty and torn and he hadn't shaved in a month. Worse, he was too broke to buy the food he needed.

> wish I hadn't come to Flagstaff—I look like a wild man now—prefer canyons to laying around a town like this....

Back at Marble Canyon, "Shine" Smith, the local preacher, was running the trading post and insisted on outfitting Holmstrom with whatever food he needed. Holmstrom, reluctant to accept such a gift, took a piece of brown paper and wrote out a check on his Coquille bank. (Smith deposited it, and the check went through Flagstaff, Phoenix, Los Angeles, San Francisco, and Portland and was honored in Coquille. The Portland Branch later inquired about putting the check on display, but Holmstrom chose to keep it.)

The locals filled Holmstrom in on river gossip:

> No one who knows Dodge likes him—agree he is a fine boatman and swimmer but very unpleasant & overbearing—wife left him—say he has been in some difficulties & must stay out of way at Ferry—He and Clark live in old cabins at Lees F—All like Clark—His wife died short time ago—went broke in citrus ranch—Spencer is only 21 years old.
>
> Mrs. Pete Nelson says knew fellow who thought killed man above & came through Cataract in pig trough—but I think it just must have been Glen Canyon....

On the 7th of November Holmstrom carried, dragged, lowered, and hauled his new oars and supplies down the cliff to his boat. Late that afternoon, exhausted, he headed downriver. He made camp in a stiff wind at the head of Badger Creek Rapid.

MAJOR POWELL had christened the sixty-one mile stretch between Lees Ferry and the Little Colorado River "Marble Canyon," for the towering polished layers of limestone that form its walls. Most consider Marble a part of Grand, the largest canyon of them all, with rapids to match. Badger Creek and Soap Creek, fierce and rocky, are first, and many early trips had portaged one or both.

> Oct 8—8:45—Just ran Badger Creek—intended all along to line it & felt kind of blue this A.M. when I got up—after breakfast though felt much better & kept looking at rapid and thought I saw way to run it—drop over top on right side of main channel, which runs square into rock below—& suction below rock sort of pulls boat to right, so as to miss rock—worked fine—waves are large but only water I took on was from the sidewinders.
>
> Kolbs ran this in 1911 but one boat bumped & both filled with water—Geo Survey ran in 23 but hole was knocked in 1 boat—probably many others have—possibly Dodge's outfit—but it is bad just same—it was cold & I hated to get wet so early was one reason I ran it I think—Lazy, too—Soap Creek next which I will portage even if it looks good.
>
> 1:10—Well I am sure getting to be a first class liar—came to Soap Creek—went down to look at the best way to portage—didn't look so bad—very large waves that would surely wreck things on left—but on right a little narrow channel—very swift—no doubt the same one Kolbs used in 11—they upset both boats—but it didn't look too bad—big job portage—unloaded—apologized to myself—& ran it.…

So it went, Holmstrom cautioning himself, promising not to run the next one, then running it despite himself.

Mileage in Grand Canyon is measured from zero at Lees Ferry, and at mile twenty Holmstrom stopped to scout North Canyon Rapid. It looked simple enough to slip off to the right of the main wave train.

> didn't look carefully enough—boat was drawn over into center—one wave came over side & gave me 2½ gal water & drenched me—I could see I was being drawn into center of biggest wave but was not worried much as I was sure it would rise over it—was sucked into trough & no further—bow was forced down on rock in trough and boat stuck there.
>
> All I could see was water on all sides—none came in though—why I didn't upset or go clear under I don't know—too good a boat I guess—oars looked awfully small & useless in the circumstances so I let go of them & grabbed gunwales & expected to go over, under, or end over end—but she came loose—shot out of wave cornerways & headed for ledge on left out of big waves—grabbed up oars & ran rest OK.

Am going back up there ½ mile in A.M. & try to analyze it & see for sure just what my mistake was—Mostly carelessness, I am sure—that makes twice I broke my word to myself today—by running Soap C & by being careless—I think the scare is the best thing that could have happened to me—as I am sure it will tend to make me more careful—am on my way now for sure—no turning back now if I had any desire to—which I haven't—not even a fly could climb out of here....

A series of vigorous rapids followed one after another for the next ten miles. Holmstrom scouted and ran each of them without any further problems. Rounding a bend, he came upon Vaseys Paradise.

beautiful—would be in midst of some millionaire's sunken garden in Santa B—but ten times more so in all this desolation—one big spring and several small ones gush out of the marble cliff about 100 feet up—& the whole cliff is covered with flowers & creeping vines & bushes.

It really hurts to go through here in a way—there are so many wonderful things & on such a grand scale I cannot begin to describe them or even remember them all I know—& pictures are almost worse than nothing as they do not show things as they really are.

Last nite the ¼ moon came around looking for me but I was camped under a vertical cliff—the moon came down over the upper walls of limestone but could not get down into the narrow inner gorge where I was— tonite I picked out a place where the moon is shining now & will till late— seems like an old friend—things have been going so good & easy I am sure I am in for some bad luck soon.

At noon on November 10, Holmstrom rowed into the azure waters of the Little Colorado River. After just two-and-a-half-days' rowing he was already through Marble Canyon. Buoyed by his success so far, but increasingly anxious about the rapids to come, Holmstrom pushed on. Below the Little Colorado was Grand Canyon proper—walls towering four thousand feet above him, so steep in places he could no longer see the outer rim. At five o'clock he pulled into camp at the foot of Unkar Rapid. The Upper Granite Gorge lay just around the bend. He did not want to chance it this late in the day.

Nov 11—didn't rain after all—worried though—still cloudy—my suspenders broke in 2 places as I was about to get into boat this A.M.—spent some time repairing them—sure was lucky it happened here though—Just suppose I had been going through a bad rapid & they had broken—would have had to drop oars & grab pants & probably would have wrecked boat and drowned....

Hance Rapid is one of the tougher rapids in Grand Canyon. Unlike many of the other major rapids, Hance is an extremely long, steep rock pile with no easily navigated line at low water. Many early parties portaged down the rocky left-hand shore rather than attempt this boulder field. Holmstrom studied it for a long time from the left shore, then carried his cargo to the foot of the rapid. He rowed across the river and climbed high on the right bank for another perspective. The route he chose involved working against constantly changing currents through a maze of boulders. Many modern boatmen, even veterans, sometimes get lost out there. Holmstrom greased it.

Reloading his boat, he headed on into the depths of the Granite Gorge. The scenery changed abruptly. Since Green River, Wyoming, the Colorado Plateau's flat pastel layers of sedimentary rock had been at river level. Now they towered in the distance, and Holmstrom entered the dark, twisted, ancient rock of the inner gorge. Climbing out had been unlikely before; it was now impossible. Most of the major rapids are in the next forty miles, and some cannot be portaged.

Powell's men called the next rapid Sockdolager—a nineteenth century term for a knockout punch. Unable to portage or line, the Powell Expedition had run it and swamped. The next rapid, Grapevine, looked just as bad and, rather than run another Sockdolager, they lined laboriously along the crags on the right shore.

Holmstrom looked each of these over and then ran them, skirting the worst of the waves, coming through dry. After lunch, a mammoth wave in 83-Mile Rapid stopped him abruptly and shot him out the side. An hour later he pulled in to the beach at Bright Angel Creek, amazed. What he thought would take two weeks, he had done in just four days.

Bright Angel Creek—a clear, rushing stream named by Powell to contrast with the Dirty Devil River upstream—was a favorite stop for early river expeditions. Here, at the deepest point in Grand Canyon, the Bright Angel Trail led up to the South Rim. On the rim were a train, hotels, access to main roads, and one of the country's more relentlessly public boatmen: Emery Kolb. At the turn of the century, long before a national park was established, Emery and his brother Ellsworth arrived on the rim with a photography outfit. They built a home and studio at the top of the Bright Angel Trail and for years earned their living photographing tourists as they departed down the trail. One of the brothers then ran down the trail to their makeshift darkroom near the only water source: the springs at Indian Gardens three thousand feet below. After developing the film and making prints, he would run back up to the studio to sell them when the tourists returned to the rim. The Kolbs were in pretty good shape.

In 1911, the Kolbs decided to photograph the Canyon by boat, retracing Major Powell's route. They wrote to Julius Stone, who had completed his trip with Galloway and Dubendorff two years earlier. Stone sent them plans for boats and advice on how to run them. The Kolbs also acquired one of the newly invented motion picture cameras, intent on making a movie of the trip which they could show at their studio and on lecture tours.

Although neither of them had much boating experience, Ellsworth was brawny and Emery, by far the smaller, adroit. On September 8, 1911, they left Green River, Wyoming, quickly learning to row, when to line or portage, how to right a boat, and how to repair a wreck. They arrived at Needles, California, on January 20, 1912. Ellsworth chronicled their adventure (and it *was* an adventure) in *Through the Grand Canyon from Wyoming to Mexico*. Their still photographs were excellent, and the movie, though jerky and fragmented by today's standards, was a hit on tours. It ran daily at their studio for the next sixty-five years.

Emery returned to the river to lead the 1923 USGS survey of Grand Canyon. In 1928 both brothers went into the Canyon to search for the missing Hyde couple. At Diamond Creek, they built a boat from rotted lumber and ran the Lower Granite Gorge in the dead of winter, only to find the Hydes' sweep scow floating empty in an eddy. In Separation Rapid, they flipped their boat, Ellsworth wearing a five-gallon can as a life jacket. They finished the trip at Spencer Canyon with their clothes frozen solid. By 1937, Emery Kolb was, if not the best boatman, the best *known* boatman in the Canyon.

The morning after arriving at Bright Angel Creek, Holmstrom hiked to the rim.

> Climbing trail—reached top of granite—for some reason everything almost looks sort of green—even my hands—maybe I am poisoned.
> I'm rich!—Almost to top of rim and starved—thinking of the burned biscuit bottoms I threw away last nite—& so weak I could easily lie down & die in trail when I find a piece of cheese the rats have been gnawing on in edge of trail—I trim it up a little & am now sitting in the trail eating it—mmmm....

When Holmstrom arrived at the South Rim, he was surprised to find that word of his solo journey had spread. A reporter interviewed him. Associated Press wired the story across the country: *Oregon Man Near Colorado Canyon Goal.* Equally surprising was a letter from home. Anna, his eighteen-year-old sister, had married her beau, Floyd Smith.

Vincent VanMatre, who was working at the South Rim, remembers meeting Holmstrom that evening. In particular, he remembers Holmstrom's descriptions of the extremes of sound down in the canyon—the unearthly silence of some stretches of river and the deafening roar of the rapids. "He was," said VanMatre, "very unassuming and modest and seemed to understate his accomplishment." Unassuming indeed. Holmstrom's only quotes in the AP story were "I was scared all the time," and, when asked why he was doing it, "Just for the adventure, I guess."

Stopping by the local radio station, Holmstrom was interviewed again. He had not dropped in for publicity, but because he had heard the radio station was in touch, by short wave radio, with Frank Dodge. Holmstrom hoped to say hello and let Dodge's group know he was on his way. Unfortunately, the radio was not working well enough that night to know if the message got through.

Next, Holmstrom, ragged and unshaven, looked up the Kolbs. Although Ellsworth had long since moved to California, Emery, his wife Blanche, daughter Edith, and grandson "Sonny" showed him around the South Rim and put him up for the night. Emery, always glad to meet another riverman, suggested they join for a trip the following year. Perhaps they could shoot more film for Kolb's show. The emphasis was on *Kolb's*, however. The first to make movies of the Canyon, Kolb claimed a proprietary interest in the river. In the past, this had caused ill feelings between Kolb and other boaters, and would do so again. For now though, he and Holmstrom were the best of friends. They talked late into the night, with Kolb offering advice and suggestions: rapids to look out for, possible escape routes, and friendly contacts over in Boulder City, Nevada. Kolb even mentioned a fellow at the head of the reservoir that might tow Holmstrom to Boulder Dam.

Unkempt as he was, Holmstrom tried to decline the use of the Kolbs' lovely guest bed, offering to sleep on the floor in the basement. Mrs. Kolb would not hear of it.

In the morning, he finished writing letters to his ever-growing list of correspondents, and a detailed one to his mother relating his latest adventures.

> I wish you could be here—some time I am surely going to bring you over here—the whole thing—canyons, mountains, River & all is so wonderful I hate to leave, and all I can bring away is the memory of it, but that alone surely makes the trip worthwhile.

That afternoon Holmstrom picked up more supplies and headed down the Bright Angel Trail. Kolb and Sonny, eager to see Holmstrom's boat, trekked down with him and spent a chilly night by the river. Holmstrom gave them his sleeping bag and curled up under his poncho.

The next morning Kolb asked to see how Holmstrom's boat handled. Holmstrom obliged, and Kolb and his grandson hopped in and cast off. A mile down river, Kolb pulled to shore with high praise for the boat, and said good-bye. Holmstrom did a final repack of his boat, threw out a bag of wormy raisins, and shoved off on the final leg of his trip.

THREE OF THE BIGGEST RAPIDS on the Colorado come in succession over the next six miles. Each put Holmstrom to the test. Horn Creek, an abrupt drop into several enormous waves, was first. Although he tried to hold tight to the right shore, Holmstrom was flung toward two crashing waves that threatened to overturn his boat. He dropped his oars and grabbed the gunwales as the waves broke over him. One oar dove beneath the boat, bending its oarlock. Holmstrom wallowed through.

Granite Falls looked malevolent, with the river hurling itself toward the right cliff, creating a series of unforgiving, rebounding waves. Holmstrom managed to pull the boat off the left shoulder of the waves, avoiding the worst of the rapid. Although he lost his right oar again, he came through dry.

Hermit Rapid followed. Again the current seized his upstream oar and dragged it beneath the boat with a resounding crack. He was where he needed to be though, and other than taking on several gallons of water, had a decent run. His "lucky oar" survived the thrashing.

Boucher Rapid was long but easy, as was Crystal Creek Rapid. (Transformed by a flash flood decades later, Crystal is now one of the most challenging on the river.)

> camped just below Crystal—tired & hungry—not much sleep last nite—Kolbs used the bag & I tried to sleep on the sand under the rubber poncho—but not much warmth in that & my sleep was disturbed by an absence of heat—nice place here—lots wood—good beach for boat—Tuna Rapid just below sound bad—Hope the tuna doesn't bite—By the way—had some for lunch—fight fire with fire.

Holmstrom was back in his element, alone, with his boat to row, a river to run, and only himself to talk to. The next morning he was hard at it again, running a half-dozen major rapids before lunch. Tuna Creek Rapid went smoothly, but within a mile he dropped into a small reverse wave and nearly flipped. Agate and Sapphire Rapids went well. Then a few rapids later, in an unnamed drop above Ruby, he lost both oars again and was nearly sucked over in a vigorous boil. Ruby, a tricky one, went as planned. Then lunch.

With the water low, Serpentine Rapid presented a challenge. He needed to make several moves: right, left, right again and then line up precisely at the final ledge, to drop between the rocks on the left and the cliff on the right. Holmstrom looked it over, then ran it flawlessly. Bass, Shinumo, and Hakatai Rapids—a rock here, a steep crashing wave there, each run cleanly.

Then came Waltenberg. Kolb had warned him about this one. At low water it was a long, steep maze of boulders and holes. The left side was vicious, with steep reverse waves and jagged rocks. A wrong move there meant disaster. The right was too shallow. On Christmas Eve, 1911, the Kolb brothers had tried both runs. Emery started down the shallow right side and piled into the rocks. Standing on a boulder next to his marooned boat, he watched Ellsworth head down the left, get caught in a hole, recirculate, and overturn. Ellsworth washed down river, followed by his boat. Emery pried his own boat off the rock and careened into another, smashing a hole in it big enough to crawl though. He caught his half-drowned brother clinging to a cleft in the rocks above the next rapid, and struggled ashore.

Given the options, Holmstrom chose the right side. He took his knocks, none as severe as Emery's, and continued through two more rapids to the calm corridor below. He had made it through the Upper Granite Gorge, upright and intact.

this was the 1st camping place I found below—Lonesome as no rapid roaring—just sound of current against banks — Had to peel biscuits on bottom — haven't too much grub — plenty unless trouble — but am going easy on it — feel well satisfied with day's run 14 miles — had been dreading Waltenberg — should have fairly easy going tomorrow for about 15 miles — Am not properly worried about not being able to get out of canyon.

I sit here like a king in front of my fire, governed by no man made laws — of course I can't make the wind stop blowing the smoke in my eyes & things like that, but it is fine anyhow — tomorrow nite I may be clinging to some rock in midstream, but no use worrying yet.

The boat takes on more personality all time — my fate and its are pretty well sealed together — If it is broken or sinks so do I.

Still think Serpentine a nasty, nasty rapid — the creek is called that name but it might well apply to rapid as it twists around like a snake & is more than treacherous.

Thoughts of home are very pleasant but it sure seems a long way off — the moon is bright tonite & almost full — For first time in my life I can see the man in the moon — large bushy eyebrows much like Mr. Holmes — my old friend — the moon....

A king in front of his fire. Holmstrom had found his spot—an unlikely spot to be sure, for an Oregon gas attendant. But here, alone in the towering canyons of the desert Southwest, surrounded by some of the greatest whitewater on earth, Buzz Holmstrom was as content as he would ever be.

Before lunch the next day he made fifteen miles without trouble. Then, at Specter Rapid, he crabbed an oar—the waves snatched it, bending the oarlock and yanking the oar beneath the boat. The boat turned sideways in the wave train. Clutching the remaining oar with both hands, he spun the boat straight as he headed into the next wave, and sailed though. At Bedrock Rapid, Holmstrom made a few quick evasive maneuvers to keep off the rocks. The next rapid, however, had him worried.

Dubendorff, like Waltenberg, was a prolonged stretch of water mined with boulders and rocks, some obvious and above water-level, others threatening damage and disaster just below the surface. The left channel, with its frothing holes and churning waves one after another, looked impossible. The right side was shallow and choked with boulders.

Holmstrom knew it would be a difficult run before he arrived. He had been warned, and he had read about it. In 1909, Seymour Dubendorff flipped here, gashing his head on an oarlock. The Kolbs, gun-shy after Waltenberg, portaged it. Clyde Eddy sank a boat here and Lewis Freeman, on the 1923 USGS trip, smashed a hole in his boat. Holmstrom later wrote of his elaborate preparations:

Before going any farther I will explain that there are several things I felt must be done before starting through a rapid and I have found other river men share the same superstition.

The painter must be coiled and laid on the seat be side me exactly right, the oars must be turned a certain way, and the bailing can put in its proper place. My hat had to be set at a special angle and the life preserver fastened properly. I must always take a fresh chew and spit on my hands to give them a better grip on the oars—Then bracing my feet I was ready for the worst. This all seems silly now but was deadly serious then.

As the boat was carried swiftly down toward the waves I tried to sing, but if there had been time I would have laughed at my own voice for it was so frightened and quavering as to be scarcely heard....

Holmstrom had picked out a thin route, so deceptively tricky that many modern boatmen still miss it. His journal describes it vividly:

on left above rapid put prunes & raisins in bag—unloaded rest on right—In center at head of Rapid is sort of rocky island with most all water going on left—would be pretty easy to line a boat down right to lower portion—which is clear of rocks—Main current on left runs through a few very large waves which could be run easy & then into a bunch of big rocks—mostly just under water—which would smash a boat so quick—but at foot of island water begins to turn to right through some rocks, & run into clear right side of lower end—I dropped over head as close to island as could possibly get & hung right against it & slipped between two rocks at lower end of island & through lower end—Bone Dry.

The whole thing hinged on whether or not I would be sucked out into the main current & waves leading into the left end of last drop—or whether I could hold against the island, as there is a strong current away from it at top & once in the waves one could not pull out.

I was some worried & sized up the country for escape & it did not look very promising—Don't get as scared as I should now though.

Felt swell when got through this Rapid & better yet when I thought of the last 2 lines of Barnacle Bill I had been trying to think of—almost fits my case. "My whiskers grew so bloomin' fast—the sea horses ate them instead of grass." Mine are almost that bad.

Camped at lower end of Dubendorff, where I have the boat all loaded again — quite a long portage of duffel over soft sand and rock bar — cooked some prunes & raisins for supper — eat them after dark as I have reason to believe that it was not the raisins that I replaced at Bright Angel that were wormy....

Holmstrom now moved with deliberate speed. He stopped briefly at Deer Creek Falls, where a hundred-foot waterfall cascades from a crevice in the sandstone. At noon he reached Kanab Creek; Dodge's group had been here when Holmstrom radioed from the South Rim. He found a clean camp and a pile of firewood waiting. He lunched quickly and pushed on. After a quick scout he ran Upset Rapid, making a tricky cut to the right to avoid a desperate hole at the foot. He came through dry, and kept rowing.

> 3:00—am in walls much like Marble Canyon—high, narrow & sheer & smooth since above Kanab—out of granite below Deer Creek—am going to take picture downstream—can see rays of sun from above left cliff—don't reach down to river though....
>
> Should look forbidding downstream—dark & rough & no way out, but doesn't look that way to me at all—probably because I am just through a bad Rapid & no bad ones ahead for a way—when I think I considered selling the boat when through I am ashamed of myself—It has saved my life many times already & still has a job ahead—100 more miles of Bad Rapids.
>
> About 25 miles downstream is Lava Falls where I will sure have to portage if not before.
>
> 2:00 A.M.—Rain finally came—woke me up at 1:30—wind roaring up on cliffs—rolled up bed & put under rock as I don't want to get it wet—awful job to dry it out then—Fixed up fire & now sitting on my rock table thinking of my tent I discarded—It was heavy though & if the rain doesn't last for days I am better off without it—This is fun now but would no doubt lose its humor if prolonged—actually slept a little on the rock shelf—but woke at 2—sky clear—wind gone & so went back to bed—woke up—& watch was stopped at 5:30—Leaped up as it gets light soon after 6—Now am all through eating & all chores done & it is still pitch dark here in the bottom of the canyon although the moon is still lighting up the upper part of the south wall—that watch is interesting—no wonder it sometimes seems a long time between meals & again very close together.
>
> 6:45 — Had a little extra time so washed face hands & teeth — Hadn't figured on that till end of trip but as well do it now & not have to bother then — Just mush & coffee this A.M. — Flour is going down awfully fast — shove off now....

The days were getting shorter. If he were to catch Dodge's group before they finished, Holmstrom had to move fast. He had seen fresh signs of their trip—footprints, camp sites, notes scrawled in the sand. Now, as he neared the finish, Holmstrom put an increasing importance on catching them. He rowed past Havasu Creek, the beautiful blue-green stream that flows in from the Havasupai Indian village, without stopping to explore. A quick lunch at Fern Glen Canyon, and he was back on the river, headed for Lava Falls.

Lava Falls is one of the largest and most violent rapids in Grand Canyon. By 1937, there was still no account of any boatmen having run it. Holmstrom had not portaged since Big Drop Three, back in Cataract. The portage had been exhausting, and the temptation to run Lava Falls was strong. He might be the first to do it; it would be quicker and easier; but was it worth the risk?

> Looked at none till Lava Falls at 1:45 mile 178—25 for today—1 mile above

Falls huge pillar of lava in center of River—played with idea of running Falls on R for 15 minutes—decided to port on L—crossed back to R for poles to slide boat on—started port at 2:30 & done with boat at 5—take duffel down in morning—Just might run, but it is very, very bad.…

FRANK DODGE'S TRIP had been going well. Dodge ran a tight ship—too tight for some people—but they had come through the Granite Gorges upright and had ample time for their geologic work. At Upset Rapid, Dodge had gotten too far left, headed into a yawning hole, and vanished entirely from sight. Climbing back aboard his boat below the rapid, he rowed to shore. Washed out? No, he said. When it looked as if the boat would hit a rock, he jumped out. Raised in Hawaii, Dodge was a lifelong swimmer, more comfortable in the water than out.

Dodge first earned notice on the 1923 USGS expedition at the same rapid. As the boatmen prepared to run it, Dodge stationed himself at the foot of the rapid in case anything went wrong. Head boatman Emery Kolb went into the hole, capsized, struck his head on a gunwale, and appeared disoriented. Dodge dove in, swimming at the perfect angle to intercept Kolb and his boat. He climbed on the boat, pulled Kolb up, and brought him to shore. Colonel Birdseye, who had been skeptical of Dodge's abilities, immediately promoted him to boatman.

In 1927 Dodge was hired as lead boatman for a movie-making trip that ended at Hermit Creek. In the early 1930s he lead two survey trips through the lower gorge. Now, at forty-six, he was considered one of the best boatmen around. When Holmstrom began writing to him for a job in 1936, Dodge had already picked his crew—Owen Clark and Merrill Spencer, two boatmen he had run with before. Besides, Holmstrom's letters had not impressed him. Nor had the name.

Dodge, in his autobiography, wrote,

> I couldn't help but size him up by his letters as a punk kid, though having some experience on other streams, would not be a reader and so would be ignorant of this stream. That if he did get through it would be purely luck. From Tapeats Creek down, the gang began to razz me in fun. They'd make believe they were asking Buzz questions such as, "Buzz, how many rapids did you line or portage?" Answer, "Hell, me line these rapids? No, I ran every one—I wouldn't bother with such as these, etc., etc." Well, I thought when and if he catches us he may very well be a blowhard kid and though I've never had a bit of jealousy in my system regarding the river, it would be hard to listen to a kid, riding his luck, to tell me my mistakes.

Indeed, the party had received the radio message from Holmstrom that he was on his way, and much of their campfire talk concerned his chances of making it. John Stark, one of the geologists, known as "Cactus Jack," had taken to leaving notes in the sand and on driftwood for Holmstrom, on the chance he might overtake them.

HOLMSTROM spent a miserable night below Lava Falls. The wind howled, blowing grit and embers in his face as he tried to cook. Exasperated, he went to bed early, pelted with sand, sparks, and spray.

> Nov 19—8:00—Boat loaded below Falls—cloudy again this A.M.—will take some pictures & shove off—got up early & took drink of water out of bucket in dark—at daylite discovered two drowned rats in it—Before drowning however they had eaten some butter for me—Between rats & myself the butter is not holding out very well—On looking at the Falls this A.M., am quite sure I could run it but would portage every time unless there was some very good reason for trying it.
>
> 8:40—actually ready to leave Lava F now—got thinking possibly those rats drowned themselves in remorse for eating my butter....

He made twelve miles before lunch, and another seventeen by late afternoon, when he stopped at a fresh camp. Pulling in, he found a slab of driftwood on a tripod of sticks. Cactus Jack had written "Hello Buzz" in large letters on the board. A can of cocoa rested by the smoldering campfire. Holmstrom camped for the night, profoundly touched by the welcome from boatmen he had yet to meet.

> Nov 20 5:30 A.M.—eating break—still bright moon lite—surely pretty—rapids roar below—across river on top of cliffs a sleeping giant—at least 1 mile long—sleeping on his side—can see clearly from head to toe—all the cliffs & rocks are surely pretty in the moonlite & starlite—6:50 all ready to shove off only waiting for a little more lite as quite a rapid right below—sunrise is beautiful—moon still in sight in the west as though to show the sun the way—in the east above the dark cliffs the sky is the bluest blue I ever saw & runs through different shades up to the pink & red clouds—makes me mad to try to describe it as there are no words that will do the work.
>
> My overalls are developing a good sized hole where they touch the seat of the boat the most—off at 7....

As soon as he could see well enough to negotiate 209-Mile Rapid, Holmstrom launched. Hot on the trail of Dodge's group, he hoped to catch them that day, perhaps at Diamond Creek, a large tributary on the south shore. Perhaps, Holmstrom hoped, they would stop there for a day or two.

THE TWENTIETH OF NOVEMBER
Is a day we'll all remember
For around the bend at Diamond Creek there came another boat
And a bearded youth sat rowing
With a red hat plainly showing
Buzz Holmstrom had come down more than a thousand miles afloat.

He was eager and excited
Scarcely ate as he recited
His adventures from Green River and his eyes they fairly shone,
As he told of his ambition
Which had nearly reached fruition
To be the first to travel down the Colorado all alone.

Thus wrote Cactus Jack in his *Doggerel Log of a Canyon Trip*, adroitly capturing the spirit of Holmstrom's arrival. Never in Grand Canyon history had two river parties met. Never had anyone run it alone. The entire trip was as excited to meet Holmstrom as he was to catch them. As he pulled in and stepped out of his boat, he held up the "Hello Buzz" sign, wanting to know who had written it. He thanked Cactus Jack for "the biggest morale boost of my life."

Geologist Bob Sharp took careful notes:

> Buzz caught us at 11:15 A.M. at mouth of Diamond Creek—Height 5' 8½" weight 155–165 lbs—husky—nice build—Heavy black beard—fairly large head—nice patches—hair dark brown—hair thinning in front—eyes blue gray.... Buzz obviously very glad to see someone—mentions lonesomeness—talks very fast and at good length—good natured....

They shook hands, exchanged stories. Each wanted to know what the other had done at Lava, at Dubendorff, at dozens of other rapids. Holmstrom was amazed by the size and weight of Dodge's expedition boats, telling the men that his own feat was nothing compared to what their boatmen had managed. *They* were the heroes.

Head geologist Ian Campbell asked Holmstrom if he'd ever been scared. "Gosh, Dr. Campbell," he replied, "I've been scared ever since I left Green River." They loved it. They loved him. Here was a man equal to the place, a man more humble than the Canyon was grand.

Standing back, aloof from the excitement, was stiff, overbearing Frank Dodge. But his preconception of Holmstrom was crumbling. Finally, he came over and held out his hand. Holmstrom, awed at meeting the famous Frank Dodge, grasped his hand and shook it heartily, beaming. Years later, Dodge described Holmstrom's first few minutes in their camp:

> Something shone out of his eyes, something of wonderment and relief that the worst lay behind him and that he was with friends and only a little more to go. I think if one man can love another that we all loved Buzz from that moment on.

Holmstrom spent the rest of the day with the men, rowing down to Travertine Canyon, where they camped together. Holmstrom was interested in the geologists' work and fascinated by a garnet outcrop they discovered there. At meal times, wrote naturalist Edwin McKee, Holmstrom was ravenous—his personal food cache was down to one can of beans.

Around the fire that night, the men of the survey party wrested more of Holmstrom's tale, from the finding of the Port Orford Cedar log to spending his last dime in Flagstaff. They talked of rapids run and rapids to come. Dodge described the two major cataracts still ahead, Separation and Lava Cliff, and the route through each.

The next morning the boatmen were reluctant to take leave of each other. A bond—a boatman's bond—had formed. In his journal Campbell wrote:

> Didn't get going very early, as wanted to have sun to take farewell pictures of Buzz, & he seemed loath to leave—tho he had to rush to get back to the job he hoped he still had. A true amateur—said he expected to make no money out of his trip—"the most money I can make will be by going right back home and going to work again." He had with him Jack's wooden board on which Jack wrote all our names. Said he was going to have it framed—& it was something he'd never take any amount of money for. We asked him if he hadn't noticed any writing in the sand, & he said yes, "Hinds for president" which brought a loud cheer. He surely has sharp eyes—knew our boats were mahogany because of a small splinter pulled loose on the Lava Falls portage.

As Holmstrom prepared to leave, the men came over and offered him a collection of money they had taken up, a little something to help him get home. Holmstrom was overwhelmed, but refused it. As he climbed into his boat, Frank Dodge held out his hand once more and clasped Holmstrom's hand. "Buzz," he said, "you're all right."

DOWNSTREAM, Holmstrom scouted 232-Mile Rapid, whose waves could hurl a

Frank Dodge and Buzz Holmstrom, boatmen

careless boater to the right shore and into a nest of fang-shaped rocks. Emery Kolb believed that Glen and Bessie Hyde had met their demise here in 1928, for he had found their scow just a few miles below. Holmstrom dropped down the center, pulled safely off to the left side, and went on.

Separation Canyon threatened next. Three of Major Powell's men, half starved and sure that the river was getting worse, quit the expedition here and hiked out to their demise. Holmstrom memorized the route — zig here, zag there, another zig down below — and ran it. A half-mile downstream, a wave stalled him, knocking him sideways and shooting the boat out on edge. Five more miles brought him to the last major rapid on the Colorado: Lava Cliff; Spencer Canyon; Bold Escarpment. It went by many names and had an evil reputation under all of them.

In 1869, the first of Powell's two remaining boats broke loose as they attempted to line it around the rapid — George Bradley rode the boat into the maelstrom. In their attempt to rescue him, Powell and two others swamped the second boat; Bradley rescued them instead. On an icy afternoon in January of 1912, the Kolbs had portaged this one. Clyde Eddy had run it at flood-water simply because there was no way around. Stone, Galloway, and Dubendorff had lined it.

Lava Cliff. If Holmstrom could get below this one, his worries were over. He scouted the rapid for quite some time.

> can't get down far on L but could see enough—nice clear stream at Spencer— start slowly through channel between submerged rocks at head on L—pull over to left cliff—drop through small reverse wave near cliff & near enough to a big rock to touch it—rock is almost against cliff on L—to R of rock— steep drop & very deep trough & monstrous reverse wave—didn't want to go through that—next to rock better place—not so deep trough—went through there OK—current shoots boat against cliff—big boil rebounds— stern eases against cliff & pull around bow first away from the cliff & through OK—about 3 gal water....

Holmstrom landed at the foot of the rapid and climbed back to the top. He wrote a long note to Dodge's trip, thanking them again, and telling them just how he had run Separation and Lava Cliff. "I will be sorry to leave the Canyon & River," he concluded, "Your Friend, Buzz Holmstrom." He tucked the note into his last empty bean can, left it where he was sure they would find it, and climbed back to his boat. On a cliff, he painted a large greeting to them from "Barnacle Buzz." Then he rowed to a beach on the right and made camp.

A few miles downstream, he would enter Lake Mead, still filling behind Boulder Dam. Better to camp here, he thought, by a rapid. That night by the campfire, he wrote and wrote in his journal. He had done it. He had actually done it—yet something gnawed at him.

Camp on right at lower end Rapid — mile 247 with the last bad one above me — the Bad Rapid — Lava Cliff — that I have been looking for — nearly a thousand miles.

I had thought — once past there — my reward will begin — but now — everything ahead seems kind of empty & I find I have already had my reward — in the doing of the thing — the stars & cliffs & canyons — the roar of the rapids — the moon — the uncertainty — worry — the relief when through each one — the campfires at nite — the real respect & friendship of the river men I met & others.

This may be my last camp where the roar of a real rapid is echoed from the cliffs around & I can look at the stars & moon only through a narrow slit in the earth.

The river & Canyons have been kind to me — I think my greatest danger is ahead — that I might get swellheaded over this thing — I am going to try to keep my mouth shut about it — go back to work in the old way & have it only for a memory for myself — I have done no one any good & caused a few people great worry & suffering I know.

I think this river is not treacherous as has been said — Every rapid speaks plainly just what it is & what it will do to a person & a boat in its currents waves boils whirlpools & rocks — if only one will read & listen carefully — It demands respect — & will punish those who do not treat it properly — some places it says — go here safely if you do it just this way — & in others it says — do not go here at all with the type of boat you have — but many people will not believe what it says.

Some people have said "I conquered the Colorado River" — I don't say so — It has never been conquered — & never will I think — anyone who it allows to go through its canyons & see its wonders should feel thankful & privileged.

Sometimes I feel sorry for the river — it works every second of the ages carving away at the rocks — digging its canyons — carries a million tons of silt per day — & again I feel sorry for the mountains & rocks with the river gnawing at their insides — but I guess my sympathy doesn't seem very important to either of them.

I know I have got more out of this trip by being alone than if a party was along as I have more time — especially at nite — to listen & look & think & wonder about the natural wonders rather than listen to talk of war politics & football scores.

The River probably thought — he is such a lonesome ignorant unimportant & insignificant pitiful little creature — with such a short time to live that I will let him go this time & try to teach him something — It has not been so kind to many prouder people than I.

I fooled along all yesterday P.M. — going through 3 miles of very easy water below Diamond Creek with the boatmen while the geologists studied rocks — camped with them — swell lot of fellows — all their good sides show up now — offered me everything — food — etc. — told them during the conversation was short of money — this A.M. when I was ready to leave — one came up to me & told me how much cash they had altogether & offered me that — I did not accept — of course — made me feel good though.

The boatmen are doing a swell job — wet all time — Boats & load weigh over 2,000 pounds each — & hard to handle & very wet — much more difficult to run rapids with than mine.

They lined Badger — Hance — Walt — Dub — & Lava Falls — Intend to run the rest — but will surely get wet here — they told me just how to run Lava Cliff here & it did help me though I am sure I would have done it so anyhow — I like Spencer especially — very quiet — Its all just part of the days work to them — Dodge is the head boatman & inclined to be a little overbearing — I think though a riverman without an equal — Clark is fine — quiet & capable.

Have about 30 miles of Rapids yet but all pretty easy I think — will continue to be careful though — felt lucky here — recognized places here shown in pictures where others had toiled portaging & lining — & within 15 minutes of the time I reached the head — I was at the foot — load & all.

A perfect nite — every star in the sky lighted up brighter than usual — still —the moon comes up later now —

Buzz Holmstrom's journal ended there, at the foot of Lava Cliff Rapid. He spent another four-and-a-half days on the water without writing a word. Perhaps there was nothing left to say. Perhaps there was but he did not know how to say it. A few miles from his last camp, he hit smooth water where his map showed rapids. At first he was confused, then realized he had reached the stagnant waters of Lake Mead, farther upriver than he expected. As the current dwindled, the silt began to settle. Dismayed, Holmstrom filled his bucket with the last of the silty water. He had been drinking it for two months and had come to feel that was what he should be drinking.

Toward the end of his first day below Lava Cliff he emerged from the Grand Wash Cliffs, where Grand Canyon abruptly ends. He camped near Pearce Ferry. The next night he was out on the ever-expanding shore of the reservoir, amazed at the size of the man-made lake. An old timer back at Hite had told Holmstrom the greatest danger of the trip would be rowing up one of the wrong arms of the lake, getting lost, and starving. Vigilant, he kept rowing. With the afternoon winds kicking up whitecaps, he rowed most of the night. The next evening he made it as far as the Virgin River, where Powell's trip ended—or at least to where the river, now hundreds of feet beneath him, would have been. A tour boat stopped to talk, and offered to tow him on in. He declined. He had rowed this far. No sense quitting now.

On Thanksgiving Day, Earl Brothers, a Boulder City promoter, was taking pictures at Boulder Dam. Around noon, he noticed a tattered man in a small rowboat working slowing across the reservoir. The man rowed steadily closer until he hit the concrete face of the dam with a deliberate *thunk*.

Brothers had heard that a lone boatman was running the river, and figured this was the man. He took several pictures. The boatman, bearded, weary, and bedraggled, pulled ashore and carefully moored his boat. At the Western Union office in Boulder City he sent a telegram to his mother:

OKAY AT BOULDER DAM.

HALDANE.

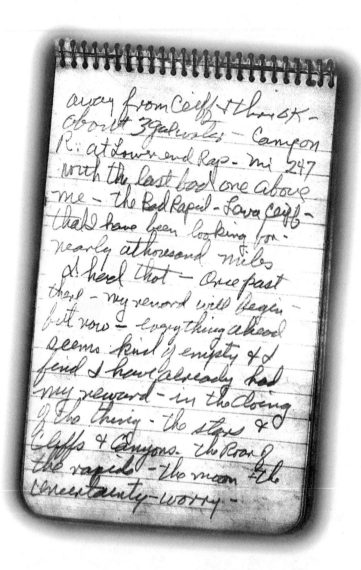

away from Cliff + there OK -
about 3 galumbs - Camp on
R. at Lower end Rap - mi 247
with the last bad one above
me - the Bad Rapid - Lava Cliff -
that I have been looking for -
nearly a thousand miles
I heard that - Once past
there - my reward will begin -
but now - everything ahead
seems kind of empty & I
find I have already had
my reward - in the closing
of the things - the stars &
Cliffs & Canyons - the Roar of
the rapids - the moon & the
uncertainty - worry -

above: A page from Holmstrom's original journal
opposite: Squaretop Mountain, Lower Green River Lake

Reluctant Hero

1938

*B*OULDER DAM: the "Great Pyramid of the American Desert." Three years before Holmstrom bumped into its massive concrete face, the diversion tunnels had been closed; Lake Mead was still filling at a rate of seventy-five vertical feet per year. After the dam's completion in 1935, Boulder City, built by and for dam workers, dwindled from its peak population of six thousand to less than half that. Those who remained were counting on a new boom: tourism. The world's largest structure, Boulder Dam had tamed the turbulent Colorado and was now creating the world's largest man-made lake. In 1937 alone, more than half a million tourists came to see the project. The Boulder Dam Hotel, a new resort inn, was already attracting celebrities, although not for the scenery. Nevada had the most lenient divorce laws in the country, but a six-week residency was required before the decree, and the Boulder Dam Hotel was the most luxurious in the state. If a person wanted more excitement than was available in the dry, sedate, government-controlled town, Las Vegas was just a few miles north, still a small, seedy city of sin. Surely Boulder City was about to become a major tourist Mecca.

The staunchest promoter was Glover E. "Roxie" Ruckstell. His invention of the Ruckstell Axle, an essential part of the Model-T, had made him a millionaire. His latest passion was aviation. He started Grand Canyon Airlines, a small fleet of Ford Tri-motors offering tours and service to the South Rim. Las Vegas had yet to build an airport, and Ruckstell had exclusive air rights at Boulder City and Grand Canyon. He launched a tour boat operation on Lake Mead and obtained an exclusive twenty-year government contract to operate on the lake. From a dock near the dam, boats roared up the expanding reservoir into the inundated lower Grand Canyon, while tour guides told fanciful tales of the area and pointed out freshly christened landmarks: Paradise Portal, Gabriel's Sentinels, Angel's Slide, Cleopatra's Terrace, Tower of Babel, Vulcan's Rouge Palette.

If one wanted transport around Boulder City, Ruckstell had the taxi service and limousines to do it. Land tours could be arranged to Death Valley and the Valley of Fire. Ruckstell's Grand Canyon–Boulder Dam Tours (GCBDT around town) had recently absorbed the Boulder Dam Hotel as well. Poised for a boom, Roxie Ruckstell was still expanding rapidly, and searching for publicity to fuel it all.

Jim Webb, a former co-owner of the hotel, still acted as manager, as well as vice-president of GCBDT. He was on the tour boat that had offered Holmstrom a tow across the lake. Now he treated Holmstrom royally, putting him up at the hotel. He alerted whatever media he could find, calling attention to GCBDT's concerns as well as to those of the new celebrity. Media coverage that had begun at South Rim began to snowball. *Daring River Man Makes 52-Day Solo Trip Down Green, Colorado Rivers! Oregon Boatman Conquers Turbulent Colorado River!*

The biggest Holmstrom story on the wires was by Florence Lee Jones of Las Vegas and filled about a quarter page of those newspapers that carried it. Jones produced a fair telling of the young filling station attendant's adventure, detailing the running of rapids, the solo portages, even his mistrust of the clear lake water. But as much as the stories tried to paint a mighty conqueror, modest Holmstrom shone through. "I guess I was lucky on the trip," Holmstrom explained. "Everyone told me it was almost surely fatal to try going through the Grand Canyon alone, but it seemed the river was at the right stage and the boat worked better than I had expected, and everything worked in together." Although the folks at GCBDT were pressuring Holmstrom to stay until more media people could get in from Los Angeles, he was eager to get himself and his boat home and back to work. After two nights in Boulder City he caught a bus north to retrieve his car and trailer.

Winter was well established in Wyoming when Holmstrom arrived. The river had frozen over and so had the old Dodge. To get it warm enough to crank, Holmstrom built a small fire beneath the engine. He spent a day visiting with the Hills, who had stored his car for him, and went to see the Holmes family at their ranch. He had nothing in the way of a winter wardrobe and, as he wrote home, "about froze my ears off" driving down to Salt Lake City in the roofless Dodge.

There Doc Frazier, whom he had met on the way to the river at the end of September, was overflowing with excitement about Holmstrom's trip and insisted that he stay with him and his wife. Frazier had movies of his own trips on the Yampa, Salmon, and Colorado. He had friends who needed to meet Holmstrom, he said, and he called every river person in town.

Frazier liked people to get their due, to be recognized. On many of his expeditions he brought along a plaque to place in honor of someone who had not, in Frazier's mind, been adequately noted. Now he was trying to get Holmstrom to be reasonable about the publicity angle. In a letter a week later he pressed, "Now, Big Boy, put your modesty behind you and cash in on this."

Holmstrom, of course, had no concept of glory and was squirming amid all the adulation being whipped up by Frazier. Two evenings of being the center of attention were two too many. He declined the entreaties to stay another night and headed south toward Boulder City at midnight, December 2, in his topless car.

While Holmstrom had been retrieving his car, Uncle Roy and Aunt Emma had made a quick trip to Boulder Dam, hoping to see their celebrated nephew. Holmstrom found a note from them when he got back. He also found Clarence Bean.

Bean, Holmstrom's old pal, who was going to go on the Salmon but could not; Bean, who was going to go down the Colorado with Holmstrom, but chose a sailing adventure instead. The sailing adventure had never left the dock, and Bean had spent the last five months in San Diego and Tijuana, doing refrigeration work. On hearing of Holmstrom's triumphant arrival, Bean abandoned ship and headed over to Boulder City.

The first thing Holmstrom wanted to do, Bean later recalled, was go camping. Camping! So they headed over to Lake Mead, camping on the shore without enough gear to keep them both warm, sharing the scant covers. One night was enough of that. But they hatched a plan. Maybe Frazier was right. A little money might be okay. Maybe the story should be written, and together perhaps they could write it. They went back to town and began.

Grand Canyon–Boulder Dam Tours made a few big splashes in the local newspapers that week. First came an announcement of a major overhaul of their lake tour program. Bigger boats, more trips, new docking facilities, and more tour guides in captains' outfits. Filling a half a page the next day was a major spread on the wonders to be encountered on a tour of Lake Mead. There would be jobs, and that did not go unnoticed by Holmstrom. He talked over the possibilities of work the next summer with Sidney Bazett, one of GCBDT's publicity men, and promised to keep in touch.

Meanwhile, the Boulder City Chamber of Commerce had their eye on Holmstrom's boat. They would be happy to take care of it. The boat would make a nice display; maybe a centerpiece for a museum. Why let it rot in the rainy Northwest? Holmstrom agreed. If he needed it again, he could come and get it. Until then the boat would be fine in Nevada, and he could travel lighter without it.

Free lodging in Boulder City trailed off. Holmstrom and Bean headed over to Las Vegas and got a room at a cheap hotel. A lot of other things were cheap in Las Vegas at the time, and it is difficult to say how much of the time they spent on their writing project. By the 14th of December, however, they were out of money and on the move, headed for Los Angeles. About half way there, in the high, desolate Mojave Desert outside of Victorville, California, the old Dodge gave up. The ten dollar car was finished. Holmstrom sold it to a junk dealer for five dollars on the spot and another two-fifty when he sent in the title from Coquille. All in all, not too bad a deal. They caught the bus to Los Angeles.

The five dollars did not last long and they were tossed out of their hotel for non-payment. Bean caught a bus back to Coquille. Holmstrom stayed in California a little longer, living on ten-cent hamburgers. He had a deal brewing with the *Union Oil Thrills Show*, an interview. Sure enough, Frazier had been right. There *was* going to be a little money.

Back in Coquille, Bean brought firsthand word of the hometown hero. He did not tell too many stories—he left that for Holmstrom. But the local folks were excited about Holmstrom's imminent return and sent telegrams of congratulation and encouragement to Los Angeles on the evening of the interview.

At 6:30 in the evening, a few days before Christmas, Holmstrom stood in the NBC studio, palms sweating, with Mr. Whitman. The real interview had taken place during the days leading up to the show. Now the two men read aloud a four-minute scripted piece, live before a nationwide audience. The result, naturally, was an overcooked version of Holmstrom's trip, playing up the danger, the rapids, and the isolation. Even so, Holmstrom managed to work in a bit of humility.

Whitman: How did it affect you?
Holmstrom: Well, it was this way. It may sound funny to you—but after weeks of being alone with the river I began to think of it as a friend—as a companion. It seemed an enemy at first but after a while I began to understand it, and it showed me just how to run the rapids. It seemed as though it said to me that if I'd be careful nothing would

happen. I could understand how the Indians came to worship nature, because out there with nothing but the roar of the river, and the stars at night, and the canyon walls I began to see things in a way I never had before.

Whitman: I can understand that. Tell me, just how dangerous is the river...

Holmstrom even managed to slip in the Barnacle Bill story, remembering the lost lines half way through Dubendorff, and concluded with a classic line.

Holmstrom: You know Mr. Whitman, you'll probably think this is strange.
Whitman: What's that?
Holmstrom: The spell of the canyon is awfully strong and it holds something of me I know it will never give up.

Another tidbit of the Holmstrom gospel had made it nationwide. What was more, he got paid for it. One hundred dollars, as much as he had saved up for his whole trip. But it bothered him. He had promised himself not to go blabbering about the trip. "I wrote xmas greetings to Barnacle Buzz and got a short note in return," wrote Frank Dodge to Ian Campbell. "Said he gathered in $100 for answering questions for four minutes. Radio. Sort of apologized for that. Broke, you know. I'll never get over that guy."

Holmstrom had promised his mother he would be home for Christmas, and he did not have much time. He hired a gyp cab, a car that, once it had enough people headed in a similar direction, started driving. It took him east to Santa Fe, then back to San Francisco, then north along the coast to Redding, California, where it finally either broke down or the driver refused to go farther north with just one passenger. Holmstrom hitchhiked the rest of the way, walking in his mother's front door at 3:30 P.M. Christmas Day and sitting down to a late holiday dinner.

Things had been happening since Holmstrom left Salt Lake City. One of the folks Frazier had called that night was Hack Miller, a sports writer for the *Deseret News* and a river runner himself. Each time the Colorado River Club went on another trip, Miller would write a major story. The writer had heard of Holmstrom's exploits from Frazier and also from the road crew Holmstrom met along the river at Hite. Although Miller did not make it to Frazier's that night, Holmstrom's adventure, and subsequent visit to Frazier in Salt Lake, were the subject of yet another river story in that weekend's *Deseret News*. Hack Miller's story, in and of itself, was no bigger than the piece filed in Las Vegas, nor was it widely distributed. But a copy of Miller's story that Frazier sent off in the mail was about to have a major impact on Holmstrom's life. The recipient was Wesley W. Stout, editor of the *Saturday Evening Post*.

Stout was enthusiastic about Holmstrom's story. He contacted writer Robert Ormond Case in Portland to try to get a story, and wrote other river men around the Southwest to see if Holmstrom was for real. Case, a classmate of Ian Campbell's, wrote to Holmstrom, asking for an interview. Two days after Holmstrom arrived in Coquille, he headed to Portland to meet Case. Case would not need to do much, Holmstrom figured; he and Bean had already written the story. Well, not quite. Holmstrom and Bean had tried, but the fact is, their piece was not very good. Labored and amateurish, it was actually a step down from Holmstrom's original journal.

Holmstrom had photos to go along with the story, but they were disappointing as well. The little Argus had failed to capture the scenery and, of course, there were no action shots. No problem. With a few lengthy interviews, Holmstrom's journal and manuscript to work with, and a literary license, Case would make it work. With some of Holmstrom's better pictures and a few from Frazier, Kolb, and others, he could put together a good spread.

Back in Coquille a few days later, Holmstrom had the uncomfortable duty of speaking three nights in a row at the Roxy Theatre telling the local folks about the big adventure. As much as Holmstrom did not like speaking, he could not seem to say no. So he dragged Bean along for moral support, had a beer or two, and got up and talked. The Coos Bay Chamber of Commerce wanted him to speak, as did the Lions, the Rotary, and the Boy Scouts.

Buzz was not the only Holmstrom of note in Coquille that year. A few months earlier, Frances had also realized one of her dreams. Metropolitan Press, in Portland, published *Western Windows*, a slim volume of her poetry, bringing her work to prominence in the Northwest.

Before long Holmstrom was back at Walker Brothers' Service Station. As always, there was a place for him. But something had changed. Holmstrom was no longer content there. He just did not fit in, or so he felt. Perhaps he had really spoken from the heart in that interview: the river *had* claimed a part of him. The other thing that was getting to Buzz was how everyone around town was making such a big deal about the river trip, as if he were someone special. He had not minded at first, but he had meant the trip to be a private thing—he had done it for himself. It was over now. He was back home and it was not anything anyone needed to make a fuss about.

To Campbell he wrote:

> Up here there is no one knows anything about the kind of boating we have done. The thing that makes my trip seem worthwhile to me is the friendship of yourself and the other men who have made the trip and know what it is like. Here they all think that because they saw my name in the paper I have done something wonderful. I am fed up with talking about the thing, and I

would almost venture to guess that by this time you have somewhat the same feeling. It seems as though there is not much to looking back at something like that. Already I find that I have a longing to go back to the canyon country, but I made a new years resolution to stay here. But you know how well those resolutions sometimes last.

Two weeks later he wrote to Earl Hamilton:

I am ashamed of myself for not answering your letter before. I have been in such turmoil since I got to the dam. I hardly know for sure whether I am coming or going....I am back working at the old job. Not much fun either.... I will probably never make any money out of [the trip] but I feel a lot richer anyhow for I have something nice to remember that can never be taken away from me....

Another two weeks passed and he wrote to Cactus Jack Stark:

It has worked out just as I was afraid it would at the last rapid, Lava Cliff. I am thoroughly disgusted with the way people here talk. I might be talked into thinking it was quite a job myself, but when I start to think that, I just stop and remember you fellows, the boatmen running the boats and loads of more than a ton in the same places I ran my light one, and thought I was doing something, and also I think of you taking the same risks I was and on top of that going ahead with the geology and taking the hardship and risk as part of the days work necessary to get at your real job. Your trip will do some real good while mine was just a selfish sort of proposition.

Meanwhile, Holmstrom was looking at a few options that might get him out of town for a while. Arthur Gordon, whom he had met at Boulder City, wanted to put together a road show, towing the boat around the West, charging for lectures and a glimpse of the boat. Gordon had first thought they should join up with a circus, but then read of a fellow who was making ten thousand dollars a year on a solo tour with John Wilkes Booth's mummy. That is what they should do, he told Holmstrom.

Holmstrom mentioned the idea of a road show and lecture tour to Carl Brandt, Robert Ormond Case's agent, who was handling the Holmstrom story. Brandt said that without good photos to project, any lecture tour would fall flat. Correspondence trickled off with Gordon.

Sidney Bazett, with GCBDT, wrote Holmstrom asking if he would be a lake captain for them. They could offer Holmstrom a career. He said Buzz was just the sort of sharp, hard-working guy they were looking for. Holmstrom took this offer a little more seriously, and looked into getting his Coast Guard license.

THEN CAME THE *POST* STORY. On February 1, Case sent Holmstrom a check for

$450. The *Post* was really going to run it. Three weeks later it hit the newsstands. "He Shot The Colorado Alone," read the cover. There would have been a picture of Grand Canyon on the cover as well, but they could not find a color shot in time. No matter. In those days, everyone read the *Post*, and everyone read the story.

It was good. It told a bit about Holmstrom and then turned it over to Holmstrom to tell the tale—Holmstrom as written by Case. But it sounded like him: humble, matter-of-fact Buzz, the filling station attendant from Coquille.

An interesting detail of the story finds its roots in the Holmstrom-and-Bean account. They had wanted to put a climax in the story, and since Holmstrom had portaged the mighty Lava Falls, there had to be a rapid he had actually run that would serve their purpose. They chose Dubendorff. In their account, Holmstrom worked up to the dreaded Dubie for weeks and finally conquered it, singing *Barnacle Bill* as he rowed. The rest of the trip was cake. In the *Thrills* interview, Dubendorff again comes across as the major hurdle to get past, and throughout Case's story, the Demon Dubendorff was the rapid that would make or break the trip.

> Well, I looked it over for fifteen minutes and then turned back to the boat. There was no use waiting; when you've got 'er figured, it's time to go. I could feel my heart beating. It seemed like it was beating down lower than usual, down in my stomach. I remembered that British officer at Waterloo, when he climbed into the saddle and found that his knees were shaking. "Shake, damn you," he said, "You'd shake worse than that if you knew where you were really going."

Letters started pouring in by the sackful from admirers, curious readers, old acquaintances, kooks. Most anyone who had ever run the river wrote: Clyde Eddy, Glen Kershner from the Pathé-Bray trip, Robert Bartl from Eddy's trip, everyone from Frank Dodge's group. Seymour Dubendorff's childhood neighbor sent a long letter. The nephew of Andrew Hall, one of Powell's men, wrote, as did the husband of nineteenth century river runner Frank Brown's cousin. Everyone was exuberant, everyone wanted pictures, everyone wanted to hear from Buzz Holmstrom. One fellow wanted him to help found a morally uplifting program for the nation's youth. Another woman, who called him "Buzzie," sent a hand-illustrated bible that had taken her eight years to finish.

One letter, though, caught Holmstrom's interest. It was a fan letter, but a thoughtful one, from Betty Lowman, an intelligent and talented young woman from Washington state. She was living alone in a small cabin on a mountaintop on Puget Sound, and had noticed the *Post* story when she was in town buying provisions. She took it home to her cabin, read it through, and while her dinner got cold, wrote Holmstrom a letter. Lowman, more than most anyone else who wrote to Holmstrom, could identify with him. A year earlier she had taken her small Indian dugout canoe and rowed it, alone, from Anacortes, Washington, to Ketchikan, Alaska, over a thousand miles.

> Time after time in reading of your trip I thought, 'We had identical feelings!'—
> in so much as a man and a woman can have comparable feelings.... [the trip
> gave] me a new appreciation of that priceless self respect one can only know
> in realizing a dream such as yours—and insignificantly—such as mine.

Holmstrom wrote back a flattering letter, telling her about his trip but asking her a string of questions about hers, wanting to know details, and how it might be for him to try the trip himself, as his feet were getting itchy. Lowman responded with a long account of her nine-week trip.

Lowman, like Holmstrom, had grown up around boats, living on an island in Puget Sound. Each summer, all the menfolk went north to the fisheries, but being a girl, she was not allowed to work up there. Her father captained a fishing boat in Ketchikan, so Betty Lowman made up her mind to row there and see him. She left with two oars, a sleeping bag, her camera, and ten dollars. On her way she made friends with Indians, fishermen, missionaries, and whomever else she met. Seven weeks into her trip she capsized in a storm, losing everything but the boat. Carving new oars, she continued, living off the land and whatever handouts she received. Most everyone she met thought she was nuts. At the end of the summer her father gave her a ride home on his fishing boat.

"The trip should not be much of a problem for a fellow like you," she said. And as to what Lowman had gotten out of her adventure, she had found the reward, as had Holmstrom, in the doing of the thing.

Betty Lowman's letters were the exception, however, and the tedious ones continued to pour in. Holmstrom, who never felt he was much of a writer, felt obliged to answer each letter, often apologizing for taking so long to respond. His fame—or whatever it was—was becoming a burden.

The real catch was that there was money to be made from his notoriety. The *Thrills* show had paid a hundred dollars. The *Post* article paid $450. That was good money in 1938. There was his mother to support; and Rolf was still in school. Carl, working as a logger, could not support them alone.

Then came a letter from a boatman in Portland. He was of Norwegian descent, a fellow Viking and Oregonian. Amos Burg had a great deal in common with Holmstrom. Burg had gone to sea as a teenager, working his way around the world. Both Burg and Holmstrom had gotten the river fever and gone off on major expeditions. Burg canoed the Snake River from its source to the sea. And the Columbia and the Mississippi, the Yukon, and the Mackenzie. Other rivers as well, most of them alone. Both Burg and Holmstrom were solitaries. Burg shunned the revelry of other sailors on his ocean voyages, reading the *Encyclopedia Britannica* cover to cover while at sea, and exploring the countryside at every port. Both men were now nationally famous explorers—for many years, Burg's stories had appeared in the *National Geographic.*

There was one big difference. Burg knew how to sell his photography, his writing, and himself. The *Geographic* routinely sent him to report on distant parts of the globe. His annual lecture tour was in high demand and he was at ease speaking before large crowds. He knew, as well, how to travel the world with nary a cent to his name. He was savvy about self-promotion, whereas Holmstrom, if he had his way, would never tell a soul.

"Your voyage down the Colorado floored me," Burg's letter began. After a brief showering of praise, Burg led up to a proposition. Perhaps, suggested Burg, they could do a trip together. By combining Holmstrom's skill and newfound fame with Burg's photographic and media talents, they could make some money doing what they both enjoyed. Perhaps, wrote Burg, they could recreate Holmstrom's solo trip on film. Burg could row along in another boat with the camera gear, filming Holmstrom's runs. The 1939 Golden Gate Exposition was coming up in San Francisco. If they could get some really good photos — still shots, movies, and color as well — Holmstrom might be able to do a show there. A plan was born.

Julius Stone, who had rowed the Green and Colorado in 1909, sent congratulations and a copy of his book, *Canyon Country.* Holmstrom was delighted and began corresponding with Stone, confiding in him the plan to do a trip with Burg. Stone encouraged Holmstrom to go ahead with the plan. His only regret was that, at eighty-three, he was too infirm to accompany them.

Doc Frazier and Hack Miller wrote, inviting Holmstrom along on a July trip down the Middle Fork of the Salmon with the Colorado River Club. He would love to, Holmstrom wrote back, if he could find the time.

Meanwhile, another offer was shaping up. A telegram arrived asking Holmstrom to appear with his boat at the Northwest Sportsmen's Show in Minneapolis. They would pay him a hundred and fifty dollars. Holmstrom asked for more. They countered: two hundred dollars? Two hundred plus expenses, replied Holmstrom, and it's a deal.

But first Holmstrom was off to Portland to get his captain's license from the Bureau of Marine Inspection and Navigation. He would need that if he were to go to work on Lake Mead. On April 4, license in hand, he returned to Coquille.

Holmstrom had to be in Minnesota on April 13, but his boat was still in Boulder City. It might be a fun road trip, especially if he had company. His old pal Thurman Hickam was working at Smith Woods Products, and Holmstrom began urging him to take a little vacation. Hickam made all sorts of excuses but finally relented. Meanwhile, Holmstrom looked for a car to tow the boat. He hated to ask Hickam to subject his Studebaker to the task, so he laid siege to Clarence Barton, who had his '26 Buick for sale. Barton wanted thirty dollars. Holmstrom offered twenty-five. They split the difference. "But it was worth it," Holmstrom later said.

He told Ed Walker he was leaving the gas station again and did not know just when he would return. But Holmstrom did say that if things got too frantic in the summer, he would drop whatever he was doing and come back. Walker both envied and encouraged Holmstrom's adventures. There would always be work for Holmstrom at Walker's.

Holmstrom and Hickam headed south along the coast, through the redwoods, then down the Central Valley of California. From there they turned east and crossed over to Boulder City. With boat in tow, they headed southeast to Kingman, Arizona, and joined the mother road, Route 66, eastbound. It was a long drive; much of the road was still unpaved, curvy, winding, and, in places, pretty steep. The Buick was a champ, though, and only quit once, when Holmstrom lost a bet that they had enough gas to get to the next station. Nine miles short, out of gas, Holmstrom started walking. Although he got a lift part way to the station, he walked all the way back without a single car coming by.

Once they got to Minneapolis, the fun was over for a while. Holmstrom tried to be the showman they wanted him to be, while Hickam, with a free pass, toured the show. To kick the week off, Holmstrom was interviewed on the radio again. It was all heroism this time and Holmstrom was only able to slip in a tidbit of self-deprecation: "You travel through what amounts to a lost world insofar as the average man is concerned, for very, very few have ever seen it. Only a few animals and some other fools like myself."

Holmstrom's distaste for self promotion became more evident. To his mother he wrote:

Crossing the Navajo Reservation

I think it is not the easiest way to make money—one show like this is sure enough—It will be over Sunday night—I am sort of like a freak in a sideshow— I say about six words every afternoon and evening. The auditorium seats about 12 thousand people—it has been clear full a few times.... In the same hotel we are staying is a fellow, Harold Williams, from Florida who wrestles an alligator in the tank—sure a nice fellow. Harold I mean.

After enduring the week in Minneapolis, they headed westward. Stopping in Salt Lake City to visit Frazier and Miller, the pair then wound their way south through Bryce and Zion Canyons. At Marble Canyon, Holmstrom showed Hickam how he had climbed in and out of the Canyon at Navajo Bridge. Hickam preferred watching the precarious climb to joining Holmstrom, and took pictures from the rim. Next they headed over to the South Rim and together made the hike down to the river and back. From there they returned to Boulder City, where Holmstrom signed on with Grand Canyon–Boulder Dam Tours. Hickam took the bus home to Coquille. For him it had been a terrific trip, one he told folks about for the rest of his life.

GCBDT was glad to have Holmstrom. As one of their lead captains, he would draw in more tourists for the two-hundred-mile round trip lake tour. In a fine new captain's outfit he could regale them with tales of whitewater heroism and death-defying feats. A great idea, but they did not know Holmstrom very well. He balked at the uniforms and showed up shirtless, in an old pair of pants. When a crowd of tourists came around the docks, Holmstrom mysteriously disappeared. When they could coax him into one of the tour boats, he was often too timid to say much, especially around women. If someone were persistent enough to break through Holmstrom's reticence, he would talk, sometimes at length. Not about feats of derring-do, but of his friends: the canyon, the moon, and the river, and how they helped him and spoke to him.

The shining and heroic captain was a bust. Holmstrom was sent up the lake to Pearce Ferry to work, away from the tourists.

Pearce Ferry remains one of the bleaker outposts of the Great American Desert. In the 1800s, Harrison Pearce operated a small ferry for the Mormon Church there. That went beneath the waves of Lake Mead and GCBDT established a small tourist facility on the shore. There was a boathouse, a dock, a small place to eat, and tent cabins. On the mesa above, an airstrip for tour planes had been scraped out of the desert on the fringes of the world's largest Joshua tree forest. Nearby was a Civilian Conservation Corps camp. In the spring, workers in boats towed the driftwood jams off the lake to burn, maintaining a clear waterway for the tour boats.

Temperatures were topping one hundred degrees when Holmstrom arrived, and soon approached 120. It was warm for the Oregon native, but the change got him away from the tourists. Phil Poquett, who with his wife Em managed the place, took an immediate liking to Holmstrom; he was a hard worker, friendly, and multi-talented. "But abnormally shy," thought Em Poquett, "and a little moody. Almost neurotic, really. You almost had to pry any kind of a story out of him, and when a tour boat would come in, poof, no Buzz."

Holmstrom found Pearce Ferry tolerable for the time being. When the Poquetts were away he ran the place, doing the cooking and keeping up the tents. But most of the time he cleaned bilges and scraped paint. Not great work, but he could be alone doing it. The biggest excitement came when the hundred-foot shale cliffs, saturated by the rising reservoir, collapsed into the lake and sent waves crashing across the docks.

When Holmstrom went into Boulder City, he often looked up Frank Dodge. After the Carnegie trip, Dodge had gone down to Yuma, Arizona, and built a small sailboat. He had towed it up to Lake Mead, built himself a small dock, and was living on the boat. He and Holmstrom proved to be birds of a feather, often sitting out on deck and talking endlessly of the Canyon. "The other night," Dodge wrote to Campbell, "Buzz and I had a rum party and reran the whole Canyon." But as many river stories as they shared, Holmstrom did not tell anyone, not even Dodge, what he and Burg were planning.

Back at Pearce Ferry, Holmstrom worked his shift, sent homesick letters to his mother, made plans with Burg, and tried to figure out how to get a show together for the upcoming world's fair. In early June, he flew to San Francisco for a radio interview with the *Allis Chalmers Family Hour*. Another scripted piece, but again flavored with Holmstrom's home-grown humility.

> Well, I honestly thought I would not come out of the Canyons alive. But down in those immense gorges it came over me how really small and insignificant a man is. Then it did not seem to matter so much. The river, the rapids, the canyon walls, stars and moon, took on real friendly personalities.

While he was in San Francisco, Holmstrom worked with his connection at the fair, Ted Huggins. Huggins was a Standard Oil public relations man; Holmstrom had long been an employee of Standard Oil at Walker's service station. Huggins, an instigator of the fair, was coordinating exhibits and events. He was enthusiastic about Holmstrom's participation and put him in touch with one of the concessionaires who would be running sideshows along the strip called the Gayway. In the main part of the fair would be the big national pavilions. Out on the Gayway were the sideshows and exhibits set up for profit, with a charge for admittance. Holmstrom would need a place for the boat and somewhere to show the film as he narrated it. Huggins, friendly and enthusiastic, did what he could, but it was really up to Holmstrom to make it happen.

Amos Burg was back and forth from Oregon to New York, tying up loose ends on other projects and ordering a new boat. A *completely* new boat, in fact: an

Jennings Pierce interviews Holmstrom for the Allis Chalmers Family Hour

inflatable rubber raft. Lifeboats were now being made of rubber, but few had ever tried one on whitewater. Burg thought it would be just the ticket in such rocky water, and contracted with Goodrich Rubber to have one fabricated. Meanwhile, he and Holmstrom corresponded about what sort of cameras and film would be best. Black-and-white movies for ease of reproduction; color movies to wow people; large format black-and-white stills for blow-ups. And large 5 x 7 color transparencies for display mounts at the fair. Burg would put together a film for distribution and they would split the profits fifty-fifty. The world's fair would be Holmstrom's deal.

In June, 1938, the prestigious Explorer's Club in New York notified Holmstrom that he had been accepted as a member. Frazier, Stone, and Eddy had signed his application. What was more, Burg, also a member, had arranged for their trip to be to an official Explorer's Club Expedition, #84. They would fly an Explorer's Club flag.

As the summer went on, though, Holmstrom began to have doubts about their scheme. Although he did not realize it at the time, his solo trip the year before had brought to a close the era of expeditions on the Colorado. Things were changing fast. In May, Holmstrom had received a letter from Norman Nevills of Mexican Hat, Utah. Nevills had been taking tourists for hire down the San Juan River for a few years and was planning a trip through Cataract and Grand Canyons in July, with passengers. What's more, two of the passengers would be women. How could a show about Holmstrom's heroic solo trip remain relevant when it was now becoming a tourist trip that anyone could do? In a letter to his mother he worried: "I guess I told you about the fellow… going down through Glen Canyon in a hog trough, and if that weren't enough trouble, now these women are in the canyon—if they make it, it will be time for me to go and hide somewhere."

Sure enough, the Nevills trip launched amid great fanfare from Green River, Utah. Nevills had built a new style of boat for the trip, vaguely similar to the classic Galloway style, but much wider, for stability. He built his boats of the new wonder material, marine plywood. Nevills brought along Don Harris, a USGS stream gager from Mexican Hat, as one of his boatmen. Harris had had plenty of free time over the winter and had helped Nevills build the boats. The clients were two women from the University of Michigan at Ann Arbor. Dr. Elzada Clover was a botanist, whose primary reason for the voyage was a botanical study and collection along the river. She brought along a twenty-four-year-old assistant, Lois Jotter, both as a helper and for decorum—it was unseemly for a lone woman to be on a trip with men. Two young men would join them; Gene Atkinson, a biologist, would row the third boat, and Bill Gibson would serve as photographer. Nevills had his eye on his business. If this trip went well and there was enough publicity, a steady stream of tourists would be drawn to his fledgling business. The boats had a fresh coat of white paint and "NEVILLS EXPEDITION" written boldly on the side of each boat.

The trip went well for the first 120 miles of flat water leading up to Cataract Canyon. Then things went awry. A boat got loose at the first rapid, and Harris and Jotter had to chase it down. The river was high and some of the rapids did not look runnable. They portaged for days on end in the desert sun. In Gypsum Rapid, Atkinson flipped; they chased his boat for miles. Nevills became increasingly cautious—too cautious, thought some of the younger folks. A rift began to develop with Nevills and Clover on one side and the rest of the group on the other. Exhausted, but through Cataract Canyon, they began to relax, drifting leisurely through the 160 miles of Glen Canyon. Nevills and Clover were in Nevills's boat, and "the gripers," as they called themselves, floated some distance back. By now, they were several days behind schedule.

In the outside world, the media fussed about the "lost" expedition. All eyes were on the Nevills trip, and Holmstrom and Burg's promotion scheme seemed increasingly unlikely. Holmstrom hitched up his boat and headed for Green River, Utah. There a reporter for the *Chicago Tribune* quoted Holmstrom as being "honestly worried" about the Nevills trip. It had only taken Holmstrom ten days to cover the same distance on low water, and Nevills had been out eighteen. By their own schedule, they were four days late. Holmstrom would go to their aid.

Holmstrom took his boat down to the Green River boat ramp. Then word came in: Nevills had arrived at Lees Ferry. The media descended on the Nevills trip. This was big news; reporters interviewed the two women repeatedly. The group, however, was in disarray. The rift had not healed. Don Harris worried that, late as they were here, they would not finish soon enough for him to get back to his job, decided to leave the trip. It was unclear if the expedition would go on. Nevills headed for Mexican Hat with Clover to find another boatman. Jotter, Gibson, and Atkinson remained at Marble Canyon with instructions to repaint the boats.

The next afternoon, Holmstrom pulled in, having driven down from Green River. He explained to Jotter, Gibson, and Atkinson that he had worried about their safety. "Of course'" he added candidly, "I thought there might be some publicity for me, too." The three were delighted to meet the famous Holmstrom. They poured out their story, not omitting their differences of opinions, painting an unflattering picture of Nevills. Holmstrom listened, sympathized with them, and talked of the river. He told them what lay ahead and assured them that, having survived Cataract Canyon, they should have no trouble downstream. That night he bought them dinner. Jotter confessed in a letter home that she "developed a bad case of hero-worship."

The next day they talked and wandered around Marble Canyon Lodge. Holmstrom treated them to lunch. Afterward, he hitched up his boat and prepared to return to Boulder City. Before he left, however, they all walked out onto Navajo Bridge, 460 feet above the river, to say good-bye. Holmstrom gave Jotter something to take along on the trip: his waterproof match case, with a compass on one end and a magnifying glass on the other. Promising to see them when they arrived at Lake Mead, Holmstrom was gone.

Jotter wrote: "We practically wept at parting on the bridge today; laid deep plans to be lost in the next stretch so that he could come look for us."

Inside the cover of her diary Jotter kept a list of bets she had made. A bet with Clover of two pounds of Bonbons from whoever fell out of the boat first; one with Atkinson for a milkshake if he left at Lees Ferry, and so on. To this she added "Buzz—$5.00 & 3 marriage proposals if go to Boulder." The bet was compounded by a statement Holmstrom had made in the *Saturday Evening Post* story. He was speaking of the loss of Glen and Bessie Hyde on their 1928 trip when he said, "Women have their place in the world, but they do not belong in the Canyon of the Colorado." He was going to have a hard time living that one down.

When Nevills got back he had two new boatmen. Gene Atkinson, after a long fiery conversation with Nevills and Clover, headed back to Michigan. Back on the river, the rift began to heal. The new boatmen, Del Reed and Lorin Bell, soon learned enough about rowing to survive. At Phantom Ranch, upon Nevills's invitation, Emery Kolb joined the trip as guest and advisor.

"I GOT QUITE A SCARE yesterday," Holmstrom wrote to his mother from Pearce Ferry. "Someone showed me a paper which said I was on my way down into Marble Canyon with the Nevills party—I thought I was here all the time till I read that.

On Navajo Bridge, Holmstrom gives Lois Jotter his waterproof matchcase

Now I don't know what to think—maybe I am drowned by now."

The news of the Nevills trip was not particularly accurate, but there certainly was a lot of it. Holmstrom wrote to Burg that he did not think much of Nevills, nor did his photographic set-up seem adequate. Hope for the Burg-Holmstrom trip remained. Holmstrom also reported to Julius Stone, one of the few others that knew of the planned trip. Stone, who wanted to see Holmstrom's project succeed, agreed that the Nevills publicity would be a flash in the pan. Stone also sent a check for five hundred dollars, no strings attached, telling Holmstrom to be sure he had top-flight photographic gear. Astonished, Holmstrom wrote back, uncertain how to accept such unsolicited generosity. "Make no apologies or explanations about keeping the check," replied Stone. "I intended it to be of assistance to you in providing the proper equipment so that you may be certain to accomplish all that you set out to do in the way of pictures on your next trip, and if this is achieved I will be more than amply repaid."

Holmstrom's comings and goings from Lake Mead had even Frank Dodge mystified:

> Buzz has been again to Frisco. He's very mysterious and seems to have several irons in the fire, what with affairs going on and perhaps another trip for pictures. Same old Buzz, just as likable, as modest and truthful as ever, which I imagine is why he lasts. He is on the company payroll but comes and goes of his own free will on his own business. He should be sitting on top of the world with no more gas filling duties. People take to him like flies to molasses.

On August 1, Holmstrom was on board a GCBDT plane flying low up the reservoir to check on the Nevills trip. The pilot found them drifting out onto the head of the lake, circled a few times, and headed back to Boulder City. Several hours later a GCBDT tour boat roared up the Canyon and pulled up to Nevills's boats. Buzz Holmstrom was at the helm, all smiles. Doris Nevills was aboard to welcome the expedition, along with several local dignitaries and newspapermen. They motored downstream a few miles to Emery Falls and stopped for lunch. The press continued to hound Clover and Jotter, to the point they could hardly eat their sandwiches. Lunch done, the group took a blistering hike three miles up the steep slopes to Rampart Cave to look at the remains of a prehistoric ground sloth. The

Three eminent boatmen, Lake Mead, 1938. Buzz Holmstrom, Emery Kolb, Norman Nevills

hike exhausted Clover, and Holmstrom had to haul her over the last boulders to the shade of the cave, where she collapsed for a few minutes. When they got back down to the lake, another boat pulled in with more GCBDT folks on board, and Holmstrom turned his boat over to one of the other captains so as to ride up front with the river party.

Holmstrom, however, was uncomfortable, and for reasons other than the heat. Although he was delighted to see his friends and other river-folk, they were now getting the publicity that he had hoped would go toward the Burg-Holmstrom trip. And although he needed publicity and might get some by his presence on the boat, in his heart he truly abhorred limelight. Then there was the matter of Kolb. The last time they had talked was when the Kolbs had entertained him at their home on the rim. They had talked about doing a joint trip to augment Kolb's show—now Holmstrom was secretly planning a rival movie. Kolb, he knew, would be furious. Smiling outwardly, Holmstrom squirmed.

Back in Boulder City, the Nevills group lingered in the showers. They did not get to dinner until eleven. At midnight the younger folks, which presumably included Holmstrom, headed into Las Vegas to see the sights. "A cockeyed idea," wrote Clover. They did not get back until three in three morning.

The next day the Nevills group was escorted around town, interviewed, photographed, wined, and dined. On a tour of Boulder Dam they met Frank Dodge. Dodge had seen the group earlier but his natural suspicion of new folks on the river, combined with the less favorable things he had heard of Nevills, kept him at a distance. Although they did not talk much at the time, Dodge later confessed to being pretty well smitten by Jotter. Tall, strong-boned, with an infectious smile and a sparkle in her eye, Jotter seemed to have the same effect on most boatmen. Holmstrom, too, had a crush on Jotter.

Lois Jotter, left, Dr. Elzada Clover, right

"It's a pity," Jotter admitted more than fifty years later, "but at the time I just didn't think it right to date a man who was shorter than me." Even though Holmstrom may have had to pay off his five dollar bet that she would not make it through, Jotter did not collect the three marriage proposals. Hero worship, yes; romance, no. And, as it turned out, women *did* have their place on the Colorado. Before Jotter left Boulder City, Holmstrom autographed her pith helmet: "To the girl who proved me badly mistaken."

The next day the Nevills party disbanded. Jotter, Gibson and Bell left for California; Kolb and Reed headed to Grand Canyon; Nevills went to Las Vegas to check on his wife, at a doctor's office with a badly infected thumb. Clover, however, stayed in town for another three days and spent a great deal of that time with Holmstrom, talking about the river, looking at pictures, and viewing the film footage from the trip. During that brief time, they became close friends. Holmstrom even confided something that had been troubling him. It turned out that bit about women not belonging on the Colorado had outraged Glen Hyde's sister, and she had written him an angry letter. Holmstrom wondered if Clover would write and apologize for him. He had been meaning to, but the letter never seemed to get written. Clover said she would be happy to set the record straight.

Sensing Holmstrom's longing to be back on the river, Clover told him he should do another trip soon. He hedged, saying that some sort of proposition might be in the works. Clover invited Holmstrom to join them for a trip on the Green River the following year.

Nevills was still in town, and before long Holmstrom reconsidered his estimate of him. Nevills was a river man, the same as Holmstrom. Nevills, to be sure, had a powerful personality. He ran countless river trips over the next twelve years, and his charisma was much of what made them work—if you liked him. When he rubbed someone the wrong way, he alienated them, sometimes permanently. Few who ever met Nevills were indifferent about him. In Holmstrom's case, friendship grew between the two.

Holmstrom painted his gray boat bright red that week, Burg having suggested the change for color pictures. Clothes spattered with paint, he took Nevills and Clover down to see the boat. In honor of his benefactor, Julius F. Stone, he had named it the *Julius F.*

At the end of the week Nevills and Clover left for Mexican Hat, Utah, to float the San Juan River, and Holmstrom began packing. "He left here on a dark night," wrote Frank Dodge, "saying nothing to anyone." Holmstrom's career with Grand Canyon–Boulder Dam Tours, which Sidney Bazett had hoped would last decades, was over after three months. (It would not have lasted much longer in any event. Within a few years, an overextended GCBDT went belly-up and came to be known as GDSOB by local investors and creditors.) For Holmstrom, the only thing that felt right in the tour-captain trade was the hat. For years afterward, Holmstrom wore his jaunty captain's cap, cocked a little to one side. HOLMSTROM ARRIVED in Salt Lake City, on August 9. He hoped to meet Burg there, but there had been repeated assembly delays on the new rubber boat. It would be at least another week. Hack Miller took Holmstrom fishing one day, climbing down into the gorge of the Duchesne River. Holmstrom visited with Doc Frazier, recently diagnosed with diabetes. Although Frazier's river running would be greatly curtailed, he still planned to float Glen Canyon in a

Amos Burg

few weeks. Julius Stone, at the age of eighty-four, would be joining him. They were planning to erect a plaque at the Crossing of the Fathers. With any luck, Burg and Holmstrom might catch them there.

Burg finally arrived, boatless. In Holmstrom's old Buick, they towed the *Julius F.* to Green River, Wyoming. A few days later the new raft arrived on the Union Pacific. Bright yellow, it weighed only eighty-three pounds. Burg, following Holmstrom's lead, named it *Charlie* for Charles Wheeler, a steamship magnate who had donated two hundred dollars to the expedition. An odd contraption in which to run rapids, to be sure, but with twenty-six airtight chambers, it might withstand a few punctures. According to Goodrich, it would float five thousand pounds. The two boatmen spent a few days fashioning a wooden frame to support Burg, his gear, and the oarlocks. As they packaged their equipment, they realized they had more than they could carry; they would have to leave a few cameras behind.

Over the last few months, they had discussed the route of the trip. They would cover all of Holmstrom's run from the previous year, but why not more? For quality photos, Burg thought they should start at the source of the Green, up in the Wind River Mountains. For that matter, they might as well go clear to the Gulf of California: from the mountains to the sea. It had a ring to it; and no one had done it. From early in his boating career, Burg had chosen the longest routes possible, source to sea, for the Snake, Columbia, and Mississippi. They agreed to start at the head of navigation.

They had been staying at Jim Maher's Covered Wagon Auto Camp outside of town, and now that they were ready, Maher agreed to truck them up into the mountains. From Green River, Wyoming, the broad, sagebrush-filled valley of the Green wound north 125 miles, finally narrowing and bending around to the east into the high country. The bend continued around to the south as the river doubled back into the heart of the Wind River Mountains. There the valley abruptly ended at the Green River Lakes. On August 26, Jim Maher dropped Holmstrom, Burg, and their gear on the shore of the lower lake.

A more spectacular place to start a river trip would be hard to imagine. From an 8,000 foot elevation, the sheer-walled granite peaks tower another four thousand feet above the lakes. Squaretop Mountain dominates the view, flanked by White Rock to the east and Tabletop to the west. Between Squaretop and White Rock, past Upper Green River Lake, the embryonic Green River winds a few more miles up into Knapsack Col on the flank of Gannett Peak. There, in a glacier-ringed cirque, the Green River is born. To the north at Three Waters Mountain, the drainage splits three ways: east to the Bighorn, Yellowstone, Missouri, and Mississippi; northwest to the Snake and Columbia; and southwest to the Green and Colorado. Burg and Holmstrom would come to know all these river systems intimately.

The next morning Burg set out with his cameras to scale White Rock, using the fire warden's horse to carry the bulk of his gear. Part way up the mountain, the horse got skittish, launched itself over a cliff, and tumbled nearly three hundred feet down the slope. Miraculously, neither the horse nor the cameras were hurt—minutes later the horse was calmly eating oats. The tripod, however, was destroyed. Horseless, Burg finished the climb and returned to camp exhausted, going to bed without dinner. Holmstrom stayed in camp all day, tending the smoldering fire.

In the morning they rowed across the lake and towed the boats up the half-mile stream to the upper lake, crossed it as well, and hiked up toward the source of the Green. Surrounded by the snow fields of Wind River Mountains, they had lunch. Formally beginning their descent, they returned to the boats, retraced their route, and made camp at the far end of the lower lake.

Amos Burg had been right about the scenery, but he was wrong about the river. The next morning they began four days of utterly miserable boating. Immediately upon leaving the mountain-ringed lakes, the Green enters a broad sagebrush valley. Five miles of fast rapids give way to slower water and great winding loops. The meanders hatch their own meanders. Even during high spring run-off this stretch is shallow and rocky—the low water of late summer made it far worse. They chopped through logs, dragged boats under fences, and towed their way through shallows. Although Burg's raft was able to slither over many obstacles, the *Julius F.*, hard and heavy, was abused. Burg calculated they were making one mile south per hour, and they had sixteen hundred to go.

Cold, rainy weather took away what little enjoyment remained. A rancher at Warren Bridge told them they had at least two hundred miles to go to get to Green River, Wyoming. The meanders got worse and the current slowed. In riffles, the stream accelerated, slamming the *Julius F.* into the uncushioned rocks. At Daniel Bridge they decided that if they hoped to finish the trip they would have to portage back to Green River. Gulf of California talk ceased.

Jim Maher came up the next day and trucked them down to his auto camp, where they spent a day or two refitting for the long run to Jensen, Utah. Burg had invited a couple of people to join them for the next leg of the trip. Charlie Wheeler, his benefactor, wired that he could not make it, but Phil Lundstrom, a friend from Portland, was there to join them.

Lundstrom had rowed on the Oregon State College crew at Corvallis and proved a good hand with boat and camera work. Holmstrom, Lundstrom, and Burg—a regular squareheads' reunion, Holmstrom called it. Lundstrom was six-foot-two, slender, and quiet. "Uncommunicative," said one reporter who interviewed them, "without being unpleasant about it." Lundstrom had met Burg at Gault's Boat Harbor in Portland, where both men often headed out to explore the sloughs of the Columbia delta. Lundstrom had a twenty-five foot cruiser, which he and his fiancée Betty used to poke into the river's-inlets. A graphic artist as well, Lundstrom drafted a handsome map of the expedition's route, and Burg had several hundred of them printed as postcards on which to mail out his journal entries.

Back in Salt Lake, Doc Frazier had decided that they should have a mascot, and sent a raccoon to accompany them. "We were going to take a coon for a mascot," Holmstrom wrote home, "I was to tame him—the best I could do was to tame him to the point where I could pet him with my left hand if I let him gnaw on my right—I sent him back to the fur farm."

The storms that hit them in the mountains got worse; most of the local creeks flooded. The Dry Creek bridge washed out. Additional water was good for the trip, but Holmstrom correctly predicted a quick drop in levels, followed by slimy, muddy shores. On September 3 they headed downstream to the town of Green River, carrying Jim Maher and Adrian Reynolds, editor of the *Green River Star.* Below town one of the lum-

Phil Lundstrom at the tie-boom in Green River, Wyoming

Entering Flaming Gorge (now beneath Flaming Gorge Reservoir)

ber workers opened the tie boom and let them through. Burg wrote in his journal, "The adventurous voyage and my dream of 15 years had actually begun. A thousand cataracts lay between us and Boulder Dam."

They had four times the water Holmstrom had launched on the year before. The going was easier. The storms finally passed and the days turned hot and sunny. Burg got sunburned; Holmstrom was sick to his stomach for a day. On the second afternoon they landed at the Holmes Ranch for lunch with Adrian Reynolds's family and the Holmeses. They took the rest of the day off, had dinner at the ranch, and listened to Holmes's outlaw stories late into the night.

With the water still high, they made good time down to Flaming Gorge, with none of the shallow-water problems that had plagued Holmstrom the year before. Ashley Falls was more powerful, but both boats slipped through without difficulty. They camped deep in Red Canyon near Dutch John Draw. Holmstrom wrote in his journal:

> yesterday was Phil's birthday—I baked him a cake tonight & we will take a picture of it in the morning with a miners candle on it & then eat it—maybe—I put in condensed milk—Pep—bisquick—dry prunes—cheese—walnuts—4 eggs—sugar—lard—cocoa. It doesn't look bad & Phil has been thinking of many excuses to taste it tonight but I'm firm in waiting till tomorrow....

They took most of the next day off. Holmstrom went for a hike up the draw and found that he could not stop climbing. By late afternoon he was on the rim looking down on the tiny boats beached along the ochre river. Every so often he stopped to write about where he was, what sort of plants were about, what smells filled the air, how the rocks looked. The canyon was far prettier than he had realized, but it was getting late. He headed back to camp, where he reported on the fate of the cake:

> the cake fell during the night—pretty soggy—got up at 5 A.M. & started to build frosting—put in eggs, sugar, water & Klim Powder—beat a while & nothing happened—tried to cook in the cup—transferred to pie pan—nothing again so put in kettle—cooked & beat it till it resembled a compromise between wallpaper paste & omelette—smeared it on anyhow to form the name phil—the photo of it went off better than the eating—I don't know yet just what was the matter with it—perhaps it should have had more baking powder—I just threw it away this evening as the blow flies got after it pretty bad this P.M.—We were going to try to eat it like mush tomorrow with milk—anyhow it wasn't burned—if that's an item.

Burg noted that they had heard a rock fall during the night and supposed it to be Holmstrom's cake. He added that he accidentally dropped his share overboard.

At Red Creek Rapid, the first one Holmstrom had portaged a year earlier, the extra water made a big difference. Wrote Lundstrom:

> There seemed to be no possible way of running boats through safely, but Buzz and Amos are undaunted and each selected a different course, certain that his was the only way and the other's was suicidal. Buzz took the deeper channel through the crashing breakers, while Amos preferred the shallow, sliding over many boulders on the way. Both came out without a scratch.

Indeed, their styles were different. Burg's boat lacked the rigidity to withstand the big waves. When the going got rough, the *Charlie* would snake, flop, fold, and turn sideways. Slipping over the shallows with his flexible floor seemed best. Holmstrom, on the contrary, had a rigid boat which the shallow rocks would damage, but he had the punch to blast through the big waves. In many of the rapids, each of them could find a run for his style of boat. Other times, there was only one route, and one boatman was at a disadvantage. In the headwaters, it was Holmstrom, but as they moved downstream, it was more often Burg.

The higher water helped when they got to the Canyon of Lodore as well. At Disaster Falls and Triplet, where Holmstrom had lined the year before, both boats ran without incident. Hells Half Mile looked too violent for the *Charlie*, and they portaged it around the main drop. After a smooth run of the upper part in the *Julius F.*, Holmstrom pulled in to pick up his cargo. Recalled Lundstrom:

> we all pushed out together from Amos's portage, myself in Buzz's boat, and we hardly got out into the torrent when we banged up on a rock that jarred the whole boat with a sickening crash. It was a moment of fast tugging to get off right side up and I think my heart stopped beating as I felt the splinters grind off the boat. We ground on to two more submerged boulders, but the staunch *Julius F.* held and we bobbed safely out to the rolling water at the foot.

That afternoon in Whirlpool Canyon, a fierce rain and hailstorm ambushed them. Holmstrom remembered a good overhanging ledge. "We curled up in it," wrote Lundstrom, "and held our boats on painters, while the boulders roared past the mouth of the niche. Luckily the boats were far enough out in the stream not to be hit by rocks." That night Holmstrom wrote:

> Yesterday Amos opened can beans at noon near Rippling Brook & left opener on can—threw empty can & opener in river—doggone—I gave him the dickens but did even worse at the same stop for I left my sheath knife there—didn't discover it till we got here—beautiful fold in rocks at head of whirlpool—Colors—but so dark no chance for color photos. Amos left his hat at Red Creek & now wears knotted handkerchief on head—with whiskers & dark tan looks like a pirate—Phil is turning dark and whiskery too.... Now starting for Jones Hole Creek to see about Doc's cache & fish, though probably too muddy—Sort of hope so as I have promised to wash up if clear....

Holmstrom was funny about washing. He was most at ease when grubby, dressed in well-worn, preferably tattered clothes. Burg remembered their landlady in Jensen washing Holmstrom's favorite dirty shirt. He was outraged. In the few pictures of him in a clean suit, he looks as comfortable as a wet cat.

They stopped at the Ruple Ranch, where Mrs. Ruple, having heard by radio of their coming, put on a catfish fry. The Ruples were headed into Vernal that night and promised to take word to the Hatch clan of the trip's progress. Holmstrom, Lundstrom, and Burg headed into Split Mountain Canyon. That evening they were reduced to opening the cans of food with an ax.

In the morning Burg, rowing close to the shore to avoid the bigger waves in the main current, hit a large pourover sideways. The reverse wave below rearranged his load and nearly flipped him. After that, wrote Burg, he left the run up to *Charlie* and things got a lot better.

As they neared Jensen that afternoon, they were obliged to stop at Coyne Thorn's ranch for a watermelon lunch in their honor. A few miles farther down, another welcoming committee called them ashore. Finally in Jensen, they checked their gear and were whisked into Vernal for a Lion's Club fete. Frazier, back on his feet, had come east from Salt Lake, and all the local river runners were there. E.C. LaRue, the head geologist from the 1923 USGS trip in Grand Canyon was in town and stopped by as well. From Vernal, Phil Lundstrom hurried back to Portland to his job and Betty.

Over the next few days, Burg caught up on his letter writing. They mailed their exposed film, visited the Dinosaur Quarry, restocked their provisions, and readied their boats. Burg wrote:

> At Jensen we emptied the boats and stored our equipment at Aunt Atta's hotel where we had a room and took meals. For 3 days the screen door

slammed as visitors arrived from the ranges to ask what would happen if *Charlie* struck a sharp rock or ran over a tack. Aunt Atta's bountiful table left us feeling as stuffy as gorged alligators. Jensen is a wide place in road where two men lean back in their chairs with their hats curtaining their eyes and chew tobacco.

Nationwide, publicity was improving. On September 15, *Ripley's Believe-it-or-Not* featured Holmstrom's solo run. Holmstrom's mother had sent Ripley's some information about it a few months earlier, and Bill Belknap, down in Boulder City, sent them a photo for their sketch.

They did not have a monopoly on the media, however. For nearly three months that fall, the weekly *Vernal Express* had at least one article per issue about river running. A particularly unwelcome blow was the article running next to the story about their Lions Club party. A trio of French kayakers had just launched at Green River, Wyoming, with plans to go clear through Grand Canyon. One of them was beautiful Genevieve DeColmont, the twenty-two-year-old bride of the party leader.

A week later the *Express* carried a Tribune Intermountain Service release: *Four Separate Parties Seek River Thrills.* Besides the Burg-Holmstrom trip and the French kayakers, Frazier and Stone had launched their Glen Canyon trip, and Roy DeSpain was heading up a Utah Department of Fish and Game trip through Lodore Canyon. "In fact," the article read, "it has been suggested—jocularly—that traffic lights be installed along the already beaten path to eliminate the possibility of crack-ups." Holmstrom and Burg were not amused.

Another more sinister story ran that fall: dams on the Green River. The first proposal to dam Lodore, Echo Park, and Split Mountain was being seriously discussed and eagerly supported by the local chamber of commerce. Drilling and testing would soon begin. Months earlier, tiny Dinosaur National Monument upstream from Jensen had been enlarged to protect the Lodore, Split Mountain, and Yampa River Canyons, yet the dams being planned would inundate every mile of river within the monument.

Holmstrom and Burg moved on. It took four days to cross the flat Uinta Basin, four days of fighting flies and mosquitoes, squinting into the sun, and constant rowing. At noon one day Burg noted that it was 130 degrees in the sun and one hundred in the shade, but there was no shade. In Desolation Canyon the current picked up and they stopped for a few photographs. Now that it was just the two of them, it was harder to set up for pictures.

At the Seamount Ranch they met Elmer King, a lonely caretaker who gave them all the melons they could carry. The rapids were not difficult through this stretch, and even though the water continued to drop, it was still higher than it had been the previous year. Although Burg and Holmstrom did not agree on everything, they got along fine and respected each other's abilities. "Buzz is a superb boatman, very rhythmic in thought and action," Burg wrote, and "is accurate as a knife thrower." "Amos," wrote Holmstrom, "is the best boatman I have seen—a very hard worker."

Just a week out of Jensen they tied up by the bridge in Green River, Utah. As earlier, word preceded them and locals held a series of receptions. Bert Loper stopped by to visit. Don Harris heard they were in, and drove down from Salt Lake City. Norm Nevills came up from Mexican Hat, and made plans to meet them at the confluence of the Green and Colorado. He figured he could come down the Colorado side from Moab in one of his boats and motor back up afterward.

They had missed Phil Lundstrom's assistance in Desolation and let it be known they were looking for a helper to go downriver with them. Several men stopped by to declare their availability, but one fellow in particular came by every evening.

Willis Johnson, called Bill by his friends, was a short, stocky young Mormon from Thistle, Utah. He and his brother Hal had been losing wages to the company store at the mines near Salt Lake. Moreover, Hal had tangled with a sheriff and it was time to leave town. They decided to try their luck picking cantaloupes, but as it turned out, Hal also picked a fight with the Green River sheriff, and ended up in the local jail.

Johnson had rowed on lakes while fishing with his father and knew his way around boats. He was cheerful and strong. What clinched the job for him, however, was his ability as a storyteller. Each evening, as Burg told it, Johnson would get about halfway into a good story and then have to leave. Same thing the next night. They had to take him along to find out what happened.

They wrote letters, shipped film, hobnobbed, and prepared their boats for Cataract Canyon. Holmstrom cleaned and tightened up the *Julius F.*; Burg built a canvas spray shield around the cockpit of *Charlie* to keep more water in the river,

Willis Johnson

less in the boat. Holmstrom did a little sewing: "Pants going bad—had them off patching them at G R in tent when visitors came & had to lay low for awhile—may have to take day off & sew on some canvas."

They expanded their larder for the long leg to Lees Ferry, topping off their supplies with a few dozen of the finest Green River melons, donated by the townsfolk. Their overloaded boats looked like fruit stands. Burg noted, "Watermelon party tonight by Civic Club and what melons!"

As they made final preparations to leave, Bert Loper told the locals that the next time they would hear about these guys would be in the obituary column. In fact they would probably drown in The Auger, a few miles south of town. Loper's motives, Johnson believed, were honorable. Loper merely wanted to keep the local lads from drowning themselves.

In a fragment that survives from an otherwise lost manuscript, *Oars Against the Rio Colorado*, written by Johnson about his journey, he told a story of their departure that day.

> I didn't see Amos's girlfriend of the past few days in the crowd but I suppose he said his good-byes to Maxine in private last night.…Not far below town a man on a horse galloped into view along the far shore, waving and shouting, and occasionally firing his shotgun. Must have been a military farewell of sorts. From where we were, it looked like that "committee-of-one" resembled very much pretty Maxine's father.
>
> But already Amos, wiry built and tall, captivatingly good looking, so witty and worldly, is pushing eagerly ahead of us with only an occasional glance over his shoulder. Such enthusiasm is seldom seen.

A few miles below Green River, they stopped at Crystal Geyser, a failed oil well turned natural wonder. They were lucky to capture a minor eruption on film, with shirtless Holmstrom showering beneath its carbonated water. They awaited one of the hundred-foot eruptions, but as dusk approached, none came. They pushed on.

The wide vistas of Labyrinth Canyon provided superb still photos, among the best of the trip, and Burg made several posing Holmstrom against the winding desert gorge. Johnson took turns spelling each of them at the oars. As promised, he proved to be adept at rowing—so much so that he kept his eyes on the driftwood for a usable boat for himself. Holmstrom, for better or worse, remained the head cook:

> Neither Amos or Bill feel very good—I make apricot cobbler—first bunch dried apricots too wormy to use at all—second bunch I pick off all I can—put in water & warm & they crawl out & I skim them off—make fine cobbler—even tastes good.

To which Burg added: "The tea tasted funny. Buzz had forgotten to take the dish rag out of the tea pot."

Just above the junction of the Green and Colorado, Holmstrom and Burg made the climb to the rim to photograph the confluence. The view was spectacular, hundreds of square miles of impassable canyon country on every side. Wrote Holmstrom:

> climb up in 1½ hrs—easy climb—limestone ¾ way up—Pines ¾ way up—few scrub cedar up here on top—rocks rounded—mosques & minaret—red & white—nice pools clear water on rocks—welcome—La Sal Mts to south—upturned strata at junction—Colorado looks bigger—very red—decided contrast with yellow of Green—as far as can see down Green quiet—can hear water up here—many pictures—all kinds of deer sign—squirrels & lizards....

They camped at the confluence that night and readjusted and retightened their loads. Nevills, who had planned to meet them there, did not show up; motor trouble had sent him back to Moab.

Holmstrom had been toying with Burg, telling him of bottomless whirlpools and the vast number of deaths in Cataract. Burg took it in stride, and though admittedly nervous, headed bravely into Cataract the next morning. As usual Holmstrom ran the big breakers down the middle with Johnson clinging to the stern deck, swallowing the waves. Burg, in his floppy inflatable raft, snaked down the side. When Burg happened to end up in the big waves, *Charlie* sometimes folded up, giving Burg the appearance of a hot-dog in a large yellow bun. Johnson found a driftwood boat, named it *Levi*, and let it run itself while he watched from Holmstrom's boat. *Levi* fared poorly.

At Mile Long Rapid, Burg lined along the shore while Holmstrom ran the center. A mile farther, they stopped at Big Drop Three, the one Holmstrom had portaged the year before. The water was still considerably higher than the previous year and the tight left channel looked runnable. Because it was too late in the day to attempt the tricky rapid, they crossed to the right side and camped on a sandbar.

The next morning they crossed back to look at the channel. Said Burg:

> Buzz...pointed to a channel down the left side, but I could see little else but great boulders over which the Colorado fumed and thundered. Lined *Charlie* so his bow wouldn't flip back and hit me on the head.

Johnson was dubious.

> It looked almost hopeless to run it.... We set up two of the movie cameras on the shore midway through the rapid at a good vantage place and signaled Buzz that we were ready.

Holmstrom lined up for the drop, to this day one of the more deceptive rapid entries on the river. He described his run:

> Left channel crooked at head—dodge to right of hole below submerged

> rock—strong current to right as water starts over—I am too far to right—but strong boil comes in from right & shoves boat back OK—just hang on & go through dry—It seems to me though that it's the most dangerous place so far.

Holmstrom had not missed a run this trip. The four rapids he lined or portaged the year before—Red Creek, Lower Disaster Falls, Lower Triplet, and Big Drop Three—he had now run. The only rapid he had not yet run lay more than three hundred miles downstream in Grand Canyon: Lava Falls. To Holmstrom's knowledge, it had never been run.

Holmstrom was relieved to be through the Big Drops; too relieved. Twice that afternoon he struck rocks, the second time hard enough to crack the hull. Not seriously, however; a small repair in camp made it as good as new.

Johnson loved the trip. He was not getting paid, of course, but it beat mining or picking cantaloupes. Soaked half the time, baking in the sun the other half, he was forever smiling. On the occasions when Holmstrom and Burg disagreed about something, Johnson was immediately between them, defusing the disagreement with a story and a smile. "We never sulked," wrote Burg, "nor did we argue too unintelligently, even when under the utmost strain."

Dark Canyon Rapid, today submerged beneath Lake Powell, still had to be reckoned with. While Burg could slip along the shallow shore, Holmstrom had to ride the deeper wave train right up to the wall—then manage to miss it.

By this time, Holmstrom was master of the stern-first Galloway technique, and ran most rapids looking downstream, pulling upstream, sliding off to the side of the bad spots. But there were occasional places where this did not work well. Diagonal waves could defeat attempts to move laterally, whereupon a boat would be surfed out to the middle, the very place the boatman had hoped to avoid. Dark Canyon was one of these.

The Hatch boys had a different approach to rapids; they cranked downstream backwards, the bow of the boat breaking through the waves. Although they wrecked more often, there were situations where this technique was preferable. Holmstrom had talked at length with Frazier, Swain, Hatch, and others about this bow-first technique. They could not understand why Holmstrom did not use it; he could not understand why they did.

It stayed in Holmstrom's mind, however. There was more than one way to skin a rapid, and he began experimenting with the bow-first technique. By using the bow-first technique when making an entry move, he could punch through a rapid's initial lateral waves. Then the bow, hitting slower water near shore, spun the boat around into the traditional Galloway pose. At that point, well off to the side of the wave train, the boat was in the perfect position to complete the run.

At Dark Canyon Holmstrom tried this hybrid technique, punching out of the main-wave train and spinning. It worked well—a new trick, and one that would serve him well in Grand Canyon. (Today, this hybrid technique is common. The move is called "Powelling," or "downstream ferrying," and is an integral part of rowing technique. Holmstrom, however, had to devise it for himself.) Camped at the foot of the rapid, Holmstrom, Burg, and Johnson added their names to the growing list of river runners painted on the wall.

> My pants clear gone, & Amos gives me one of his—too long & too small around—otherwise good fit—make fine biscuits—cheese & nuts—storm—lightning thunder & rain—moon comes out about 10 & the canyon is sure pretty—very narrow—loud noise from rapid—fine.

By lunch the next day they were out of Cataract and through Narrow Canyon. They stopped at the Chaffin Ranch, where they heard of another lone boater. Jack Aldridge had passed through a few weeks earlier in a crude boat of his own making, hoping to do a bit of prospecting on his way to Boulder Dam. A painter from Palm Springs, California, Aldridge had stopped in Mexican Hat on his way to the river and studied Nevills's squared-off San Juan punt boats. Then, at Green River, Utah, he bought a stack of pine lumber and nailed his craft together. Aldridge had survived Cataract Canyon and visited with the Chaffins. Continuing on, he said he might stop at the San Juan River to prospect.

The Chaffins restocked Holmstrom and Burg's trip with melons and other fresh food; although they begged them to spend the night, the boatmen wanted to make a few more miles.

For the next few days they rowed through the spectacular flat water of Glen Canyon, poking into narrow side canyons, exploring Indian ruins, making miles. After investigating one of the many alcoves Powell had named, Holmstrom wrote, "I believe Music Temple is the most beautiful place I ever saw." Holmstrom and Johnson went wandering up a side canyon one afternoon, lost track of time, and came hurrying back to the boats after dark. Burg was long gone; he had left hours before to make camp. Holmstrom and Johnson pushed off to find him. After floating an hour or so they heard what sounded like a rapid drawing near. They were just about to pull over and bivouac for the night when they saw Burg's fire, burning brightly, just above the noisy riffle at Aztec Creek.

The next morning at first light, Burg and Holmstrom headed up the side canyon for Rainbow Bridge. The hike was beautiful; they scrambled from pool to pool, up a small clear stream in a narrow, sinuous sandstone canyon. Rainbow Bridge was overwhelming. They were amazed too, to find that there were more than two thousand signatures in the register ahead of them, many of the visitors having hiked in by way of the long overland trail from Navajo Mountain. The last names signed were Russell Frazier and Julius F. Stone. Stone, at eighty-four, had made the march up to the bridge just ten days earlier. Although Holmstrom and Burg had hoped to catch up with Frazier and Stone on the river in Glen Canyon, time had slipped away.

Glen Canyon near Oak Creek (Now sub-merged by Lake Powell)

The following day they passed the new plaque Frazier and Stone had installed, commemorating the long-lost and recently rediscovered Crossing of the Fathers. In 1776, two Franciscan priests and their party had crossed the river at this spot, returning to Santa Fe from a failed overland attempt to reach California. That night, the boatmen camped at the foot of the cliff just upstream from Navajo Bridge, choosing to replicate Holmstrom's climb in and out of the Canyon rather than using the far easier access at Lees Ferry. They climbed to Marble Canyon Lodge and checked for mail.

They learned that the film they had sent to Paramount had developed beautifully: well exposed, good composition, solid action shots. Very good news. Frazier had left a note as well, filled with admiration and encouragement for Holmstrom and Burg's boating. He also had some bad news for the Lone Voyager film. While the French kayakers were doing fine, yet another trip had launched from Wyoming —Stewart Gardiner, solo, in a German folding kayak was on the water headed for Jensen. Meanwhile, Jack Aldridge, the lone boater who had launched from Green River, Utah, was missing and had not been seen since leaving Chaffin's ranch two months earlier. Would all these stories bring more attention to Holmstrom's tale, or would they drown it out? Inundation appeared more likely.

Although he claimed to hate writing letters, Holmstrom wrote often and kept in touch with a large number of his friends. He wrote his mother at every opportunity.

Other relatives received letters regularly, as did Coquille friends and most of the river runners he had met in recent years. But he made an extra effort to keep in touch with Lois Jotter. While most letters carried the usual news, the ones to Jotter were, if anything, almost affectionate. Years later Willis Johnson said Holmstrom had talked at length about Jotter and confessed he had really fallen for her.

From Green River, Holmstrom had written, "I don't know why I made such a parting remark at Boulder—I really think you fit into the river life just as well as any man I know & a lot better than some.... Sure would like to hear from you...."

Jotter wrote back. Letters were waiting at many of the stops along the way. From Marble Canyon, Holmstrom wrote,

> I'm beginning to think perhaps women could really do some good on a trip like this by keeping everyone cheerful and the general appearance a little better—for instance if a woman were along I probably would have taken the bath I have been promising Amos I would take ever since we left Green River Lakes—maybe even have shaved....
>
> I can't picture you all powdered up and painted up & all dressed up in a dress—just like white folks & I don't think I would like you as well that way as all tanned and weatherbeaten & run down at the heels a little, in an old pair of slacks with the sweater you didn't like....

As he had the year before, Holmstrom took the bus to Flagstaff. He mailed the exposed film and bought new supplies, getting back to the bridge after dark and climbing down the cliff by flashlight. Holmstrom launched the next morning with cotton in one ear for an earache, sand in the other ear from the wind that had blown all night—and still blew. He had slept little during the last two nights on the bus; a little whitewater improved things. Although heavy rains in the high country had given them rising water all the way through Glen Canyon, the water level was now starting to drop. Even so, it remained a good deal higher than last year. The rapids were less rocky, making for more carefree runs down the deep-water channels. For Holmstrom, much of the trepidation of last year's run had dissolved. He and Johnson delighted in the big water. At some rapids, Johnson stayed ashore to run one of the cameras. He quickly learned to hold the movie camera rock steady, panning the scene by slowly rotating his whole body at ankle level. So steady was his hand that he earned the nickname (after a newspaper accounts along the way had garbled his name) of "Bill Willis Twillis Twilliger Rock of Gibraltar Johnson." At rapids where only one camera was necessary, Johnson crouched down out of sight in Holmstrom's cockpit, the waves pouring down his neck.

Burg, on the other hand, was finding the water a bit too big for floppy *Charlie*. Whenever the going got rough, *Charlie* buckled and folded, allowing little comfort or control. Worse, there was not much point in trying to cheat off to the side in many of the big rapids—often the edges were even steeper and more full of holes than the center. As a result, the trio had to portage or line *Charlie* around most of the big rapids. For Burg, though, it was not a matter of running them all. He was along to get the pictures and survive.

At South Canyon they went exploring, looking for a skeleton Frazier had discovered on his 1934 trip. They found it, still lying at the foot of a cliff, one arm and one leg broken, apparently from a fall. Johnson's watch had ceased working some time ago, so he took it off, scratched his name on the back of it, and slipped it onto the skeleton's good wrist. A subsequent expedition reported finding the remains of Willis Johnson in the canyon.

A few days later a sobering sight brought them to shore at the foot of Lava Canyon Rapid: a relatively new boat, wrecked and washed up on the beach. On inspection they decided it must be Jack Aldridge's—it fit the description. There was no sign of Aldridge, nor had there been any trace upstream. His remains were never found.

A few miles later they set a huge driftwood pile afire within sight of the Desert View Watchtower on the South Rim. This was the traditional signal that a river party was alive and headed for Bright Angel within a day or two. That afternoon, at Hance Rapid, Holmstrom attempted the same difficult run he had made there a year earlier. This time, rather than portage his gear down the long trail to the foot, he tried running with a full load. He regretted it. Unaccustomed to moving a full boat that quickly, he missed his move and came in late. The *Julius F.* hit a rock and careened through with little grace.

> Now I could have gone to the right between two buried rocks—or turned & went through sideways wave bow 1st & missed rock I hit—but anyhow I didn't & the buried ones are awfully hard to see from above—Rowed harder in Hance than I ever did before—If I had unloaded would have been OK— Oh well—must patch boat at Bright Angel as a little water in front hold.

They headed downstream into the Granite Gorge late in the day, slipping through Sockdolager almost dry. In the small rapid below Sockdolager, a sucking boil-line nearly flipped Burg. They camped at dusk just above Grapevine Rapid, cold and wet.

They started early the next morning:

> 85 mile Rap deep trough & hi reverse wave—Line Amos's boat—I tow it out above rapid & turn loose as can't push out far enough from shore—goes O.K. then I run bow 1st & nose into quiet water at right missing big waves—there are sure times when a little bow 1st is O.K.

A few miles farther on, an unexpected wave turned the *Julius F.* on edge. Johnson and Holmstrom hurled their weight to the high side and managed to stay upright. An hour later, they pulled up on the beach at Bright Angel Creek and made camp early.

The next day, Burg and Holmstrom hiked to the rim. Anna Holmstrom had another surprise for her brother. The previous year, while at the South Rim, he had learned of her marriage. This year, Holmstrom found out he was an uncle. June Smith had been born while her uncle was running the Colorado.

Burg was able to reach friends at United Press and have his account of the trip sent out on the wires. He released a second story detailing the finding of Aldridge's boat, mentioning, of course, the Holmstrom-Burg trip as discoverers. Holmstrom wrote to his mother about a third story that went out:

> If you read or hear something I said about the trip, don't take it too seriously, as a newspaper man here sent out some quotations from me before he ever talked to me. In fact, I haven't talked to him yet and some of the things I'm supposed to have said make me cringe a little....

They saw Emery Kolb briefly—he was none too happy about their filming. Kolb had always felt river photography was his domain; now here was Holmstrom in competition with him. Kolb felt betrayed, and had little good to say about either Holmstrom or Burg thereafter. Holmstrom was uncomfortable. Although Kolb drove them back to the trail head, it was a quiet drive. By dark they were back at the river.

Johnson had stayed at the river, his tennis shoes worn too thin for a major hike. He busied himself around camp, getting gear in order for the next leg of the trip. "I washed Buzz's undershirt," he recalls, laughing. "It was getting so stiff I was afraid it would break."

The next morning Holmstrom and Johnson went up to Phantom Ranch, the small tourist outpost a mile up Bright Angel Creek. They stopped at the little store to pick up some groceries—potatoes, coffee, onions, butter, cocoa, and sugar. They shared a beer with Mr. Shirley, who managed the place, and asked to settle up. No charge. Thanking him profusely, they got a couple more beers for the trail.

"We thought they were three-point-two percent beers but they were *six* percent!" said Johnson years later. Half drunk, they headed back to the beach, flopped down on the sand and got to talking. Holmstrom, who normally kept to himself, opened up, and so did Johnson. "That's when we really got to know each other," recalls Johnson. "We talked about everything."

On the first leg of the trip, Phil Lundstrom, who had known Burg before the trip, said he preferred riding with Burg, that he and Holmstrom had never really connected. It was the reverse with Johnson. Although he and Burg got along fine, and would go on more trips together in the future, it was with Holmstrom that he really identified. Fifty years after Holmstrom's death, Willis Johnson still shakes his head in sorrow over the loss. They were brothers. Buzz, he said, was the best boatman there ever was and the best friend anyone could ever be.

Burg wrote profusely all during the trip, and at each brush with civilization would spend days catching up on his writing. He then mailed his journal entries to his secretary, who typed them onto several sets of Lundstrom's map-postcards. These were addressed to the National Geographic Society, Frances Holmstrom, Colonel Birdseye, Julius Stone, and several others. The secretary then stamped the cards and sent them in a large envelope back to the post office where Burg had first mailed the journal entries out—Jensen, Green River, Marble Canyon, and so forth—where they were postmarked and redelivered. Thus each of the persons on Burg's list received a typed set of his journal cards with the appropriate postmark. The posting date was off by about a month, but that did not matter. Burg was good at promotion.

"Oct 24—hope Amos gets all writing done today so we can start tomorrow," wrote an impatient Holmstrom. No luck.

"Oct 25—stay over."

"Oct 26—off at 11:00"

They took Wilbur and Florence Stuart from the USGS gaging station for a short splashy ride down to the foot of the Bright Angel Trail. Leaving them there, the expedition was finally off on the last long leg of the trip. Burg lined at Horn Creek and Granite Falls. Holmstrom shot on through with little problem.

The next day got off to a rough start. At Hermit Rapid, Holmstrom lost both

Holmstrom and Johnson below Granite Falls, Grand Canyon

oars and spun sideways through several waves before he was able to regain his oars and straighten out. About a half mile below, Burg, for the third time that trip, remembered he had left a camera at the head of the rapid. Holmstrom and Johnson rowed upstream as far as they could and climbed the rest of the way back to retrieve it. Then in Boucher Rapid, Holmstrom's left oar handle got caught in his pocket. "Now that seemed funny, but not at the time as I couldn't free it for a second or two & they counted there...."

Below Tuna Creek, Burg was caught against the right cliff and lost his right oar as the tubes of his raft sucked beneath the surface. Holmstrom and Johnson swept downstream, unable to help. After a short struggle, Burg pried himself loose, regained his oars, and caught up.

After that, Turquoise Rapid looked especially bad to Burg. The center wave train was huge and there was no way to avoid it by lining, nor any shore to line from. He wrote:

> Viewed this with anxiety and it took several recitations of Ulysses calling upon his comrades "To shove off and smite the sounding furrows" to arouse enough shaky kneed courage to shove off in *Charlie*. At the foot intrepid Buzz complimented this performance and added soberly, referring to *Charlie* "That thing isn't safe."

The next day was no smoother. In the morning Holmstrom tried to punch out of the wave train at Ruby Canyon Rapid with the bow-first technique and did not make it. He ended up backing down through the big stuff, cockpit submerged, and his sweater and map swept overboard. At Serpentine Rapid he was carried frighteningly close to the right cliff at the bottom, but washed clear. Burg lined both rapids.

That afternoon at Waltenberg Rapid, Holmstrom tried to skirt the big waves, sliding off to the right into shallower water. He smacked two rocks, one of them fairly hard. Pulling into camp at the foot of the rapid, he found that he had broken a three-by-eight inch hole in the side of the *Julius F.* This was the third time he had damaged the boat this trip, still remarkable considering how heavy a load he was carrying and how low the water was. By this time, they were running on a little less than 10,000 CFS—a stage that even modern professional boatmen consider "a little bony."

Holmstrom's rowing style continued to evolve throughout the trip, and he used the bow-first entries more often and with better results. "This bow first is a lifesaver some times," he wrote. After finishing his patch at Waltenberg, he told Burg he would be more careful from here on out. He had only enough material for one more patch.

A day later, as they were carrying gear around Dubendorff Rapid, Burg noted,

As we portaged, picked up relics of Eddy Expedition which they cast off to lighten loads after losing a boat here in 1927. Bill, with spirit of retriever generously shares all his booty with us, carrying nothing for himself unless he first offers it to us. His ready laugh, willingness and appreciation is so likable that he is tremendous lesson to me. What most of us excuse in ourselves as being human is mostly downright orneriness. Bill has some of the qualities that the whole human race might acquire in a half million years.

Holmstrom ran Dubendorff in the same manner as he had the year before; Burg lined it. They rowed another twelve miles to camp at Kanab Creek. Thirty-six more miles the next day brought them to the head of Lava Falls, the only rapid Holmstrom had not yet run. Although Holmstrom had not talked much about it, it had been on his mind: he wanted to run it, but thought he should portage, but…

After scouting, Johnson wrote,

This trip Buzz has run every rapid but it looks like this rapid will have to be portaged. If it does, it will be the first time Buzz has had to line or portage this trip. We believe Buzz to be the best boatman in the world, but I don't suppose he will attempt this death trap of the Colorado River.

Holmstrom had other thoughts:

Have looked Lava F over & will try to run it in the A.M. on right—will line *Charlie* down & have ready below but I don't think it would be much good as if one misses there it's probably just too bad.

They went to bed without discussing it further. Burg:

All night the subdued thundering mutter of Lava Falls hung in the air of the worst stretch of waters I had seen from the Continental Divide. Up at daybreak to gaze down on a foaming mass of holes and breakers and rocks through which no channel existed.

Holmstrom:

Ran Lava Falls about 50 times in my mind before I went to sleep and about that many more after, and I made it OK just about half the time. Had an awful time getting to sleep—couldn't eat much supper and not much breakfast.

Burg:

To share no part of his decision, I kept silent but at breakfast Buzz admitted half-bashfully like a schoolboy bringing an apple to teacher that he would run. Lined Charlie to foot to have in readiness.

Holmstrom:

On pins and needles—this waiting around before running them is just terrible—this A.M. unloaded boat—carried to foot on left—Lined down Charlie—then Amos climbs left and makes some pictures and then comes down near river and sets Bill up with 35MM and makes some still shots and then goes down to cross to left below for pictures of running—I cross over above to right & wait for him to get ready—seems as though he never will—this A.M. rapid looks worse than last night and I think I will go crazy waiting—it just doesn't look possible this A.M.

Burg:

Could see Buzz was growing increasingly nervous.

Holmstrom:

Ready at last though, go down to head and pull in below big rock on right bank to get in position—miss first time and make a circle in eddy and then try again—go just right—bow straight across to left and go into lower end of hole—just right—any closer and would go into hole and any further down would carry into waves on right—boat hangs there a second and suction pulls over to left into proper place—turn bow down and cut into edge of hole below on left of waves—just right place and bow stops almost in dead water and current carries stern down turning boat crossways of river headed to left—pull straight across and into clear and go through easy waves in lower end dry—and happy—I scarcely know just what happened myself—didn't take long—It was just like a giant hand took hold of the boat at the upper end and set it over and steered it through—I would hesitate before running it again—it's the worst one I ever tackled—the boat works just perfect.

Burg:

As he passed my camera at lower end he let out a triumphant 'Yippee!' In that moment he became the First Voyager to successfully run all Colorado River rapids.

Johnson:

How he battled the swift current that tried to hurl him into the holes and ledges and yet won through is a great wonder. We were so overjoyed and happy that later we climbed back up along the right shore of the falls and Buzz explained to us just how he run it. It was very exciting for a while.

He had done it, and as it turned out, he was the only boatman to run *all* the major rapids, including Separation and Lava Cliff. No one else ever got the chance. Since Holmstrom's run a year earlier, Lake Mead had risen seventy-five feet, burying the last two major rapids in a thick blanket of silt.

And although Holmstrom was the first to publicly acknowledge running Lava Falls, earlier accounts of the feat have since come to light: Flavell in 1896, Glen and Bessie Hyde on their ill-fated 1928 sweep scow run, and Jack Harbin a month later on his search for the Hydes. Holmstrom was one of the few to run the rapid before the catastrophic 1939 Prospect Canyon debris flow further intensified Lava Falls.

THE WEATHER SOURED ABRUPTLY; howling winds assaulted them and temperatures plummeted. Lunch was half sand, as were dinner and breakfast. After the excitement of Lava Falls, the long calm stretch below with its dreary, heavily-faulted walls, was anticlimactic. The post-Lava slump hit Burg hard:

> The voyager feels an awed wonder in these gloomy depths. All those who have traveled here have emphasized the depressing effects that the dark forbidding walls have had upon them. Even conservative Stone writes that the difficulties usually justified their anxieties. Above Bright Angel with spirits buoyantly fresh, expeditions recorded their passages in several places by inscribing their names on canyon walls; since Bright Angel there has been no such exultation in conquest. Impatient, too, of any delay we pushed on....

That night, in a whirling cloud of sand at Diamond Creek, their campfire blew out. Huddled in the tent, they ate a cold dinner from cans.

The next morning broke calm and they moved on. They ran several tricky rapids without much trouble and in the early afternoon, arrived at Separation Rapid. Burg entered first, but the current barely quickened before it slowed, pooled, and died in the rising reservoir. Neither Separation nor Lava Cliff ever surfaced again. Holmstrom, Burg, and Johnson camped on a deathly quiet spit of sand two miles below. Wrote Holmstrom: "Seems funny to be on the lake again safe & sound—feel somewhat like last year—sorry to be here in a way—Boat pretty well battered up—but a new bottom would fix her up as good as ever...."

Burg's final entry, in part lifted from Powell's journal, ended here:

> We run *Charlie* and *Julius F.* through the final breakers into calm waters of Lake Mead and pitch camp. Dangers and triumphs over, our freedom is ecstasy. The river flows by in silent majesty. On this beach I taste a moment of perfect peace. Tomorrow we row out of the western portals of Grand Wash Cliffs to Boulder Dam and our voyage will become a memory. But the fascination of these hazardous steps in the drama of human endeavor is, I hope, only a prologue. For like Ulysses, "My purpose holds, to sail beyond the sunsets and the baths of all the western stars..." and in the end say, "I am a part of all that I have met."

Early the next morning, Burg began rowing down the lake. Holmstrom and Johnson caught up with him around dusk. They had a quick dinner and rowed on in the twilight. In the darkness, they heard the trickling of Emery Falls as they slowly passed by. Observed Holmstrom:

> 3 hours more puts us at Pierces Ferry—beautiful moonlit eve—Emerge from
> the Grand Wash Cliffs by moonlight—certainly a beautiful way to finish the
> canyon trip. The river has been more than kind to us this trip.

Phil and Em Poquett were delighted to see the three boatmen at Pearce Ferry. They offered them the tent cabins and helped arrange to get them towed down to Boulder Dam. Holmstrom and Johnson declined the tents and slept on the shore beneath the stars. The next day the up-lake wind was too fierce to fight; they rested and ate with the Poquetts. The change in cuisine from Chef Holmstrom's fare was greatly appreciated. Holmstrom wrote the last lines in his journal that morning:

> Probably no boat today so we will rig Phil's outboard on Julius & start down
> as soon as possible—Out of spuds.

The wind kept up, and the following afternoon they came up with a new plan. They hoisted *Charlie* onto the deck of the *Apache*, one of the large GCBDT tour boats that Poquett operated. They climbed aboard and towed the *Julius F.* against the wind to Hemenway Harbor, two miles above the dam, arriving around five in the afternoon on November 8, just seventy-five days from the Green River Lakes.

A small crowd gathered to meet them. Johnson's brother, sister, and mother had driven down from Thistle, Utah, and Holmstrom's Aunt Emma and Uncle Roy had come over from Santa Barbara. A few reporters were there as well, snapping photos and asking questions. This was the last chance for a little publicity to boost Holmstrom's chances of getting his world's fair concession off the ground. As he walked around the front of the boat to step off, he grabbed a rope to steady himself. The rope was loose and Holmstrom, suddenly off balance, fell unceremoniously into the lake. It was the first time he had fallen in the whole trip. Johnson, highly amused, never dared to tell Holmstrom he had untied the rope seconds before.

As soon as the Western Union office opened the next morning, Holmstrom sent a telegram home to his mother in Coquille.

OK AGAIN

HALDANE

11AM

THERE WAS LITTLE ENCOURAGING NEWS in Boulder City. Although Ted Huggins telegrammed Holmstrom to hurry over to San Francisco with beard intact and boat in tow, it was becoming obvious that the concessionaire Holmstrom had to work through was getting cold feet. The cost of erecting and operating a small auditorium and display area for one of many river runners appeared exorbitant.

Burg headed to California; Holmstrom caught a ride with Johnson's family as far as Salt Lake City. He took the bus from there to Green River, still planning to go to San Francisco and give it his best effort. Returning through Salt Lake City, he checked in with Doc Frazier, Hack Miller, and the rest of the gang. Miller wrote a full-page spread about Holmstrom's latest conquest. First to run them all! Miller included Holmstrom's description of running Lava Falls, and added another slice of Holmstrom's humble pie:

> I didn't know what went on. I would swear I didn't dip an oar. I felt as if I were in a nut shell and some all powerful hand reached out and guided me through the rapid. How long I was in there I don't know. I never hit a rock nor did I pick up a drop of water. I can hardly wait to see the movies to see what really happened. I might have lost consciousness for all I know. That is the most humble feeling I have ever witnessed.

Holmstrom hurried on to Boulder City, loaded up the *Julius F.* and headed to San Francisco.

The fair was to be held on Treasure Island, newly built in the middle of San Francisco Bay. For years, the Army Corps of Engineers had hauled loads of rock out to the north shore of Yerba Buena Island, and after walling in some four hundred acres of shoal, pumped it full of dredgings from the floor of the bay, creating a new island. The plan was to build a new international airport there. They had just completed two of the most spectacular spans in the world: the Golden Gate Bridge and Oakland Bay Bridge. At its midpoint, the latter provided access to the new island. It had been Ted Huggins's idea to hold a world's fair on the island before the airport opened, and the Bay Area cities eventually agreed.

It was a time to celebrate. The beautiful new bridges were complete, the country was finally emerging from the Depression, and a promising future was in the air. It would be a brief carefree moment, however, as Europe was already plunging into World War II.

An ephemeral city rose out of the muck. Dozens of pavilions, monuments and displays in the Art Deco style went up overnight, centering on the immense Tower of the Sun. Acres were planted with flowers; trees were hauled in; pools, fountains, statues, murals were constructed. Each night, thousands of colored spotlights lit the buildings and grounds. Few who saw it would forget the bejeweled phantasmagoria.

Holmstrom met Burg on Treasure Island and set about salvaging his dwindling prospects. Years later Burg offered his perspective on what happened:

> A deal that looked good to him the year before had insurmountable problems. He would have to have an auditorium (small), have a film operator and a ticket seller. He would be charging for an exhibit where all the others were free. And the space rental was big. And Buzz was modest and shy, not a talker. He just decided he couldn't do it.

After a few disappointing days, the inevitable became obvious. Burg had a photo assignment at Mount Shasta and left. Holmstrom drove back to Coquille, towing the *Julius F.*

In Coquille, Holmstrom was still a hero. For weeks he had been in the national press. He had run *every* rapid. The Lions Club requested him as a speaker, as did most of the other clubs in town. But Holmstrom was not in the mood. He wrote Lois Jotter:

> I sure fooled the natives here—they had a number of speaking engagements fixed up for me—and I turned them all down—not going to talk at all—they can guess what happened—should be more interesting for them that way— I'm plumb tired of talking about it.... I don't know what I'll do now—I quit my job here and could go back to work but would throw a friend of mine who just has a new baby out of work so don't want to do that. And I quit again at Boulder with a promise to go back at the end of the trip but the managers have changed twice since then. I'm afraid that is off now. If the worst comes to the worst I'll go down to the seashore and grab myself a ship going to some distant spot—preferably Paraguay....

Reentry had been difficult for Holmstrom the previous year. It was even worse this time. To Earl Hamilton he wrote:

> Well, here I am back again, safe and sound—dissatisfied as the dickens and itchy footed. Don't know what the ultimate result will be—maybe serious.
> To tell you the truth I'm like a lost soul—I don't seem to belong here or anywhere else now—why don't you hurry up and get to be a doc and we will go to South America?

The letters he wrote that fall had their high points too. Holmstrom joked and never blamed anyone for failure at the San Francisco World's Fair. It just did not work out, he said, and now they would probably have to eat the film. To Stone he wrote:

> I have caught up on my clam-digging, fishing for salmon and duck hunting... in fact the fellow I was with almost got caught by a game warden last week when we were fishing as we didn't have our licenses along—after he was gone we found it easy to fish our pole up off the bottom of the river tho....

And around town, he was still good old Buzz. George McClellan remembers driving around with Holmstrom in the old Buick, boat in tow. At one point McClellan noticed that Holmstrom had been trying to slow down for a while, for *quite* a while, in fact. Finally, with the use of the emergency brake, Holmstrom brought the car to a stop. McClellan remembers, "I said, 'Buzz, why don't you get these brakes fixed?' He said, 'No use me havin' brakes. Everybody else has got 'em.'"

A new surge of fan mail came in December of 1938. Paramount Studios bought some of Holmstrom and Burg's footage and released it nationwide in a newsreel. Holmstrom relented and appeared at its premiere in Coquille, narrating an extended version of the release. But he was not happy. He did not know exactly what he wanted, he just wanted out. After Christmas he wrote Jotter again.

> I'm getting a little crazier every day—I've got to stay home another month or two but I don't fit into things around here now and don't seem to anywhere else either. The things it used to be fun to do aren't fun any more.

It was not an entirely gloomy letter; it included local news and a photograph with this note:

> You probably don't remember but down at Boulder just before you left you made the remark that I kind of looked like Cupid—I'm enclosing a picture taken there about 3 months later and wanted your opinion as to whether I look like Cupid in it too.

After his Mount Shasta project, Burg had gone back home to Portland. His father was ill, and died within a week of his return. Once family affairs were settled, he headed back to New York to market the rest of the film. But it was a hard sell. Holmstrom's trip was just not unique any more. Expeditions were *out*, river running was passé. Burg worked with several studios, but their offers were few and discouraging. He continued to send updates, and Holmstrom talked more seriously about going to sea.

In a letter to Julius Stone, he cut to the essence of his dilemma.

> I'm all in a turmoil inside—I know that if I ever expect to have anything or amount to anything I should settle down here and now. But I just naturally don't seem to be able to—my feet are itchy and I have a desire to go some place—anyplace—perhaps South America on a freighter [as an] ordinary seaman—However it seems as though any place I can think of is just a poor substitute for the River. I'm hoping before too many years I may have a good logical excuse to spend more time there—and I guess I'm not the only one who has felt that way about it.

Holmstrom had the classic symptoms of a malady boatmen have suffered ever since: withdrawal from the incredible elation of the River. The River, where everything is natural, scenic, and simple, where problems can be solved, the phone never rings, and goals are within immediate reach. To have discovered that world, lived in it, understood it, and savored it—then be compelled to leave it, with no certainty of ever returning—can inflict a peculiar strain of depression.

On January 16, 1939, E.G. Nielsen of the Bureau of Reclamation wrote Holmstrom. Colorado River ferryman Arth Chaffin had recommended Holmstrom as a prospective boatman for some studies on the Green River, scheduled to begin in a few weeks. Would Holmstrom be interested? Holmstrom wired back that he would be there. The return cable shattered his hopes, at least for the time. The bureau was most interested in him; however the trip had been postponed until fall.

Burg continued to write. Matters with the film were even bleaker. He had been able to sell some footage, but scarcely enough to cover the expense of marketing. He would keep trying.

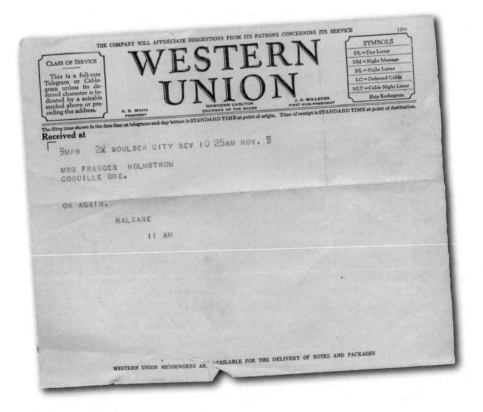

A Swell Idea

1939

THE PUBLICITY that floodlit Holmstrom's Colorado trips brought him unexpected, even unwanted, mail and adulation, importunities and proposals. Perhaps none more unexpected or welcome than an inquiry from George E. Housser of Walsh, Boll, Housser, Tupper, Ray & Carroll; Barristers & Solicitors; The Royal Bank Building; Vancouver, British Columbia. Solicitor Housser inquired whether Mr. Holmstrom (soon to be "My dear Buzz") might consider navigating a party by boat across North America.

Holmstrom, despite misgivings, once again at Walker's Standard station, was so eager to make a favorable impression that he borrowed his mother's typewriter for his reply:

Coquille, Oregon
Feb. 25, 1939
Dear Mr. Housser:

I received your letter of Feb. 21 concerning your client's Coast to Coast trip.

I have a friend [Amos Burg] who made a photographic trip from Wyoming to Boulder Dam with me last fall. He has been down the Snake from Jacksons Hole to Astoria [1925] and down the Yellowstone all the way on down to New Orleans [1922], and I am writing him today for whatever information he may be able to give. He is somewhere in the East now but I should have an answer within two weeks.

The only boating I have done on that stretch of water is a fifty mile stretch on the tail end of a trip of three hundred miles down the Salmon which empties into the Snake fifty miles above Lewiston.

Sternwheel freight boats go up to Pittsburg Landing, something like seventy-five miles above Lewiston in Hells Canyon on the Snake. Above Pittsburg Landing is about forty miles of bad going which I am afraid has some boxed rapids, and if it has there would be no going up it, but I'm going to check on that from my friend. It would certainly be great to get up through that place for then the only place on the Snake that might call for a long portage is a short canyon in the upper river. Certainly the most laborious and difficult portion of the trip would be passed when Jacksons Hole was reached.

I would suggest fourteen foot boats, 4'6" beam, 3 or 4" rake, with decked over, watertight compartment. These boats could be made of waterproof plywood with a total weight of not over two hundred pounds and a suitable hookup on the stern for an outboard motor. Being beamy and flat they won't draw much water which would be mighty handy in the upper rivers.

Our camping equipment on the Colorado was adequate and light. A light linen tent. A good ground cloth, for surely there will be some rain. Sleeping bags. A life preserver for every person. Leather soled shoes with tacks [corks] for working in the water on wet rocks. A light gasoline lantern. On stretches where there is a shortage of driftwood a small gasoline stove for cooking. As much dried food as possible through the long uninhabited stretches of the West.

As I write this letter I get more and more enthusiastic. I would like to go and my services are available. The job I would leave here is a very ordinary job.

I'd like to know more details such as how many are going and when. I would like very much to talk to your client, but would suggest waiting till I hear from my friend. Again I think it's a swell idea.

Sincerely,

Buzz Holmstrom

P. S. Please pardon my poor typing but it's better than the job I'd do by hand.

He put the matter in the back of his mind and went on changing oil and tires.

In Vancouver, however, Housser's client eagerly contemplated the long-held dream. Born in England, Edith Clegg married a London businessman, E. Burnuff Clegg, who sold textiles to the Chinese. Early in their marriage, the couple lived in Japan for a year and a half, while Mr. Clegg learned aspects of textile manufacturing from the Japanese.

In 1898, on a trip to China, Mr. Clegg passed through Vancouver. He was so captivated by the city that in 1923, a few years before his retirement, he immigrated there with his wife and four daughters. Although his wife Edith never attended a university, she was well educated and well-read—a woman with wide interests who soon took an active part in city affairs: a member of the British Columbia Historical Association and the Vancouver Folk Festival, an amateur actress, a "little theater" devotee, and Girl Guide Commissioner for British Columbia.

She lived in a commodious house with a veranda that extended all the way around its exterior. The house was located in the West-end of Vancouver about a block from Stanley Park. A gardener looked after the lovely grounds, and a maid, summoned by hand bell, looked after Clegg's domestic needs. To the nine grandchildren of her four grown daughters, Mrs. Clegg was known as "Grandmother Jane." She was a woman who believed "there was a place for everything and everything had to be in its place... she was very highly organized... she liked things to be tidy," recalls her granddaughter, Katie Brown.

> If Grandmother were there, you had to make sure that your hair was combed and that your fingernails were clean and that you washed your hands. If you were washing the dishes, there was certainly no mistaking that they were properly done, and that if they weren't properly done, they were handed back, and they were to be done again.... There were certain standards from which you did not slip if Grandmother Jane was there, and that had to do with your deportment and your efforts.

They also knew her as a proper lady, with a fondness for tasteful, well-tailored clothes (she always wore a hat), and attractive costume jewelry.

Grandmother Jane maintained a summer house in Sechelt, on the coast north of Vancouver, a rustic camp that she meant to keep that way. It consisted of a main house and sleeping cabins; wood stove, iron cots, no running water, outhouses, a draft horse for hauling logs. Katie remembers:

> the children had to make sure that the kindling box was full, and that the wood was brought to the house; and we had kerosene lamps, and every morning our job was to clean the chimneys, fill the reservoirs, and cut the wicks, and you didn't do anything else and it didn't matter how fascinating an invitation had been received or whether it was a magnificent day, you had

those certain chores to do first of all, and when they were done, then other things could occur.

Despite her gentility, Mrs. Clegg had one unusual routine: she always slept outdoors. At her home, her bedroom had a screened sleeping porch upstairs; at "Camp Sechelt," she had another screened porch and slept on an iron army cot with a tick mattress. Always outside.

At some point in her reading about Northwest history, this uncommon woman became engrossed by the saga of Captains Meriwether Lewis and William Clark. She even, at some point, wondered whether their journey might be retraced, river-wise, to St. Louis, even to the head of the Ohio River.

In February 1939, after her husband's death and while on an office visit to her legal advisor, George Housser, she rather uncharacteristically confided the fancy. Housser recalled the *Saturday Evening Post* article, "*He Shot the Colorado Alone*," and suggested Holmstrom was the man who could make her fancy a reality. He offered, moreover, to write on her behalf. Encouraged by Holmstrom's reply, Housser wrote again, requesting that the boatman meet with his client, who would drive to Coquille to discuss the journey.

In early March, apparently without waiting for another reply from Holmstrom, Mrs. Clegg arrived at Walker's station. She spoke with Ed Walker, who summoned Holmstrom from under a partially lubed auto. The attendant-boatman appeared, stared slack-jawed at Mrs. Clegg, turned on his heel, and left. She waited, obviously perplexed.

In a few minutes Holmstrom returned and accepted her offer, which she then pegged at $150 a month, to lead the expedition. Yet again, a bemused and toler-ant Ed Walker had lost his prized gas jockey. (Months later, when Clegg asked Holmstrom about his puzzling behavior at their first meeting, he explained that it had never occurred to him that the client might be a woman. At least he had been conditioned to the idea by the Clover—Jotter expedition on the Colorado.)

Agreement reached, Clegg went about her groundwork with a thoroughness for which she was famous, at least in her family. One daughter reminisced:

> I'm sure that Mother got herself in very good trim in preparation for the journey. When going to visit friends on a ranch once, she 'rode' a log... for two hours a day to develop her saddle muscles. She was a passionate and cool-headed planner. She believed that the success of any venture, whether giving a dance or climbing Mount Everest, depended first on the planning. She gave magically festive parties and, with her plans always firmly in place for the happiness and sustenance of her guests, she was a volatile and stimu-lating hostess. [She had] books, about Lewis and Clark, about the Mississippi, the Missouri, their tributaries, their history,... rolls of tracing paper, carbon paper, paper to make copies of maps and mile-long sections of rivers showing

every rapid—and many more intricate and official maps.

Holmstrom had to lay his own keel work. He knew the Columbia by sight; he knew that if boats had gotten down the Snake River, he could probably get up it—although he harbored nagging doubts about sheer reaches such as those he had seen on the Colorado, where no boat could be lined or portaged. He knew the Missouri and Mississippi as navigable mudwater runs—Burg had recounted his adventures there. But the rest of the waterways were more of a mystery to him than they were to her.

Based on his experience with the Rogue, Salmon, Green, and Colorado Rivers, he designed two boats of spruce in accord with his earlier recommendations, partially decked fore-and midship with cargo holds covered by watertight hatches. Each boat was to have a pair of handles at its bow and stern. Since Holmstrom had a long list of supplies and preparations, Art Ellingsen, the most experienced boatwright in Coquille, did most of the carpentry at his boatworks in nearby Arago, Oregon.

On March 16 Holmstrom wrote:

> Dear Mrs. Clegg—
> The rain that poured down steadily while you were [here] has stopped now and we are having some dandy weather—so warm in fact that it makes me feel a little uneasy about the snow melting up in the Rocky Mountains. However—I guess the heat wave is only local and temporary.
> I have been driving around so far this week with Arthur Ellingsen getting material together and today he actually started construction.
> We planned to finish one before starting the second one so that we can test the first one and find out its weakness—if any....

Four days later he wrote again:

> Dear Mrs. Clegg—
> The first boat is coming along fine. It should be in the water by Friday—tho it will have to have a couple of coats of paint and a little more work after that. But it will give us a chance to test it out. How it will carry the load & how fast it will go—How it handles—
> You know there is a continual wind up through the Columbia River Gorge & also well up into the canyon above Lewiston. Now this wind always blows upstream so I think we can rig up a very light mast and square sail & help the motors along tremendously—
> I've got two dandy fellows lined up for sure and another I'm pretty sure of—so if you come down next weekend you can get all the dope on the boats.
> Sincerely,
> Buzz Holmstrom

Clegg paid the bills; Holmstrom made arrangements: suppliers, deliveries, crew. His food list included standard fare: canned milk, hardtack, beans, jam, eggs, bacon, flour.

Cargo included Clegg's duffel, tent, maps; tools, spare motor parts (especially propellers), spark plugs (seventy-five cents each), grease tubes, gas cans; a snake-bite kit ($1.50).

Holmstrom contracted with a larger, commercial river boat on the Snake to cache food and twenty-five gallons of gas about every twenty-five miles, and he marked the sites on his maps. (It cost $11.99 to send 1,284 pounds from Lewiston to be distributed upriver at intervals along ninety miles by the steamboat *Idaho*.)

He wrote more letters of inquiry about the river, one of them to the Lewiston Chamber of Commerce. The reply was of little value:

> Dear Sir:
>
> In answer to your inquiry of March 14, it is possible to work a small boat up the Snake River Canyon to Weiser but it would have to be a very small and light boat that could be carried around various obstructions in the river. The trip has been made with such a light outfit .
>
> There is little information available on a trip from Lewiston to Weiser up the Snake River. However, we hope what information we have given you will be of help. If there is anything further we can do, please let us know.
>
> Yours very truly,
>
> Lewiston Chamber of Commerce.

By the first of April, one boat was finished, the other well underway. Holmstrom had received Clegg's check for the Johnson outboards he needed to purchase ($177.50 each) from Schroeder & Hildenbrand, a general hardware store in Marshfield, Oregon. He selected Sea-Horses, Model KA, 9.8-hp, weight sixty-four pounds. Twin horizontal cylinders, side by side instead of opposed, fired alternately, not simultaneously. They had built-in underwater exhaust and 360-degree steering, which allowed one to pivot the motor 180 degrees for reverse. The fuel required a mix of oil and gas.

Holmstrom, while no stranger to outboard motors, was not a veteran motor-man. He had been around them as a teenager; he put some hours on them at Boulder Dam. But when it came to anything linked with rivers, he was a diligent observer. In a letter written to Stone a few months earlier, he recalled scrutinizing Doc Frazier's home movies of their motorboat run up the Colorado from Hite, Utah, almost to Dark Canyon:

> Frank Swain surely knows how to handle the outboard. When we [Holmstrom, Burg, Johnson] came on down below Dark Canyon I wondered how you were going to get up over some of the rapids, but Doc's pictures show Frank's technique of going up the still water up to near the head & then

shooting out into the current. I was thinking it would be rather embarrass-
ing to have the motor stop up near the head of a crooked one.

He would embrace and, if possible, refine the technique.

On April 5 Holmstrom wrote Clegg: "Everything is going fine. I gave the check
for $150 to Schroeder & H and am enclosing their bill for the difference.... The
second boat is coming along very fast. Earl Hamilton & Clarence have been helping
& I'm sure we will be able to get away from here on Wednesday—April 19—so we
could leave Vancouver [Washington] Sat. Apr. 21—I'll keep you posted often and
hope we can make it then & it will be convenient for you."

Holmstrom had settled early on his crew. Since a backup boat was necessary
for Hells Canyon, and extra men were needed in the event of portage, he needed
boatmen who were fit, compatible, available. His first choice was Bean, whom he
had known longest and boated with before. Then Earl Hamilton from Coquille,
who had finished three years at Oregon State University, intent on going to dental
school in Portland. Hamilton could earn a dollar a day at the mill in Coquille;
Clegg's offer of $150 a month was extravagant in comparison. His proficiency with
motors and boating would be invaluable.

Holmstrom's choice to round out the crew was Willis "Bill" Johnson, the coal
miner from Thistle, Utah, who had accompanied him and Burg on the 1938 Grand
Canyon expedition. Johnson was strong, a willing worker, a somewhat seasoned
rower, a cook, and above all, good-humored. He quit his job with Utah Copper at

the open pit mine in Bingham, Utah, figuring that his friend and company doctor,
Russell Frazier, could help him get rehired
when the time came. Johnson was making three dollars a day at the mine; Clegg
offered them each $150 for the month. She
bought all of them new sleeping bags.

By April 15, Johnson was en route to
Coquille, where he would meet Bean and
Hamilton for the first time, and Holmstrom
wrote Clegg, "We are doggone near ready to
start.... We will be in Portland some time
Wednesday. Go out to Gault's boatyard &
set up housekeeping there. There [is] going
to be quite a lot of fussing around to do
in Portland & we thought it would be better to go up a day earlier than we at first
planned."

As usual with such expeditions, fussing

around took longer than expected. It was Sunday morning, April 23, 10:15 A.M., before the boats and crew on the south shore of the Columbia at Portland were ready to depart Gault's Boatworks. The fanfare surrounding the launch was private: Clegg, who had spent the night at the Evergreen Hotel, eschewed publicity, at least at this point. Altogether nine friends were there, including Amos Burg.

Clegg had chosen the names for the boats: one was the *Mongoose*, after the small mammal famous for its fearless ability to kill snakes; the other was the *St. George*, after the man who reputedly killed a dragon, but also in tribute to George Housser. A wreath with gold ribbons was hung on the prow of the *St. George*, considered the flagship, although both boats were identical.

They motored into the current, running with a steady upstream wind under a lid of threatening gray cumulus. After a little over an hour, they stopped on Button Island for lunch. Even without the carburetor screens plugging from lint off the new fuel filters, it was already apparent that the 9.8-hp Johnsons were underpowered for this task.

The Columbia, the legendary twelve-hundred-mile "River of the West," flows to the U.S. from farther north than any other river outside Alaska. With a watershed of 258,000 square miles—a wide web of waters, indeed—it is the third-longest river in the country. Five miles wide at its mouth between Point Adams and Cape Disappointment ninety-five miles west of Portland, it empties into the Pacific at an average rate of 150 billion gallons a day. It dwarfs the Colorado. The day they got underway, the flow was 190,000 CFS, an average flow. If things went well, boatman Holmstrom would visit the other large rivers, but he knew the first day that it would not be soon. From then on, he referred to running the outboard as "churning with the eggbeater."

Late afternoon, off Crown Point, they made their first camp in a cedar grove on Reed Island. Crown Point marked the entrance to the dark basaltic ramparts of the Columbia River Gorge, a fifty-mile reach where the ancient river had carved down through the Cascade uplift, leaving numerous tributary creeks and rivers pitching riverward in feathery waterfalls. A rainstorm broke while Johnson baked biscuits in the Dutch oven.

The next morning the boatmen were up at five, rigged a rain shelter out of ponchos, and made breakfast. They were on the water by eight, the boats moving at a maximum speed of seven miles an hour.

Highway construction was underway along the Oregon shore. In 1932 the Army Corps of Engineers had completed its master plan to build ten dams on the Columbia, and the plan gained the support of President Roosevelt. By the time the Clegg party came up the river, the Bonneville Dam, fifty miles east of Portland at the head of the tidal reaches, had been completed for a year, and ten thousand men had been at work for five years on the Grand Coulee Dam in central Washington.

Profound changes were in the wind.

The boaters watched salmon leap in the shallows as they made their way toward the fish ladders at Bonneville. The current stiffened and Hamilton walked along the shore with Bean, while Clegg rode seated opposite Holmstrom on the forward deck with her legs inside the cockpit. When the motor quit in one of the riffles, she seized the oars and rowed for shore, while Holmstrom tinkered with the carburetor yet again.

The boats entered the new lock system built into the dam to replace the one that had been in operation since 1896. It bypassed the fierce Cascade Rapids, a remnant of an

Earl Hamilton, Edith Clegg

ancient landslide. The Cascade Locks, then the largest in the world, filled in fifteen minutes; lifted fifty feet in this manner, the party surmounted the once-dreaded rapids. The group continued to motor up the reservoir in the rain.

The party ate lunch in the Oregon town of Cascade Locks, motored for another hour, and camped on a grassy point on the Oregon side, across from the settlement of Stevenson. It rained all night.

Fashioning a bonfire in the morning, they dried out some of their gear, and once they were back on the water, the rain broke off. The rims of the gorge were still darkly forested with pine and fir, the shoreline splashed with color: blue lupine, red Indian paintbrush, yellow balsamroot. Flocks of swans and geese floated unperturbed by the boats' passage.

Even from the boats they could see the snowy stocking cap on Mount Adams, shining forty miles to the north. A few miles below the mouth of the Klickitat River, they passed a basaltic islet in midstream, Memaloose Island. For centuries it served as the platform-burial site for local Indians. Now, above exposed skulls and bones, a prominent white obelisk stood visible from the river: a monument to Vic Trevett, early pioneer and friend to the Indians, who had allowed him to be buried there.

After bucking wind-whipped whitecaps all afternoon, they spent the night across from present-day Lyle, Washington. Surreptitiously, Clegg had purchased an apple pie when they stopped for lunch in Hood River and served it as a surprise. Hamilton noted, "She sure is spoiling us with too good food." The sound of trains, steamers, even planes, rattled their sleep.

On April 26 the party got underway earlier than usual. Hamilton, running the *St. George,* began to chafe privately at the late starts. By midmorning they were at The Dalles Rapids, enchanted by the sight of Mount Hood, impressive as a Hokusai woodcut of Mount Fuji, glowing twenty miles to the south. They went into a riverside community, The Dalles, for groceries and sixteen gallons of gas.

On leaving The Dalles, 190 miles from the Pacific Ocean, they breached the Cascade Range and moved into the region known as the "Inland Empire." This was sheep and cattle country—dryer and hotter than the coast. Trees thinned, then disappeared altogether, replaced by sage and bunchgrass. The boats worked the eddylines and labored through Three-Mile Rapids, bulling their way through driftwood to the entry gates of The Dalles–Celilo Canal. The canal had been in operation since 1915 as a way to bypass The Dalles, where the river was compressed into a narrow chute, and Celilo Falls. After motoring ten miles up the canal through a series of gates to the last lock, they stopped to climb the lock ladders and watch the Indians, precariously perched on rock outcrops above the falls, fishing with dip nets for chinook salmon. Along the shore, Indian women in colorful clothing washed their laundry. Hamilton wrote, "they sure were giving them a pounding and were wetter than the washing." (In fewer than twenty years, Bonneville Dam and The Dalles Dam [1957] together would inundate Cascade Rapid, The Dalles, and Celilo Falls—a fifty-five-mile stretch of rough water that caused hardships for all voyageurs, including the Lewis and Clark Expedition.)

Camp was a pleasant willow grove a mile above the falls, on the Oregon side of the river. Hamilton, as was his custom now, attended to the maintenance work on the Johnsons, while the others saw to the boats, camp, and cooking. Holmstrom built such a large fire that sparks burned sizable holes in the shelter awning, and Clegg stayed up late sewing patches on it.

Day four was wearisome: the river was rising, the current more insistent, and Bean sheared a second pin and bent a prop. Hamilton took turns walking ashore with Bean and Johnson to see if that would help the pace, and it did. They stopped at Rufus, Oregon, and each member lightened his kit further, shipping by bus and train the two-hundred-pound surplus east to Lewiston, Idaho.

As they passed beneath the Columbia Hills on the north side of the river, they saw Maryhill Castle, the French Chateau mansion built by railroad magnate Sam Hill for his bride, crowning the hill. Each member of the party remarked on the mansion. Not a single boat passed them in either direction all day. At one point, when the current became too swift, they carried the gas cans along the shore. Holmstrom sheared two pins on driftwood before they made campfall on the Washington side, across from the mouth of the John Day River. Hamilton puttered with the motors and gas lines, and shaved; Holmstrom washed his shirt, which "sure needed it"; Clegg did her own washing; Johnson and Bean made supper. Nearby, scores of cliff swallows pasted pellets into their mud nests.

The current through four rapids the next day made them glad they had shipped their spare supplies ahead. Bean motored over rocks twice and Holmstrom's motor quit on him several times. But the afternoon wind still favored them, as did the weather. Flocks of Canada geese formed arrowheads against the sky, flying north with the spring. The boatmen made good mileage and camped three miles short of Arlington, Oregon. Clegg did not even want her tent pitched for the night. The boatmen used the gas lantern for light by which to write in their journals.

In Arlington the next morning, Clegg telegraphed home. Hamilton mailed his diary notes to his wife Phyllis in Coquille. They made a few purchases and ate lunch, then cast off again.

Now well outside the gorge, but nearly seventy miles from the confluence with the Snake, Hamilton increasingly began to fret about the plodding pace. An oil barge, the *Mary Gail*, hauling gas and oil upriver, churned past them coming and going. He remarked, "Current is so swift we make awful poor time. I'm afraid we may give up. It will take us a whole month to get to Lewiston at this rate. [*Mary Gail*] has 800-hp diesels—we sure could use 799 of them. We should have 16-hp motors, instead of 10." Later he revised his estimate to 22-hp.

Bean hit rocks again, sheared pins, chewed up the prop vanes. Hamilton, who had to make repairs, decided that Bean "uses poor judgment." At the end of a fifteen-mile day, they camped on stony, mile-long Thanksgiving Island with heron rookeries, redwing blackbird flocks, geese, killdeer, and western gulls. The avian racket contributed nothing to a night's rest.

The following day, a deserved respite: lovely weather, easier current, a single rapid, the sweet scent of sage on the breeze. At Boardman, Oregon, they picked up minor supplies and eight gallons of gas. Island after island slipped behind their wake, some of them, such as Blalock, were several miles long. They camped on the Washington side above Paterson cable ferry, at the mouth of Cold Springs Creek, under a full moon in a sheltered cottonwood cove fleeced with grass and lavender lupine. Hamilton wrote, "Making a little better time today so Buzz doesn't seem so discouraged."

The next day, Monday, May 1, the river once again impeded their progress—it had risen about two feet in the night and pin-shearing driftwood floated everywhere. The spring flow of the Columbia was now 254,000 CFS. Two government boats dredged the channel at Umatilla, where the party stopped for supplies, and Clegg endured a female newspaper reporter who had heard they were coming.

So far the party had escaped unwanted notoriety. But now, back in British Columbia, the mystified *Vancouver Sun*, reported in a front page story that the "chic, talented widow, prominent figure in Vancouver's social and club life, whose lovely old home has been the scene of many smart parties," had departed on a "hunting, fishing, and exploring trip." Its competitor, the *Vancouver Province*, added that "friends thought she had left for Toronto" and, since the Columbia was at the "height of spring freshet," that the object of the trip was "river lore study." Elaborating the next day, the *Province* reported: "It is believed here that the emphasis should be placed on the exploring, as Mrs. Clegg is said to be very much interested in developing Northwest rivers, especially in regards to navigation. One of the rivermen said no effort would be made to take pictures, write articles, or otherwise cash in on the adventure. The party planned to be gone about three weeks."

A week later, the same newspaper tacked again: "Photography is her main interest in the trip and would be a determining factor in the distance and direction after they push on from Lewiston. She termed the expedition a 'community venture' and said it is the prettiest trip I ever made. The party averages twenty-five miles a day."

Once Clegg, Bean, and Holmstrom finished their business in Umatilla, several residents offered to give them and their parcels rides back down to the river. The group waved good-bye and motored upriver to Umatilla Rapids. Three of them walked around the rapid while Holmstrom and Hamilton drove the boats through. They halted for lunch within view of Indians who had erected fishing scaffolds overhanging the rapid.

The expedition pitched camp for the night on the Oregon shore, under the shadow of Hat Rock. Severe sunburn troubled Hamilton: "My face feels like it is on fire." He found trying to shave in the evening "misery." In the belief that it kept him cool in hot weather, he was still wearing wool underwear. Perhaps his physical discomforts explain why he was growing increasingly agitated about the lack of progress. "Don't see why we should fool away so much time. No one seems to want to hurry & it sure gets on my nerves. Guess it shouldn't because I'm getting paid by the day. I at least like to earn my money though." Bean was still shearing pins with an irritating frequency. By now, everyone knew he was an inept boatman, but no one had the heart to insist that he relinquish the motor altogether. They also knew by now that the *St. George*, run by Holmstrom, was indisputably the faster craft. For relief, Hamilton went fishing in the creek and felt better when he caught "the one and only."

The following day, the country acquired new bluffs alongside the river, with rolling farmland flowing away to the limited horizon. Farms looked more prosperous. Clegg walked for six miles and felt better for the exercise. She spotted a beaver in the river, a porcupine on shore. Once they reached Wallula Junction above the mouth of the Walla Walla River, they paused an hour for lunch. Now both shores were within the state of Washington. It was here at Wallula Gap that

Lewis and Clark met the Walla Walla Indians. At Wallula, oil barges now off-loaded into storage tanks and retreated back downriver because the river above that point was too shallow for them.

Emerald-green wheat fields rimmed the plateaus above the river. Shortly after passing beneath a railroad bridge that spanned the Columbia, they spotted the long-anticipated mouth of the Snake River, "definitely a landmark on the journey," but motored on past it to Pasco, Washington, where they could get supplies and perform errands. Hamilton had run the *Mongoose* all day without a single problem. After some difficulty, they found a suitable camping spot just below the city gun club. Holmstrom and Hamilton walked a mile into town to learn what they could about the availability of gasoline on the Snake. One fellow they visited with informed them that he had gone fishing up there the other day and "killed twenty-eight rattlers." On their way back to the camp with four new spark plugs and freshly cleaned old ones, the boatmen stopped to remove their shoes and, despite the gravel, walked barefoot all the way back. Clegg, however, wrote, "Pasco is a nice, gay little town. I could get a shoe shine at last."

It was high noon the next day before the expedition was ready to retreat to the Snake River and begin the assault each of them anticipated as the most difficult stretch of the entire journey.

The Snake is the tenth-longest river in the U.S. and the largest tributary of the Columbia—on the West Coast, only the Columbia carries more water—and the Snake's volume is two-and-a-half times that of the Colorado. From south-central Yellowstone Park, it flows westerly through Wyoming to the base of the Grand Tetons, then shifts southwest in a graceful scythe across the plains of southern Idaho. In the course of its thousand-mile journey, it exacts tribute from forty rivers in six states. And where the river forms the north-south border between Idaho and Oregon, it has sliced, rim-to-river, the deepest gorge in the continental U.S.

The Clegg expedition entered the muddy mouth of the Snake, and the whine of their Johnson outboards promptly informed them that the current here was swifter, more resistant, more likely to check their advance than that of the Columbia. Although the flow of the Columbia where they left it at Pasco had reached 279,000 CFS, and the Snake was running half that flow, the gradient of the Snake was greater and its width smaller. After a mile, between a railroad bridge and a highway bridge across the river, they stopped for lunch. Clegg, Hamilton, and Johnson decided to lighten the load by walking with packs. Johnson, alert for rattlesnakes, killed the first one.

On the river, Holmstrom and Bean, wading waist-deep, lined Five Mile Rapid on the right side. They lined the next rapid as well, partly to save gas. They finally camped on the left bank in what, judging by the abundance of bones (including a baby's skeleton), skulls, and arrowheads, was evidently an Indian burial ground.

No sooner had they settled into their beachfront camp than a nearby rancher, who had tracked their progress for the last couple of miles, arrived to run them off. On learning they were not firewood rustlers—firewood being a scarce commodity in these parts—Mr. Rogers apologized and then stayed to visit long past his welcome. "We thought he would never go," sighed Clegg.

Once dinner and chores were over, the group huddled around their campfire. Hamilton nursed blisters on his feet; Holmstrom nursed hopes the river was dropping. The conversation turned reflective. They had been on the river for eleven days, knitting into a team. Clegg maintained a certain reserve, however. Hamilton wrote in his journal that night, "Mrs. C has lived in almost all of the foreign countries. She sure doesn't talk about what she has, does, or anything else. I'm rather curious but don't dare ask questions. Maybe she might let something slip before the trip is over." They turned in later than usual.

The next morning they got their earliest start ever: Clegg awakened them at four by pounding on a can. Hamilton lamented, "Didn't have time to dig up any more Indians." Clegg, Johnson, and a reluctant Bean began to walk along the left shore, shoved by the ever-present upstream wind; Holmstrom and Hamilton took the boats. The river was higher by another six inches and muddier by far than the Columbia. More lightly loaded, they climbed Fishhook Rapid without a stutter. The river, now engorged between low basaltic bluffs that supported railroad tracks on each side and higher bluffs that supported dry-land wheat farms, coursed with uprooted trees. The boats dodged. After seven miles, they pulled in and picked up the hikers, went another mile, stopped for lunch, then stopped again at a crossroads settlement for twenty-four gallons of gas. Holmstrom took a turn at walking, while Clegg rode with Hamilton. Johnson killed another rattlesnake.

That evening, after buying three gallons of motor oil from a rancher, they camped on a small island, where a rancher's market-garden furnished lettuce and radishes.

Johnson and Clegg walked the next day, following the railroad tracks. They passed a siding called Winddust. When she observed to a worker there that it sounded unpleasant, he replied laconically, "It is." In the afternoon they watched a teamster bring a wooden water wagon to the river to fill before heading back up to his rimrock ranch on the plateau. Even horse herds had to be brought down to the river twice a day for water.

At a fourteen thousand-acre sheep ranch, they bought ten gallons of gas. Johnson's knee was troubling him; Hamilton's feet were badly blistered; Holmstrom's feet sore; but Clegg "walks fast & long—stands it fine." The men called for camp a mile below the community of Ayer. During the night a wind gust collapsed Clegg's tent, and zippered inside, she was trapped until her shouts brought the boatmen to her rescue. A groggy Holmstrom pulled his shirt on over his sweater and in a barefoot dash, lanced his soles with cockleburs. He helped

Holmstrom and Hamilton, burning the beans

collect Clegg's laundry, which had been scattered from her impromptu clothesline.

At Ayer the next day, Clegg attempted to cash a ten-dollar traveler's cheque at the Railway Express. No one there had ever heard of such a thing. A telegraph message to Pasco finally brought the necessary approval. They bought food and two quarts of oil, learned the water was eight feet higher than normal, went back to the river, and ate late lunch upstream at the mouth of the Palouse River. A steel bridge for the Union Pacific tracks spanned the river here, 282 feet high and over 1,400 feet long. Hamilton remarked that he would hate to be up there in a wind.

Everyone but Bean took a turn at walking. Marmots whistled warnings at their approach; they spotted several sage grouse. The weather was warm and windless. They lined the boats a hundred yards at Palouse Rapid, ran Pine Tree and Texas Rapids. Holmstrom, uncertain how far it was to Central Ferry, the next supply point, worried that they had only thirty gallons of gas left. The good news was that the river had crested, at 144,000 CFS.

They found, according to Clegg, "a charming, shady, sheltered place" for the night just above Riparia, deserted when the railroad division moved downriver to Ayer.

The following day they resupplied and lunched at Central Ferry—a store, gas station, and auto cabins where a highway bridge crossed the river. All but two of them walked after lunch, through farm and cattle country, horses and sheep. Dryland wheat fringed the rimrock two thousand feet above their path. Occasionally they saw the cable trams farmers used to shunt their sacked wheat down to the river where ships could load it. The expedition's motorboats were such a rarity here that people on shore, assuming they were sturgeon fishermen, stopped to stare. By campfall that evening, two miles above Penawawa, they had covered twenty-six miles. At a price.

Hamilton's feet revealed ghastly blood blisters. Fearing infection, he walked on the sides of his feet. "I can't stand to walk on them anymore." He decided to talk to Holmstrom about whether he was really needed in Hells Canyon. Holmstrom, who was wearing thin tennis shoes, had sore feet as well.

The next day, on reaching Almota, Clegg remarked for the first time on "Lewis & Clark's camps." (Lewis and Clark camped at present Almota October 11, 1805.) They enjoyed ice cream cones, then Holmstrom asked her about Hamilton taking a train to Lewiston. She absolutely forbade it. Hamilton recorded:

> [she] told Buzz that I would be the last one she would want to leave… forbid me to walk anymore till we got to the canyon… said let some of the others do a little of the walking for a while. She walks 6–8 miles every day and none of us can outwalk her. Sure is tough as shoe leather and is a peach of a person.

They collected twenty gallons of gas at Wawawai ("council grounds" from the Palouse word "wa," meaning "talk"), an area of apple and peach orchards just beginning to experiment with the idea of "you-pick." That afternoon, Holmstrom encountered Jack Shelby at the river's edge, the miner whom he had met three years earlier in the lower Salmon canyon. Shelby had been down the Snake, and they gleaned updated, encouraging information: he could not remember a reach where it was impossible to line or portage. He cautioned, however, that no one had gone up river farther than Granite Rapid in Hells Canyon. He had other more pleasant news: in about ten miles, they should have a reunion with the Luoto brothers, who had been operating a sweep boat mining rig on the Salmon in 1936 when Holmstrom ran it. Four miles more, and the crew went into camp. A chagrined Hamilton noted that he had sheared his first pin on the propeller shaft. At least the expendable pins saved the propeller itself.

They were on the river early the next morning. Clegg, walking, saw her first "China pheasant" ever, and later, the first cactus of the trip. The Luoto brothers, camped at John Creek, welcomed the boaters into their spotless scow and showed them photographs of the upper Snake canyon and its rapids, "which looked hair-raising," said Clegg. They built this sweep boat at Robinette (nine miles above present Brownlee Dam, but now submerged), installed the car motor to operate their placer-mining pump, wintered in the canyon at Warm Springs on the Idaho side above Granite Rapid, and worked their way down the Snake when the weather warmed. They intended to go back and do it all over again. They, too, bolstered Holmstrom's confidence, assuring him he would make it through the canyon.

After an hour, the group pressed on toward Lewiston. They lunched in the shade of a pine tree—only the second they had seen in days—and after a run of twenty-four miles, pitched camp in early evening on a sandy, freshly washed island in sight of the interstate bridge that linked Lewiston, Idaho, and Clarkston, Washington, on opposite sides of the river.

"Lewiston at last!" said Clegg, "It feels good to have got here." The expedition had been eighteen days on the rivers.

They walked to town. Clegg wanted a facial, Hamilton wanted a bath, Holmstrom wanted mail and their supplies (it was his birthday, but no one mentions it, including him), Johnson wanted some extra shoes, Bean wanted a nap.

Then as now, Lewiston, although 470 miles inland from the sea, was a port town, dealing in grain and wool, livestock and lumber. Sternwheel steamboats still moored at its docks lined with warehouses and granaries. The expedition spent two-and-a-half days in town, purchasing supplies and making arrangements for deliveries upriver for ninety miles, as far as Johnson Bar.

William Pressly Brewrink operated the twin-engine, gas-powered *Idaho,* a dependable, fifty-eight foot craft that could carry eight tons of supplies to the sheep ranches in the canyon. Since 1912, he had been running a power boat on the river, and obtained the first river-route mail contract on the Snake. The year before the Clegg expedition, he lost the mail contract to a garage mechanic, Kyle McGrady, who purchased the *Idaho* and converted her to a twin-engine diesel with three rudders. It averaged seven mph upstream. At times he used a 33-hp Evinrude outboard as backup. Holmstrom made up four caches of "grub and gas" to be dropped at approximately twenty-mile intervals: the Grande Ronde River, Divide Creek, Somers Creek, and Johnson Bar. McGrady's charge, depending on distance, ranged from 45 cents to $1.25 per hundredweight.

Clegg went up to the Lewis and Clark Hotel for a bath which cost her one dollar. She did her laundry, got her shoes mended, bought some film, and shopped for groceries for the trip. The men took the boats out of the water and worked on the hulls. Then all members of the expedition shipped every superfluous item ahead or home, including the stove and lantern, and even coffee because it was heavier than tea. The boatmen took only the clothes they had on. Johnson wrote in his journal: "We won't be too surprised if we aren't able to make it up through for all the rivermen here tell us it is impossible but we are a little optimistic and are going to give it a good try."

Friday, May 12, they set out at noon. Practiced boatmen and hardened hikers, they felt ready for the milltails of Hells. The flow of the Clearwater averages 15,000 CFS. Above its confluence with the Clearwater at Lewiston, the Snake is noticeably narrower. All the expedition members could ride and they made good time—five miles before a late lunch just short of Asotin, Washington. While they ate, they observed the sternwheel steamboat, *Lewiston,* churn upriver for a load of wool.

Above Asotin, Clegg, Bean, and Johnson walked, following a dirt road past farms and orchards. In camp that night Clegg recorded the shared anticipation: "We are all feeling rather excited to be on this leg of the journey and are hoping for the best."

They awoke to the whack of a beaver tail off shore, and after hotcakes, bacon, and tea, were underway by seven. This time Bean and Johnson walked. They followed the dirt road on the Washington side, completed the year before from Captain John Creek to Rogersburg at the mouth of the Grande Ronde. Along the way, they photographed Indian pictographs, examined the sixty-pound catch of some sturgeon fisherman, visited with placer miners, noted the yellow blooms on the cacti.

The group lunched at Billy Creek, then stopped at the Grande Ronde for their first cache. Holmstrom noted that they were two days ahead of schedule, but they had to take it all on board, even though it meant they were overloaded. An onlooker at the Grande Ronde informed them "it was suicide to take boats like that into Wild Goose Rapid." Holmstrom confided to his journal, "We shall see—probably have to line it as we are very heavy loaded." Although they had to unload four gas cans in order to allow Bean to run the *Mongoose* up a steep riffle, they motored up the left side of the rapid without difficulty. By nightfall, they made twenty-three miles.

The next day, the loads, coupled with the strength of the current, persuaded everyone but the pilots to hike the stock trail along the Idaho side of the river. The going got rougher; the boats ground their way through a series of reefy rapids where the current accelerated as it shallowed—McDuff, Cochran Islands, Cottonwood—and picked up the hikers in between to help with gear portage. The river narrowed, the canyon got rockier, treeless, and bald save where bunchgrass stools splashed the slopes with a pale green cast in the midafternoon light. A twelve-mile day, and earned.

May 14, up at 4:30 A.M. Mush and tea. More hiking for anyone not running a motor. No trails. They reached the confluence with the Salmon; Holmstrom noted it with a grin and a nostalgic glance, but his concentration was now on the engorged river above the confluence. At the confluence, the Snake was flowing 102,000 CFS, but since almost 40,000 CFS of that was from the Salmon, the current eased somewhat above the confluence because the flow was rapidly diminishing on the Snake. The growl of the motors ricocheted from the river-polished black basalt walls. Clegg, Bean, and Johnson groped their way along the Oregon shore, often well above the river.

The boats pounded up through the three stages of Mountain Sheep Rapid, then worked the Idaho side of Deer Rapid just below Eureka Creek (earlier, Deer Creek) a mile below the Imnaha Bar. The current and strong waves forced Holmstrom to unload a part of his supplies on the Idaho shore before attempting his run. Kneeling on the seat to hold the bow down, he operated the motor with a rope extension and gathered momentum as he raced up the eddyline below the rapid. When he hit the tailwaves in the main rapid, the boat went airborne "up in the air like a ball," veered into the next wave, and pitched him headfirst over the bow into the river. He had forgotten to wear his life jacket.

Holmstrom recalls:

> go down & hear motor churning right over my head—it goes away & I come up—easy swimming at first—see them all running for the boat [*Mongoose*] below—Doc was about 200 feet away over a rough boulder bar but he gets there first—cuts the painter & jumps in—at first thought cinch to swim out but now can see that it isn't for I'm drawn out into lower end where bad boils and down I go—getting pretty tired—after a while I come up & see Doc can't make headway with oars as backcurrent so he starts motor & comes for me—I'm very tired now—just about the time he reaches me I get into another boil & down I go—I feel bottom of boat overhead & then go on down—very dark & seems like I'll never come up—hold breath—pretty soon it gets lighter come to top—Doc throws kapok jacket & I can't quite get it—as on other side of boil—he rows boat backward towards me & it sure looks good—about all I can do is reach up & grab drive shaft of motor & then he comes back grabs my hand & works me around to the side & hauls me in—no small job itself as I'm not much help—tears my pants—my only ones—dumps me off ashore as I'm too tired to be any good....

Hamilton and Bean took off in the *Mongoose* after the riderless *St. George* and captured it a mile-and-a-half downriver, swirling in an eddy with its motor off. Hamilton brought it back upriver to the beach where Johnson was ministering to an exhausted Holmstrom, lying face down on the beach like a spent salmon. Then he motored across the river to pick up an anxious Clegg, who had watched the near-drowning helplessly from afar. "It was the greatest comfort to see Buzz move first one leg and then the other.... I knew he was alive."

After a desultory attempt at lunch, the spent boatmen recrossed the river and made camp on the bar below the mouth of the Imnaha River. There Clegg had a close encounter with yet another rattlesnake—the largest of many they killed. She wrote, "We are all feeling tired, emotional strain, I suppose, but we eat a very good dinner. I had said to St. Christopher [patron of travelers] that I won't smoke till the end of this trip—a kind of gratitude." Holmstrom's

entry is briefer: "To bed tired."

Morning broke cold and gray and rainy, but the rain eased momentarily. Holmstrom was hatless, since his "fine seagoing hat" had floated away in the accident, and watchless as well—it had quit after immersion. They rigged one boat with bow and stern lines and used it to ferry their loads across the mouth of the Imnaha, which was too high to wade, to reach a stretch with less current. Two miles farther upriver at Divide Creek on the Idaho side, they collected their second cache.

More cautious than the day before, they lined at Divide Creek, White Horse Rapid, and the one above it. They set up camp in the dark after fewer than three miles (three hours on the engines), under renewed rain, "all feeling a bit dejected," according to Clegg.

In the morning, as the rain faired off for breakfast, the group recouped its buoyancy. "Buzz looking quite himself again," said Clegg. It was a six-rapid day, lugging gear around some of them, a lot of carrying and wading and lining—"altogether a heavy day for the men," wrote Clegg. They passed John Spencer's ranch at Doug Creek, homesteaded in 1914; a mile upstream from it, at Dug Bar, they motored past the historic site where Chief Joseph's band of Nez Perce crossed the river in spring flood before the War of 1877. Another two miles, and they powered past the mouth of Deep Creek on the Oregon side, where in 1887, thirty-one Chinese miners were massacred for their gold dust. A five-hour day on the motors, but camp was a gravel pit at the south end of David and Sarah Van Pool's cattle ranch at Big Sulphur Creek on the Idaho side. Not even enough wood for a fire.

In the dawn's half-light, they could see the clouds breaking up—a hot day seemed likely. Except for the heat, the day went much like the one before: motor, portage, motor, some walking ashore. Clegg walked all day. At Lookout Creek, Holmstrom encountered Duncan Conrad, whom he had met on the lower Snake three years earlier.

That evening they pulled into Somers Creek, marking a ten-mile day, and sorted out the waiting cache. Dad Wilson had a sheep ranch three miles up the creek, and the visitors found his enormous wool sacks stacked along the shore. Since the wind was kicking up and clouds threatened again, they stretched their tarps between the sacks. The group spent a cozy night despite the rain.

Morning rain made reluctant risers. They waited it out, ate a late breakfast, loaded the supplies, and cast off at noon, leaving fifteen gallons of gas behind for lack of room. They made only three miles before camping at the upper end of a valley; there they collected driftwood for a large fire and dried their clothes, while Clegg mused that she thought the somber canyon walls, lion-colored hills, and breadth of silky river made this the most beautiful camp so far.

The boatmen were on the river before six the next morning. Immediately they lined the boats for several hundred feet, then portaged part of the load nearly half a mile. Some walked along the Idaho side four miles to Pittsburg Landing, location of the Circle C Ranch, which was owned by the Campbell brothers of New Meadows, Idaho. Johnson, stick in hand, killed three rattlesnakes along the way, and observed, "... it is likely we will be bitten before we are

through the trip... they never warn you with their rattles... until we have started to exterminate them."

They did not stop at Kirkwood Bar, where Grace and Len Jordan were busy raising their family and running several bands of sheep. Instead, they hurried on to a camp above Salt Creek for the night, where, content with ten more miles behind them, they listened to the novelty of a frog chorus.

In the morning they stopped at Temperance Creek Ranch on the Oregon side, a livestock operation run by Ken and Hazel Johnson. Hazel invited them in to have coffee with her. A 32-volt Windcharger windmill furnished power for house lights and a refrigerator, and the garden provided strawberries; ripe cherries glistened on the trees. Holmstrom, with an eye on the fields, noted, "...raining on their 25 tons hay they have just cut—farmers luck as bad in this country as at home."

A mile or so farther up the trail, Clegg spotted and Johnson killed the new record in their rattlesnake pogrom: eleven rattles and a button.

Meanwhile, across the river, the boatmen lined Sheep Creek Rapid and just before noon, reached Johnson Bar on the Idaho side. This was the limit of commercial upstream navigation—even today the traditional end of the mail run—and the site of their last cache. The party set up a rain fly while they sorted their groceries and, still ahead of their calculated schedule, decided to send some supplies back to Lewiston in order to leave more room for gas. Now distance would be measured by time rather than miles. Before reloading, they pulled the boats out of the water and examined their hulls.

The party then proceeded up canyon, managed a two-hour lining through a rough pitch, and halted a half mile farther. The hardest part had now begun, and the river served notice. Writing about the shoaly slope just completed, Johnson said, "...we took quite a battering from the surge of the water from the rapid hammering the boats against us. We were many times in water up under our arms and the water was chilly. We are bruised and sore and tired tonight." Holmstrom agreed: "Glad to be on the last leg of the canyon."

In the morning they could see Hat Point across the river, part of the rim over-looking their camp: at 6,892 feet, it towered over a mile above them. It also marked the start of the two most arduous days. They had to line the boats at Rush Creek Rapid; carry all their gear and supplies; and within a half mile repeat the effort at Sluice Creek Rapid—all of this under a cold rain. At each rapid they had to experiment on both sides of the river, probing the unrelenting currents for possibilities.

So swamped were the boatmen that they could not cross over to get Clegg, even though she was cold and hungry, until late afternoon. A mile-and-a-half advance one day—less than an hour on the motors. Just over that the next, as they worked their way past Bills Creek to camp. The boatmen's diaries are barely comprehensible. Holmstrom: "...hardest days of work yet...." Hamilton: "It was an awfully tough lining show.... The surges were very bad and the shoreline terrible with granite boulders." Johnson, in a single entry for both days: "Yesterday and today are two of the most grueling days we could possibly have and yet keep going. We were into one tough rapid after another; most of them have no names and we had to portage the boats and loads up through the ledges on several occasions. This is some of the swiftest water I have ever seen and it is easy to understand now why no boats have ever made it up through here before."

For Clegg, the going was so tortoise-like that she hiked back by trail to Johnson Bar to pack a few groceries from the cache. Since someone had already collected them, she did not log much fruitful mileage either.

On Wednesday, May 24, the clouds dissipated, but the river currents did not. The boatmen breakfasted early on mush and hotcakes, then motored to the foot of Waterspout Rapid and made a lengthy portage of gear before running the boats up. They ran No Name Rapid, lined at Bernard Creek, and camped in late afternoon sunshine on the Idaho shore in the marrow of the canyon. None but packers and sturgeon fishermen visited this reach. The benches above the river were the last ungrazed western range as yet unexploited by stockmen.

Holmstrom rose at daylight to patch his ragged pants into a semblance of modesty. They ran the boats empty up to Three Creek Rapid and lined them over the top on the Idaho side. They lined once more before lunching at the foot of Granite Rapid, a throbbing slant of whitewater at any flow, and tricky at the 17,000 CFS they were battling.

After lunch, they spent the rest of the afternoon getting above Granite. With motors, they worked the boats to the head of the rapid on the Oregon side, finally lining them over the lip. Next they portaged all their dunnage from the base of the rapid to a spot fifty yards above its tongue. Then they motored upriver along the shore and crossed to a cramped sandbar on the Idaho side for the night. Looking back at the rapid, Holmstrom said he would prefer not to run it; Johnson said it was one of the most dangerous they had come to. In any event, they took a quiet pride in their accomplishment—the first party since 1819 to bring any sort of a boat above that point. (Completion of three dams by Idaho Power Company in Hells Canyon [1959 to 1968] left Granite Creek Rapid one of the rougher on the river.) It was not over by any means, but they had done what they had been told they could not do. Elation kept Holmstrom and Hamilton awake in their sleeping bags, and both decided to use the opportunity to patch their tattered pants. Holmstrom tells the story this way: "Mine are badly torn in the crotch. It's about half dark and I cut off a big piece of canvas and try to sew on—and in A.M. find the patch itself has a very big hole in it—but it's smaller than the first one. Tomorrow maybe I'll patch the hole in the patch." A case of no holes barred. And so to bed, with the redolence of syringa blossoms and the sound of crickets creaking in the grass and a steady stream of harmless caddisflies flowing overhead, feeding the bullbats.

The next morning they all took a deep breath—Holmstrom observed that, "The canyon where we are now is the prettiest yet I think"—and pressed on. With loaded boats, and the usual walkers on shore killing snakes as they went, Holmstrom and Hamilton motored two miles to Wild Sheep Rapid (earlier, Two Creeks), which was nearly as treacherous as Granite. This they ran up near the head; then all hands carried the boats fifty feet and lined them about twice that far, moored them, reloaded, and paused for lunch.

Lunch included sturgeon meat purchased at Wild Sheep from fishermen Chet Maynard and his son, who sent their catch (they had a five-hundred-pounder in tow) wrapped in wet burlap, by pack string to Johnson Bar, where it was boated to market in Lewiston. Snake River sturgeon, being anadromous, migrated from the sea, and the Maynards speculated that the noticeable decline in numbers was caused by the Bonneville Dam rather than overfishing. Clegg bought thirty pounds for $2.50 and it lasted five meals. "Delicious!" she exclaimed.

As was his custom on every river he ran, Holmstrom kept an observant eye on the geology: checking mineral composition, recording unusual outcrops, speculating about formations beyond his reach. "…some nice pinnacles way up on Ore side—from a distance seems to be granite as is quite gray—but turns out to be basalt—the last granite went under the river just above our camp above Bills Ck." And again the next day, "…at camp last night see some black volcanic rock full of green specks about size of peas…."

After lunch, the boats ground their way upriver another two miles, and the men selected a camp at Warm Springs, situated among scattered yellow pines, a campsite that had been abandoned centuries earlier by Indians; the lodge depressions were still visible. The walkers beat their way along the shore, following an overgrown trail and killing more snakes than a famished mongoose. They built a pine knot fire, ate, and admired the view: "...finest scenery yet.... "

Another early start. They backpacked loads and lined the boats on the Idaho side at Brush Creek. The walkers' difficulties increased from this point onward because the trail on each side of the river ended—they trudged over ledges and in and out of folded drainages. Wherever necessary, the boats ferried the hikers to the more favorable side. The boatmen lined a side channel at Hells Creek. Said Holmstrom, "All we can do to get thru & its well we do as there is no shore on either side." In early afternoon, they pitched camp in Oregon, opposite Deep Creek and at the foot of Steamboat Rapid.

The sight and sound of that rapid running along the base of a cliff was anything but soporific. As Holmstrom scribbled, "It's going to be terrible to get by... we intend to hold the boats & start motors—they simply must push the boats up the rest of the Rapid—then we will have to carry stuff over terrible trail on top ledges—long—we will be lucky to camp at head of rap tomorrow night...." For the first time on the journey, he sketched a rapid. Johnson was busy expressing his own reservations: "This may prove our downfall. This rapid is so rough that it may take us till noon to get by it, if we get by it at all.... the sides of the canyon are unbelievably rugged."

At six the next morning, they attacked. Hamilton took the unloaded *Mongoose* up first. The other boatmen pulled him as far as they could, then held him while he started the engine. Motor whining, he slowly worked his way almost to the top but then sheared a pin and dived for the oars. He rowed back down, started over, and this time made it to the foot of the last pitch, about 150 feet. Holmstrom walked back down the shore, killed a rattlesnake, and brought the *St. George* up. They ferried duffel, ran the last stretch, and noon found them reloaded above the rapid, "lucky to be thru so soon" (three hours for each boat). Exploring the deserted Red Ledge copper mine on a nearby slope, they camped a mile upriver from it.

On the morning of May 29, Clegg groused, "Was awakened this morning by the sound of a car—reaction, 'how horrible,' a car in my canyon!" (The car was visiting the mine downriver.) The boatmen, fatigued from Steamboat, rose later than usual. Once on the river, it was smooth water until Sawpit Rapid, (earlier, Thirtytwo Point Rapid) which they had to line, as well as an unnamed rapid just above it.

Buck Creek Rapid (earlier, Plummer Rapid) snatched their collective breath with its ferocity. Where it shelved off at its base, the holes kicked like mules in a stall. Downright dangerous. (Decades later, veteran river runner Don Hatch described it as "the damnedest thing I ever saw.") They unloaded the boats again and portaged again. Holmstrom's "very rough portage," has the ring of his characteristic understatement.

Squaw Creek (earlier, Black Point) was next, and if not worse, was not much better. Holmstrom thought it might be the worst of all to run; perhaps at that stage it was. Another strenuous line and portage—"long & bad." They finished at 4:30 P.M. and decided to camp on a sandbar on the Idaho side. Holmstrom again: "…very hard day's work—slickest mossiest rock I ever saw—wonder we haven't broken our necks." Another day, another five dollars.

Clegg, meanwhile, had hiked up slope and visited with an elderly recluse, "old Plumbob," as he called himself, and he sent her back to camp with strawberries and cherries, much to the delight of the boatmen.

It rained during the night, but the boatmen were too weary to rise; they simply tossed their ponchos over their bags and went back to sleep. Come morning, they lined Doyles Creek Rapid, where Holmstrom sheared a pin and Johnson grabbed the oars to save them from a quick retreat.

They heard Kinney Creek Rapid well before they saw it. Nine months earlier, a flash flood roared down the creek on the Idaho side and temporarily dammed the river. After a few minutes, the river broke through, but it left a residual dam, a steep rapid—"more of a falls than a rapid"—in between, and a minefield of boulders below. They lined the boats to the tail of the rapid, removed the motors, carried the boats 150 yards to the top of the rapid, and stopped to study the run with a critical eye. Johnson said, "No boat could live in that rapid"; Holmstrom, however, said, "…the rapid has the greatest fall of any I ever saw—could be run OK in a boat tho."

After lunch they ran glassy water for another half-mile and set up camp in a ponderosa pine grove on the Oregon shore. Shouts from the road across the river announced the arrival by car of Hamilton's wife Phyllis, his mother and step-father, uncle and aunt. Hamilton motored over to get them; they brought dinner and joined the group.

An air of triumph pervaded the moonlit camp, lending a festive mood to the evening. The hills drew back, announcing the limits of the canyon. Johnson rejoiced in his diary, "We are through Hells Canyon. Nothing can stop us now."

The expedition's achievement was an extraordinary feat. It had been done only once before, in 1819, almost 120 years earlier to the week. Donald McKenzie, a partner in the North West Company, who was determined to prove that the Snake River could furnish a downstream channel for the furs of the upper Snake River country, left from a fort near present-day Walla Walla, Washington, and went at the Snake against the grain: his six boatmen with a "barge," poled, paddled, and cordelled their way up the canyon. The indefatigable McKenzie, who weighed over three hundred pounds, took two months to reach the southern end of the canyon above the rapids, and the ordeal left him with reservations: "Yet from the current and the frequency of the rapids it may still be advisable and perhaps preferable to continue the land transport…." Holmstrom's party was the last to accomplish such a coup before dams erased six major rapids.

Clegg gave the expedition a day off. They loafed, visited, wandered back down to Kinney Creek to photograph the rapid. They went up the creek and called on "old Plumbob" in hopes of more strawberries and were not disappointed.

While Clegg enjoyed a foursome of bridge with the visitors—"one very dirty deck of cards... made me quite homesick"—Holmstrom and Bean hiked cross-country upriver on the Oregon side to visit Clydeus Rosalure Dunbar, locally known as "Wheelbarrow Annie" because she used a venerable, rickety wheelbarrow to move her hay. Annie smoked roll-your-owns, slept in her barn, looked out for horses and cow, dog and chickens, pheasants and rattlesnakes. At night she hiked with a lantern to Homestead for necessities. Holmstrom thought her "the dirtiest person I ever saw"; she may well have regarded him likewise. Clegg, although she did not visit, was more sympathetic: "They said she talked well, like a person with a good education and a good background.... There must be a story behind her. She lives absolutely alone in the poorest way, dresses like a tramp (or very much in my own style of the moment) but seems to have money to send away for things." On passing her by boat at a distance the next day, Clegg spotted her on shore waving, and wrote, "I thought she looked rather pathetic and would like to have stopped and talked."

Thursday, June 1. Time to move on. Hamilton took their visitors back across the river, where they took some of the load as well as Bean and Johnson to Homestead, Oregon, several drainages north. Homestead was the location of the Iron Dyke copper mine, which had ended production five years earlier. They counted on getting groceries at a small store that still subsisted there.

Phyllis rode upriver with Hamilton, and Holmstrom carried Clegg. They pulled in at a beach less than a mile above Homestead, only to be informed that their unextinguished campfire above Kinney Creek had ignited a grass fire. The men rode back in a car to the site and fought the fire, which had grown to a mile square, until they controlled it.

The next morning they purchased candy, beer, cigars, and gas at the store, and awaited the arrival of the Forest Service fire warden. Following the warden's stern lecture, a remorseful Johnson plead guilty and paid a five-dollar fine, although he neglects mentioning the incident in his diary. Then he and Bean, together with Phyllis and some of the supplies, rode ahead fourteen miles in the vehicles to await the boats. The rest of the visitors left for Coquille. Even with passengers, the boats covered seventeen miles before camp above Wildhorse Rapid, which they ran.

They were in Robinette, Oregon, before noon the next day, eleven river miles, partly because Bean and Johnson accepted a ride offered by a passing driver. Robinette was a tiny terminus of the Oregon Shortline Railroad, and there they bought gas and shipped all but the essentials ahead to Weiser, Idaho.

The country had opened up into arid farms, fields, orchards, a trace of green still clinging to the gentle slopes. The river, however, was wider and shallower, with a plenitude of barely submerged rocks called "sleepers" or "gators" causing footaches for the outboards. By this point Holmstrom had sheared three more pins than Hamilton, who was keeping count—a matter of interest and pride, at least to him. To lighten the load, Bean and Johnson accepted another ride on the road to Home, Oregon. They reported to the others that it made them carsick.

Because the river was dropping fast—the spring flood was over and irrigation canals were siphoning off their shares—they had to line Bayhorse Rapid and Eagle Rapid. Until now, Holmstrom and Hamilton had sheared a total of twelve pins. Indicative of changed water conditions, one day they sheared six, another day nine. They then ordered six dozen from Portland!

Clegg walked along the shore from Home to Huntington, Oregon. At the Huntington Bridge, she and Holmstrom walked two miles into town to get gas, then got a lift back in a car. Camp was a small, dirty cove below the bridge at the mouth of Burnt River. The wind blew hard and cold.

The next morning, June 5, Bean and Johnson caught the train twenty miles to Weiser. Then they hiked a mile downriver to meet the boats—which had dodged their way upstream, as Holmstrom said, "...tensed up continually expecting to hit a rock at any time"—in order that they might all arrive as one party. In midafternoon, with eight gallons of gas to spare, they all moored in a cottonwood grove on an island at the bottom end of Weiser's Main Street, where the Weiser River flows into the Snake. At this point they had been traveling forty-four days.

Time for festivities. Once camp was arranged, Clegg went into town with Holmstrom and purchased three bottles of liquor for their celebration on the beach. "We had a very merry time, joined in the end by two newspaper men," she said. "I went to bed early. The others went up town & went a little too far with their

Up Hells Canyon: Hamilton, Holmstrom, Bean, Johnson

joy and didn't feel good the next morning." With boatmen, ever thus.

Neither Holmstrom nor Johnson wrote anything in their journals for the next two days. Hamilton, however, left a clue. "Buzz and Bill get awful drunk. Start up town and I go along to bring them home. Get eats and all order steaks. Buzz & Bill get sick & I eat three steaks. I had to carry Buzz & Bill home. They went out like a light."

The following morning: "Boy are Buzz & Bill sick. Get up late." A portion of the recovery day was spent attending to apparel. Clegg mentions, "Our clothes barely lasted us into Weiser. My shoes and Bill's were flapping—all trousers in a dangerous condition, Buzz's shirt well ventilated, even the Doc slightly damaged." Hamilton got a bath and new clothes. Holmstrom shaved, then weighed and discovered he had lost twenty-two pounds. Johnson found a gray suit, but delayed shaving until the next day. Bean took a room in the hotel. Clegg had a bath, shampoo, facial, and did her laundry. Reporters, who Clegg called "most leech-like," arrived in camp with questions. Hamilton said he could safely say five hundred people came down to their camp during the course of the day to see them and their boats. Many brought gifts—eggs, pies, cakes—others wanted photographs or autographs. Clegg sent the crew into town for dinner, while she "minded the camp and amused the visitors."

In the morning Holmstrom wrote his mother a modest appraisal of the trip to date: "Really, the snakes were the biggest danger we had." Then the men pulled the boats out of the water, sanded the bottoms and replaced the guard strips, put a coat of varnish on each, and went up town again to see a movie at the Star Theater: *Adventures of Marco Polo* starring Gary Cooper, who survived sandstorms, shipwrecks, and avalanches en route to the Orient.

Everyone in town now knew them from their newspaper photographs and wanted to talk to them about the voyage. Clegg carped, "...there is no privacy... they... want to know about the trip, past and future, and are so nice and friendly that one likes them—but it does take time."

That evening, however, the five of them cooked a private dinner in camp. Bean and Johnson, as planned, were paid off. Jokes and recollections were shared. After dark, Clegg wrote, "We shall miss Bill very much. He was so faithful and friendly and deeply interested in the journey." For his part, Johnson wrote, "We are all very sorry to part for the trip has been so lovely and successful...." He waited to see them off the next day, and gave Clegg a box of chocolates. Bean left on the train to Oregon.

Departure was delayed until midday because they had to wait for the noon train from Portland bringing the shear pins and spare spark plugs. A large crowd came down to wave them off. Under a cloudy sky, Weiser soon slipped astern.

As the boats muled upriver, Clegg lamented, "Mosquitoes for the first time... landscape a mudflat—I want my canyon." Hamilton was also feeling morose: "Rather wish I wasn't going on, it's sort of an anticlimax. Will only be a job now."

Even the unflagging Holmstrom says, "...not interesting here... wish back in Canyon...." They made twenty miles and camped on a small island just below Ontario, Oregon.

Once again the expedition began calculating distance by mileage. Past Homedale, now wholly in Idaho, they skittered upriver through barren flatlands, cultivated islands, graveled shoals and shallows—sometimes "too shallow even to row"—shearing pins and dinging props and seeking potable water at ranch houses. Hamilton complained, "[this] isn't a river here, it is merely a collection of wet stones." At one point, in exasperation, he filled Clegg's canteen from the river and punned in his diary, "...boy would she boil if she knew it."

Newspaper articles and radio reports excited folks with nothing better to do to peer at them from the tops of haystacks or through riverside willow thickets along the shore, waving them in with bribes of vegetables and then taking their photographs. One ranch wife insisted on showing Clegg poems and quilts she had made; Clegg noted that evening, "...the quilts were the more successful." Holmstrom called the river "Mizerable going"; Hamilton was disenchanted and homesick and it showed: "Don't see how anything can live in this country." Clegg was irritable and bossy. On June 11 they stopped at Walters Ferry for gas, then pressed on to record a thirty-five-mile day.

The next day, with the help of employees from Idaho Power and a truck, they surmounted Swan Falls Dam, and relaunched for Grand View, a forty-mile-plus day. Moods lifted: the water was clearer, they saw doves, crows, magpies, mallards, geese, egrets, pelicans, sandhill cranes; jackrabbits along the shore, sturgeon in the shallows. The country elevated to rimrock; the wind provided a helpful, following shove.

In the morning, Holmstrom bought a pair of "smoke glasses as sun hard on eyes on water." And the water that day was hard on boats. With the flow down to 19,000 CFS, they had to line one rapid, then unload the boats and portage over a wet, steep, rocky shore for another; then stop and do it all over a third time. An eight-mile day. Not one with much to smile about, as Clegg's diary entry reveals. While walking along the bank, she stopped to visit a ranch family. They sent their boy on a mile-long trip to fetch her some spring water. "The son has a fixed grin and at first I thought he was mentally deficient. But he doesn't seem queer when you talk to him." And when the wind collapsed her tent in the night, she did not even bother to ask for help erecting it; she just slept on top of it.

Thereafter, mileage improved. In Glenns Ferry by noon, and facing five dams ahead as well as two-hundred-foot Shoshone Falls and Twin Falls, Clegg decided to do all the portages in one drive to Minidoka Reservoir, a distance of over a hundred miles. She went to the Commercial Hotel for a bath, while Holmstrom and Hamilton hunted for a willing truck and driver. By the time they had located one, she had eaten dinner, so she sent them uptown for their dinner, and she stayed with the boats.

The next day they had the boats loaded in the truck before noon and were on their way. They drove through Hagerman Valley, past Thousand Springs, and had lunch in the town of Twin Falls. After lunch they wasted two hours trying to talk a Johnson dealer into taking their two 9.8-hp motors in trade on a new 22-hp Johnson worth $270. No go. They did learn from the salesman, however, that because of diversion dams, it would be better to continue by highway to American Falls, where a major federal irrigation dam had been constructed in 1927. They took his advice, and by nightfall were camped out in the rain on a mudflat without natural shelter or wood. They ate a cold supper in Clegg's tent and went to bed shivering: from the heat of Glenns Ferry, they had climbed almost two thousand feet and their clothes were insufficient. Suddenly, the floodlights along the dam came on and robbed them of their assumed privacy.

Roused early by wind, they dragged the boats two hundred feet down the muddy shore. It was bitterly cold, the sky gray as a bruise. Holmstrom had to borrow socks and a sweater from Clegg, then the two of them walked into town—he, according to her, looking "as blue as the sweater"—where he got gas and oil and she purchased groceries. They motored off at midmorning, up the choppy, twenty-five-mile reservoir, hunting with growing frustration for the inlet of the Snake through the willows and cattails. Wet and cold, they mistook the mouth of the Portneuf River for the channel and wound up camping for the night at the same place where they had eaten lunch.

The next morning, in a desperate ploy to fox the wind, they broke camp without waiting for breakfast and picked up the threaded, meandering channel only two miles from camp. The river, down to 1,500 CFS, was so shallow through the Fort Hall Reservation bottoms that they had to walk at times and only made about seven miles before camping by the bridge at Pingree. They got a lift three miles from a ranch wife, but since they could only locate a quart of oil at the crossroads of Thoms, telephoned for a delivery of gas and oil from Riverside.

Cold and windy and tiresome. Said Clegg, "We haven't been warm for nearly three days"—they reached Blackfoot in the afternoon. Actually, the town was two miles from the river, as the men learned by lugging four gas cans in need of gas, while Clegg stayed with the boats under a bridge out of the rain. With a rodeo going in town, no one was available to help with transport. They found some shelter in a grove of willow and cottonwoods a mile farther upriver, and built a witchburner of a fire.

Above Blackfoot, six rock irrigation dams jammed their passage; they ran two and lined four. Flow increased; they speculated that it was the result of continued rain and a release from the dam at Jackson Lake in Wyoming. After wading in freezing, knee-high water all day, Hamilton noted that they had been out for sixty-one days.

Walking to the camp that afternoon, four miles above Shelley, Clegg stopped to visit a rancher with eleven children. She found them enjoyable and was charmed when one child informed her, "We are gen-u-ine pests." As for the day, she said, "The last four days have been dull and trying and miserably cold… impossible to make much progress."

When a run of only a mile the next morning brought them to yet another old dam, they retreated three miles and telephoned for a truck to take the boats the remaining ten miles into Idaho Falls. With consent of the sheriff, they left the boats in Memorial Park in the center of town. Clegg bought all hands a good dinner and champagne—the first Holmstrom had ever tasted. His diary that night records: "5 men commit suicide this year at Idaho Falls." The men slept by the boats; Clegg slept at the Bonneville Hotel: "a bed for the first time since April 23rd!"

Wednesday, June 21. They were now two months from Gault's Boatworks. Clegg bought pants, shirt, jacket—"this trip is certainly hard on clothes." As planned, the boatmen loaded the *Mongoose* and both engines and their duffel on the truck. They left the *St. George* for Hamilton to crate and ship by rail back to Oregon. While the *St. George* was unarguably the faster boat, and although both boats were in the same condition, the *Mongoose* carried a load better. They had a parting drink in the hotel bar and lunch in a coffee shop. Hamilton decided to accompany them with the driver over the Continental Divide "just for the ride."

The weather faired off to a radiant blue sky and the ride was ideal. They went by way of St. Anthony, Idaho, over Targhee Pass (7,072 feet), and through West Yellowstone and its Norris Basin. To everyone's regret, they passed north of Old

Faithful but were rewarded with sightings of bear, deer, elk, antelope, moose. It was summer solstice, the longest day of the year, but by the time they pulled into Gardiner, Montana, drove a mile out of town, and carted the boat down an overgrown trail to the river, it was dusk. They eased it into the water and tied the painter to a pine tree for the night.

Holmstrom and Hamilton shook hands, and then, good-byes said, Hamilton headed back to Idaho Falls with Mr. Dilley, the driver. Now only two were bound for the sea. They settled in for their first night on the Atlantic side of the divide.

Morning broke with pressing business: Mrs. Clegg was down to $1.09. She had arranged for money to be sent her in Gardiner, and in the morning it was with considerable relief that she found it waiting at the post office, along with a stack of mail. Holmstrom took care of his errands and was informed by one resident that the Yellowstone was "a desperate river." By two in the afternoon he was rowing Clegg through the swiftwater rapids of Yankee Jim Canyon on the desperate river— back with oars and clearwater and constricted canyons, back in his element. And finally, they were back on the trail of Lewis and Clark: on the return trip in July 1806, William Clark had run the Yellowstone from below present-day Livingston, Montana, down to his meeting with Meriwether Lewis on the Missouri.

The *Mongoose* sailed along through the redrock canyon and out into verdant Paradise Valley, the Gallatin Range to their west, the Absaroka Range—called the "Snowies" by early settlers—to their east. At seven hundred miles in length, the Yellowstone is the preeminent river of the Great Plains. Holmstrom, with Clegg, was intent on running 550 miles to the Missouri—all but the last few miles of it in Montana. At Billings, the river averages 7,000 CFS; at its mouth 13,000 CFS—this year, it was 13,000 CFS even at Billings.

Burdened by the weight of the two motors, and buoyed by the release from their drone, they stopped long enough to ship them ahead by rail: one to Livingston, the other to Billings. After lightening their load, they made good time. Holmstrom let Clegg row at times. She stuck on a rock and he pushed her off, "no harm done." They made Livingston on the afternoon of June 23, shipped the first motor on to Billings as well, and slept in the city park by the river, kept awake by a drum corps entertaining American Legionnaires attending the state convention.

In the morning before shoving off, they met a fisherman who, convinced they would not make it through Yankee Jim Canyon, had come down to watch for their bodies. Clegg called him "a cheerful soul." They floated north beneath vertiginous, 10,000-foot peaks such as Sheep Mountain on the east and Electric Peak on the west. Creeks spilled in on each side.

The river widened through the Great Bend as it swung from north to east, running through sandstone bluffs with bottomlands softened by flickering cotton-woods shedding their downy seeds, and wild yellow roses in bloom along the banks.

Violet-green swallows twisted over the river and back to their pockets in the bluffs; a wavering chevron of Canada geese straggled north. Livingston Peak reared to the south, the Crazies ten miles to the northeast, the Bridgers to the northwest. Their river elevation was still almost a mile high. They logged a fifty-mile day.

Two mornings later they rowed into Billings, which with its population of twenty-five thousand, was the largest town in the Yellowstone Basin. In 1875 Grant Marsh, under contract to the U.S. Army, had piloted the sternwheel steamer *Josephine* to a point just shy of present-day Billings, establishing the record for the highest point of navigation on the river. (On the Mississippi, Marsh had been a mate on the *John J. Roe*, a boat so slow, Mark Twain wrote, "that when she sank it took the owners five months to discover it.")

Clegg had settled on replacing the Johnson with a Model PO, a faster, heavier 22-hp. Holmstrom located a truck, pulled the boat out of the water, and took it to the Murphy Auto Cabins, where he wheeled it into the garage and took over the cabin for himself. Clegg went up town and took a room at the Northern Hotel: "This hotel is very comfortable—almost grand." She wired Portland for the new motor, then located a tinsmith to make food boxes to replace their wooden ones.

They settled in for what proved to be a ten-day stay. When a couple of days later a telegraph from Schroeder & Hildenbrand in Oregon informed Holmstrom that they could not sell a Johnson outside their sales territory, he ordered one from the dealership in Seattle. (The Billings dealer told Holmstrom he was lucky to sell one outboard a year.) It did not arrive until three days later.

In the meantime, Clegg had a facial, manicure, had her hair done, even visited a chiropodist, shopped for clothes, then called on friends in Billings. George Housser drove out with his son, Trevor, and took her on outings south to Yellowstone National Park and east to Custer Battlefield National Monument and to a Crow Indian celebration at Lodgegrass on the Fourth of July. They visited the local country club, and Billings's red-light district, about which she said, "Personally, I think it is an offense to go unless you are going 'on business'; I never went to see the Yoshiwara [Japan]." She enjoyed a round of cocktails and dinner followed by bridge games. Sometimes Holmstrom joined her for dinner; one night he took the friends' children to the movies.

With his river routine momentarily interrupted, Holmstrom's thoughts curved toward his river cronies Doc Frazier, Amos Burg, and Willis Johnson, whom he knew were dodging their way down the Middle Fork of the Salmon that same week. Perhaps some part of him, the boatman's bond, made him hanker to be with them, but it did not pay as well. During most days, however, he was busy with river preparations, among them repainting the *Mongoose* with red decks and white hull. On picking up the new engine, he was dismayed to find a crack in its mount, but rather than wait for a replacement part, he arranged a rivet-patch overlay. That done, he towed the boat up to Lake Elmo, five miles north of town in Billings Heights, and gave the new engine a workout. He brought it back to the garage and reworked the controls. That night, he informed Clegg that they were ready to launch.

On July 6, at a very reasonable hour, friends saw them off at the East Bridge. Four hundred eighty-three miles to the Missouri. The river was shallow but running a healthy 15,000 CFS. Though they were heavily loaded, Holmstrom still favored oars. They rowed over thirty miles, but missed Baptiste Creek, the pull-in for Pompey's Pillar, where William Clark carved his name July 24, 1806—the only glyph surviving from the expedition. Clark named the outcrop for Sacajawea's son, born in 1804 at the winter camp with the Mandans. Clegg was so disappointed that they camped early and she walked back four miles to see the inscription. "The rock is shaped like an enormous birthday cake [200 feet high]. I just got back to camp by dark, and enjoyed the walk."

They floated through grassland, the faint violet shadow of the Beartooths barely visible on the northern horizon. This was buffalo country, as Clark wrote, "…country thick with buffalow & keep a continuing bellowing in every direction." Mule deer were now the only wild, quiet reminders.

They boated past the mouth of the Bighorn River, where in June 1876, Captain Marsh took the sternwheel steamer *Far West* to within fifteen miles of Custer's Last Stand in order to rescue Reno and Benteen's wounded soldiers, and then ran 710 miles to the hospital at Bismarck, North Dakota, in fifty-four hours, averaging thirteen mph. In comparison, the Clegg expedition shuffled. They found a channel to the right of the diversion dam at Hysham and ran it, then lined the one at Forsyth.

Using the motor and now running on 17,000 CFS, they passed Miles City and covered over a hundred miles in one day. A steamboat on this reach, two years after the Northern Pacific extended its rails to Miles City in 1881, had been held up several hours while seventy five thousand buffalo crossed the river. A year later, instead of hauling two hundred thousand hides, all that was left for steamer cargo were buffalo bones, headed east to be ground into fertilizer. Now the only delay for the *Mongoose* was the dam at Intake—insurmountable gates, abutments, and rock walls. They had to call for a truck to come twenty miles from Glendive, Montana, to haul them out of the canyon, around it, and back down to the river. That night the wind kicked up and scattered their campfire, and a fierce lightning storm forked overhead. Mosquitoes argued over drilling rights and left Holmstrom with swollen hands, arms, and mouth in the morning. Their last camp in Montana.

As they boated along this reach, they were passing through some of the larger coal reserves in the world. At one camp, they had watched a black seam afire in the cliff across the river: "After dark there was a burning point in it, just like a big taillight." In the morning, smoke filtered out of fissures. (The region was only thirty years from becoming an extensive coal mine and oil field.)

The last few miles to the Missouri were slow going. Mudwater again. Looking upstream from the confluence, Holmstrom glimpsed the site of Forts Henry, Buford, Union: where Maximilian Prince of Wied and his artist Karl Bodmer walked; where John James Audubon sketched a white wolf; where George Catlin rested on a cannon and painted Indian chiefs; where Jim Bridger stretched his blanket; where Mike Fink, the archetypal boatman, doubtless liquored, lifted his faithful "Bang All" and shot his friend Carpenter by deliberately missing the tin cup balanced on his head, and then was shot in turn by Talbot, and his body buried.

Holmstrom's first encounter with the Missouri, however, was inauspicious: "Only place to land at Williston is at garbage dump—I step ashore & go in mud to my knees—then tie boat to old car frame. Can't get water—after seeing all the sewage that goes into river don't feel inclined to drink it."

July 13, more than two-and-a-half months into the journey, and they were on the Big Muddy. Holmstrom notes, "Better going on the Missouri—tho not as big as I thot—at junct doesn't look as big as Yell[owstone]." He was right, of course. Although not as large as the Columbia or the Mississippi, the Missouri is the longest river in the U.S. (2,945 miles). In flow, which is 76,000 CFS at its mouth, it ranks a distant sixth. At the mouth of the Yellowstone, as Holmstrom alertly observed, the Yellowstone's spring flow is usually about 2,000 CFS greater than the Missouri's 11,000 CFS. This year, however, the upper reaches of the Missouri were running 23,000 CFS.

River pilots on the upper Missouri—the two-thousand-mile reach from Fort Benton, Montana, to Sioux City, Iowa, called the river the "Sandy" because it flows through an area of alluvial, easily eroded soils, not only muddying the water but destabilizing the banks and carving large meanders. Construction of the Fort Peck Dam in Montana in the 1930s closed a proud, hundred-year history written by crack steamboat pilots who survived snag-strewn channels and savage storms on the upper river. The last steamboat departed Fort Benton the same year that Johnson Motors produced its first outboard—just eighteen years before Holmstrom came down the river.

The upper Missouri displays other peculiarities: it has two annual rises, the low-snow runoff in April; and the high Rocky Mountain runoff in June; rainfall that averages fourteen inches at Fort Benton grows to forty inches at St. Louis. As the Clegg expedition came downriver, the runoff had peaked, but the flow was a high 23,000 CFS and the storm season was just getting underway.

Six years of drought, the Dust Bowl years, with their consequent devastating impacts on farms, were appallingly apparent all along their Missouri passage. Farms were short of drinking water or, often as not, abandoned. Holmstrom: "... haven't seen a single farm with running water... sometimes pump 5 min before get even a trickle of water." Clegg: "The ranchers are few and far between on this river." And the river was quick to seize low-lying ground. "The woman said it was the last year they would be there as the river would wash away the ranch-house next year.... The river is always changing its course and doing a good deal of damage in the process." Holmstrom: "One man lost 600 acres this year." As a precaution, the boatman slept on the bowline, and one night felt it move under his sleeping bag. He got up and found that three feet of bank had caved in on top of the *Mongoose*.

The depressing condition of the country, coupled with the bleak plains and the Norwegian settlers, prompted Holmstrom to make a literary reference to the Norwegian-American novelist Ole Rolvaag, whose classic on struggling pioneer farmers, *Giants in the Earth,* had been published a dozen years earlier. Holmstrom remarked that the region was like a page out of the novel. He learned from merchants that the area had been good grazing ground, but high prices offered for wheat had persuaded ranchers to plow ground that was never meant to be plowed. Topsoil blew away like talcum powder in a dry wind, farm prices fell, farms were abandoned, mortgages foreclosed.

Cottonwoods toppled into the river hourly, leaving little in the way of firewood. For decades "woodhawks" had harvested what trees were available for the steamers, which burned on average twenty-five cords in twenty-four hours. At least once, Clegg and Holmstrom used a lump of coal for their fire. Then they got a kerosene stove.

Their routine became one of an early search for water and gas, then miles against the wind—"bad wind"..."Windy very all day." Because of the wide or vertical mud banks, Clegg had to ride in the boat. "I had expected to walk which would have been very good for me; I get no exercise now... everywhere you step out of the boat, you are up to your ankles in gumbo. It makes everything in the boat so dirty, you just can't keep it or the boat clean." They spotted the site of Lewis and Clark's winter camp with the Mandans, but the steep bluff prevented them from visiting it. They both commented on the fact that they had not seen a commercial boat since Johnson Bar on the Snake, although they did see numerous old grain scows and steamers dry-docked, abandoned high on the shores. They motored on through a "chocolate froth."

In mid-July, at Bismarck, North Dakota, with Clegg feeling "very depressed about the trip," they stopped and hired a taxi to see the Badlands, 135 miles away. Both plainly enjoyed the excursion, the landscape and its geology, and they treated themselves to dinner at the Prince Hotel before going back down to the boat for the night.

That night Holmstrom wrote his mother a letter in which, for the only time, he expressed his discontent: "It is unbelievable how little time I seem to have even to write letters. From the time I wake up in the A.M. till [I] go to bed there are a lot of things ahead to do. Making camps like we make is an awful job itself. Since Bill and the rest are gone, it leaves an awful lot for one person to do."

They were traveling due south now, toward South Dakota. Rain, hailstones, wind that uprooted cottonwoods and tossed them into the river. By the time they reached Mobridge (Missouri Bridge), South Dakota, in the Standing Rock Sioux Indian Reservation, the hailstones were lethal; Clegg took a room in the hotel and Holmstrom huddled in her tent snugged to a tree. The wind here blew "harder and hotter and dustier." People in the hotel told Clegg that before this summer, they could not remember seeing the black hills green.

In the morning, she brought breakfast down to the boat for Holmstrom, and then they were off before the dew was off the hay, boating along the edge of the Cheyenne Indian Reservation. The wind punched the water into whitecaps and they had to pull off for a couple of hours. They soon settled on a camp.

They arrived at Pierre, South Dakota, at noon and picked up a bundle of mail. Clegg found it "a funny little town for a capital; it shows signs of the Depression and 10 years of crop failures." Even the number of legislators had been reduced for reasons of economy! The two of them ate dinner uptown, but Holmstrom insisted she sleep at the St. Charles Hotel. (Here, as all along the Missouri, they had taken to locating a Boy Scout whenever they had to leave the boat temporarily at a community, and he would watch it in their absence.)

Hot, windy, hazy. Another lightning storm. Grassrope, Culdesac, Chamberlain. Maddening meanders. "Motor goes slower all the time." They got gasoline and camped.

The following day, Clegg noted the prettiest twelve-mile stretch of river since they left Livingston. But as they traveled along the Nebraska border, heading easterly, Holmstrom continually fought the motor. The river was dropping, the current lessened. He hoped he could make it to Yankton. A sternwheel steamer, the *Sara S*, surged past them at five mph, pushing a scow upriver. She was bound to pick up cottonwood logs that would be sliced into veneer for egg crates. They stopped at a large stone ranch house, which proved to be the Bonhomme Colony of the Hutteische Church. They went up to visit.

The pacifist colony from German Tyrol had been there since 1872, living a communal life. Clegg and Holmstrom found the members very friendly, talkative, contented, even jolly. Their dwellings and clothing were spotless. The women wore "peasant skirts and loose bodices and sunbonnets with colorful linings." Hard workers all, but no one had to work after age forty-five, except to peel potatoes. They raised hundreds of pigs, drank but did not dance; their only music consisted of singing. Marriage choice was free, but only to someone within the church. Store purchases were voted upon once a year. If someone fell ill, he or she was taken to a doctor in Yankton (where they were called Mennonites). When Holmstrom and Clegg left, a dozen of the woman accompanied them down to the river and loaded them down with fresh apples.

Ten miles short of Yankton, the motor quit for good. Holmstrom rowed the rest of the way, arriving about noon. A friendly game warden drove him and the outboard in his own car to St. Paul, Minnesota, a distance well over two hundred miles, to see about repairing the engine. Clegg stayed behind at Yankton's Curry Hotel.

Warden Gunnerson and Holmstrom drove all afternoon and into the night. The next morning at the St. Paul dealer, they pulled the engine apart and found it ruined by water pushing a bearing into the cylinders. They placed a call to the factory in Waukegan, Illinois, where Arvard Olsen said "give him a new one." Holmstrom: "Sure glad to hear that." They started back at eleven and arrived in Yankton at seven that evening, just as Clegg finished her first catfish dinner. Holmstrom wrote, "... tired & sleepy & happy with new motor."

Two days more, and they were past Sioux City, from which point downriver, the Army Corps of Engineers maintained a deeper channel and stronger current with dredges, pilings, and stone wing-dams. Willows woven into mats stabilized the shoreline, but the pilings made it difficult to find campsites. The left shore was now Iowa. Clegg: "Woke early to clean half Iowa off my trousers and shoes which took me 45 minutes."

From Omaha, the river runs 650 miles without a dam, but is channeled for barges. With the new motor and a channel, they could make fifty miles in a day. "Lots of work going on. Pile drivers, derricks, shovels, dredges, scows.... The farmers are grumbling that the dyking and narrowing... is causing more floods than ever. They want a levee with a road on top." (Levees actually do increase the frequency and raise the height of flooding.) The *Mongoose* cruised into Omaha—Council Bluffs toward evening, the Lewis and Clark Memorial limned against a salmon-tinged sky. Holmstrom hooked a Boy Scout watchman and went to dinner with Clegg, stopping on the way to buy a new pair of pants because when he jumped ashore, he went into mud up to his knees. She took a room at the Hill Hotel; he returned to the boat, which was moored by a sewer.

The next morning, they took a taxi ten miles west of the city to Father Flanagan's Boys Town and were given an extensive tour. (Their interest was sparked by the popular movie, starring Spencer Tracy, which had been released a year earlier.) Then they crossed the bridge into Council Bluffs and visited the Lewis and Clark Memorial. Made of flaking concrete, it looked better from the river. Clegg: "We had great difficulty in getting to it, as no one knew exactly where it was."

They moved south rapidly, past the mouth of the Platte, marking the end of the Great Plains; a brief stop at Nebraska City to repair the prop damaged by a piece of oak and to buy a new one. Short of water, they stopped at a bunkhouse and tool-storage boat for river workers, and the watchman filled their canteens. He informed them that they purified river water and also used old ice to cool it. That afternoon, Holmstrom was so sleepy that they stopped so he could take a nap, until Clegg awakened him after two hours.

The next day they cleared the Kansas-Missouri state line, slipped past St. Joseph (Holmstrom: "biggest and foulest sewer yet"), then Atchinson and Fort Leavenworth, "all looking attractive from the river, and what is rare being attractive right down to the river bank. The river is usually a rather squalid backdoor to a town." By his own admission, Holmstrom was not feeling well. They camped below Leavenworth, and powered into Kansas City at 8:30 the next morning. Holmstrom made a log entry that was short, seamanlike, in a shaky hand: "Don't feel good."

He and Clegg had discussed the merits of altering the hull of the *Mongoose* by removing the four inches of rake, thereby increasing its speed on these flat waters. On learning of an elderly, experienced boatwright employed by the Star Boat Company, Holmstrom trucked the boat there to have the work done. He must have been feeling ill indeed to leave his boat in the hands of a stranger.

He was a sick man, a lot sicker than he conceded. Feverish. He insisted he was fine but slept most of the day. Clegg took a room at the Muehlebach Hotel and wandered around the city studying its architecture.

The next day at noon, with Holmstrom still groggy, indifferent to food, and gulping quart after quart of water, Clegg took his temperature: 101.5. She hunted up a hotel where they could both afford to stay and found a doctor. When Dr. Stofer's thermometer read 102.5, he suspected typhoid, common in the area, or possibly pneumonia, and advised getting Holmstrom into a hospital. Clegg took him to St. Lukes Hospital in a torrential thunderstorm at dusk,

She moved to the Brookside Hotel, which was closer to the hospital, and checked on him in the morning. Holmstrom was comfortable. The doctor was still uncertain about his typhoid diagnosis. Clegg spent the afternoon walking miles about the city. Back at the hotel, nothing so thoroughly convinced her that she had left the West behind as her dinner confrontation. Having had a facial and shampoo, wearing her best shirt and trousers, "feeling extra respectable," she was met with a gasp by the female maitre d' at the dining room door: "Oh! You aren't going into the dining room like that?" Clegg was persuaded to take her dinner on a tray in her room. "Oh well; I suppose this is the Middle West."

She checked on Holmstrom again but found him sleeping. His fever had peaked. Clegg: "WHAT A RELIEF!!!!!" Then at Doctor Stofer's invitation, she spent the evening visiting with his family.

The following day, Holmstrom was showing signs of renewed life. Clegg spent another day with the Stofers, and in the afternoon, Holmstrom was released, feeling, according to him, "weak but OK." Clegg had found a hotel, the Ambassador, where they might both stay. "If they don't like my trousers here, I think they would expire at the sight of Buzz and I would hate him to feel uncomfortable."

Holmstrom had been sick for a week, in the hospital for four days. In retrospect, it could have been typhoid, which requires two weeks for incubation. He decided to get a typhoid vaccination. Clegg did likewise.

The first concern for a reinvigorated Holmstrom was his boat. On looking over the boatwright's work, he was pleased. The next day he got the *Mongoose* back in the water and tested its redesigned hull. He found that the alterations had increased its speed—in fact, the boat tended to plane. A black tempest opened over the river, and instead of departing, the pair decided to spend another night in the dry comfort of the Robert E. Lee hotel by the river. Since the storm was still there in the morning, they waited until noon; when it eased, they launched.

The Missouri swings due east at Kansas City. The channel was marked with red-and-white buoys, and they made good time on a rising flow of 35,000 to 45,000 CFS—Lexington, Booneville, Waverly—boating beneath wooded limestone bluffs, both exhilarated to be back on the river.

The days flowed together: Sandy Hook, Jefferson City (where a local wanted to show them the "scenic" penitentiary), Chamois, Hermann with its vineyards. At St. Charles, Clegg made a telling commentary: "...terraces down to the river and flower beds, all arranged to look nice *from* the river. What a change! They like their river in these lower reaches and I haven't noticed any garbage dumps or sewers."

Their only problem was a leaky boat; water soaked the floor in the stern compartment. On reaching the Mound Hill boat harbor in St. Louis, Holmstrom unloaded the boat and pulled it out of the water. He found that the shipwright in Kansas City had neglected to replace three screws.

St. Louis news photo

Clegg called friends, the Arbuckles, who lived on a farm in the Ozarks fifty miles from the city. She and Holmstrom were invited to spend the night and did. The Arbuckles had a city house on Washington Boulevard as well, and they all returned there by noon the following day. Clegg visited a beauty parlor, played Chinese checkers with the daughter, and in the cool of the evening went for a driving tour of the city. Holmstrom bought a river cap, wrote some letters, fiddled with the boat, admitted in his journal "...don't like St. Louis very well."

In the morning, they left St. Louis, the second-largest inland port in the country, and headed south down the Mississippi between the borders of

210

Missouri and Illinois. Now they were on the real "Big Muddy," Mark Twain's river, one whose flow at its mouth was nearly eight times that of the Missouri, making it the largest watershed in the U.S. From its confluence with the Ohio River at Cairo, Illinois, the upper Mississippi extends north 790 miles. Here, however, it was not as large as its reach through the lower Coastal Plain, not even as large as the Ohio. But the dredged, nine-foot-deep channel coupled with a brimming 130,000 CFS provided a strong assist to the outboard. And both boaters noted the change from muddy to sandy banks, a consequence of the Mississippi's glaciated headwaters. Clegg appreciated the change: "The Mississippi is much more attractive and beautiful than the Missouri—it has an air!" In two days, they were at the confluence with the Ohio River.

While the Ohio River (a Seneca word for "great river") is the third-largest in the U.S., at its confluence with the Mississippi it is the larger of the two, an average 280,000 CFS compared to the upper Mississippi's 198,000. It is the mother of Appalachian rivers, draining the western Appalachian Plateau, draining ten wet states along a line that marks the southern glacial advance during the ice ages. Moreover, between 1780 and 1820, it was the birthplace of most western forms of transport boat: ark, flatboat, broadhorn, keelboat, steamboat. In September—November 1803, Meriwether Lewis brought a fifty-five-foot modified keelboat down the river for his meeting with William Clark. Mike Fink, "half-horse, half-alligator," earned his fame here. From here, Abraham Lincoln made flatboat trips to New Orleans between 1828 and 1830. Robert Fulton's second steamboat, with paddle-wheels midship, ran the Ohio to New Orleans. (Ohio steamboats, unlike their wood-fueled Mississippi counterparts, were largely dependent on coal.) These boats made the Ohio the "thoroughfare for the West" from 1780 to 1860. Eventually, fifty dams turned it into a rosary of reservoirs for barges that carried more cargo than the Panama Canal. (Twenty-one high dams have replaced the original fifty.)

All of those dams, fitted with locks, were in place as Holmstrom swung the *Mongoose* easterly into the clearer, jade-green current of the Ohio. The river was running a copious 66,000 CFS. Nine hundred and seventy miles and fifty-three locks to Pittsburgh. At least the locks were free. After the previous night's rain, welcome sunlight flashed off the water. Behind the levee on their left stood the dilapidated Halliday Hotel, used for a time by General Grant as his headquarters during the Civil War. Suddenly, on this glassy run, Holmstrom met a new hazard: he sheared a pin on a garfish, large as a log but harder to spot. It would not be the last—he hit five in one day.

Holmstrom found the river a "very clear contrast" with the Mississippi; Clegg found it "perfectly lovely." They motored past the mouths of the Tennessee and Cumberland Rivers flowing in from Kentucky on their right. Past Paducah, then old Shawneetown—made famous by the flatboatmen and keelboatmen in their day, and now a state historic park. Occasional islands. Clegg wrote, "The shores are more like

lake shores, hills and bays and woods and clearings, and happy looking houses...." Past the mouth of the Wabash River on the north, Evansville on the Indiana side, Owensboro on the Kentucky side. Clegg made an excursion to get her first look at a tobacco field. More ferries than bridges here. With camps harder to find, they took to using abandoned ferry landings. Holmstrom swiped a few ears of corn from a field, and it was so good that Clegg vowed to watch for campsites near cornfields.

They liked the Ohio with its sidewheel steamboats, even though at night the wash sometimes imperiled Holmstrom's sleeping bag. One night they built a large campfire, and Clegg said they stayed up late and had a long talk. Shadows became evening. "This river gets prettier and prettier," she reveled.

They meandered east between Kentucky and Illinois. Some of the towns along the river were still mucking out from the foul monsoon of 1937, when it rained nineteen inches in twenty-three days. At Leavenworth, Illinois, the town had been rebuilt on a bluff above the old town.

August 22, month four. They awoke to a fog-shrouded river, a fog so impenetrable that it delayed their departure for over an hour. When it lifted, they shoved off for Louisville, arrived at the locks that had replaced the infamous Falls of the Ohio (a twenty-four-foot drop over three miles); waited for an hour for the lift, and just before noon, tied up at a boat harbor. Holmstrom called Dr. Hendon, a surgeon-friend of Doc Russell Frazier, who took him on an overnight visit to his farm, while Clegg checked into the Brown Hotel—"charming... long white corridors like a ship"—went to the bank and then bought some books. Unlike other rivers, while they motored on the Ohio, she had time to read.

The following day after lunch together, Holmstrom and Clegg visited a flood-damaged museum in the basement of the public library and went on to the local historical society, where the president proved to be the great grandson of William Clark's sister. On examining an original letter by Clark to his brother exhibited there, announcing the expedition's return, Clegg commented, "Very neat writing, very odd spelling." Both Clegg and Holmstrom agreed the grandson looked "absurdly like" the portrait of Clark. Afterwards, since the day was well spent, they decided to go see Churchill Downs racetrack. That done, they dined at the hotel.

Dawn touched the river a painterly, reflective green; they were on their way within the hour. Holmstrom remarked, "Sure liked Louisville." As though to compensate for the layover day, they covered sixty-five miles: northeasterly past Madison, Indiana, and Carrolton, Kentucky, past the inviting entrance to the Kentucky River ("It was a heartbreak to pass it by...."), and camped at Rising Sun, Indiana, just across the river from Rabbit Hash, Kentucky.

On this water, now down to about 18,000 CFS, the new motor was averaging almost ten miles an hour. They reached Cincinnati before noon. Holmstrom's impression: "—dirty—not very nice town." Clegg, however, had discovered that a showboat on the waterfront was having a performance that evening; her lifelong interest in theater was piqued, and she determined that they would stay overnight and take in the show. She got a room at the Colonial Hotel, "comfortable and very clean... very old-fashioned and rather poor." Nothing that happened thereafter improved their impression of Cincinnati.

After being assured that it was a place where they could eat in their river attire, they got a ride to the Netherlands—Plaza Hotel for lunch. Holmstrom was refused: "Not without a coat." They lunched elsewhere. Before the play, he went to meet Clegg for dinner at the Broadway Hotel. As he tells it, "...2nd rate [hotel] ask at the desk for her—describe her broadbrim western hat & trousers—the clerk is horrified—'Well, I guess she wouldn't eat here—not with trousers.' They seem to be mighty conservative."

The play was packed but Clegg's review was more rant than rave: "The play was shockingly cut, so badly that there was no continuity. They burlesqued it. They were very difficult to hear. There wasn't one note of sincerity or simplicity in the acting. Why people go on coming I don't know and wish I could have found out." Obviously, they were not going to play Peoria.

Cincinnati fell astern, fast. Two mornings later, Holmstrom was gassing the *Mongoose* 170 river miles to the southeast, in Huntington, West Virginia. Even though the flow had fallen to 7,000 CFS, they now averaged over sixty miles a day. The reservoirs behind the locks were sometimes forty miles long. Clegg read her books and abridged her diary: "I say very little about these days on the Ohio because though they are delightful, there is very little incident. They are beautiful and peaceful and pastoral, and yet a lot of history lurking around."

History lurked in the bushes like a ghost when they spent the night of August 28 on Bleunerhassett Island, off Parkersburg, West Virginia. The point of the island had been the location of the estate and mansion belonging to Harman Bleunerhassett, an Irish-born English landowner, who had married his niece and come to America to escape the reach of scandal. Popular, lavish entertainers, they were ruined when Harman became involved in a conspiracy with Aaron Burr. They left the island to live in poverty and the mansion was burned. Clegg and Holmstrom walked the site in the evening but could find no trace other than garden terraces and naturalized flowers.

They traveled up the chain of water past shoreline trees and shrubbery so subjugated by vine maple and Virginia creeper that it seemed almost black. At Wheeling, West Virginia, since they simply could find no place to camp, they moored at a boat dock at one end of the toll bridge and carried their heavy packs across to the Wheeling Hotel at the other end of the bridge. Holmstrom asked the toll collector whether they owed him anything, and when the man said "only cars and trucks," Holmstrom replied that then he should charge them because they were certainly doing the work of a truck.

The next day they motored past Stuebenville, Ohio, and the Carnegie Steel mills, and Holmstrom jotted, "…pools of water—some brown some black… different colored streams of water coming into river—acid kills all fish." No sheared pins here. At dusk, after eight locks, they reached Pittsburgh, headwaters of the Ohio.

Holmstrom had put so many miles on the new Johnson that it needed a professional tune-up. Clegg took a room at the Roosevelt Hotel—"expensive and not very good"—and Holmstrom went elsewhere. She recorded, "We weren't allowed into the cafe-grill there—Buzz furious." Traveling with Clegg for over four months, Holmstrom must have been sensible to certain delicate balances on the social scale, but these repeated instances of Midwestern snobbery must have gravelled him in a visceral way. Nothing in his western upbringing had prepared him for the arrogance of encrusted privilege.

If anything, Pittsburgh was worse than Cincinnati. Clegg: "Coming up the river to the point between the Monongahela and the Allegheny Rivers was fine; the only point of view from which Pittsburgh looks human… I would like to have slipped through… on somewhere up the Allegheny…." Holmstrom left the motor in the hands of a dealer while he and Clegg toured the downtown Golden Triangle, the universities, Old Fort Duchesne. Then Holmstrom went back to check on the motor.

He returned for dinner with bad news: the Johnson dealer, while testing the motor, smashed the *Mongoose* into the dock with such force that he punched a hole in the bow beneath the water line. They would fix it, of course, but it would probably mean a delayed departure.

They got away the next evening at dusk, so eager that they took a chance that they would find accommodations at the yacht club five miles up the Allegheny. Unfortunately, at Oakmont there were only rooms for transients, and Clegg did not consider herself one. It was getting late and they wandered through the streets aimlessly, "hot, rather cross and tired," until they lucked upon a house with two large, clean rooms for rent. "We got a good country supper at the restaurant." Spirits lifted. But there was a joker in the deck. It was September 1, and for the second time since Louisville, word of war preparations percolated to the expedition. With its Luftwaffe and two thousand tanks, Germany had attacked the Republic of Poland. Clegg wrote, "The news is frightful and as far as I can see amounts to war. Bitter! I didn't think it would come—wolf, wolf I suppose."

The three-hundred-mile Allegheny drains northwestern Pennsylvania and flows south to Pittsburgh, where it joins the Monongahela to form the Ohio River —the Allegheny actually supplies eighty percent of the water at Pittsburgh that makes up the Ohio. They followed the Allegheny—a paltry 1,500 CFS this late in August—upstream toward southwestern New York. Clear in the morning, the day soon turned hot as a banked stove; dark clouds coagulated, loomed menacingly, then loosed a blinding rain. Holmstrom had to duck the *Mongoose* into the bank because he could not see. The sky cleared and they went on meandering upriver between railroad tracks on each shore. A chain of eight locks took them up the river to Brady Bend. And there, seventy-eight miles north of Pittsburgh, the river gave out, worn to a thread, a piddle of less than 1,000 CFS. Said Clegg, "Not enough water to float the boat, even rowing. We seem to have hit the all-time low for the Allegheny water."

Holmstrom went off to hustle a truck, but this time it was difficult to find anyone who was licensed to haul out-of-state to New York. Finally a fellow named Bob Blatt agreed to chance it.

They left the river after nightfall, boat in tow, driving under moonlight that bronzed the Allegheny Mountains and the creeks that trickled out of them. The truck and the rough roads made sleep out of the question—it took them four hours to cover a hundred miles to Warren, Pennsylvania, where they stopped for coffee and hamburgers in a cafe.

They reached Buffalo, New York, in the predawn, another hundred miles. They eased the *Mongoose* into the Niagara River about fifteen miles upriver from Niagara Falls. The Niagara drains Lake Erie into Lake Ontario, and although only thirty-three miles long, flows at a prodigious 200,000 CFS. They were too tired to even go look at the falls. They watched dawn paint the river an opaline blue, then stowed their gear and motored five miles down to a boatyard at Tonawanda, where the Erie Canal begins. A fellow there informed them that England had declared war on Germany. Clegg was stunned. She had been out of touch, missed the impending signs. "I didn't think it would be war again. I *must* get to England." It was her mother country; her sister was there.

They took a bus to the Hotel Buffalo and checked in but could not sleep. That Sunday evening, September 3, they listened to President Roosevelt's speech, which put the blame for aggression squarely on Germany. In 1938 Britain and France had given guarantees to Poland; the day after German planes bombed Warsaw, Britain and then France had declared war on Germany. Roosevelt promised, "...this nation will remain a neutral nation, but I cannot ask that every American remain neutral in thought as well. Even a neutral cannot be asked to close his mind or his conscience." Within hours, German submarines sank eight British ships, including an ocean liner.

Monday morning Clegg and Holmstrom were on the bus back to the dock early, but a wind and rain storm descended, raking the water, intensifying, then abating in time for a midmorning departure. They motored into the canal.

The Erie Canal extends from Buffalo to Albany, New York, over 350 miles, connecting Lake Erie and the St. Lawrence Seaway with the Hudson River. Funded by the New York state legislature at a cost of seven million dollars, it was completed in 1825 as a toll canal, and opened Eastern markets to the farm products of the Old Northwest. It was also the reason for the location of several large cities—forming their economic muscle and sinew; in fact, for almost half a century it made Buffalo the largest city between Philadelphia and Chicago. Early barges were pulled by horses, and packet boats could make the trip in ten days. Eventually, railroads destroyed the canal's long-haul advantages. Later, however, the canal was enlarged, improved, and converted to the New York State Barge Canal.

When Holmstrom and Clegg stopped at Lockport to get their permit, they were dismayed to learn that the canal was open only to boats of sixteen-feet or more with inboard engines. The lockman wavered, then capitulated. Clegg: "Having come so far, I think he hadn't the heart to refuse us."

They made forty miles the first day through wooded lake-like reaches, and picked up a stretch of the Seneca River, draining Seneca Lake. One of the glacial Finger Lakes, it eventually flows into the Oswego River. Never exceeding their ten mph limit, more often putting along at an enforced six mph, they cruised past banks of goldenrod, wild grape, and morning glories, past small colonial towns with white houses under leafy trees. Some stretches of the canal were higher than the country on either side. Often, wooden tugs passed them going the other way, towing up to five scows, each with a wheel to steer. Sometimes Standard Oil tankers glided past; none of them left a wake. They found a pleasant, sheltered camp near a double railroad bridge, the end of a misty, cloudy day and the start of a cold night. Freight and passenger trains hurtled by every ten minutes or so.

The next day, still cold, they motored through Cross Lake, pulled in for lunch, and reached the west end of Oneida Lake, about fifteen miles inland from the shore of Lake Ontario. A forceful wind had grown all afternoon, and Holmstrom was uneasy about the twenty-two-mile crossing. At the last lock they had been told not to attempt the lake; however, at lake-edge the government weatherman in the tower told them the lake was not that rough, that it would likely be rougher the next day, and to simply follow the Standard Oil tanker—aptly named *Providence*—through the lock and across the lake. This they did, though not without apprehension.

At the halfway point in the crossing, Holmstrom had to stop and gas up. When they started the motor again, the *Providence* was an alarming half-mile ahead. *Mongoose* had gone from rocking horse to see-saw to roller coaster. The following gale shoved breakers in endless rows ahead of them. Neither end of the lake was visible. Seeking shelter was pointless, impossible. The fierce furrows of steaming whitecaps went on and on. Trough and crest, trough and crest. But the motor never faltered. They spotted the breakwater, seething under an oceanlike surf. Holmstrom: "...then happens what has been threatening ever since middle of the lake—several whitecaps close—[I] slip back over the first one—try to slip back over the 2nd & it's so steep boat shoots down the front like a surfboard & whole forward half goes under—take on 10 buckets—near shore tho & make it OK.—I sure like the Johnson for not quitting but don't like the weather man for sending us across."

They were wet, tired, and hungry, but with no place at the resort to build a campfire, they went to the Sylvan Home Hotel, and the kindly landlady filled her kitchen with their wet clothes. Clegg said, "I didn't think we could make it. However we did, and was I thankful to get to Sylvan Beach. Was I scared!"

Down at the dock, Holmstrom met a man with a forty-foot cabin cruiser who had been waiting since yesterday noon to make the crossing. Too rough for him. Moreover, Holmstrom learned that over the years, at least twenty-five ships had swallowed their anchors on the lake. "We sure feel good to be here safe—tired."

On the afternoon of September 7, still in the Mohawk Valley, Clegg photographed a herd of cows. It was a deliberate gesture—honoring the men of the Lewis and Clark Expedition, who on September 20, 1806, on the return voyage, had shouted with joy at the sight of a herd of cows on the outskirts of La Charette, just a few miles upriver from St. Louis. That evening, Clegg and Holmstrom camped above Little Falls in, according to his estimate, "a very poor place."

The following afternoon, in a long, slashing rainstorm, they stopped for hot coffee and lunch midway between Utica and Schenectady, at Canajoharie, a town where a Beech-Nut Company plant was located. Despite soaking clothes, dripping slickers, and life jackets, the welcome they received at the local diner dispelled apprehensions acquired in the Midwest. Clegg wrote, "The Beech-Nut factory is the pleasantest looking factory I have ever seen; near the river, standing in a garden, glass and white paint, it might be an enormous hotel by the look of it. The tiny town is gay and attractive." The town had a population of 2,500. Eight hundred, mostly women in white uniforms, worked at the plant, packing strained baby foods; producing candy-coated gum; and printing labels, wrappers, and cartons. Holmstrom mentions that the town and business had not felt the effects of the Great Depression.

They were now on a reach of the Mohawk River, a central New York lowlands river, largest tributary to the Hudson. Since foul weather continued to dog them, they left the boat at the locks at Amsterdam, a carpet manufacturing center about twenty miles above Albany, and walked a mile into town to dry out and warm up at the Thayer Hotel. They then decided to spend the night there.

In the morning the sun dipped out of the clouds and they were in a cheerful mood as they walked back to the boat. Only 450 feet above sea level, but that meant nine locks down to the Hudson, past the former ninety-foot Cohoes Falls. They came through the last lock onto the Hudson River at Troy in midafternoon. Tidewater!

The three-hundred-mile-long Hudson is the only river that completely transects the Appalachians. Flowing due south from its source in Lake Tear of the Clouds, for about forty miles it cuts a palisaded valley with a deep, wide trench. "This is our lordly Hudson hardly flowing / under the green-grown cliffs." This was the river of the Iroquois; of English navigator Henry Hudson, who in September 1609 sailed his *Half Moon* up to the limits of navigation; of Captain Kidd, who purportedly hid his treasure on several of its points; of Washington Irving's Ichabod Crane and Rip Van Winkle; and of Robert Fulton's first commercially successful steamboat. It is a tidal estuary for the last 150 miles, one of the larger in the world; for the last seventeen miles, it forms the border between New York and New Jersey, and when it reaches New York Bay it is nearly a mile wide.

They motored along the east shore to Federal Lock 1, assisted by a 3,000 CFS current, staying out of the path of larger boats. The plum-colored Catskill Mountains, clothed in cherry, beech, and maple, dominated the western horizon. Below the lock, the Hudson turns tidal—it is only a foot above sea level—and they were grateful for the motor. The *Mongoose* muttered past sandbars, islands, marshes; willow and ash trees leaned from the shore.

The upper river was polluted with what Holmstrom took to be wool drifting in the current. He guessed there must be a blanket factory in the vicinity. What he observed were actually pulp wastes from factories making boxes, tissue, and wallpaper out of Adirondack pulpwood. Clegg was feeling deeply depressed.

> Troy is horribly squalid... no letters, the trip seemed to be ending in a slum as well as in a war.... I'd had my heart set on having a really nice camp for the last night... it looked as if it would be impossible to find one.

Six miles to Albany. The scenery improved but the weather did not: chilly, with a leaden overcast and a clammy rain. On a briny wind, ring-billed gulls swirled overhead. Past Germantown, then Millionaire's Row on the eastern shore: the Mills chateau, designed by Stanford White for Ruth and Ogden Mills, heirs to a banking fortune; the unrivaled Vanderbilt mansion; Franklin Delano Roosevelt's Italian-Renaissance-style Hyde Park. Across the river on the west were extensive properties belonging to Father Devine (1875–1965), a black religious cult leader from Georgia, who founded the Peace Mission Movement; tens of thousands of members who, after surrendering their possessions, lived communally through co-operative labor without pay. Sayville was one of their "Havens." Clegg and Holmstrom thought it "looked very grand."

A headwind beat the river into a froth and they docked at Poughkeepsie, home of Vassar College, took rooms at the King's Court Hotel and went out to see a movie—*Young Mr. Lincoln,* starring Henry Fonda as the president, making riverside speeches to his girlfriend.

Monday morning, a bluebird day. Past the massive granite dome of Storm King Mountain, West Point U.S. Military Academy, Peekskill, Jones Point. They were boating through the Hudson Highlands, green mountains that frame the gorge, where the river is two hundred feet deep. The blustery breeze was now gusting to fifteen knots and the tide was contrary, making progress wet and difficult. They motored under a railway trestle and found a cozy mooring secluded by cattails. Opposite their camp was a gas station and restaurant with cabins surrounded by beds of petunias. They had dinner, then Clegg took a cabin for the night. Holmstrom slept by the boat.

On September 12 Clegg was up in the dark and down at the boat as soon as the river gathered pink color from the sky. They re-embarked and drifted for a moment in the glory of the sunrise, a Hudson River School landscape by Thomas Cole. Holmstrom jerked the motor to life. Through Haverstraw Bay, more lake than river and lathered with whitecaps; then Croton Bay; through Tappan Zee, nine miles long and two miles wide, with salt marshes and birds crying over them; past the Palisades, soaring five-hundred-foot volcanic cliffs that rise vertically

from the river for fifty miles south to Staten Island; under the George Washington Bridge connecting New York and New Jersey. They moored at the ramshackle Undercliff Boatworks, their boat singular among the more expensive craft. They had been four months and twenty days on their journey. Like Lewis and Clark, they had reached their "Travellers Rest."

They called for a taxi and went together—via River Drive, appropriately—to Wall Street, where Clegg picked up her mail at a bank. On the way, they passed the uptown pier at West 50th, occupied that day by the RMS *Queen Mary*, primed battleship gray. As the flagship of the Cunard White Star Line, it could not get sea-going insurance against "Acts of War," and therefore sought safety in a neutral port. The *Normandie*—black hull, white superstructure, red funnels—pride of the French fleet, was moored a hundred feet away. Soon enough, she would burn, but the *Queen Mary* would serve as a troopship ferrying American and Canadian soldiers to the United Kingdom; at twenty-eight knots she was too quick for U-boats.

Clegg and Holmstrom took a bus, adjusting to a rhythm not their own, looking for a hotel—"all of which Buzz found too grand or too expensive"—and compromised on the Hotel Jackson—"repulsive." Clegg closed her diary: "It feels great to have really reached the Atlantic, and the journey was great—even if it has ended in a war." The next morning she moved to the New Weston Hotel at 50th and Madison.

Later in the week, in a brief wharfside ceremony, and with Holmstrom at the oars, Clegg donated the *Mongoose* to the Bayside—Queens chapter of the Girl Scouts of America. She shipped the outboard motor back to Portland to be sold. As soon as she and Holmstrom settled accounts, he sent his mother a check. The next day, Clegg gave him an expensive waterproof watch, its back engraved: "Coast to Coast."

The evening of September 22, she sailed from the West 18th Street pier for Southampton, England, on the U.S. *Washington* (a six-day crossing), to begin a year's stay.

For his part, Holmstrom now possessed a better understanding of American watersheds than any other boatman in the country. He knew fifteen significant rivers intimately. Even his friend Amos Burg, with his canvas canoe and rubber raft, was a rudimentary boatman in comparison. Haldane "Buzz" Holmstrom stood alone, nonpareil in his occupation.

Circling the Eddy

1940-1941

*H*OLMSTROM SPENT THE LAST WEEK of September, 1939, touring New York City. He visited the prestigious Explorers Club, of which he was a member. There he met sailors, river runners, mountain climbers, and the famous photographer, William Henry Jackson, who was ninety-seven at the time. Holmstrom called on river runner Clyde Eddy, who chauffeured him around the city. In a letter to his mother, Holmstrom wrote, "The pleasantest most interesting place I've been was the American Museum of Natural History—a huge place where you should spend days & days." In a subsequent letter he said, "…I've seen NY properly—as I've ridden on the elevated trains—am quite expert on the subway and have eaten in the Automats." The most telling lines of all, however, were these: "I'm leaving today for home & glad to get going as it's the lonesomest place I was ever in."

He told a reporter, "...I felt more lonely in New York than I ever did in the depths of Grand Canyon. The rocks and rapids were never meant to be friendly. But in New York I found myself alone among 7,000,000 people. I got lost in the Times Square subway station and was treated like a freak when I asked for information."

He took the train south to Washington, D.C., to see Colonel Claude Birdseye of the 1923 Grand Canyon survey. Birdseye was just leaving town, but they visited for an hour, exchanging river tales. Holmstrom spent the next few days at the Smithsonian Institute. "Could gladly have spent a month there." But other than the museums, the East Coast was unappealing. He caught a Greyhound west to Detroit to call on friends, Lois Jotter and Elzie Clover.

To Holmstrom's disappointment, Jotter was away collecting evening primrose seeds for her dissertation. His fondness for Jotter may have received another dampening—Jotter was now dating Victor Cutter, the aspiring academian she would soon marry. Elzie Clover, however, was in town and delighted to see him. The friendship that had grown between them a year earlier at Boulder City would last throughout Holmstrom's life.

Clover took him to the University of Michigan at Ann Arbor, where she was a professor. The grounds, the library, and the science building all fascinated Holmstrom. His scientific inclinations were evident, not only to Clover, but to her colleagues. Professor Bartlett, the department head, encouraged Holmstrom to pursue his academic interests.

But the Midwest did not suit him any more than the East. He wrote home, "I don't like Detroit either—there are no cars on the streets here older than last year's model." Well, there was at least one—a few days later he bought a 1931 Model-A Ford and began driving west. Although snow slowed him for a day in the Rocky Mountains west of Denver, he soon arrived in Salt Lake City. Doc Frazier, whom Holmstrom hoped to visit, had just departed as physician on Admiral Byrd's expedition to Antarctica. Holmstrom drove seventy miles south to Thistle to visit with Willis Johnson and family.

Holmstrom and Johnson knew that Burg had sold a short film of the 1938 Colorado trip. Hoping to see it when it showed in Salt Lake City, they inquired—theaters were unaware of it. A few days later the two men were in a Salt Lake theater when *Conquering the Colorado*, starring Buzz Holmstrom, flashed onto the screen. It surprised them both. The footage Burg had edited together was crisp, well composed, and exhilarating. The soundtrack was pure hyperbole, written by Burg and narrated by an exuberant Lew Lehr:

> As the water grew rougher, his spirits rose! Didn't he have the finest boat in the world? A boat he cut himself from the cedar forest? Hadn't it brought him safely through, where others had gone down? Water filled the cockpit!

Waves tried to tear him out of his boat! On and on they tore through the river like indestructible spirits! Bring on your rapids! This is a boat! And a man! Try to stop us from getting through! The river tried every trick it knew, charged him madly toward the canyon walls! But Buzz was now a superman, with superhuman strength! He defied the river to do its worst! He was master! He was stronger than the river, and his boat was stronger than either of them!

Johnson howled. Holmstrom cringed. Although *Conquering the Colorado* was a hit across the country, it was a far cry from what they had hoped to produce. Of the many hours of black-and-white film exposed, a scant ten minutes made it to the screen. And of the eighteen hundred dollars Burg received from the sale, he and Holmstrom each cleared, after expenses, a mere five hundred.

Burg did not dwell on it. He traveled, lectured, sold articles, sought assignments, and planned new trips. Holmstrom, never an opportunist or a self-promoter, could only dream of finding work he loved. In the years to come, as he labored at menial jobs, he sometimes envied Burg.

Holmstrom had left Coquille for the Clegg voyage in April 1939, six months earlier. Now it was time to see his family, time for immediate plans. But after each of his last two trips he had gone home to a discontented winter in Coquille. He decided to break the pattern: he went with Johnson to the Bingham Mine thirty miles south of Salt Lake City to get a job.

The Bingham Mine was the first open-pit mine in the world, the place where massive removal of low-grade ore first proved profitable. As war kindled in Europe, copper prices recovered dramatically, and demand suddenly outstripped supply. Shifts ran night and day. Anyone who knew Doc Frazier and Sheriff Swain had a job for the asking. Holmstrom arranged to go to work as soon as he got back from Coquille. He motored home to visit with family and friends, but by early November was back at Bingham Canyon. Like Johnson and five hundred other workers, Holmstrom was assigned to the track crew, keeping miles of rails in order.

The town and mine of Bingham Canyon were a half-hour drive southwest of Salt Lake City, two miles up a winding canyon from the valley floor. The town itself, a hodgepodge of shanties and honky-tonks with a smattering of respectable businesses, straddled Bingham Creek and wound up the side-canyons. The mountain slopes above slowly succumbed to the ever-deepening pit. Utah Copper furnished lodging for the workers, as did a few independent boarding houses. Johnson lived at the Gemmel Club, which provided good food, game rooms, billiards, and ping-pong tables. Holmstrom took a room at Cypress Hall across the street.

The work was hard, the hours were brutal, and the pay was poor: for Holmstrom and Johnson, $4.30 a day. Here, during the Great Depression, people had waited week after week in hope of a job. Conditions had improved, but it was still difficult to save any money. Throughout the winter, Holmstrom continued to correspond with E.G. Nielsen at the Bureau of Reclamation. The idea of damming the Green River was gaining momentum, and Nielsen assured Holmstrom-there would be abundant survey work in the spring.

Holmstrom grew bored with track work and transferred to the powder gang. At least being a powder monkey had an element of risk. The gang worked the graveyard shift, after the mining crews shut down. All night long they drilled and tamped charges, drilled and tamped more charges. It required care, attention, caution, patience. Shortly before dawn, they detonated the charges, sending a roar and a tremor through town, and waking the mining crews for breakfast. In a letter to Lois Jotter, Holmstrom described his work.

> I changed jobs at the copper mine—you see there are about 150 powder monkeys there—It is very hard work and rather uncertain—that is, when you go to work it's uncertain whether you will be able to walk home from work, or have to be brought home all mixed up in a basket.
>
> They used to have mostly Mexicans and Greeks on the gang, but since the last 3 fellows got blown up even the Mexicans began leaving the job, so they had to start putting dumb white guys to work on it and that's where I came into the picture. It was interesting work, though, and not really so dangerous as I have made it sound—it's true there are a lot of accidents but they are mostly due to carelessness and I certainly was careful.
>
> I had my choice of two different jobs—either the powder gang or a job on a line car—that is—a sort of lineman—putting up electric wires and such, but I chose the powder gang because the title "powder monkey" seemed much more dignified than that of the lineman who is called a "grunt."

For Christmas of 1939 Holmstrom decided to have photographic greeting cards made. In going through Johnson's photos of the Clegg trip, he found one of himself half drowned in the Snake River, with Hamilton rowing hard to the rescue. He chose this, drew a black circle around his bobbing head, astern of the boat, and had "Holiday Greetings" printed below. He sent them to his widening circle of friends.

Throughout the winter, Holmstrom earned $5.50 a night, with no room for advancement. Occasionally he and Willis took time off and headed across the valley to Thistle to hunt or fish along the Wasatch Front. On one such trip, according to Frank Swain, Holmstrom lost his temper. Four of them—Holmstrom, Johnson, Swain, and Miller—had gone hunting. After dinner with the Johnson family, they showed movies of their river adventures, then headed back up the valley toward the mine. Miller was driving; Johnson was in the front seat talking to him. Swain and Holmstrom were in the back seat. Holmstrom began talking about Burg.

Burg's letters always mentioned his next adventure. Now Burg had acquired a sailboat and was heading for Alaska in the spring. According to Swain, this had bothered Holmstrom for some time. He questioned the accuracy or fairness of the accounting for the sale of the film. Holmstrom, claimed Swain, said Burg had cheated him; he was going to get even; he just might have to kill him.

Neither Johnson nor Miller ever told this story, nor did they deny it. Perhaps liquor flavored his remarks. Or perhaps, as with many of Swain's tales, Holmstrom's words and intentions mutated over the years. At any rate, nothing came of it. Holmstrom and Burg continued to correspond. Burg visited Holmstrom at Bingham later that season, and Holmstrom stayed with Burg in New York in 1941.

To Johnson, Holmstrom appeared jolly enough. They delighted in playing practical jokes on one other or on friends. Most afternoons they shared a beer in Johnson's room. Johnson recalls a time when he and Holmstrom went to the Swains' for dinner. Swain's young son, afraid to come near the men, hid in a corner. Holmstrom made an effort to befriend him, smiling and coaxing. When the boy finally gathered his courage and timidly approached with an outstretched hand, Johnson, who had been watching, made a sudden, loud, gruff bark. The boy, terrified, would not go near Holmstrom again. "*Oh*, that made Buzz mad!" says Johnson, bursting into a series of giggles.

Holmstrom exchanged letters with Hayes Perkins, an admirer. Born and raised in Coquille, Perkins had made a small fortune mining in Africa. He encouraged Holmstrom to head for the Dark Continent. The money was good for a talented American, and the rivers, he added, were huge.

Fantasies of work abroad faded before immediate offers. In April, 1940, Holmstrom's extended correspondence with E.G. Nielsen finally paid off. An immense project that would transform much of the Green River was about to begin: dams at Echo Park and Split Mountain Canyon. A canal and pumping system would then divert much of the water westward along the base of the Uinta Mountains, across central Utah, and spill it into the Sevier River, well south of Salt Lake City near Fillmore. Called the "Colorado River–Great Basin Project," the plan had passed an enthusiastic Utah house and senate in March. The Bureau of Reclamation went to Fillmore to classify recipient land so as to properly allocate all the water that would soon be coming.

Work at the mine had become too predictable, and in early April, Holmstrom resigned as powder monkey and went to work for the federal government as a land-classifier. To Earl Hamilton he wrote:

> Last week I changed jobs again. There's a survey gang from the Bureau of Reclamation working down here at Fillmore and I'm sort of flunkying for them. It's not much of a job, but a change. You say nothing happens there— well, nothing happens over here too, but I've been moving around so I can see it happen in different places anyhow.

Within a few weeks, Holmstrom transferred to another division of the project, where his mining experience proved useful. Moreover his river running experience was invaluable. The primary dam in the project was to be three miles below the confluence of the Green and Yampa Rivers at Echo Park. Extensive drilling work was required for site evaluation, and Holmstrom arrived with the first crew. With access difficult from either upstream or downstream, their first task was to get a road close to the site. Upstream was slightly more feasible. A primitive road already wound down Blue Mountain into the Chew Ranch. From there, a stock trail meandered down Pool Creek into Echo Park. After a few weeks of blasting and scraping, they made a passable road to the river, and set up a base camp in the shady box elder grove on the south shore. Holmstrom constructed a skiff and two thirty-foot barges, each outfitted with motors, to transport men and equipment back and forth to the dam site.

The road construction and camp were technically illegal. Shortly before Holmstrom and Burg floated through in 1938, President Roosevelt had enlarged Dinosaur National Monument to include the entire canyons of Split Mountain, Whirlpool, Lodore, and the Yampa. Overnight it became the largest national monument in the country, yet it had no budget. Its only ranger was not consulted or notified that the Bureau of Reclamation was setting up operations in the monument; he complained futilely to his superiors. The Bureau of Reclamation had long dominated the Department of Interior and National Park Service complaints went unanswered. The drilling project continued.

Foreman L. L. "Red" Kreager, older, competent, and well-liked, was a good hand with a rowboat. Holmstrom was a "driller's helper," there to do whatever was needed. Most of his work centered on keeping the boats in working order and hauling men and equipment up and down the river. When he was on duty, he motored down to the site and spent a few days there, sleeping on the ledges at

Holmstrom built barges in Echo Park. Red Kreager on right

night. Once the crew completed the river-level test drillings, they began high-wall work, hoisting the immense six-ton drilling rigs by cable, hundreds of feet up the cliffs. They drilled a set of exploratory holes five hundred feet above the river. On difficult operations like these, Holmstrom's ingenuity was invaluable. Like his father in the logging camps, he often came up with innovative solutions to complex rigging problems.

Back in camp, Holmstrom began a second project. For planned downriver survey work, the Bureau of Reclamation needed a reliable whitewater boat. Holmstrom designed a plywood boat similar to the *Julius F*. Materials were trucked into the base camp and when not on drilling duty, Holmstrom worked on the new boat.

On a warm Sunday morning in June, 1940, Bus Hatch came down the Echo Park Road with a few boats and a few friends, and invited Holmstrom and Kreager to go on a float trip for the day. It was impossible to say no. The party headed downriver. "Let's hit all the worst places, Bus," Holmstrom said, and they did. At S.O.B. Rapid, Hatch capsized his boat in a frothing hole. He scrambled onto the bottom, drifted into the next rapid, and flipped right-side-up. Three miles downstream Kreager towed him in.

A few weeks later, Norman Nevills dropped by the camp at lunch time. He was retracing John Wesley Powell's trip, Wyoming to Nevada. He was traveling with two women again: his wife Doris, and botanist Mildred Baker. They had a novel communication system: carrier pigeons. Weekly, they tied a message to one of the birds and sent it out. Mostly falcon fodder, few pigeons made it home to their coop.

The Nevills party found Holmstrom working on the new boat. After lunch, they pulled a few of their boats out of the water for repairs and spent the afternoon pounding nails, telling outrageous stories, and laughing. The women washed their hair in the clear water of Pool Creek. Story telling went far into the night.

No sooner had the Nevills party left the next morning than two more boats rowed in, Bert Loper and Don Harris at the oars. A year earlier, Loper and Harris had run Grand Canyon; at age seventy, it was Loper's first time through, and following Holmstrom's lead, they ran every rapid. The two had become the best of friends. This year, they began at the Green River Lakes, where Holmstrom and Burg launched on low water in 1938. Loper and Harris had a higher flow. Even so, for over a hundred miles they had scraped bottom where Holmstrom and Burg had portaged. "We proved it could be done," Harris recalls, "and we proved it wasn't practical."

They wanted to stay, but Harris had to be back at work in a few days. They continued downstream. No more boaters passed that summer. With the new plywood craft completed, there was little for Holmstrom to do but work drilling shifts and write letters from Echo Park (locally called Pat's Hole, for former resident hermit Pat Lynch).

Pat's Hole
July 8, 1940
Dear Lois,

There isn't any post office at Pat's Hole where I am now but I like to put it at the top of my letters as it has a sort of romantic and historic sound... it's 15 miles downstream from Brown's Hole and 7 miles upstream from Jones Hole, and right in front of my tent is a dandy fishing hole where we go swimming.

3 miles from our camp is the Chew ranch. Mrs. Chew, who is now 76 and very healthy and active, had 14 children and as far as I know none of them chew tobacco. 12 of her children were born out here in the mountains and she never did have a doctor. One child fell off a cliff and was killed and another was killed while trying to break a wild horse and all the others are alive and healthy, but it's a wonder, as they have some sort of trouble that apparently makes it very hard for them to tell the difference between their brand and other peoples on cows and horses. The old man Chew is 88 and healthy. He says it is due to a clean life and never taking any medicine—whenever he didn't feel good he would doctor himself with whiskey and I have heard it said he would sometimes doctor himself even when he did feel good. He told me he went to the state college 2 years but I found out it was the state pen. Brand trouble. One time he took an overdose of medicine in Vernal and the J.P. fined him $15.00. The J.P. said he could pay the fine next day as Chew was broke at the time. That night C. stole a cow and calf belonging to the J.P., took them to Jensen and sold [them] for $22.00 which he used in paying his fine. The other day I asked where Mrs. C—now 76—was and found out she had gone over to Gunnison to take care of her mother who is a little under the weather.

I am working on a diamond drilling gang down here making test holes for a dam site. Another guy and I are batching. Our tent is in a brush pile—there are an awful lot of snakes, lizards, bugs and insects around—the other fellow moved out. I would sleep in my sleep bag at night and in the daytime a lizard about 14 inches long slept in it, but he would usually get up about 4 and go to catch some flies, I guess. I sort of got acquainted with him and he was nice and clean and I didn't mind much, but later a blow snake decided to move in with me at night. He was a total stranger and I moved out on to the sand bar and gave him my interest in the tent.

There are a lot of deer around here—we don't kill any as it's against the law beside being in the Dinosaur National Monument. But day before yesterday I judge some outlaw must have been hunting up on the mountain, because all at once I noticed where one, apparently shot with a gun and its throat cut from ear to ear almost, was outside—they have a lot of vitality, you know—and I guess it had run down into Pat's Hole and no doubt badly frightened had tried to climb a tree outside our tent (where we don't live any more) and got its hind legs caught in a rope there, and then hanging head down, died.

Well, we just skinned it as that seemed the thing to do—and then we just ate it as it seemed like that wasn't as big a crime as it would be to let that meat go to waste. Besides, it is sort of self defense as it would smell bad if it wasn't eaten and annoy everyone like a public nuisance...

I must close now as part of that darn deer has somehow gotten in the frying pan and I must save it from burning.

Sincerely, Buzz

Willis Johnson and a friend drove in from Bingham to visit for a few days, and Holmstrom took them on the full tour, boating down to the drill site and back. They spent a few days at Echo Park, camping with Holmstrom's fellow workers and their families. Johnson recalls Holmstrom complaining of a cut on his thigh. When asked how he got it, Holmstrom mumbled something about it being a zipper bite. After a bit more urging he elaborated: one evening his buddies had taken a gopher snake and stuffed it into the bottom of his sleeping bag. He gashed his thigh while exiting.

Johnson adds that Holmstrom eventually got his revenge by invit-

The six-ton drill rig going up to the high holes

ing the men over to his tent for a few snorts of strong whiskey. They got so boisterous that they ended on the outs with their wives, who were trying to sleep nearby.

On his days off, Holmstrom sometimes made the long journey over the mountain to Vernal, Utah, where he stayed with Bus Hatch's family. Eva, Hatch's wife, remembered that Holmstrom liked to be alone, liked to sit and think. He went to a few dances, she recalled, but never really danced. He seemed miserable there, in fact. He was modest and apologetic about accepting hospitality at the Hatch's table, but "a very nice boy," she thought. Holmstrom gave her a copy of *Western Window,* his mother's poetry book.

Bus and Eva's son Ted, who was then seven years old, recollects Holmstrom's visits fondly. Often they would go outdoors and play ball. Hatch remembers one conversation especially well. They had gotten to talking about the dangers of big rapids, recalls Hatch:

> Buzz told me about nearly drowning one time on the Snake. He said he kept getting pulled down and he couldn't breath. After a while he quit struggling,

everything quieted, and he realized that he was drowning. That near-death euphoria washed over him. It wasn't that bad. It didn't matter any more. The next thing he knew, someone had thrown him over the deck of a boat and was working the water out of him.

"So never worry about drowning," he told me, "because it's not that bad."

Back at Echo Park, Holmstrom worked shifts at the drill site, painted the new boat, tinkered with his car, and wrote letters.

> Vernal, Utah Oct 26, 1940
>   Dear Lois—
>   Still down here at Pat's H. but we should be done in another week. And not a bit too soon as it's getting doggone cold… We take turns of 2 weeks working nights and it's my turn for nights now—we go to work at 4 and work till twelve and then sleep under a ledge till 8 A.M. as we can't come home at night because the only way is by boat and the river is shallow and rocky so it's hard to travel even in the daylite. We have a large flat-bottomed scow affair with a tunnel for the propeller of the 22 hp outboard which will travel in a foot of water at about 10 mph.
>   Down at the dam site where they say now they will probably never build a dam, the sun reaches the river at 2:30 and leaves at 4 making a short working day… I'm sitting in the tent here over at our camp now, listening to the wind howl, and the leaves off the Box Elder trees dropping on the roof, and hoping that the few flakes of snow do not really mean business.
>   On my last trip in here my little car almost gave up the ghost so I decided to fix it—I have pistons, valves, rods, etc., scattered around among the leaves— the sand blows into the cylinders and bearings which probably won't help matters any.
>   I always wondered if I were a good enough mechanic to fix an automobile motor and now feel a real sense of accomplishment in having taken it apart. As for putting it back—well—I'd rather not think about that yet.

As the last test holes were drilled, the Colorado River–Great Basin Project collapsed. Estimates of cost soared to eighty percent of the assessed value of the state of Utah. The project went back to the drawing board, resurfacing under different names and configurations for decades. Meanwhile, the Bureau of Reclamation finished plans for Holmstrom to take the new boat down through Desolation and Gray Canyons. Mansfield Merriman, chief geologist for the Echo Park survey, went with Holmstrom, as did H. E. Wilbert, an engineer. Their objective was to examine several potential dam sites. Bus Hatch and Mandy Campbell drove the group forty miles south of Vernal to the confluence of the White and Green Rivers and launched them. Holmstrom wrote to Julius Stone:

> I think I told you about building a fifteen-foot plywood river boat last summer. Well, on Nov. 11 a USBR engineer and Mr. Merriman, their dam site

Late November run of Three Fords Rapid, Gray Canyon, in the plywood boat

specialist, and I left Ouray heading for Green River looking for dam sites in Desolation and Gray Canyons.

There was six inches of snow in Vernal and a cold wind. Too cold for a river trip I thought. Both men were heavy and you should have seen their extra clothes, beds, etc., so altogether we had an awful load for one boat. Added to that the river was naturally pretty low.

During the early forenoons slush ice was so thick we could hardly make any headway. It would stick to the sides of the boat and build up on the oars until they were like a couple of clubs and too heavy to use so we would have to chip it off with a hammer.

One evening I carried a bucket of water up to camp, walked over and got a cup and then had to break the ice to get a drink. We slept with all our clothes on in our bags and none too warm at that. There was no one home at the Semontan or McPherson ranches.

We made profile surveys of eleven dam sites, all but one being in Desolation Canyon, there being only one in Gray Canyon at Rattlesnake Creek. Luckily, none of us even got our feet wet.

To Lois Jotter he quipped:

One advantage of taking such a trip in November is that there's no danger of getting drowned as you'd be sure to freeze to death first.

Well—I got my car back together but it didn't run so hot so I had a mechanic do it over—you ought to see it go now…

The trip ended in Green River, Utah, on November 18, 1940. Holmstrom, thirty-one years old, was once again unemployed. During the summer he had written letters to numerous government agencies, looking for some sort of boating work back in Oregon—survey work, port work, *any* work. Dick Neuberger, an influential reporter (later Senator) who had befriended Holmstrom, asked Oregon Senator McNary what might be available. No offer was forthcoming, and Holmstrom returned to Coquille.

As always, he was glad to see his family and friends. A popular man, Holmstrom was welcome anywhere, any time. His mother hoped her son would remain home. He found employment at Smith Wood Products, driving the Hyster forklift. Pay was a nominal eighty cents an hour, but a bit better than Walker's. Although shunting lumber was not what Holmstrom had in mind for the rest of his life, the men at the mill were friendly, and his good friend Thurman Hickam worked there with him. For years, Hickam had been the undisputed master of the straddle-bug, a tall, un-axled lumber carrier operated from a cab atop the four long, wheeled legs. After-hours Holmstrom, Hickam, and the rest of the gang gathered at Bill's Place to unwind; shoot a few games of snooker, share a few beers, and swap stories.

Frances tired of her dilapidated house, sold it for what she had paid for it, and bought a house in a wooded cul-de-sac at the end of Hall Street. If anything, the place was more in need of repairs than the house she had sold, but the location was an improvement. With trees on all sides and a stream flowing by, the place made her feel like she was back on the farm in McKinley.

After taking a careful look at the new house, Holmstrom decided to undertake some repairs. That would keep him busy and close to home. Since Carl had enlisted in the Navy and was in boot camp in San Diego, he could not help, but Rolf, still in high school, was handy and eager. They had barely begun before Holmstrom realized he was in over his head. He pried some of the wallboards loose

Holmstrom on the Hyster, Smith Wood Products

and found there were scarcely enough studs to hold the roof up—a gap-boarded roof that was not really *worth* holding up. Neither the wiring nor the plumbing was worth saving. Since his mother already loved the place, he pressed on. Never having built a house before, much less having remodeled one, Holmstrom remained remarkably confident.

Before long, he had the interior walls down. Then he put in enough studs to hold up the new roof he was going to install. On a clear weekend, he tore the old roof off; Rolf remembers going to bed in his room that night and seeing the starry sky above. Not even a lone rafter barred his view. The next day, as Buzz and Rolf began the new roof, one of the men from the mill arrived with his tools. Soon another worker arrived. And another. That was the way things got done in Coquille.

Wood was cheap, and for a few dollars, Holmstrom could get as much good lumber as the old trailer could carry. He got a great buy on Douglas fir flooring, and paneled the whole house with an over-run on a large Southern Pacific order. Room by room, they transformed the old bungalow into a comfortable, respectable home. His mother was elated: a cozy place in the woods, and her fledged boy back in her nest. For Frances it had been a wonderful year. To top things off, Binfords and Mort, of Portland, had published *Rich Lady*, her second book of poetry.

The house project took nearly a year. By fall of 1941, Buzz was restless, and began inquiring about jobs with the Bureau of Reclamation. In December, he received an offer. The bureau was about to begin another dam survey down in Grand Canyon, and he could sign on as a driller's helper. They needed someone to build boats as

Barges on upper Lake Mead, Bridge Canyon Dam Project

well. Although he would have to take a cut in pay, Holmstrom promptly accepted, and drove to Kingman, Arizona.

In early December, Holmstrom reported for work. He was sent back to Pearce Ferry, familiar ground on the shore of upper Lake Mead. Grand Canyon–Boulder Dam Tours was gone, but the bureau workers there welcomed Holmstrom. They began building a power boat and barges for transporting gear and equipment. Unlike the scorching weather he had endured in the summer of 1938, December's weather was quite pleasant. And although the landscape and work were familiar, he missed Red Kreager, his congenial foreman at Echo Park. The new boss, Ray Gossett, was rough around the edges. Holmstrom got along with most anyone, however; Gossett would be no exception. The boat building went well and before long he was ferrying men and gear up to the Bridge Canyon dam site, forty miles southeast into the lower reaches of Grand Canyon.

On the way, crews motored over Lava Cliff and Separation Rapids, now buried beneath fifty feet of reservoir. For almost twenty miles as they neared the head of the lake, they dodged mud flats. Because it was silting in faster than expected, reservoir navigation was tricky. Near the dam site, they encountered current and were soon on an untamed river.

As at Echo Park, Bridge Canyon plans called for a dam almost as big as Boulder Dam. Water would inundate Lava Falls, Havasu Creek, even Kanab Creek, a hundred miles upstream. If the irony of working to tame the rivers he loved ever occurred Holmstrom, there is no record that he mentioned it. Few in his day ever openly questioned the wisdom of progress and development.

As glad as he was to get back to the river, he remained restless. To Earl Hamilton he wrote:

> This is not as good a job as I had in the mill, but that mill was sure getting me down and it seemed as tho I just naturally had to make a change...
>
> The weather is fine here—cold nights, but pretty warm in the daytime...
>
> I suppose I'll be getting drafted pretty soon... We have no radio here and the war seems far away—still it is always in the back of my mind, which as you know is not far from the front—and it seems to keep a person from really enjoying anything.

Wooden Boats, Iron Men
1942-1945

WHILE HOLMSTROM boated for the Bureau of Reclamation in Arizona, the edge of war smoldered ever closer. With the bombing of Pearl Harbor on the morning of December 7, 1941, and a simultaneous devastating attack on American forces in the Philippines, he knew the writing on this wall was more easily deciphered than any Anasazi pictograph. The following morning, Congress voted a declaration of war. Three days later, the declaration was extended to Germany and Italy, which in turn had declared war on the U.S. A notice to Holmstrom from the Selective Service Board to appear for a physical examination erased any lingering doubts. In early February 1942, he left Bridge Canyon, Arizona, for Coquille, intent on enlisting in the navy rather than waiting to be drafted into the army. On February 20 at Portland, he was sworn in as a seaman apprentice, Company 106.

When a Portland newspaper reporter asked to interview him, Holmstrom answered with characteristic directness and modesty:

> I'm an apprentice seaman now and I have the same feeling of anticipation in the pit of my stomach that I've experienced before. It's a good feeling.
>
> But listen. You asked me to tell you about the Colorado River. I don't want to be like the college football player who makes All-American and then coasts on that reputation for the rest of his life. So I'd just as soon forget about those fifty-two days on the river, as far as the publicity is concerned. It's water under the bridge.

Another reporter encountered Holmstrom in Marshfield (later Coos Bay) and wrote in his column about "the quiet search for adventure that led Buzz to the navy." In part, he said:

> [Holmstrom] loves the clash of man with the elements and he knew he'd experience it again this year in the rolling expanse of the Pacific. Perhaps Buzz will pilot a mosquito boat into Subic Bay, or will help those soft-spoken Texans defend Kodiak Island. Perhaps we'll hear of him in Pago Pago or Port Darwin, or again in Ceylon or Celebes. And again we may never hear of him until he comes back from it all, as he came back quietly from Boulder Dam after the long nights alone with the river, his friend. But of this there is a certainty, wherever this strong young man may go, he will not worry. He has faith in his soul, his body and his skill. They have pulled him through too many narrow escapes to let him down now.

Reality, as usual, did not adapt itself to the dreamer's dream. Not in the military. What was remarkable, given the prevalence of "Catch 22," was how well the navy matched the man with his task. Holmstrom had no interest in killing; as a boy, he would boil worms ahead of time to avoid putting them live on a fishhook, not that it made much difference from the worm's perspective. On a river trip, if he took a weapon, likely as not the cartridges would not fit the gun. More than most, Holmstrom in a combat zone would have had to overcome a hearty disdain for weapons and regimentation and a lifelong antipathy for killing.

Promptly after induction, Holmstrom was shipped to Camp Lawrence in San Diego, California. As all soldiers or sailors must, he had to adapt to the loss of personal freedom. It may have been harder for him than for others. In an April letter to Elzie Clover he wrote, "I don't know if I would ever get to like Navy life or not. It certainly is different—to put it mildly. Sometimes I get to thinking about some of the camping and boating trips and don't feel very happy—but all that seems a long way off now.... That old expression about 'spending his money like a drunken sailor' is a lot of baloney, if my case is any example, because now I have been here about six weeks & my total pay so far after they took out their deductions is $7.00, and out of that there are several articles you must buy.... It's time for church now—& there again we have no choice."

Holmstrom spent his first eight weeks in basic training—boot camp; his second eight weeks were passed in a cabinet shop with forty-two other men selected after boot camp to be carpenter's mates (nick-named "termites" by other sailors). He remarked that it was about as interesting as "piling a load of wood in the woodshed." Then they began building wooden models of items to be cast in metal—work of close tolerances and calculated allowances for shrinkage. They did foundry work, carving sand molds for their patterns and casting them in bronze—trying to learn a craft in four weeks that normally required a four-year apprenticeship.

Following the casting instruction, Holmstrom was put to work planking and caulking a forty-foot navy motor launch called a "whaler," a project in which he took an extraordinary interest. They used cypress planks, tapered the edges to fit, then caulked the seams with cotton cord and white lead. Nevertheless, Holmstrom wrote his friend Hamilton, who was now a licensed dentist, "I enjoy the school very much but am doggone sorry now that I am in it. I'm afraid that a carpenter at sea is going to have rather an uninteresting time of it. You can't get on a gun crew—have anything to do with the small boats & a lot of the better things. You just stand by pretty much until the action is all over & then clean & patch up. But I found it is easier to get into the school than it is to get out." A bit later, he told his mother, "Really, I've got in a lot of practice at carpenter work here.... I am getting so I can make boards fit together better than I used to...."

At the outbreak of World War II, the U.S. Army numbered less than two hundred thousand. (Six years later, 3.2 million men and women were serving in the navy alone.) While Holmstrom received his training during the summer in San Diego, the war flamed on two fronts. President Franklin D. Roosevelt and Prime Minister Winston Churchill gave first priority to the defeat of Germany. Only fourteen percent of Allied resources were devoted to the War in the Pacific, yet they were responsible for preventing the expansion of the Japanese perimeter by sending troops to occupy the South Pacific Islands of Fiji and New Caledonia, seven hundred miles east of Australia.

During this time, Holmstrom wrote Clover that he dreamed of going camping, sleeping with a big driftwood fire under a starry sky. San Diego, however, had mushroomed into a city of three hundred thousand and military liberty was restricted to a maximum of twelve hours and within the city limits.

While in boot camp, Holmstrom met Dick Hollister, whose last name placed him in roll calls and rotations immediately ahead of him. Hollister, nicknamed "Slim," was from Montana and had been intent on being a radioman, but he did not know Morse code. At six feet, five inches, he contrasted with Holmstom, who was almost a foot shorter. Despite the differences in their appearances, they enjoyed

Mutt and Jeff

Chauncey Coor

each other's company and became fast friends. Chauncey Coor, from Arizona and recently married, joined them in carpentry school, and the three men often spent liberty hours together; they went to bars, shows, even the zoo. Since Coor was six feet tall, they were a stair-stepped trio. Holmstrom, however, was twelve years older than either of the others.

As the three top members of their class, they were friendly competitors on every test. Holmstrom graduated third in their class of forty-three, with a general classification test score of 96. His other marks: arithmetic, 90; English, 88; spelling, 96.

In August 1942 all leaves were canceled, and the top three graduates were selected for torpedo boat maintenance and repair school. Their transfer orders were to Melville, just north of Newport, Rhode Island—to the Motor Torpedo Boat Training Squadron Training Center—signed by commanding officer, Lieutenant Robert J. Bulkley, Jr. None of them had any idea that torpedo boats even existed, let alone knew what one was. Even the acronym, MTBTS, was a complete mystery.

MOTOR TORPEDO BOATS, or patrol torpedo boats, popularly called PT boats, were a relatively new and untested development in the U.S. Navy. In December 1941, the navy had only twenty-nine of them, twelve of them at Pearl Harbor. The concept was not yet forty years old. The first torpedo boat was built in Italy in 1906 and used successfully against the Austrian navy. Since then, the British and the French had led efforts to improve and refine the concept.

European experiments in the motor-torpedo-type boat had renewed U.S. Navy interest. The newer boats—sixty to sixty-eight feet in length, with two to four torpedoes, machine-guns in power-driven turrets, and an average speed of forty knots—were seen as useful for coastal defense and for freeing larger vessels for offensive action. The navy's General Board authorized, and the Secretary of the Navy approved, an experimental program on a limited scale. Congress appropriated fifteen million dollars to be spent at the discretion of President Roosevelt, who also approved. The navy announced a design contest; armament was to include at least two twenty-one-inch torpedoes, four depth charges (PT boats were not sub chasers; the charges were used if they caught a diving sub), and two .50-caliber machine-guns.

In 1939 the winning designs were already obsolete: Hubert Scott-Paine's British Power Boat Co. had developed a vessel that exceeded American requirements and was less costly than the proposed American boats. On September 5, 1939, as Holmstrom was preparing to cross Oneida Lake with Mrs. Clegg, the first British boat, PT 9, arrived and was unloaded as deck cargo in New York—interestingly, the same day that President Roosevelt's neutrality proclamation embargoed arms shipments to all belligerents, including the United Kingdom.

The first satisfactory U.S. Navy boats were copies of PT 9 built from plans under license to the Elco Naval Division of the Electric Boat Co. at Bayonne, New Jersey. In order that the boats could carry four twenty-one-inch torpedoes, their size was increased to seventy-seven feet. Higgins Industries at New Orleans built a seventy-eight-foot model with somewhat heavier armament. Later, Elco increased the length to eighty feet, with more freeboard than the Elco 77. Elco turned out 320 of the boats and Higgins, 205.

The boats were powered by three twelve-cylinder, water-cooled Packard marine engines—three props and three rudders. They burned 100-octane aviation gasoline (rubberized fuel tanks stored three thousand gallons for a three hundred mile range) and were originally rated at twelve hundred horsepower. The horsepower rating was eventually beefed up to fifteen hundred with no increase in weight. Although much plywood was used in PT construction, the hull itself was two layers of mahogany planking laid diagonally over laminated wood frames. A coating of airplane fabric impregnated with marine glue was ironed on between the two layers of mahogany, and four hundred thousand screws held it all together. The resulting hull was light, strong, resilient.

In relation to its size, the PT boat carried the heaviest armament of any naval vessel. They also had smoke screen generators to evade enemy fire. They could make forty knots fully loaded. The boats, however, had no armor: they were vulnerable to attack by shore batteries, fighter planes, and destroyers, and therefore operated almost exclusively at night and at close quarters. The early boats had no radar; however, within a year almost all of them were equipped with semi-reliable radar that gave them eyes in the dark. Called "mosquito boats"—half airplane, half submarine—they operated with a crew of ten, plus two officers, all volunteers.

By the time Holmstrom, Hollister, and Coor arrived at Melville (traveling by train to Boston and Providence, then bus), Japan had conquered all of Malaysia; Netherlands East Indies (Java and Sumatra); northern New Guinea; and the Philippines, including Corregidor. Burma had been overrun and Japanese troops occupied Korea, Manchuria, and large parts of China. Its goal of an impregnable Greater East Asia Co-Prosperity Sphere was within its grasp. Then in the first week of May 1942 came the inconclusive Battle of the Coral Sea (southeast of New Guinea), when an American task force intercepted a Japanese fleet headed for Port Moresby on the southeast coast of New Guinea. One month later, more encouraging news came from Midway, between the Hawaiian and the Aleutian Islands, where Admiral Chester Nimitz's Pacific Fleet cost Admiral Isoroku Yamamoto's Combined Japanese Fleet four aircraft carriers in a single afternoon. No one fully appreciated the Allied victory at the time, but the tide had turned—Japan would not win another major battle in the Pacific.

While the 1st Marine Division was fighting to take Guadalcanal in the Solomon Islands southeast of New Guinea, Holmstrom and Hollister (Coor had decided the PT boat squadrons were not for him and transferred out) absorbed a week of instruction in the assembly and disassembly of pontoon dry-docks at the U.S. Naval Construction Center across Narragansett Bay in Davisville, Rhode Island. Lacking A-frame dry-docks in the South Pacific, a more portable arrangement was required. Holmstrom: "It might be an awfully handy thing to know." He had a chance to watch the Seabees, the navy's construction battalion (CB), in action, and was impressed: "They are a pretty rugged looking bunch of fellas. The type you would find around a big construction job like Boulder Dam or Grand Coulee. They don't march very well or know anything about ships, but they work just as hard as if they were getting time and a half and afraid of losing their jobs."

The following week, Holmstrom and Hollister completed five days of instruction under the supervisor of shipbuilding at the Elco Naval Division, learning how PT boats were assembled. Another handy thing to know.

Here they studied everything except carpentry: how to chart a course, how to operate radar, how to man and take apart cannons, how to disassemble a torpedo. Their grounding at Melville included survival training.

On a six-day leave with Hollister in Boston, the two of them took in the sights: old cemeteries, Paul Revere's steeple, Bunker Hill. Holmstrom recorded an amusing incident that occurred at the Revolutionary War site: a young boy volunteered a tour and a lecture on the battleground, including the facts that the monument was thirty feet in diameter and two hundred feet high. Holmstrom paid him a dime, then told him that out West where he was from they had redwood trees four thousand years old and twice as high and big as the monument. The little boy offered his dime back. Holmstrom: "But I didn't take it."

They took a day to hitchhike south to New Bedford (Holmstrom had read *Moby Dick*) and visited the whaling museum (it was closed), the whalers' chapel, and the site of the old shipyard. They hitched to Cape Cod, where he wrote Elzie Clover that "some of the summer homes owned by New Yorkers are so big that they look silly."

One of the fellows who stopped to give them a lift on the way back turned out to be the owner of the Providence newspaper and made a detour to escort them through his printing plant.

With a move south to the Brooklyn Naval Yard, Holmstrom and Hollister took up bunks on new PT boats and ate on a scow-tender. Lieutenant Bulkley had requested that they figure out what they needed to keep a squadron (twelve boats) operational for a year, and they were busy making up tool kits and lists of equipment, supplies, and materials for their eventual departure. "Sort of like making up a patching outfit for a river trip, except that there is so much here that we don't know, such as where we are going, how much damage we will have to repair, how long we will stay, how hard it will be to get more material, etc., and at the same time trying to stay away from any unnecessary stuff."

One Sunday, they escaped downtown to the Explorers Club for lunch and

spent the evening visiting with Amos Burg, who had a 16MM copy of the Colorado River film with sound. Holmstrom told his mother in a letter, "Right now it looks pretty unimportant to me, but I didn't have the heart to tell him so." Burg left on a midnight train and was off to South America, where he performed intelligence estimates for the OSS, forerunner of the CIA. Since his hotel room was paid for, they slept in it. With New York under a blackout, no one was out late.

A second excursion to New York allowed Hollister, a fervid baseball fan, to watch a World Series game between the Yankees and the Cardinals; a man on a streetcar gave him a ticket. Back at the naval yard, no one believed he had seen a game until he pulled out his ticket stub.

In late September, another brief liberty permitted them to scoot up to Boston and visit Oregon friends. With free tickets from the USO, the two of them went to the Chicago Bears-versus-Army football game. In a drenching rain, they watched Army play the Chicago professional team to a standstill, then lose 14 to 7. "I think the Chicago Bears are the best football team in the world... very few of the players are under 200 lbs. on up to one man weighing 270.... It sure was a dandy."

By October-end 1942 they had been in training for three months altogether. Attached to the Squadron Commissioning Detail at the Brooklyn Naval Yard, they were assigned to (Squad)Ron 7, the first to carry radar. Once equipped, Hollister received his orders to ship out, and Holmstrom was right behind him. They went by boat to Norfolk, Virginia, where twelve PT boats (PTS 127 to 138) were loaded onto two navy tankers. Since two carpenter mates were assigned to each squadron, both men shipped out together, but never on the same ship, making it less likely that the squadron would be left without a carpenter's mate in the event of an attack.

The tankers motored south by way of San Juan, Puerto Rico, to Aruba Island in the Dutch Lesser Antilles, just off the coast of Venezuela. At the refinery there, they took on a load of aviation gasoline. After leaving the depot, and while following a zigzag course at sea, one of the tankers was fired on by a German submarine—deckhands saw the white trail of torpedoes slice past.

They proceeded westerly to Panama, through the Canal, and off-loaded the PT boats at Balboa on the southern end of the Canal. They continued to Taboga, a small, mountainous island with a U.S. naval station on it, where Ron 7 made port and underwent six weeks of shakedown training: maneuvers, patrols, gunnery practice, torpedo practice, simulated missions, night duty—and above all, teamwork. Here, the PTs like all their sisters, received their affectionate nicknames: *Gypsy Wildcat, Artful Dodger, Little Lulu, Green Bitch*, and so on. Then they lightered the PT squadron aboard two Standard Oil tankers, the S. S. *White Plains* and the S. S. *Richmond*, and unescorted spent twenty-eight days crossing to Noumea, New Caledonia. From there they sailed to Brisbane, Australia, off-loaded the PT boats, and in order to spare the engines, had them towed by a minesweeper and the gunboat *Tulsa* (a Yangtze River refugee), through the Great Barrier Reef north over a thousand miles against fearsome weather, with several of the boats sustaining damage, toward Torres Strait, just off the tip of Cape York Peninsula—the northernmost point of Australia and fewer than a hundred miles south of New Guinea.

Midway up the coast, the ships made port at Townsville, Queensland Territory. The U.S. Navy was organizing a destroyer base there, and the officer in charge had not the faintest idea of what his equipment needs might be. He asked Hollister and Holmstrom and four other sailors to assist him in putting together supply lists. Neither Hollister nor Holmstrom had ever even been on a "tin can," as destroyers were nicknamed, but the men sat up all night with a couple of supply catalogues, and in Hollister's words, "By God, we got the job done. Buzz and I sure laughed about it later."

At Cairns, two hundred miles north of Townsville, Holmstrom and Hollister and six other men from their Ron, along with an officer, left on two PT boats and met a small Dutch freighter at sea. They transferred with their gear to the freighter and went on to Thursday Island, landing in the dark.

Holmstrom and Hollister labored ferociously on Thursday Island, readying the site for the arrival of their twelve boats. Since the water was too shallow for a pontoon dry-dock, they worked at preparing other mooring sites. Taking over a marine railway used for luggers on the island when it was a pearling station, they adapted it to haul PT boats out of the water. When the PT boats arrived, they refurbished them and painted their hulls with camouflage: brownish red below the waterline, a mottled gray and olive drab above. While there, they lived with a company of Aussie soldiers in an old hotel, ate mutton, trained in the use of their firearms, and were assigned positions on the beach in the event of a Japanese invasion, a reasonable concern. Thursday Island became part of Base 10, located in Darwin, Australia. Hollister recalls that when he and Holmstrom put their hand-tools in a rowboat and headed out to do exterior repairs on a PT boat, Holmstrom "would row like a ten-horsepower outboard" because the tides in the strait could run seven knots.

By sea, the enemy never came within range of the island, and it was just as well. Shoal water extends so far out from the reaches of the southern coast of New Guinea that it was not possible to fire a torpedo—in places it extends so far to sea that ships can go aground out of sight of land.

Leaving PTS 127 to 132 and a base force in command of Lieutenant Robert J. Bulkley, Jr., at Thursday Island, in case of an enemy diversionary attack on Torres Strait, Lieutenant Commander John Bulkeley took PTS 133 to 138 to Milne Bay, at the southernmost tip of New Guinea. Holmstrom and Hollister remained at Thursday Island.

In January 1943 Holmstrom passed the examination and qualifications for a rating change to Carpenter's Mate second class. So did Hollister. Holmstrom's proficiency rating was a perfect 40, as was his mark for "Ability as leader of men"; his seamanship rating was 39.

Throughout spring and summer 1943, Allied forces moved up the northeast coast of New Guinea in a series of leap-frog advances that often bypassed entrenched Japanese positions. Once air bases were established for support, the advances proceeded as part of General MacArthur's "Operation Cartwheel" strategy to liberate the Philippines, and eventually, Okinawa. At night, PT patrols interrupted Japanese attempts to resupply their bases with barge convoys of troops and materiél (the "Tokyo Express"); PTS also scouted enemy positions by drawing fire from shore batteries, and provided a screen for amphibious assaults from landing craft.

After several months, in June 1943 Holmstrom and Hollister moved to Milne Bay. Shortly thereafter, they motored north to Kiriwina Island, desired as an air base for use against New Britain and part of the Trobriand Islands in the Bismarck Archipelago immediately east of New Guinea. It was here that Holmstrom made numerous native friends and reevaluated some of his prejudices. Natives, maltreated by the Japanese invaders, cooperated with the Allies, furnishing invaluable labor and surveillance of enemies. Holmstrom soon came to admire their skills and industriousness, their sense of direction, their knowledge of their own landscape and waters, even their way of life. The new friends communicated with a shared cluck-cluck language of gestures and signs and pidgin. Holmstrom went for hikes on the jungle trails to visit nearby villages, gave the villagers vegetable seeds from home and showed them how to plant them. The local natives walked five miles to assist with work details each morning, for which they were paid six cents a day. Holmstrom found one young man with a searching intelligence especially likable: "He speaks fair English. He has a good personality and is real smart. Honestly, he's a good deal smarter than I am. He seems to know everything that goes on in the jungle. A wonderful memory and a natural engineer. He built a couple of buildings for us… with nothing but a knife. They do the job in a good deal different way than we do but the main thing is that they get results. I'll bet if you gave him a set of tools and showed him how they work he'd be a better carpenter than us in six months. And I hesitate to think where he would be if he had been born in the states with white skin and had all the opportunities we have all had." In another place he wrote, "I'll swear that these natives are happier than we are and have just as many things that are luxuries to them as we have." Writing to Hamilton, he said, "This place is almost as pretty as the moving picture version. There are some really good looking native girls here—but my knowledge of the language hasn't done me any good yet." Acclimated to the humid climate, he was never sick, even for a day.

At night Japanese "Zeroes" bombed and strafed the landing strip at Kiriwina.

The Seabees sprayed diesel fuel on the strip to darken it and left a white coral strip alongside, which successfully diverted the night raiders and left the real strip intact. On August 17, 1943, the 5th Air Force staged a massive surprise raid on the Japanese base at Wewak, midway up the north coast of New Guinea, and all but wiped out two hundred planes they caught on the ground, crippling Japanese air strength in the region. As Operation Cartwheel rolled on, Holmstrom and Hollister repaired damage to boats inflicted by artillery fire, and with native help built tent and mess quarters as well.

When replacements arrived, the pair went to Sydney, Australia, on a two-week recuperation leave. Hollister recalls that by buying Holmstrom at least two Aussie beers, he could tease out a few stories about the Colorado River trips. While there they had to spend a couple of days at a gunnery school, training on 20MM Oerlikon cannons—primarily an anti-aircraft gun with a 6,000-foot ceiling—with which they were already far more familiar than most of the instructors.

Three weeks more, and they were back at Milne Bay. By persuading a New Zealander with a sawmill to cut a piece out of a native tree, they replaced the keel in a PT boat thought unfit for anything but scrap. (Two years later, Hollister happened upon the same boat docked in the Philippines. He went on board and was told by a seaman that it was the fastest in their squadron.)

Both men sat for the Carpenter's Mate first class examination on the same day. Since there was room for only one advancement, the two of them shook hands and agreed to play the test completely straight. Hollister scored slightly higher and was dead certain that Holmstrom deliberately took a lower grade: "That's the kind of guy he was." Before long, Holmstrom also received his first class rating.

Beginning in November 1943, the Pacific Ocean Area Forces under Admiral Nimitz made successful amphibious assaults on the Gilbert Islands, northeast of New Guinea. In a series of coordinated advances across the central Pacific, the forces cut the Japanese supply lines and provided air bases to bomb Japan's home islands. In less than a year, MacArthur would again set foot in the Philippines. Ron 7 had lost only three boats, two to reefs.

By mid-1944 Holmstrom and Hollister were overdue for a thirty-day leave when Hollister developed appendicitis and had to have surgery. While recovering, he discovered that his nurse was from Jerome, Arizona, and had lived across the street from Chauncey Coor. Because Hollister did not want to miss the Liberty ship that would provide him transportation to the U.S., he was up and about within a week. Their replacements arrived, and in late April 1944, Holmstrom and Hollister left for San Francisco. En route the ship ran out of food and the men were reduced to eating canned plums.

When the squadron mates reached San Francisco in May, they landed at Treasure Island—the place where Holmstrom had intended to show his Colorado film at the 1939 World's Fair. First they went off to get a decent haircut, then found a restaurant and ordered the best steak on the menu. That afternoon, in one of the unforeseen encounters chance contrives, Holmstrom met his brother Carl, whom he had not seen since induction, downtown on Market Street. Carl's survey ship had been moored in San Francisco Bay for six weeks. They all went to have a drink at the "Top of the Mark" in the Mark Hopkins Hotel, but dressed in navy uniforms, were refused admittance. Nevertheless, it was a joyful reunion.

Holmstrom and Hollister headed for Coquille and a visit with his mother. Her letter to Elzie Clover is the sole light on the reunion: "We had a wonderful visit, but the inevitable end of it leaves me missing him more than before he came. He is quite thin," she observed, "very brown—at first it was a disturbing yellowish brown, due, he said, to the daily atabrine they took to ward off malaria—but it and the deeply weary look in his eyes left before he had been here a couple of weeks."

Hollister remembers looking at the repainted Colorado River boat still anchored in the backyard grass. Eight months earlier, Frances Holmstrom had written in her diary, "Painted the top of Buzz's old boat, the *Julius F.* and hope to do the rest of it tomorrow, as I don't know any other way of preserving it; save the surface and you save all."

Holmstrom and his sidekick left to visit Hollister's folks in Hall, Montana, where he had grown up on a ranch. Together they drove an old pickup with a

Hollister and Holmstrom at Frances Holmstrom's house, Coquille

wooden rowboat up a goat trail to Cooper's Lake in the mountains. There they spent a day trolling with Daredevil lures and caught ample cutthroat and rainbow trout. Hollister recalls Holmstrom holding up a fresh catch and saying appreciatively, "Isn't this a beautiful fish?" They camped overnight.

At the end of their leave, the pair had orders to report to the Brooklyn Naval Yard. They entrained for Boston, sitting on their seabags on a passenger train packed with troops from all branches of the service. Hollister was suddenly overcome with an attack of malaria; by the time he got to Boston, he had experienced a second attack and was sent to St. Alban's Hospital. His stay lengthened to six weeks. Holmstrom, in the meantime, was assigned to a new squadron: Ron 34 (PTS 498 to 509), commissioned six months earlier. Because he shipped out leaving Hollister in the hospital, his movements from this point without Hollister's recollections are cloudy.

While Holmstrom was on the East Coast, the story in Europe briefly was this: The fall of France in 1940 had left England with only Commonwealth forces for support. In early 1941 Congress voted Lend-Lease aid to save England from collapse. (Even the original PT 9 was returned to England and put in service as a gunboat.) British Coastal Forces used MTBS to patrol their coasts, to protect Allied shipping, and to prey on enemy coastal convoys. To date they had fought over four hundred actions in their home waters and sunk 270 enemy vessels, including E-boats. The E-boat (enemy boat) was the German counterpart of the MTB or PT: 106 feet long, three diesel engines, four torpedoes, deck armament, comparable speed.

By the time Holmstrom arrived back in Rhode Island in early June 1944, not only had the tide in the Pacific turned, but in Europe, air warfare had tilted the conflict overwhelmingly in favor of the Allies, who were now ready to open the Second Front promised to a beleaguered Stalin two years earlier. An air offensive was planned for the D-Day landing known as "Operation Overlord" on the northern coast of France. Four squadrons of PT boats were shipped to England—the first served the Office of Strategic Services in the swift and silent pick-up and delivery at night of secret agents on the Normandy Coast.

At midnight on June 6, 1944, under the supreme command of General Dwight D. Eisenhower, with eleven thousand planes forming a protective umbrella, four thousand transports, eight hundred warships, and innumerable small craft (including PT boats) ferried and supported the infantry who swarmed ashore at the Baie de la Seine at Normandy. Holmstrom was not among them.

Holmstrom was undergoing additional training and duties in Melville and Brooklyn. While there in July, he had a few days of leave and used them to go camping at a small lake in New Hampshire, "just doing nothing." On August 10, he departed by ship on a ten-day crossing to England, where he joined up with Squadron 34, which had been in action in the English Channel since late May and had taken part in D-Day operations. The Normandy Invasion was an operation "that eventually went according to plan, but not according to timetable." By this point, Cherbourg had surrendered and General George S. Patton had broken through the German flank and raced into Brittany, but U.S. and British forces were still battling the German 7th Army in northern France.

By the beginning of August, however, the PT boats had been withdrawn from the Normandy invasion area: some were transferred to Portsmouth, England, to work with British MTBS; others were assigned to the advanced base opened in

Cherbourg that month to patrol the Channel Islands—Jersey, Guernsey, Alderney—where Germans had hold-out garrisons.

Bob Poling, stationed on PT 508, *Mairsey Doats,* recalls meeting Holmstrom in July in the damaged dry-dock at Cherbourg. Holmstrom, who abhorred injections and passed out at the prospect more than once, was having difficulty sitting after a recent typhus shot: "Worst one I ever got." On August 25, 1944, the two of them learned Paris had just been liberated, and figuring no one would miss them, decided to risk the two hundred-mile trip on the *Red Ball Express*—the famous priority supply train for troops at the front (it displayed scarlet meatballs painted on its bumpers).

The two seamen, technically "absent without leave," hitched a ride on the train and en route traded war information to troops starved for any kind of news or gossip. They stopped at an antiaircraft station and were treated to lunch. By afternoon, they realized they were not going to make Paris in time and reluctantly turned back.

Poling clearly recalls two shards of conversation from the shared train trip: Holmstrom spoke of his cross-country journey with Clegg and said he would like to repeat the trip someday; he also said that after the war he wanted to build a cabin that looked out over the Pacific Ocean. Said he already had the spot picked out.

On September 18, 1944, Holmstrom wrote to Clover again. In part, he said, "Say, this navy is sure a fine thing for seeing the world.... We are in France now. But as far as I'm concerned personally, it's just as quiet and safe as if I was at home."

In October Squadron 34 received orders to prepare its boats for delivery to the U.S.S.R. By then, Allied armor divisions had cleared most of France and Belgium of German forces; Germany had evacuated the Balkan Peninsula; and the Russian army on the Eastern Front had swept through the Baltic States, Belorussia, East Poland, Ukraine, Rumania, Bulgaria, and Finland. Squadron 34 prepared its boats at Roseneath, Scotland, near Glasgow. They said a fond farewell to *Idiot's Delight, Hemingway Hotel, Nasty Bastard, Sassy Sue, What's Next.*

In late November, Holmstrom was back in Melville, Rhode Island, attached to the PT squadron's 11th Amphibious Force. He was there until April 10, 1945, when he was transferred south to the Brooklyn Naval Yard.

Rolf Holmstrom visited him there. His initial attempts to locate his brother were frustrated by buddies who, not knowing Rolf was related to Buzz, denied knowing any such person. On learning who Rolf was, they revealed that Buzz and a few friends were absent without leave. Rolf returned the following morning; the brothers went to Palisades Park in New Jersey, drank cider, and rode the merry-go-round and the roller coaster.

On June 21, 1945, the day it was commissioned, Holmstrom was received aboard Squadron 41 (PTS 601 to 612), six weeks after Germany surrendered but seven weeks before Japan surrendered. He traveled by sea—Cape May, New Jersey; Norfolk,

Virginia; Charleston, South Carolina; Mayport, Florida—to Miami, where the navy ran an operational training and shakedown center for Elco 80s. As he wrote Clover on August 2, "It was a fine trip, kind of like a tour in a car. I thought Charleston was the most interesting, as it's really southern & in the entrance to the bay is Fort Sumter...." He complained about the mosquitoes. Four days later, the first atomic bomb exploded over Hiroshima.

While in Miami, Holmstrom received an unexpected visit from Coor, who had gone to officers' training school and was now an ensign. From the address on a forwarded letter, Coor realized that he was residing in an hotel only a block from Holmstrom's squadron, and dashed off to see him. Again, not knowing who Coor was, Holmstrom's buddies denied any knowledge of their mate's name or whereabouts. Finally convinced that Coor was a friend, they belatedly revealed that he was top deck sacked-out in a hammock, recovering from the previous night's binge. Despite Coor being an officer, the two men went off to a bar and a show. Recalling his friend, Coor laughed, "He was kinda shy, but always giving the ladies the eye. He was fun to talk to, fun to get to tell stories, fun to be around, always kidding a little bit."

Squadron 41 was assigned to the Pacific Fleet and shipped out in early August. Rolf was in the Army Air Corps in Rio Hato, sixty miles southwest of the Panama Canal Zone, when a PT boat, out on maneuvers, stopped in for lunch. In a conversation with a couple of the crew members, Rolf learned that they were from Ron 41, and that his brother was in their squadron and had intended to accompany them that day, but at the last minute decided to remain ashore in Panama City. So they missed seeing each other by a few hours and miles.

On August 14 President Harry Truman announced Japan's surrender. Ron 41 turned back from its fleet assignment and proceeded north to California instead. (Its boats were saved for training purposes but the squadron was decommissioned in February 1946.)

Holmstrom was discharged on October 5, 1945, at Bremerton Naval Base, Washington, on Puget Sound. His discharge papers said he was authorized to wear the following service decorations: European-African-Mid Eastern Area ribbon, Asiatic Pacific ribbon, U.S. Navy Good Conduct medal. He tucked his paycheck for $272.20 into his pocket and thumbed a ride south to Coquille. It had been three years since he told his mother that putting on civilian clothes again would be even stranger than wearing a navy uniform. Tomorrow he would give it a try.

left:
The sailor

opposite:
Holmstrom's
last camp
at Rondowa
Bridge

Home is the Sailor

1946

RANCES WAS HOEING WEEDS in her flower garden and Carl had finished repairing the wood-burning stove when Buzz arrived. It had taken him nearly three days to hitchhike the three-hundred miles home. Carl had reached Coquille two days earlier; it had taken him nearly a week to reach home from the San Francisco Bay Area. An oil workers' strike was spreading across the United States, and no one knew how long the interstate bus lines would be out of service. The lumber mills in Coos Bay had shut down, as had many others along the southern Oregon coast including Smith Woods in Coquille. The war was over and the old antagonisms between labor and capital were rekindling.

That evening, Anna, along with her daughters June and Shirley, met at Frances's house for a family reunion and dinner. Anna's husband Floyd, recently discharged from the army, was expected home any moment. Frances brought Buzz up to date on the local news and reassured him that Rolf would be coming home early the next year. She wrote in her journal, "The days when grandmothers raised children, while mothers worked and men went off to war, are coming to a close."

Unable to find local work, Carl left a few days later for Klamath Falls, Oregon, where he took a job in the woods with one of the small gyppo outfits in the area. Although the future appeared uncertain, Buzz, at thirty-six, easily resumed his hometown rhythms and routines.

Ed Walker called in, and a few days later Buzz was back working at the service station as though he had never left. Frances, delighted to have Buzz around, mentioned in her journal "he even liked the service station job."

Buzz went fishing, renewed old friendships, repaired Frances's house. He chatted and played snooker with the other veterans downtown at Bill's Place, and occasionally went to church on Sundays with his mother. He entertained his two nieces, who adored their uncle. Weather permitting, the family took Sunday picnics in the old Ford up into the mountains near Powers or south down the coast to the Bandon beaches.

As the holidays approached, Buzz drove out to McKinley with Ken Hansen, his high school buddy, to help fell trees on the Hansen property. A few days before Christmas, the entire family—Buzz, Frances, Anna, Floyd, and their children—purchased a tree in town. Spirits were high as Frances and Anna busily prepared for the dinner at Anna's house.

At 8:30 A.M. on Christmas, Carl arrived with an armload of apples. He had ridden the Greyhound all night in order to be home on time. Frances wrote, "It was very dark, gloomy, and rained fiercely most of the day. But it was a happy Christmas and a lovely dinner."

DESPITE HIS SERVICE in the South Pacific and Europe, Holmstrom was restless. Plainly he had outgrown Coquille. He had run the Rogue, Salmon, and Colorado Rivers and had crossed the country by boat. He had been a driller, a miner, and a sailor. But what next? Contrary emotions tugged at him—the desire to escape from and his strong feeling of attachment to his hometown; the visions of a fresh start and yet, back at the gas station once again.

Holmstrom was a working man. Having no head for business or self-promotion, he did not see many opportunities available in Coquille, and certainly not on the rivers of the Southwest. Given the times, he was probably right. Norm Nevills's tiny commercial river running operation in Mexican Hat, Utah, had shut down during the war, and although Holmstrom had gotten along with Nevills, working for him might have been difficult. Running rivers with paying passengers may not have been beyond Holmstrom's imagination after the Clegg trip; but given the choice, he preferred the company of friends and other rivermen.

After Christmas, most of the roads in Coos County were flooded and Coquille was temporarily isolated. On December 27, Holmstrom wrote to Elzie Clover:

Dear Elzie—
I don't think I've written you since I got discharged at Bremerton, Wash. on Oct. 5—My mother had been living by herself here for a long time and so as I had a chance to go to work in a service station for a while I took it and it has really been kind of fun as I've kind of got acquainted with a lot of people I'd almost forgotten—Its not very cold here but—man how it does rain— Already we've had more rain than during the whole of last winter and right this evening it's pouring—In spite of the season of the year the pussy willows are budding out now."

"I still don't have any plans for the future—apparently don't have the ambition or ability to make any—Sometimes I think I might have a go at the merchant marine—A pretty good business as things are now is a deep sea fishing boat but that requires some money which I never did get around to save...

Holmstrom finished the letter with an anecdote:

I thought I would wash a dirty old kapok sleeping bag that I had for a long time in the machine but it swelled up till it like to have burst the sides right off the washer and naturally she didn't wash very clean. We finally dragged it outside and hung it up to dry but then we had a few freezing nights and it froze up solid—then it started to rain and not having a good place to hang it, why I took it up to a friend of mine [Hal Howell] with a basement with a furnace in it and after three days it thawed out then for about a week it dripped something fearful—A couple of days ago he told me she appeared to be getting somewhat dry but now today he says that it is getting to smell so bad that if I don't get it out of there soon he figures he may have trouble with his wife.

No sooner had he mailed the letter to Clover then he received word that his job application with the Bureau of Reclamation had been accepted.

By the New Year, the rain slackened and the roads reopened. Just as Carl returned to Coquille after a two months absence, Buzz packed for his new job with the Bureau. On Friday morning, January 4, he boarded the bus for Los Banos, a small town in the San Joaquin Valley between Stockton and Fresno, California. Thurman Hickam accompanied him to the station. Later Hickam said that Buzz seemed depressed about going and asked Hickam to travel to California with him.

Holmstrom had been hired to work on the Friant Dam, part of the Central Valley Water Project, as a "diamond drill helper" at $1.10 per hour. A few days after he left, Sam Flint from the U.S. Coast and Geodetic Survey came through Coquille looking for him; Flint had heard that the survey needed a river pilot for some work on the

Grande Ronde River the following spring. He left a message with Frances.

On the bus to California, Holmstrom became ill. When he finally reached Sacramento, he was hospitalized for nearly three weeks. At first the doctor thought he had the flu, but he subsequently realized that Holmstrom had suffered a malaria attack. Treating Buzz with Atabrine, an antimalarial drug, he recommended that Holmstrom live in a drier climate than that of his home state. By the beginning of February, Holmstrom was feeling better and wrote to Frances, asking her to send more Atabrine to use as a preventive as soon as possible. A few days later, he was working at the dam site. By early April, he had been promoted to "diamond driller" at one dollar and fifty cents per hour, fifteen dollars for a ten hour day. He had also received a letter from the U.S. Coast and Geodetic Survey, hiring him as a river pilot for the survey work on the Grande Ronde in northeast Oregon.

Sometime after his return from the war, Holmstrom began seeing Loas Morrison, an acquaintance from his high school days. Although they were the same age, Loas had been a senior when Holmstrom was a sophomore, nearly twenty years earlier. Now she was living in San Francisco. They shared a mutual, long-standing friendship with Clarence Bean, who was also living in San Francisco at the time.

When she was twelve years old, Morrison learned that she was adopted. Sources suggest that from that time on the young girl was often at odds with her middle-age adoptive parents, Sarah and Arthur. Ross Kistner, who lived next door to Loas when they were children, spoke of her as a free spirit.

> There was nothing untoward about her behavior. She was just full of it. One time Loas was driving her father's new Chevy sedan around town. The Rainbow was the confectionery shop across from the hotel where all the high school kids gathered after school. She would drive around the corner in the car and yell, "Any of you guys want a ride to school? I'll circle the block and you hop in cause I don't know how to stop this damn thing." She was just into everything.

Morrison became a competent pianist and watercolorist. In the 1920s she performed with a small band on board the sternwheelers during their weekend runs down the Coquille River to Bandon. Independent and outspoken, (some folks called her willful) Loas was known to like a drink or two. Her carefree days ended in the mid-1930s when she married Cliff Gulseth, a local car dealer; they eventually moved to Coos Bay. A few years later, they divorced and Morrison moved south to San Francisco, where she met her second husband Don Blagg. Two days after they married, while boarding an airplane for their honeymoon trip, Blagg suffered a heart attack and died. Morrison remained in San Francisco, where she worked during the war.

Loas and Buzz's friendship became a romantic one. Friday afternoons after work, Holmstrom caught the bus in Los Banos for the three-hour ride to the city, arriving at the Market Street terminal by the early evening. He had bought an old Chevy in Los Banos, but did not trust it to make the trip from the Central Valley.

They ate in restaurants, rode the cable cars, and visited Chinatown and Fisherman's Wharf. They walked across the Golden Gate Bridge to Sausalito. While they explored the city, they shared memories of their early days in Coquille. Never loquacious, Buzz was rarely at a loss for words with Loas. "I guess I'm going kind of soft or some such thing because I've remembered many times what grand bull sessions we had for those few days," he wrote to her.

Still, when he was making arrangements for a visit, Holmstrom did so with a schoolboy's politeness. If he suspected he might be late or unable to make a date, he apologized in advance. He stumbled at times: "I wish I could tell you for sure but I am pretty sure you will see me Friday evening—So Long, Buzz." Yet he never revealed his feelings for Morrison with any directness, at least not in his letters. He moved slowly, if not obliquely, toward his heart's desire. The depth of Morrison's attachment remains unknown.

He did share his immediate plans with her: The Survey was planning a project in the northeastern corner of Oregon and had offered him at least two month's work, building and piloting two boats down the Grande Ronde River, beginning in May. Though he was excited about the job, he seemed reluctant to leave Loas.

In early April he traveled to Santa Barbara to visit with Uncle Roy and Aunt Emma. Their accounts of his visit differed profoundly. Emma stated that her nephew was elated over the prospects of the new job, not at all depressed when he visited them. Roy said, "When I saw him his eyes were wrong—deep set and dead."

Two weeks later, Holmstrom returned to San Francisco to attend Easter church services with Loas. In a letter to Frances, he wrote, "It was the best thing I've done in some time." On April 23 he resigned from the Bureau of Reclamation. He said goodbye to Loas, promised to write regularly, and drove north to Coquille for a brief visit before joining the survey party.

On April 28, Frances wrote:

Loas Morrison

> When I woke this A.M. there was sort of vibrating, not loud, snore audible
> all over the house. Also there was a strange hat and coat on the sofa. But
> Carl said Rolf was in his bed. However, there seemed something fishy about
> it still. I peeked in and sure enuf there was a mound under the bed clothes.
> Still I wasn't satisfied and finally I investigated closer and found—the mound
> wasn't Rolf, it was *Buzz.*

Rolf had been discharged from the army at Fort Lewis, Washington, in mid-February 1946. Upon arriving home he ordered a refrigerator for Frances, the first the family had ever owned. Rolf had last seen Buzz a year earlier at the Brooklyn Naval Yard. He remembers being annoyed with him in Coquille because they did not have a chance to sit down and talk. "Buzz was in and out of the house, visiting old friends and preparing for the job on the Grande Ronde. He seemed preoccupied with the two boats he had to build for the trip. But otherwise, he was in good spirits and was particularly tickled about the recent purchase of the refrigerator," said Rolf.

Frances wrote of Buzz's two-day visit:

> He was thin when he came home, but seemed well, happy, eager—so glad to
> be home, running around to see all his friends, looking forward to the new job
> and to a longer visit at home when it was finished. Everyone commented that
> they had never seen him so happy. It was a visit to treasure.

On April 30, Holmstrom took the Greyhound to Portland, and then east up the Columbia Gorge to The Dalles. It had been nearly seven years to the day since he began the cross-country river trip with Mrs. Clegg on the Columbia. He rode past Bonneville Dam; at The Dalles preliminary work had begun on a new dam.

Holmstrom arrived at the survey warehouse that evening and met George Grimm, the man in charge of the project. Grimm's chief responsibility was to make sure the operation went smoothly, on and off the river. He would also assist Holmstrom with the construction of the boats. His main worry that evening was whether Holmstrom, of whom he had heard much, would be able to build two boats in the next two weeks; Grimm had a team of surveyors eager to get to work. He took Holmstrom to an old hotel overlooking the Columbia River. The owners had partitioned a corner of the porch into a small, six-by-seven-foot "sleeping room" with screens instead of windows. Not a bad place to bunk given the warm weather.

After a day of working alongside Holmstrom, Grimm's doubts about the new man's abilities as a boatwright disappeared. Holmstrom looked briefly at the blueprints and set to work. The carpenter's-mate rating he had received in the service was paying dividends. The group needed a rowboat to scout camps and rapids and to ferry men and supplies across the river as well as a scow to carry the bulk of the equipment and supplies. The rowboat was a simple matter; the scow, however, was a new challenge. Rectangular, eighteen feet long and six feet wide, and steered with sweeps mounted at each end of the boat, the scow reminded Holmstrom of the barges he had built at Echo Park before the war. Those he had piloted with motors.

From the 1936 Salmon trip Holmstrom remembered Harry Guleke, the "king of the scows." He knew, too, the story of Glen and Bessie Hyde's disappearance in Grand Canyon. Their empty scow had been found floating in an eddy. For now, however, he concentrated on building the scow rather than on thoughts about the difficulty of piloting it. In a letter to Loas he joked, "I should have got here a week sooner.... I don't know for sure how I am going to make out as I am fooling around with a type of boat that I don't know anything about, but we will sure find out."

On May 2 back in Coquille, Frances celebrated her sixty-fifth birthday. Carl gave his mother an *Inkograph* pen and Anna made an apron for Frances. The next day a mysterious package arrived on Frances's doorstep, the sender unknown. She opened the package and found twenty pounds of bacon, more than she knew what to do with. A few days later a letter arrived from Buzz, admitting responsibility.

On May 3 Holmstrom signed an "Oath of Office, Affidavit, and Declaration of Appointee," witnessed by George Grimm's immediate superior, Lieutenant Commander Ira R. Rubottom. The job description read "river pilot", pay was twenty dollars a day. Holmstrom joked with Rubottom that the survey was paying him too much—he would be quite willing to take the boats down the river for half that amount. Rubottom later wrote, "In fact, I am sure he regarded it more as a vacation than a position..."

A friendship quickly developed between Holmstrom and Grimm. Each morning they had breakfast together before starting to work on the boats. The two discussed the day's work and complained vigorously about the lack of materials and decent tools.

During his two weeks in The Dalles, Holmstrom wrote regularly to Frances and to Loas; to the latter he complained, "I've been working every day since I've been here on these damn boats... This is surely a sour letter... I swear I'll do better very soon." He wrote again on May 5:

Dear Loas—

This evening I got your letter of May 4—It surely must have made good connections with the plane—surely didn't come up on the bus like I did.

The day before yesterday it was 92 degrees here—but now the wind is blowing up the gorge something fierce. When you walk against it you have to lean over about 45 degrees.

The people who run this hotel have been nice to me. They took me out to see some people who live on a ranch on a bank of the river below town—I didn't exactly know them—but had heard of them as their daughter married a fellow from Portland [Phil Lundstrom] who knew Amos Burg—

Now instead of this fellow taking his wife on a honeymoon trip as he should have why he went on quite a long trip with Amos and I and left his wife home at work. But anyway these people are nice and don't seem to hold it against me.

I worked yesterday and today as we are in a hurry to get going—I think maybe we will leave the last of next week—We are just going over on the Grande Ronde river now—I don't know anything about it but I guess its nothing to worry about—

I'm sure glad you saw Bean. I got his address when I was home and was going to send it to you. Please give my very best regards to your folks—

So Long for now, Buzz

On May 6 Holmstrom wrote matter-of-factly to fellow river runner Doc Frazier in Salt Lake City:

I came up here to work for the coast and geodetic survey who are doing some survey work around this part of the state. Its only going to last a month or two and then I figure on going back to the Bureau…. It's very nice around here now. I'm hoping our work takes us close enuf so I can see you this summer.

On May 10 he turned thirty-seven. He wrote another letter to Frances from The Dalles on May 12, one she characterized as the "same optimistic note he usually wrote." Buzz promised "a better one next time." He wrote again to Loas.

Sunday Evening, May 12
Dear Loas,

I've been kicking myself all day for not sending something home to my mother. I didn't realize till this A.M. that it was Mothers Day when someone told me—I just finished writing her a letter—But it seems like there's nothing much here to write about.

The wind has been blowing something terrible all day and its pretty cool—but I think it hardly ever rains here—

I worked yesterday and today as we are trying to get the boats done just as soon as possible because there's a crew of surveyors waiting—This Geodetic Survey is quite an outfit—

The Grande Ronde River where we are going has been surveyed several times but each survey is different from the other and its really very important to have it right before they try to do any work—so this outfit has been called in because when they finish a survey it is just naturally right and no question.

Since I've been here I have gone to the show several times—outside of that I've just worked, ate and slept—which is really a fine thing. The fellows I've been with here at the office are a pretty good bunch of guys but I am not real chummy with any of them. I know I told you we'd be leaving but now I think it will be maybe next Wed. And I'm hoping to get a letter from you first—

So Long for now—Buzz

The night before he left The Dalles Buzz wrote to Loas his third letter in nine days.

Tues eve , May 14
Dear Loas—
At last my labors here have come to an end—We are all packed up and ready to be on our way tomorrow A.M.—I've enjoyed myself here as I've been very busy building the boat…—And then we built a small rowboat for the men to cross back and forth across the river with—I'm sure it will work all right—I'm not so sure about the barge but I don't think the Grande Ronde is so very rough and so I'm not so worried as I am curious—but there's quite a big party of men and if we lost the barge and our chow they would get very hungry indeed—
I think this trip will take from two to three weeks so you better hadn't write for a little—My address will be Box 799—It will be forwarded to wherever we are—We have the whole outfit loaded on a little trailer which looks like it is about ready to collapse—It would be an inglorious end to our trip if we should end up alongside the highway somewhere with a pile of kindling wood on our hands—
I've been thinking that when I get down there again we should surely go to see Bean—And I sure hope it will be soon—I'm not so excited about this trip as I should be and I think I know why—If I get a chance I'll write you again before we start but I'm not sure if I can.
So Long—Be good—Buzz

He attached a poem clipped from a magazine:

So this is love that I have hunted long!
And very different from the thing I sought.
Not torrent's thunder, but the merry song
Of brooks upon a hill. Not flame-tongues caught
By logs and, angry, raging to be free,
But steady gleam of friendly lantern light.
Not gales that churn the air and claw the sea,
But zephyrs that caress a star-eyed night.
This thing that's love is gentle and profound.
It brings to mind a forest deep and cool,
A peaceful shore with sea gulls hovering round,
A single flower mirrored in a pool.
Why have I always looked with restless eye
For comet's tails and lightning in the sky?

On the morning of May 15 Holmstrom and the survey crew began the tedious two-hundred mile drive to La Grande, Oregon, towing the overloaded trailer.

Before they left The Dalles, however, they stopped for one last look at mesmerizing Celilo Falls. Holmstrom was fascinated by the sure-footed men standing on the rickety wooden platforms, dipping their nets into the turbulent water. In a few years The Dalles Dam would begin backing up water that would drown the falls.

Leaving the Columbia Gorge, the party turned inland and drove through the rolling hills of northeastern Oregon. Near Pendleton, the overloaded caravan switchbacked up the steep, two-lane road called Cabbage Hill. They stopped at Blue Mountain Pass (4,200 feet) to rest the trucks. From where they stood, the dry plateau country, with its scrub and pine trees and the Blue Mountains in the distance, stretched out before them.

Later that afternoon they descended into the Grande Ronde Valley. In the unseasonably warm weather, the brakes on the truck smelled of overburdened metal and rubber. Across the valley to the east, the snow-covered peaks of the Wallowas, clear and sharp in the afternoon sun, stood like a cliché of the European Alps. For the first time, Holmstrom sighted the Grande Ronde River winding alongside the road down the valley. They reached La Grande at dusk and stopped for gas and additional supplies. Elgin, their destination, lay twenty miles north.

THE HEAD WATERS of the Grande Ronde River rise in the Anthony Lakes area of the Elkhorns, south of La Grande. With the spring thaw, the steep 185-mile river comes to life, peaking in late May or early June. The high-mountain water runs icy and clear down into the Grande Ronde Valley, where numerous tributaries give the river a milky brown look.

The Nez Perce name for the area means "valley of winding waters." The name can be misleading however. At the town of Minam, the Minam River joins the Wallowa River and a few miles downstream at Rondowa, the Wallowa joins the Grande Ronde, sometimes tripling its flow. From source to mouth, the Grande Ronde drops an average of twenty-one feet per mile, steep for an Oregon river. At peak stages the river gathers increasing velocity as it races through the forested canyon, cresting its banks into the streamside trees

The next morning, May 16, the survey party reported to Commander Rubottom at the survey camp at the lower bridge outside Elgin. Preparations for the trip were in full swing and introductions were brief. Paul Haverlah, a tall, pleasant Texan, was the lead engineer. He would be in charge of the reconnaissance and benchmark crews. He had been headquartered in Elgin the past fall and winter, completing a survey of the Grande Ronde from La Grande to Elgin. The camp cook, Theodore Moffett, had been hired by the survey the previous March. A veteran of both world wars, Moffett had lived in all the western states and now owned a small ranch in Wyoming. The men unloaded their equipment, supplies, and the two boats. It took all of them to push the scow off the trailer and into the river.

The survey (a Department of Defense project, and therefore classified information) was to begin at Rondowa, a few miles downstream, and finish at Troy, thirty-five miles beyond. At Troy, the boats and equipment would be loaded on the truck and trailer and transported over to the Snake River to complete the survey.

A local resident, Dave McCartney, advised Rubottom that the worst rapids on the river lay below town. Rubottom informed Holmstrom, and along with Grimm, the three men decided to hike along the river and see for themselves. A week earlier, the Grande Ronde had peaked at 9,080 CFS at Rondowa, where the flow was three times that at Elgin. Unusually warm weather over the last few days, however, caused the river to rise again. That morning the gage at Rondowa read 6,370 CFS. Farther downriver at Troy, additional sidestreams jumped the flow to 8,190 CFS.

As they walked along the banks of the river below Elgin, the men decided that navigating the heavily loaded scow might prove difficult along this stretch. Although there were few sizable rapids, the river was fast and shallow (one to two feet) and littered with boulders and gravel bars. The scow would be difficult to land. They agreed that the next morning Holmstrom, with one other man, would make a test run in the empty boats. The rest of the survey crew would truck the equipment and supplies to the end of the dirt road at Palmer Junction, five miles downriver, and meet them. On the way back to camp, Holmstrom joked with Rubottom and Grimm that he thought the scow should have been larger.

Later Grimm and Haverlah, the only two experienced men on the survey, reported in *The Elgin Recorder*, "We are used to roughing it and tough going. Grande Ronde Canyon and Hells Canyon on the Snake River will be taken in stride, we hope. We have followed the courses of many rivers and streams. These may be our toughest, but we aren't worrying."

The rest of the day they prepared for the launch. Holmstrom had cashed a large check before leaving The Dalles and asked Grimm to purchase a money order for him at the post office in Elgin. He wrote once more to his mother.

In the evening Holmstrom visited with Oliver Barlow and his wife Alice at their home in Elgin. The couple owned the Elgin Greenhouse, a thriving nursery on the edge of town. Besides being an excellent ice-skater and soloist in the First Christian Church choir, Oliver Barlow was an avid fisherman and boater. He had been known to hop the train from Elgin to Rondowa and spend the day fishing, returning on foot late in the evening with his catch. Both Barlow and his friend, Dave McCartney, had floated the Grande Ronde numerous times.

Friendly and good-humored, Oliver Barlow liked Buzz instantly. They spent a relaxed evening talking about the river, boating, and Holmstrom's adventures in Grand Canyon. The Barlows later reported that Holmstrom was in "good spirits and showed no sign of uneasiness."

Early Friday morning Holmstrom, with his usual mix of confidence and caution, set off down the river in the scow. Another man followed in the rowboat. Holmstrom, standing in the middle of the scow, was momentarily out of control.

He was not alarmed, however. The boulders were obvious and easily avoided; the few rapids were of little consequence. His immediate concern was the velocity of the river; he wanted to keep the scow off the gravel bars. Memories of his first trip on the Rogue and his wreck at Black Bar Falls came back. As he had suspected, steering a scow on fastwater was nothing at all like rowing.

Holmstrom had always been a quick learner and set himself to the task at hand. He lifted both sweeps out of the water and flailed, pulled when he might have pushed, even tried to use the rear sweep as a rudder. Despite his best efforts he ran aground, but it was not a major mishap. He responded and adapted and corrected, as he had always done when facing a new challenge.

A couple of hours later, Grimm and the rest of the survey crew arrived at Palmer Junction. They found the boats moored below the mouth of Lookingglass Creek, near Dave McCartney's place. The rowboat handled well. Although landing had been difficult, the scow was apparently manageable. Holmstrom, however, did remark, "I am afraid we are in for a tough time." Grimm ordered the supplies and equipment stowed aboard the scow. At noon the party embarked. Whatever further doubts nagged Holmstrom, he kept to himself.

While the survey crew walked along shore, the scow, loaded with gear, supplies, and equipment, swept downriver. Holmstrom was surprised by how difficult it was to steer. He struggled to keep the overloaded craft off the gravel bars and pourovers. Keeping the boat pointed downstream took all his effort. Despite the swift current, the scow, sitting low in the water, moved ponderously. What confidence he had earned on the upper stretch of river now evaporated. Holmstrom was worried.

Four miles downriver, he spotted the bridge that carried the railroad tracks across the combined rivers and up the Wallowa. The locals called the area Rondowa— the official train stop designation. Grimm, on the left shore beneath the trestle, signaled Holmstrom to land. As the Wallowa surged into the Grande Ronde, it tripled the flow and forced water back upstream, creating a small bay along the left shoreline of the Grande Ronde. Grimm had correctly anticipated the need for a such a landing spot. With much effort, Holmstrom managed to maneuver the scow into the safety of the eddy. When asked how the loaded scow had handled, he responded, "nicely." Camp would be the cobblestone beach at the confluence of the two flooding rivers.

Holmstrom had made it this far, but his confidence was shaken. As he looked below the confluence, he was shocked by the increased velocity of the river. The Grande Ronde surged downstream, bank to bank, with no eddies in sight. He began to seriously doubt his own judgment—how he would manage the overloaded scow in the turbulent water below Rondowa after today's difficulties. He was a day into the trip and there was *now* no turning back. That night Holmstrom, as he had two nights previously, shared a tent with Grimm. He said nothing about his increasing apprehension.

On Saturday morning, May 18, Holmstrom awoke tired and anxious. He had not slept well. At some point his apprehension about piloting the scow had given way to profound self-doubt. Moffett later recalled that Holmstrom appeared nervous at breakfast: "...of course, it was difficult for me to realize that because I had known him for only a very short time." After breakfast, members of the survey team crossed the railroad bridge at Rondowa and traveled by trail downstream to begin their work. Holmstrom accompanied them to have a closer look at the next stretch of the river. The river ran so fast and high up the steep banks that the men stepped carefully for fear of falling in. The Rondowa gage below the Wallowa River was pegged at 6,980 CFS. Downstream at Troy, the gage had jumped to 8,790 CFS.

After three miles, the surveyors stopped and begin to work their way back toward camp. As he walked back alone, Holmstrom scouted the river again. Obstacles were few, the runs clean. He noted a series of impressive waves with pourovers. No eddies in sight, the river streaked forward. Again, landings would be difficult. Still, it was manageable—at least in a rowboat. The loaded scow, however, was another story.

Holmstrom arrived back at camp just after noon. Moffett asked if he wanted lunch or coffee. Holmstrom declined the coffee, but accepted a sandwich. At one he began loading provisions—two cases of canned goods, five gallons of gasoline, a hundred-pound sack of potatoes—into the small rowboat to take downstream to the next night's camp.

Sometime afterwards, Grimm saw Holmstrom rowing downstream and waved. Holmstrom rowed ashore and discussed the location of the next camp, as well as the condition of the river. Grimm thought this stretch was particularly bad,

Holmstrom's scow on the Grande Ronde

with boulders strewn about and few easy landings. He shared his concerns with Holmstrom, who did not appear worried. The rodman later spotted Holmstrom walking back to camp on the other side of the river and called to him. He waved back.

At two forty-five Holmstrom arrived back in camp. Moffett commented on his quick trip and asked him if he wanted any coffee. He replied, "No, I'm not going to drink any more coffee." Then he added, "That river is awful bad. I just can't make that river." Moffett reassured him that if they could not make the river by boat, they would surely find some other way. For the first time Holmstrom had revealed his increasing lack of self-confidence.

Moffett went down to the riverbank to fetch dishwater. Holmstrom followed. Near the bank, a Krag rifle leaned against a tree. He asked to borrow it, saying he was going downriver to "shoot a chicken." Moffett assumed he meant a sage grouse or timber pheasant; at that time of year they were common along the river.

Used in the Spanish-American War, the heavy Krag was later adapted for hunting large game. "There won't be any bird left if you use the Krag," Moffett teased and then suggested instead that Holmstrom take one of the .22 caliber rifles in camp.

Moffett went back to the cook's tent and a few minutes later Holmstrom appeared with the cook's new .22 Remington. He asked for a cartridge. Moffett told him that he should take more than one if he was going to shoot gamebirds and offered the whole box. At first Holmstrom refused, then relented. He put the box in his shirt pocket. It was three in the afternoon when he set off down the trail. Moffett lay down for a nap.

When he awoke after a half hour, Moffett crossed the Rondowa bridge and walked to a nearby ranch to purchase eggs for breakfast the next morning. He was back at the cook's tent in thirty minutes. A short time later, the survey party finished their work and began returning. Unknowingly, they had passed Holmstrom who was on the other side of the river.

When they reached camp, Grimm asked Moffett where Holmstrom was. He informed Grimm of what had occurred and added that Holmstrom appeared to be despondent because he did not think he could safely pilot the heavily-loaded scow.

Dinner was served at six, but Holmstrom had not returned. It was not unusual for him to be late to meals and no one remarked his absence. Dinner was finished within a half hour, the dishes were washed, and Moffett had set aside some food for the tardy boatman. By now, Moffett was concerned. He decided to check on Holmstrom.

Moffett walked down the steep, narrow game trail through the woods. Above him, a dozen other game trails disappeared into the thick stands of ponderosa pine. The evening sky, still light, tipped towards dusk. The air was warm. Moffett stepped gingerly over tree roots, half-buried stones, tangled vines of the sloping bank. Below him the river raced by, clamoring up its banks.

After three-quarters of a mile, he halted abruptly. In the middle of the trail ten feet away lay Holmstrom's body, curled over on one side. Moffett stepped back. He turned and hurried back to camp. Fifty years later, Paul Haverlah recalls the scene that evening:

> Moffett came into camp walking very fast. He looked frightened, very scared. Then he said, "I found him. He's slumped over in the trail. He's gone." There was just this silence where no one said a word. We were all stunned. Then George Grimm said, "What do you mean he's gone?" And Moffett replied, "Looks to me like he's dead."

Grimm immediately sent Paul Haverlah and another man back with Moffett to stand watch. They feared that animals might scavenge the body. Shaken, Grimm then walked four miles to Palmer's Junction to telephone Rubottom, who had returned to The Dalles. He also phoned the Union County coroner, L.L. Snodgrass, in La Grande.

Late that evening Snodgrass and his assistant Tom Harris drove the ambulance to the end of the dirt road at Palmer's Junction. They boarded a speeder (a railroad trolley used by the local Union Pacific section crew) and reached Rondowa shortly before midnight. Grimm left one man in camp and led Snodgrass and Harris, along with the rest of the men, to the location where Holmstrom lay.

In the dark alongside the river, Grimm and the other men held flashlights and gasoline lanterns while Snodgrass examined the body. He found Holmstrom lying face down, just as Moffett had left him. The bullet hole was above the right ear; the bullet lodged in the skull. Harris noted powder burns around the wound and later Dr. James Haun, a physician in La Grande, confirmed the findings with his own examination. The box of shells was still in Holmstrom's shirt pocket. His thumb still clasped the trigger. The automatic safety on the Remington, designed to engage after firing, had done so. A single spent cartridge remained in the gun.

After talking with Moffett, Grimm, and Haverlah, and after observing the position of the body and the nature of the wound, Snodgrass ruled that Holmstrom had died from a self-inflicted gunshot wound. He estimated the time of death at five, possibly five thirty that evening. Snodgrass surmised that Holmstrom first must have sat down on the ground, leaning against the tree stump. At some point he tilted the right side of his head towards the muzzle of the rifle, his left hand gripping the barrel against the skin above the ear. With the thumb of his right hand on the trigger, he positioned the gun at an acute angle and pulled the trigger. Death was instantaneous. He rolled off to one side and landed in the position in which Moffett found him.

The estimated time of death, according to Snodgrass, implied that Holmstrom had spent a significant amount of time sitting there before he took his own life. He had left camp around three. The walk downstream took no more than twenty minutes. The survey party, walking back to camp along the other side of the river, did not hear a shot.

It was nearly one thirty in the morning when Holmstrom's body was placed on a stretcher to carry back to camp. In the darkness, the men took turns carrying the body, alternating positions between the uphill trail and the sloping bank. The task became a lengthy ordeal. At three in the morning they arrived in camp and placed the body on the speeder. Grimm went with Snodgrass and Harris to La Grande to meet Rubottom. He told Haverlah and the rest of the men to wait until they heard from him. Then the speeder disappeared down the tracks. Exhausted, the men crawled into their sleeping bags and fell to sleep immediately. The river raced past them into the night.

JUST BEFORE DARK on Sunday, May 19, Elbert Schroeder, the town mortician, called on the Holmstroms. Schroeder had received the telegram of Holmstrom's death that morning; then he had thought it best that Pastor Munger carry the news to the family. Now he asked Carl and Rolf to step outside—he had something more he needed to tell them. Carl and Rolf looked hopeful until Schroeder said, "I'm sorry I have to tell you this. I've been talking with the coroner, and he said the official consensus was that Buzz took his own life. That he did it himself." Carl and Rolf were stunned. Carl finally asked Schroeder how Buzz had done it. "With a rifle," Schroeder replied, "According to the coroner, Buzz died of a self-inflicted gun wound."

Schroeder told the two brothers that the body would be shipped by train the following day. Someone would have to tell Frances at once—in a town the size of Coquille, word would spread quickly. People would be talking, coming by to express their condolences, asking what they could do. *The Sentinel* would print something. The meeting lasted no more than ten minutes.

Carl and Rolf trudged back into the house. Rolf, twenty-three at the time, recalls that when Carl told Frances, "Mom, that was Elbert Schroeder and he told us how Buzz died," she got up from the davenport, asking "Well, how did he die?" Carl replied, "He did it himself, Mom." Frances froze. She looked at her oldest son in disbelief. Rolf recalls: "Then she kind of wilted as she sat down in her chair. She was devastated, just devastated by this last piece of news." Belle Knife gave her a sedative, but no one slept well or long that night. Frances woke and prayed that it was a mistake; Carl and Rolf huddled together in the other small bedroom, reminiscing about their brother until early into the morning. For days afterward, Frances repeated again and again, "He couldn't have. He couldn't have done that!"

BACK ON THE GRANDE RONDE, the search for another boatman had already begun. Immediately after Holmstrom's death, Rubottom had wired the Coast Survey in Washington, D.C., "attempting to engage new pilot. If successful and he feels project feasible at this time will proceed otherwise will assign unit to other work temporarily."

Although most of the men on the survey crew were single, Paul Haverlah had a wife and two children in Elgin. After waiting three days for word from Grimm, Haverlah gave up and hopped a train at Rondowa for the short ride to Elgin. To his mind the river, with its swift current and steep banks, was simply too dangerous for a family man. Later he tendered his resignation, assuming he would be fired for walking off the job. (The survey did not accept his resignation and Haverlah was later reassigned. Several other members of the survey also declined to go down the river until the flood waters subsided, even if their refusal meant the loss of their civil service jobs.) On May 21, Forrest Earl Eidemiller, twenty-eight, a Salmon River boatman from Orofino, Idaho, was hired.

The survey party proceeded down the Grande Ronde on May 22. They worked continuously through Sundays and Memorial Day, and completed the line to Troy on June 6. Neither Grimm nor Rubottom mentioned any difficulties piloting the two boats farther down the river. Eidemiller thought the river "pretty rough, small, fast and high." Eidemiller was not the boatman Holmstrom was, but he knew scows. On June 11 the team moved on to Asotin, Washington, to take up further survey work on the Snake River.

ON WEDNESDAY, MAY 22, Frances wrote in her journal, "Haldane's earthly tabernacle came home to Coquille today." Buzz's body, shipped by train from La Grande two days earlier, arrived on the spur line from Coos Bay. He came in a wicker basket, his billfold tucked in his hands which were folded across his chest. His body was promptly taken to Schroeder's Mortuary, just off Main Street. Because of the heat, the length of time, and the nature of the wound, the body had begun to decompose. Mr. Schroeder asked Ed Walker to inform Frances and the rest of the family; they had already had enough surprises.

Schroeder suggested a closed casket for the service the next morning, and the Holmstroms agreed. They feared that some people would come to view the body simply out of curiosity. They asked that Buzz be dressed in his regular work clothes—jeans and a flannel shirt. Later Ed Walker and Doc Hamilton were given permission to view the body. The Holmstroms chose not to.

At ten thirty on the morning of May 23, the memorial service for Buzz Holmstrom was held in Schroeder's funeral chapel. Zettie Hawkins, the local piano teacher, served as organist. Frances had asked Pastor Munger to perform the eulogy. The family sat in the front row of the small chapel; no screen separated them from the growing crowd.

Friends from McKinley drove into town for the service; members of Frances's congregation attended as well. Ed Walker and his family, Doc and Phyllis Hamilton,

Belle Knife and Mrs. Bean sat behind the family. Mrs. Watson, the Howells, Brick Leslie, Ken Hansen, Thurman Hickam, people who knew Buzz from Walker's service station, and his former classmates from Coquille High School—all arrived to pay their respects. Edith Clegg, from the 1939 cross-country trip, also attended.

Clarence Bean came north from San Francisco. For many years a rumor persisted that Bean, while in town, did not attend the services. It is also unclear whether Loas Morrison attended. The Lawhornes, who had been so close to the family over the years, could not get away in time to attend. However, over the next few weeks the two sisters regularly exchanged letters.

When asked about the service fifty years later, Rolf Holmstrom can not remember much: grief overwhelmed him that morning. He remembers a speech, but not the words; a sea of faces, but no individuals; going through the motions, but not the particulars. By the time the funeral service was over, the chapel was full and the crowd overflowed onto the front street. Coquille turned out to say good-bye to its hero, the one who had been a source of pride to many in this small logging community.

At noon Haldane Holmstrom was buried in the Coquille Masonic Cemetery near his high school. Patches of sunshine broke through the bank of clouds rolling in from the coast—a typical spring day in southern Oregon.

For Frances, the reasons why her son would take his own life were unfathomable. Little in her experience had prepared her for such a death. Since she had witnessed her husband's decline and death, her grief was tempered. When her mother and then her father died, she sadly accepted the consequences of age and disease. But the sudden death of her relatively young son left her reeling and confused. If Buzz had committed suicide, she had no understanding of why. The thought chilled her.

The rest of the summer Frances continued her daily routines, more out of habit than interest—working in her garden, painting miniature scenes on the myrtle wood pins and brooches, and performing domestic chores that could not wait. She attended church more often and visited Buzz's grave every other day. She ordered a headstone from Mr. Sanders, the local stone mason. On July 3 Emma came to stay with Frances for three weeks.

At the end of the summer, the Bureau of Reclamation sent Holmstrom's tent and belongings to Frances. Not knowing what to do with the tent, she sold it to Frank McCrarey for fifteen dollars. She wrote on August 14: "I am so glad to be relieved of it." Buzz's death certificate arrived in the mail. Under "Usual Occupation," it read "*Expert Boatman.*"

After his death, the *Julius F.* settled into the grassy hillside near Frances's house. But it so reminded Frances of Buzz that when the local postman, Billy Steward, asked about it one day, she told him to take it and put it to good use. He was an avid fisherman and turned it into a fishing boat. He took out the fore and aft compartments and modified the stern to carry an outboard engine. Frances had also given Steward instructions that once he was finished with the boat, he should burn it. She did not want it passed around. Whether it was destroyed remains an open question. Time and the coastal weather may have done the job nevertheless.

On September 3, 1946, Frances wrote, "I am very tired—inside." She realized that she alone carried the full weight of Buzz's death. Rolf Holmstrom decided his mother needed a holiday, the first in many years. Two weeks later he took Frances on a short motor trip through Oregon.

One of their stops was Elgin, where they visited with Oliver and Alice Barlow, who had talked with Buzz the night before he set off down the river. All had seemed well, according to Mr. Barlow. Rolf was persuaded that Barlow, in his kindness, may have tried to comfort Frances with optimistic stories. She left feeling somewhat relieved.

By the end of September, about the time Frances and Rolf arrived back in Coquille, the stone mason had finished engraving the marble headstone. Robert Louis Stevenson, in anticipation of his own death, wrote a poem to be engraved on his headstone when he died:

> Under the wide and starry sky,
> Dig the grave and let me lie.
> Glad did I live and gladly die,
> And I laid me down with a will.
>
> This be the verse you grave for me:
> "Here he lies where he longed to be;
> Home is the sailor, home from sea,
> And the hunter home from the hill."

Now Frances chose a line from that poem that echoed her grief. A few days later the headstone was installed. For years afterwards, on the anniversary of Buzz's death, a rose appeared at the grave.

The Unanswerable Question

O VER THE YEARS questions about Buzz Holmstrom's death on the banks of the Grande Ronde that spring evening have persisted. Of the three possible causes—accidental, foul play, self-inflicted—the last was the hardest to believe and the most difficult to explain. It made no sense. Good-natured, easy-going Buzz, "who didn't know a stranger," who made friends quickly and easily, who signed his letters to his mother, "Everything O.K.!"

Those closest to Holmstrom rejected suicide. Others were stunned, but allowed that he was capable of such an act. Few voiced their opinion that, indeed, they were not surprised. In the months following his death, his family and friends sought answers to the hard questions and gnawing doubts left behind. The yearning for some resolution to the sad mystery remained with them for years.

~

Now I do not expect that there was a river man of this river that was better acquainted with Buzz or closer to him than I was. And it is heartbreaking to even think he committed suicide and I'm still prone to think it was an accident.

— BERT LOPER, 1947

~

THE MOST ACCEPTABLE cause of death was an accident. This shifted the burden of responsibility to fate and granted a particular kind of relief to family and friends. People make mistakes, misjudge situations, happen to be in the wrong place at the wrong time. At first the Holmstroms assumed there had been an accident; even then, it had been hard to imagine Buzz being careless on the river. When they heard a firearm was involved, they were stunned.

Ten days after Holmstrom's death Lieutenant Commander Rubottom wrote to Frances:

> Like you, I believe it could have been accidental, and I have never been satisfied in my own mind that it wasn't. One of my first questions to the coroner was "couldn't it have been accidental?" I spent considerable time questioning him on the subject. But as you say he only looked at the obvious and circumstantial evidence, and without knowing Haldane, arrived at the conclusion he did.
>
> At any rate I will never be convinced that it was not accidental.

Rubottom was almost certainly trying to comfort Frances Holmstrom. Two days after Holmstrom's death, Rubottom had telegrammed the U.S. Coastal Survey in Washington, D.C.: HOLMSTROMS REMAINS BEING SHIPPED TO HIS HOME COLLECT AS PER FAMILIES REQUEST STOP DEFINITELY SUICIDE ONE DAY AFTER STARTING DOWN GRANDE RONDE CAUSE UNKNOWN BUT RIVER HIGH AND TREACHEROUS AND FEAR OF BEING UNABLE TO SUCCESSFULLY NEGOTIATE IT APPARENTLY A CONTRIBUTING FACTOR STOP. To make sure his superiors understood the situation, Rubottom added: DEFINITELY SUICIDE RUBOTTOM.

On June 8 Rubottom again wrote to Frances Holmstrom. Whatever Rubottom believed, his compassion took precedence.

> Your letter has been received and I am glad if my letter was some comfort to you.... I thoroughly agree with you, that he would never do such a thing because of fear of the mission he was engaged in.... I have talked to a number of people who had known Haldane and have had letters from others. They are unanimous in the opinion that he would not have done such a thing because of the river, and that there must have been some other reason.... I am sorry that I cannot tell you how long he had been dead when they found him.... I am sorry that I did not know that he had been having periodic attacks of malaria.... I am sorry I am unable to give you any more

information, but if what I have given you is any comfort to you I am happy to have been able to do that little bit.

Oliver Barlow thought accidental death a possibility. Although he admitted having no first-hand information about the death, he did know the river and its surroundings. "It was a wild place full of vines and rocks," he wrote later to Frances. He thought it possible that Holmstrom stumbled and fell, discharging the rifle, on the steep banks of the river. Barlow added another opinion, "From what I have heard there was too much taken for granted and there was not enough investigation of the circumstances." Grimm, the observer-in-charge, wrote to Frances, "I want to think that it was an accident but I just don't know what to think. It is one thing we can never feel at ease about."

~

FOR MANY, INCLUDING Carl Holmstrom, Doc Hamilton, and Ed Walker, there had to be an alternative explanation for Buzz's death: foul play. Ed Walker, who had lost a daughter to cancer years before, was exceptionally reluctant to accept the official explanation.

In early June, two weeks after Holmstrom's death, Frances gave Walker permission to contact Walker's old friend, Coos Bay District Attorney Ben Flaxel, about an independent investigation of the circumstances. Frances herself appealed to Sheriff Howell of the Coos County Police Department to find out what he could. She also asked Elbert Schroeder to write Mr. Snodgrass, the coroner in La Grande, once more. At one point, she even considered exhuming the body.

Over the years, a story circulated that Holmstrom had argued heatedly with the cook, Moffett. One version alleged that Buzz had refused to do the dishes; another version insinuated that the cook's wife was involved. Given the times, it is unlikely that any woman worked on the survey or visited the camp. Yet another version suggested that alcohol was the culprit. Paul Haverlah states there was no drinking in camp that he was aware of. Then, as now, the stigma of suicide weighed heavily on family and friends. Sloppy work by the coroner, the lack of an inquest or autopsy, the explicit suggestion of cowardice in the La Grande paper—all served to fuel suspicions of a cover-up. Even Clarence Bean supposed that murder was a possibility and wondered aloud what motive the cook had.

After the river survey was completed, Theodore Moffett gave a deposition on June 8 to the district attorney in La Grande. Two days later he wrote Frances:

Dear Mrs. Holmstrom,
   I am writing to you as a member of the Coast and Geodetic Survey party engaged in the survey of the lower Grande Ronde River at the time of the death of your son "Buzz." Personally and on behalf of all the members of the party I want to express the deepest sympathy. We had only known Buzz for

a few short days, but we had come to like and respect him.

I suppose that I can tell you little of the facts surrounding his death which you do not already know, but I think that it may give you some satisfaction to know that I had no doubt whatever as to his ability to handle the boats on the river successfully; and I am certain that the members of the party felt likewise that he was fully qualified and competent.... He did make the statement to me that he could not make the run, but I am personally sure that for a man of his ability this run would not have been difficult.

As you know, it was necessary for a report to be made to the Government with regard to Buzz's death. In that connection, we were requested to make written statements, and I have a copy of the affidavit which I submitted. I will be glad to send it to you if you desire it.

Again let me express my sympathy and may I tell you that all of us have the deepest feeling of sympathy for you.

Sincerely,
Theodore L. Moffett

Frances responded immediately, requesting a copy of the affidavit, which, along with all other correspondence, she gave to Ed Walker. Naturally she said nothing of her suspicions to Moffett. Walker took it and his suspicions to Flaxel, who wrote George Anderson, the Union County district attorney. In his July 23 response, Anderson, while sympathetic, could discern no evidence that would lead him to further investigation. He summed:

> Our Coroner, by the way, is Mr. L. L. Snodgrass, our local funeral director. Mr. Snodgrass has been Coroner for over 14 years, and I have worked in close cooperation with him since I took office in 1936. From my experience with him I have found him to be careful, painstaking and thoroughly reliable in his investigations, and always anxious to consult with me whenever there is any possible question on a case.... All members of the party were questioned and no circumstances to indicate the possibility of foul play were found. No theory for a motive to murder could be established and this fact, coupled with the powder marks and the position of the body and the rifle led Mr. Snodgrass to the conclusion that Holmstrom must have sat and held the rifle to the side of his head and pulled the trigger—a theory with which I agree.... Also, the present whereabouts of the cook and his gun are unknown, so it would probably not be possible for comparisons to be made.

A week later, Flaxel met Ed Walker and Frances at the service station in Coquille to discuss the situation. On July 30 Frances wrote in her journal, "No use, it seems, to keep up the battle."

In late August, however, Frances wrote another letter to George Grimm in Parkway, Washington. She wanted to know more about the character of Moffett, suggesting that perhaps he had been involved in an altercation with Buzz. Grimm replied:

As to Mr. Moffett. In my mind there can be no doubt about his part in the affair, and certainly no doubt as to his character. While he has only been with the Survey since March of this year, I have been with him most of that time and there is no question of his being reliable. I am sure he would be both hurt and indignant at any hint of such a suggestion....

Rolf says it was unlikely that his brother would have gotten into an argument, much less a fight. Buzz made friends easily, was slow to anger, went out of his way to avoid confrontations.

Suicide my eye! If he got depressed because of a little poor boating, enough to shoot himself, then I'm crazy. Someone shot him. Either a deer hunter or a distiller. I'm sorry to hear of it.

— FRANK DODGE, NOVEMBER 1947

THE EMBATTLED-COOK THEORY took on a life of its own among Holmstrom's family, friends, and the residents in Coquille. After all, miners and trappers along the Rogue River had disappeared under mysterious circumstances for many decades. Most of Coquille believed there was more to Holmstrom's death than met the eye. Gradually, however, there was a weary, grudging acceptance of the inadequacy of any explanation. Ed Walker and Frances spoke infrequently about the possibility of suicide, although it weighed on their minds over the coming years.

Given Holmstrom's fame, the number of people involved, and the public nature of the work of the Coast and Goedetic Survey, it would have taken an unusual amount of collusion to cover up a mistake or a misdeed. What may have seemed obvious to the survey crew that night took on added, even sinister, dimensions to folks in Coquille. They repeated again and again, "We knew Buzz. He wouldn't do that kind of thing." Almost certainly, however, Buzz Holmstrom did take his own life.

While "suicide" satisfied the more superficial and immediate questions surrounding his death, it also raised far more perplexing questions. Among his family and friends, acquaintances in and out of Coquille, and the river-running fraternity whose friendship he so valued, there was no consensus. Indeed, the opinions and explanations taken as a whole present a complex, sometimes contradictory, picture of who he was. Even those who knew Holmstrom well offered differing explanations: their interpretations leaned toward a single rather than a multiple cause. At the time, suicide was misunderstood and seldom discussed, tainted with failure and weak character.

Explanations of that suicide ranged from the plausible to the far-fetched.

Frank Swain made Holmstrom's reputed outburst six years earlier about Amos Burg the cause. "Holmstrom killed himself because he didn't have the courage to kill Amos," said Swain, implying that Holmstrom was a coward. Since 1940 Burg and Holmstrom had seen each other often. The tone of their letters and meetings contradicts Swain's conclusion. Burg had planned to meet with Holmstrom again that summer to discuss another river trip.

Decades later, amateur river historians begin to analyze the motives, characters, and behaviors of early river runners of the Grand Canyon. Their conjectures, flavored with popular psychology, made their way through the river-running community—specious speculations: Major Powell, even Norm Nevills were "mama's boys"; Nevills's death was a suicide in disguise; possibly Flavell was gay, so was Holmstrom. Despite a lack of evidence, such allegations lingered. One wonders why they were made at all.

Holmstrom drank; evidence of a problem, however, remains inconclusive. Jim Watson, Doc Hamilton, and George McClellan did not consider him an excessive drinker. Dick Hollister, who was always with Holmstrom in the South Pacific and on leave in Australia, claimed that Holmstrom drank infrequently. Rolf said of his brother, "Buzz knew what was important. He never lost his objectivity. Drinking was a very small part of his life."

~

Most of the poetry of Buzz was in Buzz. Interested in birds and animals. Intense, simple. He wanted to get close to life. Buzz was so complicated it finally got the best of him. Every time I talked to him I felt I was arrogant and boastful. He had the common touch.

— AMOS BURG, 1952

~

WHILE FRANCES PUBLICLY REJECTED the explanation of suicide that summer, she searched for answers. She wrote to Rubottom, suggesting that perhaps Buzz "was another War casualty." World War II had ended only months earlier; many veterans returned with physical and psychological ailments. In addition to injuries and wounds, servicemen also suffered a variety of infections and diseases, malaria among the most common. What Frances meant by the phrase "war casualty" remains unclear.

Throughout his tour in the South Pacific, Buzz stayed remarkably healthy. While it seems clear that he contracted malaria in the South Pacific, there is no mention of it in his navy medical records. The protozoa can go undetected for years, and dormant malaria may be missed by blood tests. The last time Frances saw Buzz in Coquille in April 1946, he was thin, yet not necessarily sick, from his bout with malaria three months earlier. Buzz reassured her that he was feeling better. Upon his release from the Bremerton Naval Base in October 1945, the physician in charge found Holmstrom to be "physically qualified for discharge from the Naval Service." Under "Defects Noted" none were listed.

In 1948 river historian Dock Marston interviewed Buzz's friend, Earl Hamilton, who told Marston that he believed Buzz's war experience had changed him. He reported that Holmstrom had been in the hospital in Australia, and that he later tried to get into an Oregon rest home but was not admitted. Ed Walker had tried to help. Hamilton also told Marston that the Holmstrom family knew nothing about it. No specific reason is given. One can assume it involved malaria.

Earl Hamilton's wife Phyllis and her daughter Linda agreed that it was common knowledge around their house that Buzz had been injured during the war. Linda Hamilton recalls her parents discussing Holmstrom's injury at dinner; he had suffered a head wound. Again, Holmstrom's military records add nothing. Dick Hollister dismisses the reports of hospitalization.

Hamilton was not the only person in Coquille who worried about his friend. Other members of Holmstrom's inner circle—Clarence Bean and Ed Walker— were also concerned. Buzz may have mentioned something of a personal nature to them.

In addition to malaria, might he have contracted venereal disease? After his death, his friends wondered if it might have affected his mind. "He just seemed different," Hamilton had told Dock Marston. Although many servicemen acquired diseases overseas, all venereal diseases were easily treated with penicillin then. Tertiary syphilis requires ten years to affect the brain. Holmstrom's discharge papers report no such finding from his urinalysis and Kahn blood test.

~

And now about Buzz Holmstrom, his reported suicide is wholly unaccountable to me because I had known him so well and for so long a time and had never known of any discouragement or sorrow in his life, so that I am wholly amazed.

— JULIUS F. STONE, JUNE 7, 1946

~

MORE THAN FIFTY YEARS AGO, George Anderson, the district attorney in La Grande, responded to Flaxel: "Under the circumstances I am sure you will agree that the bare statement of friends or relatives that Holmstrom 'just wasn't the type of man to commit suicide' is of no assistance. In my opinion there is no established 'type' in such instances...." Today we know better.

Nothing indicates mental illness in the Holmstrom family history. Frances never mentioned problems of that nature in her family journals. In the early decades of the twentieth century, however, people were unlikely to recognize a mental illness, much less record it. Information was limited, and rural area residents were often the last to know about the latest developments in psychology and the first to dismiss them. In the 1930s and 1940s, psychologists were relatively unavailable to most residents of the southern Oregon coast.

Only in the last thirty years have researchers, psychologists, and psychiatrists identified and begun to understand the complexity of mental illnesses, and of depression in particular. The public now knows there are categories of depression, degrees of severity, and a variety of manifestations, sometimes adhering to a pattern, sometimes not. If Holmstrom experienced such a disorder, which seems likely, he could not name it, let alone cope with it. Like most people of his time, he would have said he was "down in the dumps," or "feeling blue." He would have "gotten on with things," as his circumstances demanded and his training taught him. If the feelings returned or persisted, he would have tried to ignore them. He might have come to blame himself. The last thing he would have considered was that he was the victim of a disorder not of his own making.

Whatever form of depression Holmstrom suffered throughout his life remains unknowable. The source of his depression—biological, circumstantial, a combination of the two—remains as much a mystery as the specific symptoms he suffered.

Evidence that Holmstrom experienced depression appears in his letters and journals, and in the written accounts, anecdotes, and interviews with his family and friends. The allusions to depression are often fragmentary or indirect. "Depression" and "depressed" were terms used by laymen in ways that vaguely communicate something they sensed about Holmstrom, clues suggesting a pattern of depression.

After each of his Colorado river trips in the late 1930s, Holmstrom's spirits slumped noticeably. The euphoria he had experienced on the river was replaced by an unshakable emptiness. On one occasion he wrote, "I have done no one any good and caused a few people great worry and suffering ... The river probably thought he is such a lonesome, ignorant, unimportant and insignificant pitiful little creature with such a short time to live that I will let him go this time and try to teach him something." At the time, his letters to Doc Hamilton, Amos Burg, Lois Jotter, Elzada Clover, and Julius Stone are full of self-recrimination and inner turmoil. When he should have been enjoying his success, he was undermining it. It was hard for him to accept the hometown praise and adulation. He was irritated by their admiration, saying that they did not really understand what he had done. He lost interest in things that he previously enjoyed doing and he wanted to get away, but did not know where to go. Of course, he blamed himself for the way he felt: "I don't seem to fit in around here anymore, or anywhere else for that matter.... The things that used to be fun to do aren't fun anymore.... I'm a lost soul."

Sixty years later, Bob Sharp, a member of the 1937 Carnegie–Cal Tech research trip which met Holmstrom in the Grand Canyon, put it this way:

> If you have a remarkable experience as a young person, there is no encore. Everything else was going to be anticlimactic. Some of the astronauts have had a tough time. Grand Canyon is not that caliber, but it was the best trip I ever had. I had intellectual interests which went beyond the Canyon trip. I don't think Buzz had such a background of interests to tide him over. He had lived his dream and everything after that was dull. I believe that he could have easily deteriorated psychologically. He was a workman and just plain work was no longer satisfying. It's tough for somebody to have a marvelous experience like that. What do you do for an encore? What more do you have up your sleeve?

Earl Brothers had been at the boat dock when Holmstrom rowed up and nudged his boat against Boulder Dam on his solo trip. In a reply written on March 29, 1950, to a Marston query, Brothers wrote:

> I'm fearful that your impression that I knew him well is perhaps overrated.... Buzz did spend several days here resting up and getting acquainted. Was in and out of my office quite a bit.... I'm unable to throw any light upon his reasons for suicide. I knew him as a person of retiring nature. He was not particularly impressed with the exploitation of his feats. There was, however, something very unusual about the man. He seemingly preferred to spend great deal of time alone....

Holmstrom spent the summer of 1938 working for the Poquetts at Pearce Ferry. In his notes, Marston reported Em Poquett's sometimes contradictory comments about Holmstrom, "He was extremely quiet. Very nice to have around.... He wouldn't talk much. Had to pry things out of him. He was very shy... queer... yes, and neurotic. He mentioned his mother but no other members of his family." Later Poquett remembered Buzz as "being peculiar, very moody... He would disappear when the tourists would come around."

In November of 1947 Zee Grant replied to yet another inquiry by Marston about the possible causes: "Buzz, I met in New York where he looked me up, feeling the need of another river rat's companionship in an atmosphere so foreign to his out of doors nature. I too can't understand how he would have taken his life. However, he was a very sensitive person, of unusual intelligence, and may have had some trace of nervous depression. Some call it battle fatigue. This is my own guess."

~

Buzz Holmstrom, I think, appealed to the imagination of all those—Bill, Gene, Don Harris and I—who remained at Lee's Ferry a couple of days while Norm and Elzie went back to Mexican Hat for supplies. He impressed us all as being a very generous and sincere person, more concerned for our possible safety than that someone might equal his record on the river.

— LOIS JOTTER, DECEMBER 10, 1947

IN JULY OF 1948, Dock Marston interviewed Bill Gibson, a photographer. Gibson, who held Buzz in high regard, told Marston that Holmstrom had been depressed by what the doctor had told him while in the hospital in Sacramento recovering from malaria. If Holmstrom wanted to stay well he would have to remain in a desert climate. Marston asked a leading question: "Did he appear to be suffering from neurotic difficulties?" Marston's shorthand transcription of Gibson's reply read, "Hard to say. Introverted personality. Once knew him. Moods of manic depression, innate sweetness. He wrote Gibson two months before he shot himself."

Of all those interviewed by Marston, Roy Lawhorne was in a position to know Holmstrom best. Lawhorne had spent considerable time with the entire Holmstrom family. After Buzz's father died, he stepped in as mentor and confidant. Yet Marston's notes, however compelling, are erratic, occasionally indecipherable, and inconclusive. In his interview with Lawhorne, Marston wrote:

> He wanted to shoot a chicken and emphasized chicken. Roy says on reading coroner's letter: "That's phony. When he had those spells, he was pretty bad. It was a case of suicide. Frazier not a good source. Neither am I'" Told of going out of his head with pain. He picked up something during the war. When I saw him his eyes were wrong—deep set and dead. He tried to commit suicide before. [This is the first and only mention of any previous suicide attempt by Holmstrom.] He had superstition of appeasing river, of killing animals. Confirms Earl Hamilton. Don't know what the disease was. Was in hospital in New York but family did not know it…. Told of dreams on river. Thought of river as a personality. Roy didn't know what the disease was, but he had a spell when working in Northern California. Was very happy in job in Northern California and hesitated on Oregon job. Uncle Roy advised him against it. Buzz felt he was being loaned.

The allegation that Holmstrom committed suicide because he did not think he could navigate the scow down the Grande Ronde River was the simplest answer. Undeniably, Holmstrom had told Moffett, "I just can't make that river." The men on the survey, not knowing Holmstrom, assumed that to be the single primary cause. The allegation deserves examination, however, because it was the reason most often given by people and, doubtlessly, it masked the likelier cause: untreated depression.

The claim gained publicity in a May 21 article in the *La Grande Observer* only days after Holmstrom's death. "The suicide of Haldane ("Buzz") Holmstrom, famed river boatman, after he found he could not carry out one of his daring river stunts, was reported Tuesday by Coroner L. L. Snodgrass." In addition the article read, "The coroner listed death as suicide. He ascribed no reason, but men of the geodetic survey crew where Holmstrom was employed as a boat pilot said Holmstrom had been despondent because he could not navigate the Grande Ronde River in a specially built boat." Beneath a photo of Holmstrom, in bold letters, was the headline, "GIVES UP." The article's tone, content, and abruptness greatly upset the Holmstrom family and the residents of Coquille.

~

Buzz was a tragic hero. He never quite knew why the world passed him by. The worldliness of the world finally led him to suicide.

— ELZADA CLOVER, JUNE 3, 1950

~

IN HIS MAY 25 LETTER to the director of the Survey in Washington, D.C., Rubottom, using gentler language, agreed with the article.

> There is attached an article from the La Grande Observer, on the tragedy which appears to be the basis of all other press releases. The article seems to cover the case pretty well with many of the usual Press inaccuracies.... No definite reason for Mr. Holmstrom taking his own life has been discovered, but all reports indicate that it was because he was afraid he could not successfully navigate the river.

Yet, in a conversation with Paul Haverlah weeks after Holmstrom's death, Rubottom speculated that Holmstrom had "lady-friend problems."

George Grimm wrote to Frances,

> While he appeared to be worried over the outcome of the trip due to the fact that he was not familiar with that type of boat, at no time did he give a hint that he thought of giving up. It is absurd to think that he took his own life because he was afraid. He didn't know fear.

In an unwitting defense of Holmstrom, La Grande district attorney George Anderson wrote to Flaxel in Coos Bay:

> It is unfortunate, perhaps, that publicity was given to a theory advanced by some people that suicide was committed because of fear of taking the party down the river. This arose because of Holmstrom having gone down the river one day before in a small boat and said afterwards that he didn't believe he could make it with the larger boat and party. It was suggested that

he killed himself rather than suffer the possible stigma of being branded a coward. To me this theory appears far-fetched....

Whether challenging or defending Holmstrom's honor, they had all missed the point.

Buzz Holmstrom was no coward. Anderson, however, came closer to understanding Holmstrom than he realized. Far worse for Holmstrom than someone else branding him a coward was that he had labeled himself one. Alone, without so many depending on him, he might have taken the risk of piloting the scow down the river. Now, however, it seemed he had no choice. Disgusted, he had told Moffett, as mentioned earlier, "I'm going to shoot a chicken." Later Clarence Bean told Dock Marston, "That's just the kind of thing Buzz would have said." During their conversation, Bean also cryptically commented to Marston, "Three thousand people believe in Buzz and only three really know the truth, and why should they tell?" Bean would not elaborate.

What hopelessness Holmstrom experienced in the moments before his death appears to have been triggered by his irrational response to the situation on the Grande Ronde. How much danger the river presented remains an unanswerable question. Holmstrom's perception, correct or not, had been set in motion by a precipitating event, possibly before Holmstrom even reached the Grande Ronde. Unrequited love, a shortage of money, an uncertain future—each may have been a factor. The "final straw" occurred when he piloted the overloaded scow down the river to Rondowa and saw the Wallowa River surging into the Grande Ronde. Grimm obviously respected Holmstrom's judgment and would have followed his suggestions. Yet, Buzz said nothing. As a problematic situation on the river spiraled into a full-blown crisis, his capacity to find reasonable solutions left him.

Holmstrom had been hired because of who he was: the man who had run the Colorado River alone. "World's best boatman," Willis Johnson had called him. In fact, he had not run rivers since 1940. He had always expected much of himself and taken little credit for his achievements. If he reneged, and told Grimm he could not pilot the scow, what then? The men would be disappointed, the survey halted. He would let everyone down. Word would spread, his career as a government river guide would end. Back to Coquille and the service station—a quitter and a small-town failure. The Conqueror of the Colorado! Now everyone would know what he had always suspected: he had lost what little courage he possessed; he was just no good. In the hours before his death, the same savage reasoning that caused Buzz to believe he was incapable and therefore a failure, demanded a price. The tragedy was that Buzz Holmstrom's courage and humility disintegrated so quickly into such unyielding shame and despair.

Holmstrom, moments after arriving at Boulder Dam, 1937

A Last Word

I N THE END, the legacy of Buzz Holmstrom rests not with how he died but with how he lived. Although his accomplishments on the river will always merit attention and admiration, his attitude toward and appreciation of the rivers he ran commands our respect and emulation. Throughout his life, Holmstrom retained his native talents, his homespun humility, his abiding love of rivers. Without fuss, privilege, or encouragement, he did what he set out to do—run the Green and Colorado Rivers—then returned to his routine job at the service station.

Certainly, he was a man of his times. Yet something about Holmstrom—his lyrical appreciation of nature, his self-effacing, ironical humor, his simple acceptance of his own insignificance—appeals across the generations. On the river today he is known as a boatman's boatman.

FIVE DAYS INTO HIS SOLO VOYAGE of 1937, with nearly a thousand miles of river to run, he wrote to his mother:

Just Below Red Ck. Rapid
Oct. 9
Dear Mamma,

    I am writing this as I lay in my sleeping bag—& this is the only paper I have up here—I had no intention of writing this letter now but it is so beautiful here right now I must tell someone about it. I am camped on the left bank of the river and have my sleeping bag in a little level place I scooped out in the sand among the rocks—the fire is flickering up and down behind me & throwing flashes of light on a mountain cedar tree just above me—It has many dead limbs on it & looms up kind of ghostly but pretty too—

    Just beyond the mesquite & almost over me is a big pine tree outlined clearly against the sky with many stars twinkling through its branches and over here the stars really do twinkle—I can hear that miserable Red Ck rapid roaring back up the river and the voice of another downstream but it doesn't sound so unfriendly—

    Little waves are slapping on the sides of the boat—the compartments act on the principle of a drum—A whiff of smoke from the dying campfire blows over here once in a while but I don't mind—I can see the rim of the Canyon walls on both sides of the river—black & jagged against the starlit sky.

    Well Mamma I wish you were here & I believe if you were you would say it is pretty good too.

                                            Haldane

Acknowledgments

$\mathcal{I}$ T IS IMPOSSIBLE to adequately thank everyone who contributed to this book. From the beginning the book was a collaboration, not just of three authors, but of the many friends, relatives, and admirers of Buzz Holmstrom.

We would especially like to thank the Holmstrom family—Buzz's sister Anna, and brother Rolf, for their unstinting support and generosity. They shared not only their memories but their hospitality. It is with great sadness that we also thank Buzz's older brother Carl, and Rolf's wife Betty, both of whom passed away during the writing.

Buzz Holmstrom's friends, too, were instrumental in bringing his story to life. A list of thanks includes: Ross and Adelaide Brown, Carolyn and Amos Burg, Neil and Betty Lowman Carey, Chauncey B. Coor, Lois Jotter Cutter, Margaret Dement, the Eidemiller family, Jay Freeman, Freddie and Willie Friederick, George Gant, Phyllis Hamilton and her daughter Linda, Ted Hatch, Paul J. Haverlah, John Hickam, Dale and LaRona Hoehne, Dick Hollister, Hal and Frances Howell, June and Woody Jennings, Cora Lee Johnson, Willis Johnson, Ross Kistner, Carol Lindegren, Betty Lundstrom, George McClellan, Hack Miller, Bob Poling, Lois Sheperd Shinkle and her daughter Marie, Boyd Stone, Bob Taylor, Dorothy Taylor, Vincent M. Van Matre, Jim Watson, Percy and Josie Witherspoon.

For research assistance we must thank many individuals and institutions: Katie Brown; Mary Ellen and Dick Pugh, *Cambridge Museum, Idaho*; Patti Strain, *City Manager of Coquille*; Karen Underhill, Laine Sutherland, Diane Grua and Richard Quartaroli, *Cline Library, Northern Arizona University*; Ann Koppy, *Coos County Historical Society Museum, North Bend*; Jordi Lindegren and Molly Barrett, *Coquille Library*; Fred Reenstjerna, *Douglas County Historical Museum*; Annette Howell, *Elgin Library*; Dennis McBride, *personal Grand Canyon Boulder Dam Tours collection*; Carolyn Richards, *Grand Canyon National Park Library*; Bill Frank, *Huntington Library*; Joan Nevills Staveley and Julia Betz, *John Wesley Powell Museum, Page, Arizona*; Roy Webb, *Marriott Library, University of Utah*; Karin Gunson, *Oregon State Medical Examiner*; Susan Seyl and Michelle Kribs, *Oregon Historical Society*; Duffy Knaus, *Knight Library, University of Oregon*; and the Utah Historical Society. Any omissions are unintentional.

To those who reviewed all or part of the manuscript, and vastly improved the book: Linda Besant, Logan Hebner, David Lavender, RJ Johnson, Joyce Jones, Tom Ledbetter, Terri Merz, Jill and Mike Miller, Earl Perry, Richard Quartaroli, Lew Steiger, Susan Tasaki, Mary VanCleave, Jeff Wallach, Roy Webb.

Throughout the years of research, writing, and rewriting, our families have shown unflagging support, timely encouragement, and wondrous patience: Vince's wife, Helen, and children, Jake and Gwen; Cort's daughter, Keats; and Brad's wife, Jeri. We'll make it up to you somehow.

And finally, our gratitude to the rivers of the West, that have given each of us more than we can ever repay; to those of the river community who have lived, worked, and played there with us; and to those we have known who have been lost in the middle of rapids, on the river or off. We'll catch you downstream.

Photograph and Manuscript Credits

HUNTINGTON LIBRARY, Marston Collection manuscripts: quotes throughout text.

CORT CONLEY:
Amos Burg collection: FRONT COVER, 83, 125, 148, 161

WILLIS JOHNSON: (*Hack Miller, photographer*): ii

ANNA HOLMSTROM SMITH AND ROLF HOLMSTROM:
iv–39, 44, 102, 135, 232

GEORGE GANT: 40   BETTY LUNDSTROM: 147

CLINE LIBRARY, NORTHERN ARIZONA UNIVERSITY:
Lois Jotter Cutter Collection: 141 (NAU.PH.95.3.27)
    LETTERS: 158, 168, 169, 224, 228–229, 230–231
Carnegie / Cal-Tech Collection: 119 (NAU.PH.94.27.132)
Bill Belknap Collection: 123, 142, 143, 145, 152, REAR COVER
    (NAU.PH.96.4.113.6, 114.2, 114.3, 114.1, 113.3, 114.4B, 113.5)
Buzz Holmstrom Collection: 45-81, 138, 170, 226, 229, 283
    (NAU.PH.97.22...)

Emery Kolb Collection: LETTER, 84

OREGON HISTORICAL SOCIETY, *Amos Burg Collection:* 157

CAMBRIDGE MUSEUM, CAMBRIDGE, IDAHO:
Edith Clegg photographs and journal quotations: 171–219

U.S. BUREAU OF RECLAMATION: 221, 231, 233

DICK HOLLISTER: 238 (LEFT), 241, 246, 250

CHAUNCEY B. COOR: 238 (RIGHT)   JORDI LINDEGREN: 255

ZOE BOTHAM (*Forest Eidemiller, photographer*): 263

RIPLEY ENTERTAINMENT CORP: *Believe it or Not:* REAR COVER

All other photographs are from the authors' private collections.

Journals

BUZZ HOLMSTROM'S journals, scribbled in pencil in small pocket notebooks, reside at the University of Oregon at Eugene.

We have used a faithful new transcription of the journals by Brad Dimock that follows the originals as closely as readability will allow. Minor punctuation was added for clarity and a few abbreviated words were completed to avoid confusion.

The complete journals were published in 2003, along with Burg's, Johnson's and Lundstrom's accounts, in *EVERY RAPID SPEAKS PLAINLY*, available from Fretwater Press.

Index

Grave Creek Falls 53
Green River 88–91, 95, 144, 146, 151, 169, 224–231
Green River Lakes 146, 156, 158
Green River, Utah 98–100, 103, 139–140, 152–153, 156–157, 161
Green River, Wyoming 88–90, 109–110, 118, 145–147, 151, 166
Grey, Zane 46, 50, 53, 54, 57, 63, 64
Grimm, George 257–268, 273–274, 281–282
Guleke, Harry "Cap" 68, 69, 71–74, 103, 257
Hamilton, Earl 34, 43, 60, 87, 131, 168, 177–202, 224, 225, 234, 237, 244, 268, 273, 276–280
Hance Rapid 109, 122, 159
Hancock, Monroe 71, 72, 74, 81, 82
Hansen, Ken 29, 32, 33, 42, 252, 268
Harbor, Oregon 18, 19, 20, 21, 24
Harris, Don 139–140, 152, 227
Harris, Tom 265, 266, 280
Hart, Sylvan 74, 75
Hatch, Bus 74, 94–97, 103, 150, 155, 229–230
Hatch, Don 97, 194
Hatch, Ted 229–230, 286
Haverlah, Paul 261, 265–267, 273, 281, 286
Hells Canyon 79 172, 177, 186–197, 262
Hellgate Canyon 50, 52, 53, 61
Hells Half Mile 94–95, 149
Hickam, Thurman 34, 42, 48, 60, 134–136, 232, 253, 268, 286
High Lead Tree, The 11
Hollister, Dick 237, 240–247, 276–277, 286, 287
Holmstrom, Anna (Smith) viii, 1, 2, 14, 27–41, 44, 88, 110, 160, 252, 257, 286–287
Holmstrom, Carl viii, 1, 2, 13–45, 82, 87–88, 133, 232, 246, 251–253, 256, 257, 267, 273, 286
Holmstrom, Charles 2–32, 36–37, 41
Holmstrom, Frances 1–44, 49, 88, 130, 161, 232, 233, 246, 252–258, 267–277, 281, 286
Holmstrom, Rolf 1, 2, 5, 17, 35–38, 41, 44, 47–49, 59, 85–87, 133, 232, 233, 248, 249, 252, 256, 267–270, 275–276, 286, 287
Housser, George 171–174, 178, 203
Howell, Hal 42, 50, 60, 253, 268, 286
Hudson River 216–218
Huggins, Ted 137, 166–167
Hyde, Glen & Bessie 103–104, 110, 120, 140, 144, 164, 257
Jarvis Landing 5, 6, 18
Jensen, Utah 92, 96–100, 147, 150–152, 157, 161, 228
Johnson, Sylvester and Anna 8, 9, 21

Johnson, Seth 8, 9, 18, 19, 36
Johnson, Willis 152–166, 176–198, 203, 222, 223, 224, 225, 229, 286, 287
Jotter, Lois (Cutter) 139–144, 158, 168, 169, 174, 222, 224, 231, 278, 280, 286, 287, 289
Julius F 144–152, 159, 162, 165, 166, 167, 168, 227, 246, 269
Killam, Jack 71, 72, 84
Knife, Belle 267, 268
Kolb, Emery; Ellsworth 50, 60, 83–84, 89–93, 99, 100, 103, 107–113, 116, 120, 130, 140–144, 160
Kreager, Red 226, 227, 234
La Grande, Oregon 260, 261, 265, 266, 268, 273, 277, 281
Lava Cliff 119–122, 131, 164, 165, 234
Lava Falls 115–119, 122, 132, 155, 163–167, 234
Lawhorne, Roy and Emma 16, 21, 88, 268, 280
Lees Ferry 84, 99, 103–107, 139, 140, 153, 157
Leslie, Brick 32, 33, 268
Lewiston 65, 70, 75–82, 89, 172, 175–176, 180–182, 186–187, 191, 193
Lodore, Canyon of 91–96, 149, 151, 226
Loper, Bert 71, 84, 88, 89, 104, 105, 152, 153, 227, 272
Lundstrom, Phil 147–152, 160, 161, 258
Luoto brothers 79, 80, 186
malaria 246, 254, 272, 276, 277, 280
Marble Canyon 106, 136, 140, 157, 158, 161
Marshall, Catherine 41
Marshfield 10, 19, 21, 23, 28, 176, 236 (see Coos Bay)
Marston, Otis "Dock" 86, 277, 279, 280, 282
McCartney, Dave 261, 262
McClellan, George 42, 43, 47, 168, 276, 286
McCurdy, Phyllis (Hamilton) 34, 43, 181, 195, 196, 268, 277, 286
McKinley, Oregon 23–37, 43, 232, 252, 268
Melville, Rhode Island 238, 240, 247, 248
Merchant Marine 32, 39
Middle Creek 24, 25, 29, 30, 46, 50
Miller, Hack 129, 134, 136, 145, 167, 286, 287
Mississippi River 133, 145, 146, 174, 175, 203, 205, 211, 212
Missouri River 105, 146, 174, 175, 202–211
Moffett, Theodore 261, 264–266, 273–275, 280, 282
Mohawk River 217, 218

Phil Lundstrom's postcard map of the 1938 expedition route

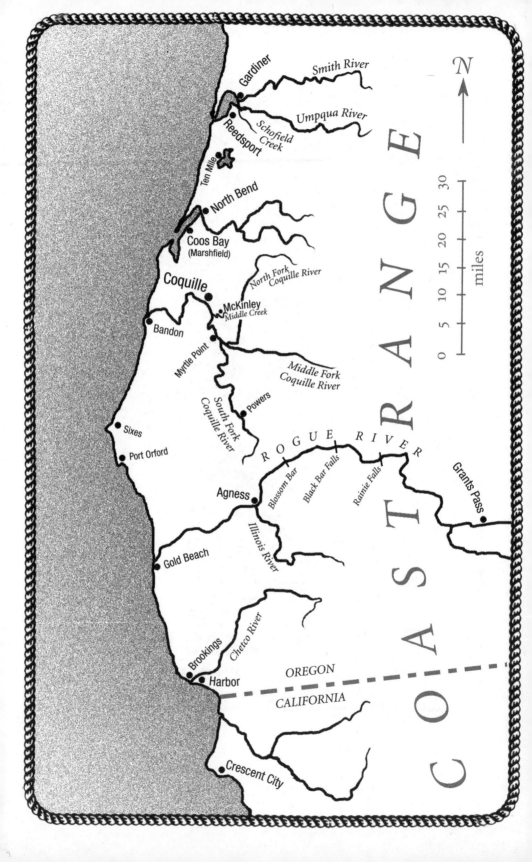